AMERICAN STUDIES – A MONOGRAPH SERIES

Volume 317

Edited on behalf
of the German Association
for American Studies by

ALFRED HORNUNG
ANKE ORTLEPP
HEIKE PAUL

VERENA REITER

Renegotiating American Nationalism

The Proxy War over Marriage Equality through the Lens of Un-Americanism

Universitätsverlag
WINTER
Heidelberg

Bibliografische Information der Deutschen Nationalbibliothek

Die Deutsche Nationalbibliothek verzeichnet diese Publikation
in der Deutschen Nationalbibliografie;
detaillierte bibliografische Daten sind im Internet
über *http://dnb.d-nb.de* abrufbar.

ISBN 978-3-8253-4889-2

Imprimé en Allemagne · Printed in Germany
Druck: Memminger MedienCentrum, 87700 Memmingen

Gedruckt auf umweltfreundlichem, chlorfrei gebleichtem
und alterungsbeständigem Papier.

Den Verlag erreichen Sie im Internet unter:
www.winter-verlag.de

Table of Contents

Acknowledgements

My fascination for the phenomenon of un-Americanism began with my master's thesis at the University of Regensburg. When searching for an interesting topic for my thesis, I stumbled across the 2013 special issue of the *Journal of American Studies* titled "The Un-American." Back then, I could not have imagined that, a few years later, I hand in a dissertation in which I further explore un-Americanism since my interest in this topic was unabated. I am very grateful to Prof. Dr. Nassim Balestrini and Prof. Dr. Eva-Sabine Zehelein who encouraged me to pursue a doctoral degree during my time as a graduate student at the University of Regensburg.

At the University of Frankfurt, I am particularly indebted to my supervisor Prof. Dr. Simon Wendt who accepted me as a PhD student and believed in my project when I was still in the midst of my eight semester and had not even graduated yet. Thank you for your continuous support, your time and your feedback, and in particular for your reliability. Whatever I needed, you never kept me waiting and I truly appreciate that.

I am also very thankful to my co-supervisor Prof. Dr. Philipp Gassert who regularly invited me to the University of Mannheim and who reminded me of the strengths and potential of my research always just at the right time when I needed such encouragement the most.

Over the years, this book has benefitted greatly from the feedback, critical questions, and input which I received in the course of various presentations and discussions in the American studies colloquiums at the University of Frankfurt, the University of Mannheim, the Ludwig Maximilian University of Munich, the University of Regensburg, and the University of California, Davis. Many thanks also go to the friends and colleagues who I met via the German Association of American Studies and in particular the Postgraduate Forum of the GAAS. I hope to keep in touch with many of you in the years to come.

One of the most memorable times of this journey was certainly my research year at the University of California, Davis. I am very grateful to Prof. John Scott for inviting me to the Department of Political Science as a visiting scholar and for letting me be part of the department's academic community since this was certainly a unique opportunity. The UC Davis

Political Science graduate student cohort of 2016 welcomed me with open arms, and they were an essential part of this wonderful time I had in Davis.

This dissertation project was generously supported by a doctorate scholarship of the Friedrich-Ebert Stiftung. I am very grateful for both the funding and the network that came with this scholarship. Many thanks go to Ursula Bitzegeio and Simone Stöhr from the FES doctorate program for their support and words of encouragement.

Most importantly, I want to thank my family and friends for believing in me and for making this project possible. To all those friends, loved ones, neighbors, and colleagues who made Frankfurt my home – thank you. Most of all, I am indebted to my wife without whom this book would truly have not been possible. Thank you for your love, your encouragement, your unbounded optimism, and the joy and happiness you bring to my life. To my mother – I could never thank you enough for your unconditional love, your support, your advice, and for always wanting nothing but the very best for me in life.

Introduction

> New York City owes a debt of gratitude to its recent guests, the Veterans of Foreign Wars. They have produced a simple test for un-Americanism. A man is un-American, they say, if he objects to the din of a VFW parade outside his window at midnight. Tests might be conducted by each post by simply sending a man with a big bass drum into a residential quarter at midnight. Observers might take note of the reactions & the test would be complete. (Malcolm)

In a September 1966 issue of *The New Yorker*, the journalist Donald Malcolm described an intriguing test for determining un-American attitudes of the American people.[1] In today's national dispute over what is American or un-American and over how the American nation is experienced and expressed, a method as simple as the one described by Malcolm would be greatly appreciated. Unfortunately, determining who or what is un-American is not as easy as that. Americans in 1960s New York might have wished for a simple and easy test in order to differentiate between who is American and who is un-American but, as the absurdity of this suggestion proves, they ultimately failed to find reliable criteria for who is a good representative of the American nation. In fact, the term 'un-American' has been used in countless contexts throughout American history but its enormous popularity has done nothing to consolidate a specific definition of the term.

What is un-American? It was "un-American" of the quarterback Colin Kaepernick not to stand during the national anthem to protest inequality in the United States, some people suggest (Biderman).[2] The Trump administration's "wealth test" for U.S. immigrants was denounced as "un-

1 Malcolm's article was printed in the "Talk of the Town" section of *The New Yorker*. In "Talk of the Town," contributors publish short insights into New York life which are often humorous and ironic in tone. Therefore, Malcolm's piece should not be taken too seriously although there is often some truth to the stories.

2 As a part of the so-called U.S. national anthem protests, starting in 2016, American athletes protested against racial injustice and police brutality by kneeling on one knee whilst the national anthem is played (Haislop).

American" since it impeded family reunification and led to a merit-based immigration system (Ramírez). Baseball pitches can also be un-American. Barack Obama's first pitch of the Major-League All-Star baseball match in 2009 was deemed as such for "its high, gently looping trajectory" since the pitch was not as straightforward as Americans commonly prefer them (Lewis, "Introduction" 875). Former President George W. Bush was said to have done a much better job with his first pitch as it was precise and "workmanlike" (875). President Trump called Democrats "un-American" for not standing and applauding during his State of the Union Address in February 2018 (J. Taylor) whereas liberals tend to believe that Trump is the "most un-American President in living memory" (Wolffe). Opponents of the Patient Protection and Affordable Care Act have dubbed this health care reform un-American on multiple occasions (e.g., Sensenbrenner, Steyn) whereas its advocates claim it is un-American to not provide access to health care for all U.S. citizens (Speier qtd. in J. Anderson). Even the superhero Captain America, the epitome of Americanness, has been accused of acting "un-American" in the movie *Captain America: Civil War* when he decided that his team of superhuman warriors, the Avengers, should not be subject to any oversight (Klein).

The idea of being American or un-American is not primarily a question of citizenship; it is a question of ideology and national self-definition. Political parties, advocacy groups, as well as ordinary Americans[3] increasingly accuse their opponents of un-American thought or behavior in order to gain political and sociocultural capital and to emphasize that they cannot accept the others' idea of American national identity. Today, these attacks in the form of accusations of un-Americanism are especially prominent in national discourse when American values and morals are at stake. Over the last decade in particular, the accusation of un-Americanism has become "the [p]olitical [i]nsult of the [m]oment" (Gage).

Although the growing polarization in the United States and the intensification of the cultural battles has led to an increase of accusations of un-Americanism, Americans have been using this rhetoric almost

[3] For the purpose of this study, persons who consider themselves Americans are regarded as such. Their status of citizenship is not relevant for this analysis. This approach avoids that long-term residents of the United States, who regard themselves as Americans, are excluded from this debate only because their citizenship or immigration status does not reflect their self-identification as Americans.

since the beginning of the republic. In its historical context, the term 'un-American' is most commonly associated with the House Un-American Activities Committee (HUAC), a committee established in 1938 by the House of Representatives (Goodman 21). The HUAC was initially implemented to investigate subversive and un-American propaganda and activities. However, the target of their investigations were mostly government employees and private citizens who had communist ties or who were believed to engage in homosexual conduct. The House Resolution 282, which approved the creation of the committee, did not provide this investigative body with clear guidelines and specifications on the limitations of its power.[4] The vague wording of their mandate gave the investigators the broadest possible scope of action and legislative freedom to probe un-Americans and un-American activities according to however they chose to define them ("Constitutional" 419).

Even though the time of the Second Red Scare (1940s to late 1950s) is long over, the problem of finding a commonly accepted understanding of the term 'un-American' remains. Those who decide to use the term 'un-American' continue to adopt one of countless possible interpretations or just rely on their own understanding. The history of the term 'un-American' does not follow a linear development. It is characterized by disruptions, semantic shifts, and multiple contexts of use. However, at least one thing about the definition of 'un-American' can be said with certainty: the term has experienced an enormous extension in meaning since the Red Scare Era and the time of the House Un-American Activities Committee.

In the 21st century, the term appears most prominently in debates in which the self-concept of the American nation is being debated as groups of Americans attempt to renegotiate and reconceptualize American self-definition to incorporate their interests and demands. People are

4 The HUAC was authorized to investigate:

> (1) the extent, character, and objects of un-American propaganda activities in the United States, (2) the diffusion within the United States of subversive and un-American propaganda that is instigated from foreign countries or of a domestic origin and attacks the principle of the form of government as guaranteed by our Constitution, and (3) all other questions in relation thereto that would aid Congress in any necessary remedial legislation. (United States, Congress, House, Special Committee on Un-American Activities)

most likely to accuse their opponents of un-Americanism in a conflict when they want to remind their opponents of their idea of American values, when they struggle to adduce convincing arguments, when they feel threatened by potential changes in society, or when they cannot grasp or verbalize their dissent and therefore turn toward this powerful language to express their opinion.

The fight over marriage equality[5] in the United States constituted a discursive context in which accusations of un-Americanism were prominent, particularly since the controversy got more intense following the turn of the millennium. In their fierce battles over whether same-sex marriage should be an American right, both same-sex marriage advocates as well as opponents frequently accused each other of un-Americanism in order to win ground. The same-sex marriage debate was a discourse over the direction which the American people as a nation would be heading and whether conservative or liberal values and morals would shape the future direction of the American nation in the end. Appealing to the rights enshrined in the nation's defining documents and insisting on their interpretation of Americanism[6] by accusing the opponent of un-Americanism has been a common tactic for the supporters of the gay rights movement

5 In this research project, the terms 'same-sex marriage,' 'gay marriage,' and 'marriage equality' are used interchangeably with all three denoting the marriage of a homosexual couple.

6 According to Kazin and McCartin, Americanism has two meanings: "It signifies both what is distinctive about the United States (and the colonies and territories that formed it) and loyalty to that nation, rooted in a defense of its political ideals" (1). I concur with Kazin and McCartin that Americanism gives us an idea of what is characteristic and distinctive about the United States, and that notions of Americanism are relevant in the context of national loyalty and pride. However, I do not agree that this is (mainly) rooted in a "defense of its political ideals" (1). Much rather, I argue that Americanism is equally connected to the nation's sociocultural norms and values, thereby, making it a description of ideas of American national identity and self-concept. In everyday American nationhood, I believe that the cultural aspect of Americanism is of even greater relevance for the American public. Additionally, I claim that ideas of Americanism, and thereby of American national identity, are negotiated, debated, reinforced, and transformed through sociocultural discourses and practices of American nationalism. In the course of this, certain subjects and their notions of Americanism prevail whereas others are suppressed and marginalized. As a consequence, Americanism has both a uniting as well as an exclusionary function.

since the early days of the fight for equal marriage rights (Hall, "Americanism" 1109). This rhetoric was quickly adapted by opponents since those were concerned about the increasing liberalization of American life and often instrumentalized homosexual Americans as scapegoats in times of struggle and insecurity.

A profound investigation of charges of un-Americanism in the marriage equality discourse reveals that, at its height in the years before the Supreme Court ruling *Obergefell v. Hodges* in 2015,[7] this debate was no longer focused on same-sex marriage. It had turned into a dispute over who possessed more sociocultural capital and who would be able to define American national identity. Ultimately, marriage equality served as a proxy war for a conflict over American character, American values and morals, and most importantly, over whose interests should define discourses and practices of American nationalism in the days to come. The marriage equality debate and the concomitant charges of un-Americanism functioned as a venue for the discursive renegotiation and reconceptualization of American nationalism. Essentially, the debate paradigmatically represents the transformation of a conflict away from its object of dispute and towards a renegotiation of contemporary notions of American nationalism.

American Nationalism, Un-Americanism, and the Marriage Equality Debate

This book is an analysis of contemporary notions and reconstructions of American nationalism and will examine this concept through the lens of charges of un-Americanism in the national debate over marriage equality. At its core, the study seeks to investigate how the American nation has addressed the challenges posed by a minority's insistence on legal and sociocultural equality as well as their demands for full inclusion into a commonly accepted idea of American nationalism. The book takes a particular interest in illustrating that sociocultural conflicts, such as the

7 In *Obergefell v. Hodges*, the Supreme Court of the United States held that the right to marry was guaranteed to same-sex couples by the Due Process Clause and the Equal Protection Clause of the Fourteenth Amendment to the United States Constitution. Thereby, the court made gay Americans more equal in legal terms. The ruling requires that all states recognize and perform marriages of same-sex couples (United States, Supreme Court, "*Obergefell*" 2; 28).

conflict over marriage equality, merely serve as proxy wars, and that the core issue is a dispute over 21st century American nationalism.

Americans' prevailing opinions on what characterizes their nation and on what defines (un-)Americanism are influenced by structural forces of normativity and normalism. This is particularly the case when it comes to the position of minorities within the nation and the degree to which they are regarded as an integral element of American everyday nationalism. As the influence as well as the visibility of gay[8] Americans increased in the 21st century, the American people were confronted with the challenge of granting this minority their rightful place within the nation and within conceptualizations of American everyday nationalism. Traditional hegemonic heterosexual constructions of nationalism and national identity were challenged by the everyday enactment of gay identity practices and by reconceptualizations of the un-American. Gay Americans turned from un-American security risks and targets of HUAC investigations to "un-un-Americanized" citizens who deserved protection and equal rights. This social shift has a lasting and powerful impact on American nationalism.

My book seeks to disclose and critique how the American nation reacts to such sociocultural transformations and how its people, willingly or by force, reconstruct their concept of everyday nationalism in order to integrate a previously marginalized minority. The questions that have fueled this project on nationalism in the United States were, among others: Which place do gay people occupy within dominant, mostly heteronormative, notions of American everyday nationalism? How have the demands of the gay rights movement, in particular the ruling in *Obergefell,* affected ideas of American nationalism? What roles, both active and passive, do sexual minorities play in the continuous process of the (re)negotiation and (re)construction of (un-)Americanism and American everyday nationalism? What is the impact of a concept such as homonationalism[9] and

8 The usage of the term 'gay' in this research project refers to homosexual individuals and for the purpose of this study includes gay, lesbian, and bisexual subjects. If the abbreviation 'LGBT' is employed, this denotes lesbian, gay, bisexual, as well as transgender people. Furthermore, the term 'queer' is used in order to include and denote all sexual and gender minorities (i. e., everyone who does not identify as heterosexual or cisgender).

9 Homonationalism describes the association between nationalism and queer people/queer life. The term was originally coined by Jasbir Puar in her attempt

does homonationalism exist parallel to or as an integral part of American nationalism?

Renegotiating American Nationalism: The Proxy War over Marriage Equality through the Lens of Un-Americanism is an invitation to the exploration of the changes which American everyday nationalism is subject to as a consequence of the gay rights movement's successes, in particular the landmark civil rights case *Obergefell v. Hodges* in 2015. The interest of this book is to uncover the extent to which this newly found equality regarding marriage translated into a greater equality regarding the Americanism of gay subjects and their full inclusion into representations of American everyday nationalism. Since there is a strong historical connection between the gay rights movement and charges of un-Americanism (Hall, "Americanism" 1109–10), the marriage equality debate was chosen as an exemplary discourse for this present project. This debate offers insight into how democracies cope with the challenges posed by social diversity and how minorities induce the majority to address their claims for recognition, participation, and equality. The clash of opinions over same-sex marriage forces us to ask fundamental questions about power relations and the close link between national identity politics and social norms, values, and beliefs. Consequently, those who determine what constitutes marriage also decide the Americanness or un-Americanness of individuals. Marriage is not only a highly politicized institution, but also a mechanism for structuring and regulating society, as well a gate-keeping mechanism for determining who is permitted to shape and define the meaning and experiences of American nationalism. The fight over marriage equality was one of the most controversial debates of the Obama era, my primary period of investigation, which makes this controversy a suitable framework for my analysis of contemporary notions of American everyday nationalism.

My book enters new ground as it is the first research project to not only treat un-Americanism as an object of study but to operationalize the term 'un-American' and develop it into an analytical lens. Charges of un-Americanism weigh heavy in political and sociocultural discourse,

to critically address the instrumentalization of queer people whereby queer rights are defended in order to justify racist or xenophobic positions and U.S. foreign policy practices. In this research project, I employ the term 'homonationalism' in order to explore to what extend gay subjects have become active agents in the negotiation of American everyday nationalism.

making it an effective oratorical strategy since the term 'un-American' has an enormous firepower. However, based on the results of my analysis of speech acts that include the term 'un-American,' I argue that 'un-American' has a far greater potential for research when it is not merely the object of study. The operationalization of the term and its subsequent development into an analytical lens will enable this study to argue that debates over same-sex marriage are ultimately debates over American national identity. Employing the term 'un-American' as an analytical tool allows for a profound insight into people's way of thinking and a deeper understanding of how the American nation addresses the challenges, transformations, and insecurities that the increasing inclusion of gay people into American society entails. 'Un-American' as a research approach is uniquely tailored for investigating sociocultural conflicts relating to American nationalism since un-Americanism and the term 'un-American' are deeply rooted in American history and culture. A detailed description of the book's methodological approach which the operationalization of the term 'un-American' offers will be conducted in chapter I.

A Word on Strategy

The research design of this study aims at highlighting the correlation and interdependence between identity politics, nationalism studies, and non-normative sexualities in the Obama era. My selection of the Obama era, in particular his second term, as a timeframe for this research project is determined by my choice of marriage equality as a discursive example. During the second Obama presidency, the way was paved for the necessary developments in the country which enabled liberals and progressives to dominate the national discourse in the United States and to propel the advancement of gay rights, not least the right to same-sex marriage. After President Obama's election in 2008, gay rights activists were already debating whether marriage could be the next major goal of the movement. Efforts were made to legalize same-sex marriage in several states.[10]

[10] At the time of the 2008 presidential election, same-sex marriage was only legal in the state of Massachusetts, and Vermont offered civil unions to same-sex couples. Proposition 8, a California ballot proposition and state constitutional amendment which would restrict marriage to the union between a man and a woman, was passed in the course of the November 2008 elections.

However, the conflict was not yet as fierce as it would become during Obama's second term when marriage equality activists were able to celebrate a number of successes as support for same-sex marriage in the country grew, in particular in traditionally Democratic states. The overturning of Section 3 of the Defense of Marriage Act in *United States v. Windsor* in 2013 and the 2015 ruling in *Obergefell v. Hodges* were two milestones of the gay rights movement which occurred during Obama's second term. Consequently, the intense disputes and debates leading to these milestones also took place within this timeframe, thereby making it the most relevant period for this project.

In addition to the chronological correlation with the marriage equality debate, Obama's second term is fascinating for a study of American everyday nationalism as it, so far, marked the final years of a liberal period in the United States before the election of Donald Trump as the new president singled a drastic change in the American nation. Beverly Gage argues that for liberals "this has created a sense of rupture . . . as if the 2016 election shifted the nation into some dystopian reality that was never meant to be," and she claims that this development is also reflected in the immense popularity of the insult of un-Americanism. Gage described this change as a "rupture"; however, this major transition had loomed large in the final years of the Obama presidency as a significant part of conservative America could no longer identify with what had become American nationalism during the Obama years. My study focusses on the time of the second Obama presidency but still keeps the ideological shift that came afterwards in mind, especially as this shift can be regarded as a backlash to the liberal politics that preceded the aforementioned.

In order to best illustrate how charges of un-Americanism shaped the marriage equality discourse during the second Obama administration, this book engages two different types of text. A core pillar of my text corpus is built on speech acts which contain the insult of un-Americanism. The speech acts assembled are from a wide range of sources which include, but are not limited to, newspaper articles, online blogs, and social media accounts. In order to understand how charges of un-Americanism work in national discourse and how this rhetoric affects American nationalism in the everyday lives of its people, the speakers are of different professional and social backgrounds.[11]

[11] It is necessary to point out that several speech acts stem from politicians and advocacy group representatives because their statements are documented;

Opinions of the court and the accompanying dissents in the form of slip opinions from the United States Supreme Court cases *United States v. Windsor* and *Obergefell v. Hodges* constitute the second major category of sources from which my study draws. Supreme Court judges try to reach decisions based on American law and history. However, they must also take sociocultural changes into account without allowing themselves to be swayed by temporary sentiments and political trends. This makes opinions of the court and dissents reliable barometers for long-term transformations in American culture and society which include changes in regard to American everyday nationalism. Supreme Court Judge Bader Ginsburg likes to quote her former constitutional law professor as saying that "the Court should never be influenced by the weather of the day but inevitably they will be influenced by the climate of the era" (Bader Ginsburg in interview with Hockenberry). Supreme Court slip opinions are a valuable primary source for research since they mirror the mindset of the American public. Compared to courts texts and the legal culture in other democracies, American judges are quite candid in their opinion and openly address their thoughts and concerns. This is a huge asset for research since judges tend to reflect national public discourse in the writing of their slip opinions and particularly in dissents. In U.S. legal culture, reaching a decision based on well-conceived rationale while avoiding influence from current sentiments in the country is not contradictory with expressing one's opinion and even one's anger and outrage in legal writing.

Nationalism Studies

Nationalism in its classical sense is commonly understood as an "ideology based on the premise that the individual's loyalty and devotion to the nation-state surpass other individual or group interests" (Kohn) or the "[i]dentification with one's own nation and support for its interests, especially to the exclusion or detriment of the interests of other nations" ("Nationalism"). However, for the purpose of this research project, I will draw on the theoretical approach of 'everyday nationalism studies' which provides an important new perspective on nationalism studies by focusing on how the nation is experienced and expressed by people in their every-

however, accusations of un-Americanism made by Americans outside of the political context were considered whenever possible.

day lives. Eleanor Knott describes 'everyday nationalism' as a subfield of nationalism studies which takes particular interest in directing "attention on the 'masses' and human agency within nationalism studies to consider the role and relevance of the everyday, and relevance of the lived experience of nationalism." Everyday nationalism is an approach in the field of nationalism studies which focuses on how people experience, negotiate, draft, and construct their nationalism through their everyday lives and discourses. Researchers of everyday nationalism aim to reveal people's fears, needs, hopes, and concerns regarding their national identity. They think of nationalism as a bottom-up phenomenon and not primarily as a top-down force.

Two scholars of everyday nationalism studies, whose theories will provide part of the theoretical basis for this book, are Jon E. Fox and Cynthia Miller-Idriss who suggest analyzing nationalism from four different perspectives of everyday life: "talking the nation," "choosing the nation," "performing the nation," and "consuming the nation" (537–38). The first perspective, "talking the nation," which is "the discursive construction of the nation" (537), makes their work on everyday nationalism particularly interesting for the investigation of how American nationalism is negotiated via charges of un-Americanism. Michael Skey, also an everyday nationalism studies scholar, proposes examining everyday nationalism with the help of five different dimensions: "spatial," "temporal," "cultural," "political," and "self/other" (Skey 11–12). Skey's approach to everyday nationalism is noteworthy insofar as he tries to understand why people struggle so intensely with sociocultural changes and transformations in their everyday lives, for instance, the new direction of American nationalism singled by granting marriage rights to gay Americans. Skey engages in the study of processes of stabilization and destabilization as well as the (re)negotiation and (re)construction of a nation. The theories of Skey as well as that of Fox and Miller-Idriss provide the theoretical framework for this study on American everyday nationalism. Due to their importance for my analysis, their work on everyday nationalism will be discussed in detail in chapter II.

Despite the commonly held myth that nations have somehow always existed, nationalism studies are a comparatively new field of research. The philosopher and anthropologist Ernest Gellner was one of the first scholars of nationalism in the 1960s. In his publication *Nations and Nationalism*, he argues that "[n]ationalism is primarily a political principle, which holds that the political and national unit should be congruent" (1).

Gellner understands nationalism as an imposition on modern societies in order to keep them together under a shared culture by providing a uniting bond. The 1970s and 1980s saw the rise of nationalism studies with publications of Tom Nairn, John Breuilly, Terrence Ranger, Anthony D. Smith, Eric Hobsbawm and, perhaps most notably, the political scientist Benedict Anderson. Anderson is best known for his 1983 book *Imagined Communities: Reflections on the Origin and Spread of Nationalism* in which he introduced the theory of nations as socially constructed" imagined communities." He defines 'nation' as an "imagined political community – and imagined as both inherently limited and sovereign" (6). This idea of nations being "imagined" stems from the fact that "the members of even the smallest nation will never know most of their fellow-members, meet them, or even hear them, yet in the minds of each lives the image of their communion" (6). Benedict Anderson sees the beginning of the concepts of nations and nationalism in the Age of Enlightenment, when the first states developed a national conscious independent of a ruling monarch and perceived themselves as a group of free people forming a bond which they called their nation. Distinctive for the United States is a civic nationalism which is characterized by the adherence to liberal values of equality, freedom, and individualism.[12]

Scholars of nationalism have traditionally researched the origins of nations and nationalism. The questions of how nations are built and upheld or how developments such as globalization affect nation states have been at the center of scholarship in this area.[13] Nationalism studies

12 Despite civic nationalism being regarded as characteristic for the United States, it is debated whether so-called "neo-nationalism," also called "new nationalism," gained popularity over the last years since right-wing populism, opposition to immigration, and nativism have been on the rise, in particular since the election of Donald Trump in 2016 (Bergmann 185). It is all the more interesting to investigate nationalism during the Obama era and the influence which the marriage equality debate had on this concept during these years in order to better understand a possible shift towards neo-nationalist tendencies.

13 As Edensor notes, "literature on nationalism and national identity has been dominated by a focus on the historical origins of the nation and its political lineaments" and that "the nation has been subject to very little critical analysis in terms of how it is represented and experienced through popular culture and in everyday life. This absence masks a supposition that 'nation' is equivalent to 'society', a popular assumption that also afflicts social scientists and cultural theorists" (1).

predominantly analyze this ideology on a macro level as nationalism is overwhelmingly understood as a top-down socio-political phenomenon, and they typically regard the state and the nation as congruent entities. In this sense, nationalism is an ideology which is supposed to unite the people of a nation by binding them together through a shared national identity and culture. It creates a feeling of belonging and community. However, that sense of unity is often created by defining the nation in contrast to other nations or even against a vaguely defined enemy from outside. Such an approach can involve placing one nation over others and feeling a superiority, which justifies a primary or even singular concern for the interests of one's own nation. In the case of the United States, research topics of traditional nationalism studies often include, but are not limited to, American exceptionalism, the United States' changing role in world politics, or the defense of the homeland. More broadly, the focus of nationalism studies has long been exclusively on developments which tackle the United States and its relation to the outside world rather than on developments within the nation. Therefore, nationalism studies regarding the United States would have been more inclined to investigate anti-Americanism than un-Americanism.[14] In this context, American identity is defined in contrast to external entities and is only rarely based on the experiences of the people within the nation itself. The diversity within people's American national identities and their experiences with inner-American nationalism consequently garner little attention.[15]

[14] Un-Americanism may not be confused with anti-Americanism or the non-American. Anti-Americanism is characterized by a feeling of hostility or dislike towards the American nation. It is mostly present in the context of criticism towards the United States and U.S. foreign policy. In contrast to un-Americanism, the insult of anti-Americanism is very rarely espoused by Americans towards fellow Americans.

[15] As the study of un-Americanism revolves around inner-American discourse, its analysis would usually fall under the concept of patriotism since the object of study and the political language concerned involve internal developments within the patria, the homeland. Whereas nationalism has been traditionally associated with a feeling of superiority and the aspiration to foreign dominance irrespective of personal political beliefs, patriotism, by contrast, concerns internal affairs and is defined by political or sociocultural issues. This differentiation between nationalism and patriotism has often been encouraged for analytical purposes. In order to distinguish between the "positive and negative

One of the most impactful turns in nationalism studies was initiated by Michael Billig in his 1995 monograph *Banal Nationalism,* in which he challenges previous conceptions about this ideology.[16] Billig's goal was to redirect the attention of nationalism scholars to the banal representations of the nation that take place within the respective nation, for example the use of flags, traditions and rituals, sporting events, or national symbols, which create a sense of national identity and community among citizens.

manifestations of national identification," Qiong Li and Marilynn B. Brewer utilize approaches from social psychology in their attempt to figure out what it means to be American and how patriotism and nationalism have transformed after 9/11. They explain that social psychology distinguishes "between 'patriotism' and 'nationalism,' with the former connoting pride and love for country and the latter referring to chauvinistic arrogance and desire for dominance in internal relations" (728). Furthermore, they add that "patriotism may also be compatible with liberalism and tolerance for diversity, but nationalism is more likely to be associated with authoritarian values and intolerance" (728). However, drawing such a clear line between patriotism and nationalism is increasingly regarded as outdated and not beneficial for research on national identity. Minxin Pei notes that if one seeks to distinguish the concepts from each other, one might find "a distinction, but no real difference" (32). She explains her critique of this artificial distinction as follows:

> Political scientists have labored to prove such a difference, equating patriotism with allegiance to one's country and defining nationalism as sentiments of ethno-national superiority. In reality, however, the psychological and behavioral manifestations of nationalism and patriotism are indistinguishable, as is the impact of such sentiments on policy. (32)

Thereby, nationalism is increasingly seen as an ideology that is not limited to foreign affairs, but one that also exerts considerable influence on internal political and sociocultural developments as well as on the construction of diverse, competing concepts of national identity.

16 Billig criticizes that "there is something misleading about this accepted use of the word 'nationalism.' It always seems to locate nationalism on the periphery. . . . In consequence, those in established nations – at the centre of things – are led to see nationalism as the property of others, not of 'us'" (*Banal* 5). Billig demands that the focus of nationalism studies should much rather be on the people within the nation and how nationalism is experienced in and represented through their ordinary lives. "If nationalism is a widespread ideology, then a different perspective is in order," Billig insists and claims that nationalism studies need a change of perspective (15).

Although Michael Billig addresses American banal nationalism at some points in his work, the United States was not the focus of his work. However, he acknowledges its significance and notes that more research needs to be done on nationalism in the United States (Billig, "Reflecting" 351). Lukasz Szulc, who criticized Billig precisely for this lack of interest in American banal nationalism, points out that the United States has yet to receive the attention it deserves by banal nationalism studies (69). Szulc bemoans that marginal or less powerful nations have been the most widely studied nations, which has resulted in a "low visibility of banal Americanism" (69). Billig and Szulc both agree that there should be increased "efforts to make the invisible visible and advance our understanding of how banal Americanism is being reproduced and universalized" (69). It is one of the objectives of this book on un-Americanism and American nationalism to draw attention to how bottom-up nationalism is constructed and negotiated in the United States. Billig's work is relevant for this aim as it was the precursor to everyday nationalism studies.

Concerning the role of gay Americans in the construction of dominant ideas of American nationalism both as minority subjects and as active agents, the existing literature continues to exhibit a noticeable lack of interest. The legal and social situation of gay and lesbian people within the American nation has been predominately discussed in regard to citizenship and the accompanying rights. In her monograph, *The Twilight of Equality?: Neoliberalism, Cultural Politics, and the Attack on Democracy*, as well as in several essays, Lisa Duggan discusses the gay rights movement and gay American citizenship within the neoliberalist framework in the United States. In these works, she scrutinizes "the new homonormativity" which she defines as "a politics that does not contest dominant heteronormative assumptions and institutions but upholds and sustains them" ("Homonormativity" 179). In *Sexuality and Citizenship*, the sociologist Diane Richardson examines the normativity and critique of the concept of sexual citizenship. She is primarily interested in how the sociocultural construction of sexualities affects the materialization of various ideas of citizenship within society. Unfortunately, both Duggan and Richardson only briefly comment on the relationship between homosexuality and nationalism. *Renegotiating American Nationalism: The Proxy War over Marriage Equality through the Lens of Un-Americanism* builds on Duggan's and Richardson's theories of homosexual citizenship but links them to everyday nationalism studies in order to illustrate how gay subjects shape the meaning and experiences of American nationalism.

How American nationalism in the context of foreign affairs and counter-terrorism caused a reconfiguration of concepts of sexuality, race, and ethnicity in the United States was addressed by Jasbir K. Puar in her monograph *Terrorist Assemblages: Homonationalism in Queer Times* (2007). Puar coined the term 'homonationalism' in order to critically question how queerness was employed by the American government "as a regulatory frame of biopolitics" (*Terrorist* 24). She examines to what degree a discursive instrumentalization of homosexual Americans, encouraged by the U.S. government's need to justify dubious foreign policy decisions, led to the inclusion of some queer individuals into American nationalism at the expense of other minority subjects. Puar's critique paved the way for further research on the intersection of queerness and American nationalism. Since she repeatedly encouraged other scholars to continue the debate on homonationalism (e. g., "Rethinking" 336), it is all the more perplexing that scholarship has not taken the multiple opportunities Puar's conceptualization offers for expanding on her research and connecting it to new fields of study. Her work provides an excellent foundation for linking new strands of research to her work, an opportunity this study will seize in chapter VII.B.

Un-Americanism Studies

Competing notions of Americanism have been at the center of a rich and ongoing scholarly discussion, which has resulted in countless publications examining Americanism and a continuous unfolding of new insights and perspectives. In light of this development, it is surprising that historiography offers only a handful of studies on un-Americanism although un-Americanism bears an enormous potential for research. Despite a growing interest in this object of study, scholarship on un-Americanism is still very much in its infancy. This significant lack of analysis is what motivated George Lewis to start inquiring into un-Americanism and its development from the 18th century to the 9/11 terrorist attack in his research project "Un-Americans: Ideological Dissent, Patriotic Subversion and Isolating the 'Other' in the USA" ("Un-Americans: Ideological Dissent"). The absence of studies on un-Americanism, particularly regarding the term's development after the Cold War Era, also surprised Lewis:

> There have, hitherto, been no sustained scholarly analyses of un-Americanism. That is despite the fact that the term has been ever-present in American political, social, and cultural life from its coining in the late eighteenth century to its ongoing development in the twenty-first. Such analytical neglect is perplexing for a number of reasons, not least because there are few scholars working on the United States who could not, if they so desired, find meaningful ways of linking their work to ideas of un-Americanism, but also because as a word and as a term "un-American" is so extraordinary. ("Introduction" 871)

Emerging from his research project was a special issue of the *Journal of American Studies* called "The Un-American" in 2013, in which Lewis and fellow contributors discussed un-Americanism from a wide range of perspectives throughout history in order to trace its development. Among the twelve topics covered were the House Un-American Activities Committee, the Daughters of the American Revolution, the Ku Klux Klan, religious groups, as well as the civil rights issue.

For the purpose of the present project, Simon Hall's contribution to the special issue of the journal is of particular interest. The author explores the historical connection between the gay rights movement and charges of un-Americanism in his essay "Americanism, Un-Americanism, and the Gay Rights Movement." Hall explains why accusations of un-Americanism occupy such a prominent position in the movement's battle rhetoric and provides a wide range of examples throughout history when accusations of un-Americanism were raised in the course of the gay rights movement. Since his writing is only of article-length, Hall touches upon the various aspects of the interconnection between un-Americanism and gay rights but cannot sufficiently elaborate on them; nevertheless, his work sheds light on a previously overlooked connection which this book will investigate in depth. It is the goal of this research project to extend upon Hall's essential work.

The special issue "The Un-American" that resulted from Lewis' research project was the first scholarly engagement with the phenomenon of un-Americanism which investigated the term 'un-American' outside of the context of the House Un-American Activities Committee and the surrounding time period. Previous research was limited to the term's usage during the Red Scare, failing to explore un-Americanism independent of McCarthy's anti-communist campaigns. Consequently, even the studies on the House Un-American Activities Committee do not offer a more comprehensive contribution to research on un-Americanism. Frank

J. Donner's 1961 monograph *The Un-Americans* may sound promising at first; however, while Donner provides an insight into HUAC hearings, he does not seem to be interested in un-Americanism per se, though the title of this book suggests otherwise.[17]

Robert K. Carr and Walter Goodman both offer a historical documentation of the work of the HUAC. For his monograph *The House Committee on Un-American Activities*, Carr conducted extensive research on the events which led to the committee's development, the committee's hearings and files, as well as its coverage in the media and the consequential public perception. At its core, Carr's book amounts to a vivid representation of the committee's work from the viewpoint of a contemporary, however, it is not a broad historical analysis. After all, it was published in 1952, twenty-three years before Congress abolished the HUAC. Walter Goodman's *The Committee: The Extraordinary Career of the House Committee on Un-American Activities*, released in 1968 and thus offering a more nuanced historical perspective, was considerably more critical in tone than Carr's study. By analyzing reports from the hearings, Goodman strove to uncover what was meant by "un-American activities" but was unable to reach a conclusion since the charge was instrumentalized and interpreted according to the whims or motivations of the chairman in each hearing. Everyone and everything had the potential to be un-American.

Historiography shows that research on the House Committee on Un-American Activities is limited and outdated. Since the beginning of the 21st century, there has been some scholarly interest in the HUAC in the context of the so-called Hollywood Blacklist and the 'Hollywood Ten,' a group of writers and directors who were accused of having communist ties and therefore subpoenaed to testify before the congressional committee. Most notable is the essay collection *'Un-American' Hollywood: Politics and Film in the Blacklist Era* in which Krutnik et al. intended to shed light on un-Americanism and draw parallels between the HUAC crusade and the 9/11 terrorist attacks among other research goals (Krutnik et. al. 17). Unfortunately, they fail to meet this objective because the es-

[17] Donner is familiar with the House Un-American Activities Committee, both in his capacity as a civil liberties lawyer and also as a defendant as he was once accused of being a member of a communist organization (Lambert). The main goal of his book is to resume the cases he fought before the HUAC and not to explore un-Americanism more broadly or to scrutinize the usage of the term 'un-American' at that time.

says are focused strongly on topics from the field of film studies and only occasionally touch on un-Americanism at best.

Another context in which historiography has explored the HUAC and to a certain extent the usage of the term 'un-American' is the Lavender Scare which paralleled the anti-communist Second Red Scare. During the Cold War, homosexual Americans were subject to discriminatory practices as they were put on the same level as communists and deemed national security risks.[18] In his monograph *The Lavender Scare: The Cold War Persecution of Gays and Lesbians in the Federal Government*, David K. Johnson introduces the reader to the gay subculture of the McCarthy Era and uncovers step by step how homosexuals came to be perceived as security risks in the eye of the public which was beset by a communist panic and frantically in search of spies. Johnson illustrates how closely intertwined questions of national security and un-Americanism are with gay life in the United States. The fact that this is not just a phenomenon of the Cold War Era but also a recurrent pattern in the 21st century is investigated in the present study on charges of un-Americanism in the marriage equality debate.

The topic of national security and the allegation of un-Americanism toward gay and lesbian citizens was also addressed by Mary K. Bloodsworth-Lugo und Carmen R. Lugo-Lugo in their book *Containing (Un)American Bodies: Race, Sexuality, and Post-9/11 Constructions of Citizenship*. They investigate how certain bodies were perceived as threatening and how same-sex marriage was portrayed as an act of domestic terrorism in the Bush post-9/11 era (9). At that time, notions of Americanism and American citizenship were discussed in the context of biopolitics and the so-called "war on terror" with same-sex bodies as well as immigrants being viewed as enemy combatants (Bloodsworth-Lugo und Lugo-Lugo 1–3). Bloodsworth-Lugo und Lugo-Lugo explore the discursive condemnation of same-sex marriage and the position of

18 During the McCarthy Era, homosexuals were regarded as un-American and even more dangerous than communists, especially if they worked in government positions and in foreign service (D.K. Johnson 2). In order to protect the United States from the threat posed by homosexuals, approximately one thousand employees were expelled from the Department of State for real or alleged homosexuality under the guise of being deemed a "security risk" (76). The popular strategy was to dismiss them from federal government, expose them in hearings, and to disgrace them publicly for un-American behavior.

gay subjects as un-American threats, however, again without treating un-Americanism as an independent concept.

Since scholarship largely ignored un-Americanism as well as the term 'un-American' until the publication of the special issue of the *Journal of American Studies* in 2013, a historiography of un-Americanism needs to also take noteworthy newspapers articles into account. In 2017, Beverly Gage, a professor for American political history at Yale University, published an article in *The New York Times Magazine* titled "How Un-American Became the Political Insult of the Moment." Gage gives a brief overview of the history of the term 'un-American' in order to highlight how the term has been an integral part of American culture since the early days of the republic. However, her focus is on the term's current usage, specifically on the months following the 2016 presidential election and President Trump's first weeks in office. "'Un-American' [b]ecame the [p]olitical [i]nsult of the [m]oment" for everyone, from the left to the right, on the political spectrum because no other line of attack more fittingly expresses the discontent of Americans, and it is "ready to be attached to any given outrage" (Gage). Additionally, Gage insists that charges of un-Americanism are not just a rhetorical trend:

> It's re-emergence reflects something far more serious about the state of national discourse. . . . [T]he word has historically gained traction at moments when national consensus seems the most wobbly and uncertain. It signals an urgent desire to find something – anything – that Americans can still agree on.

Convinced that the American nation is in the midst of a massive inner reconstruction and redefinition, she warns:

> To label something 'un-American' is to imagine America as it should have been or as it might yet be but not as it ever was. Far from bringing back a meaningless insult, the revival of the charge suggests that something very big is now at stake: not only the direction of federal policy or the partisan balance of power but America's identity as a nation.

Gage's perspectives on un-Americanism constitute the most significant contribution to this area of research in recent years. So far, Gage's article is the only publication which has examined the usage of the term 'un-American' in contemporary discourse. *Renegotiating American Nationalism: The Proxy War over Marriage Equality through the Lens of Un-Americanism* aims at filling this gap in scholarship. I trace and illustrate why insults of un-Americanism have become such a popular oratorical choice and thereby offer an in-depth investigation of the usage of the term 'un-American' in a 21st century discourse.

Contribution to Research

Bart Bonikowski and Paul DiMaggio warn that the neglect of a substantial scholarship on American nationalism is problematic for three reasons (as listed in Bonikowski and DiMaggio 950): First, the United States as a nation deserves more profound scholarly attention as it is one of the only new nations that has survived for centuries despite its diverse ethnic and racial setup. Second, "understanding how Americans imagine, feel about, and talk to one another about their homeland is a necessary but ordinarily omitted prerequisite to making sense of political contention in the late-twentieth and early-twenty-first centuries." Third, understanding American nationalism is crucial due to its enormous influence on American politics.

Renegotiating American Nationalism: The Proxy War over Marriage Equality through the Lens of Un-Americanism seeks to fill this gap in historiography and offer a study on American nationalism which takes particular interest in current reconceptualizations and renegotiations of everyday nationalism as a consequence of the ameliorated status of gay subjects within the American nation. My book describes and critically discusses the mechanisms of Americanization and un-Americanization of individuals, based on the role they play within American sociocultural as well as political discourse and the American nation. The resulting everyday nationalism is the unfinished product of a continuous engagement with the everyday enactments of the American nation as well as with the competing demands of various groups for a seat at the table of nationalism discourse. In my research, I employ an innovative methodological approach by developing the term 'un-American' into an analytical lens which helps detect issues and concerns connected to American nationalism as they are negotiated in proxy war discourses.

The limited scholarship on the everyday enactments, discourses, and ideas of American nationalism is not due to a lack of interest in this field of study. It is one of the main hypotheses of this project to see the gaps in the historiographical state on U.S. nationalism as resulting from a unique and challenging characteristic of the discursive manifestations of nationalism. Based on my theory that culture war debates serve as proxy wars for negotiations of nationalism, I argue that this unfortunate neglect correlates with the phenomenon that discourse over nationalism is often hidden within other debates, as it is in the controversy over marriage equality. When scholars seek to examine nationalism, particularly inner-American everyday nationalism, they need to turn to controversies which, on the surface, have little to do with their interest of research but actually serve as pretext for discussions on nationalism. I strike new ground by claiming that the debate of marriage equality was ultimately turned into a platform for a dispute over what defines the American nation and which ideals American everyday nationalism should represent. My book reveals new facets of American nationalism by uncovering the diverse settings in which nationalism is negotiated outside of traditional nationalism discourse.

Charges of un-Americanism are an inner-American phenomenon, just as everyday nationalism is focused on how American nationalism is experienced, negotiated, and reconstructed on a daily basis within the United States. The field of nationalism studies has been dominated by research projects which explore nationalism in relation to other nation-states but has only rarely asked how notions of American nationalism affect inner-American discourse, politics, culture, and people's everyday lives. Similarly, anti-Americanism has been the central theme of several book-length examinations,[19] whereas un-Americanism has not received adequate attention in American studies. As a consequence, this book intends to shift the focus of nationalism studies away from a comparative and international perspec-

[19] See Egbert Klautke for a historiographical review of works on anti-Americanism from a 21st century European perspective: "Anti-Americanism in Twentieth Century Europe." *The Historical Journal*, vol. 54, pp. 1125–39. *Cambridge UP*, https://doi.org/10.1017/S0018246X11000276. A critical examination and comprehensive history of anti-Americanism can be found in Max Paul Friedman's monograph *Rethinking Anti-Americanism. The History of an Exceptional Concept in American Foreign Relations* (Cambridge UP, 2012). In his book, Friedman takes U.S. foreign relations with nine countries into account and argues that the myth of anti-Americanism has often negatively affected United States' national interests. An essay collection offering a wide range of perspectives on anti-American from around the globe while simultaneously tracing the development of this concept is Tony Judt and Denis Lacorne's book *With Us or Against Us: Studies in Global Anti-Americanism* (Palgrave Macmillan, 2016).

tive and towards the developments, processes, and discourses that take place within the United States and which are the consequence of social transformations within the nation. The cultural studies scholar Winfried Fluck claims that "[o]ne of the reasons why American studies scholars are currently hesitant to acknowledge that, although American culture may not have developed autonomously, it has nevertheless developed under conditions of its own, is that they are afraid of being accused of exceptionalism" and therefore refrain from treating developments within the United States as unique ("Theories" 60). No nation is a satellite, independent of the influences from the surrounding world: however, the debate over marriage equality is an example of a controversy which was fairly independent from international developments as focused on American values as well as on American national identity and character. Shifting scholarly attention to inner-American developments is also an important step for the hitherto largely neglected interrelation between queer studies and nationalism studies. Puar's innovative concept of homonationalism benefits greatly from an examination of how the perception as well as the agency of gay Americans *within* the nation impact American nationalism.

Although I primarily seek to make a contribution to the field of nationalism studies, I also offer new perspectives on queer studies due to the book's employment of the marriage equality discourse as a paradigmatic debate. The development of the gay rights movement is adequately reflected in historiography, scholarship has discussed the pros and cons of same-sex marriage, and researchers have repeatedly delved into parallels to the African American civil rights movement. However, they have only rarely investigated how marriage equality relates to un-Americanism and in particular how the struggle for same-sex marriage impacted and transformed contemporary notions of American nationalism. Gay and lesbian life in the United States was long thought of as a parallel universe in some respect, particularly when homophobia was more common and when gays largely remained within their communities. However, times have changed as gay subjects have become omnipresent in the representations of American nationalism through everyday life, and they have become active agents in the process of shaping American everyday nationalism. I argue that the correlation between queer studies and nationalism studies deserves greater attention within the interdisciplinary field of American studies because it allows us to situate the fight for gay rights in the larger macrocosm of the American nation. Consequently, my book also makes a contribution to queer studies by examining the Americanization of a sexual minority and the transformation of 21st century American nationalism as a result of the striking successes of the marriage equality movement.

Situating and Mapping the Text

As Fluck postulates, culture can be regarded as the "key to national identity" ("American Cultural Studies" 288) and it offers "a common horizon for national self-definitions" (287). Consequently, this book on current notions and reconceptualizations of American nationalism is situated in American cultural studies. The interdisciplinary character of this field offers conceptual approaches that help assess how the American nation addressed the challenges that resulted from the gay minority's insistence on full inclusion into the common conceptualization of American nationalism. *Renegotiating American Nationalism: The Proxy War over Marriage Equality through the Lens of Un-Americanism* draws on theories and practices from the fields of sociology, political science, law, and linguistics, among others. In the course of its exploration of the renegotiation of American nationalism, my book links the previously unconnected fields of everyday nationalism studies and queer studies, and it also offers new insights on American rhetoric and ideology, identity politics, regulatory normativity, and landmark civil rights cases.

Despite the necessity to chronicle parts of the history of un-Americanism and the marriage equality movement, my study of contemporary American nationalism as a dynamic phenomenon of American culture is not a historical project. However, I wish to take into account that the discourse examined in this research project is treated as an event of the past for reasons of analytical practicality although the debate over same-sex marriage and the concomitant renegotiation of American nationalism are far from being over. The impression is created as if past and present seem to diffuse in this investigation of American everyday nationalism ahead and in the wake of the Supreme Court ruling *Obergefell v. Hodges*. Thereby, this study is also an engagement with contemporary history as my research object "is still smoking" ("noch qualmt"; my trans.; Tuchmann 31)[20] while it is written about. Consequently, I would like to

[20] In her 1982 book *In Geschichte Denken*, the historian Barbara Tuchmann discussed whether one should or can even write about history "while it is still

borrow from Puar and understand this cultural studies project also as "a historization of the contemporary moment" (*Terrorist* xxvii).

In chapter I of this study, I elaborate on an innovative methodological approach which I designed for this research project. I operationalized the term 'un-American' and developed it into an analytical tool with which I illustrate why the debate over marriage equality is in fact a renegotiation of American nationalism. After explaining the appeal of the term 'un-American' in discourse, I trace its development from an object of research to an analytical tool and describe how this methodological approach can be employed by scholars before highlighting the unique benefits of the term 'un-American' as a research tool.

Everyday nationalism studies, which provide the theoretical framework for my study, are the focus of chapter II. After a review of Michael Billig's work on banal nationalism, I introduce the theories and research of Jon E. Fox and Cynthia Miller-Idriss as well as that of Michael Skey. Their work on everyday nationalism is the conceptual framework for my investigation of contemporary ideas of American nationalism in the light of the elevated status of gay subjects within the American nation. As identity politics plays into this context, processes of identity formation are also addressed in this chapter.

In chapter III, I explore the history of un-Americanism in the United States and provide a brief overview of the development of the term 'un-American' from Jeffersonian times until the late 20th century. The focus of this historical chapter is on the era of the investigations of the House Un-American Activities Committee and the crusade against gay Americans during the so-called 'Lavender Scare.' This timespan lay the foundation for un-Americanism as a regulatory mechanism for proper American behavior, as a language for the designation of insiders and outsiders, and as a charge which would shape the debates of the gay rights movement from its inception in 1950s to the controversy over marriage equality in the Obama era.

While the first three chapters introduce the methodological, theoretical, and historical framework of this study, chapter IV marks the beginning of the analytical part of this book. In "Charges of Un-Americanism and the Debate on Marriage Equality," I briefly trace the road to marriage equality in the United States by adducing the most important legal and

smoking" ("die noch qualmt"; my trans.; Tuchmann 31) as this often results in a lack of distance to the events concerned.

political moments which shaped the evolvement of the discourse over same-sex marriage in the United States. The focus of this chapter is on the analysis of speech acts which include accusations of un-Americanism in the debate over marriage equality in the years before the historical 2015 ruling of *Obergefell v. Hodges*. In order to recognize the impact of the usage of the term 'un-American' on the debate on marriage equality and in order to understand how this controversy eventually became a dispute over competing notions of American nationalism, I scrutinize and contextualize the reciprocal insults of un-Americanism in this dispute.

Chapter V is dedicated to the analysis of two milestone court rulings in the fight for marriage equality. In *United States v. Windsor* and *Obergefell v. Hodges*, the United States Supreme Court addressed questions of equal rights, the character of the American nation, and the obligation to include a minority into American everyday nationalism. In *Windsor*, Section 3 of DOMA, which had excluded same-sex couples from the terms 'marriage' and 'spouse' by definition and denied the federal recognition of same-sex marriages, was ruled unconstitutional. The process which began with *Windsor* reached a new peak with the ruling in *Obergefell* which ordered the nationwide legalization of same-sex marriage. The majority opinions and the dissents in *United States v. Windsor* and *Obergefell v. Hodges* mirror the sentiments and concerns of the American public in the national discourse over same-sex marriage and American nationalism. I argue that *Obergefell* is the most important turning point in the process of the "un-un-Americanization" and rehabilitation of gay subjects within the American nation. In addition to the examination of two court rulings, I reflect on the controversial debate over whether the decisions in these cases were the result of judicial activism and assess the possibility of a societal backlash to the rulings in *Windsor* and *Obergefell*.

Chapter VI, "Polarization, American Values, and the Nation," builds on the results of the analyses from chapters IV and V and excavates the underlying and often ensconced reasons which cause Americans to engage in mutual insults of un-Americanism. Before the ruling in *Obergefell*, many of the core promises of the American nation were not upheld for same-sex couples and their families. I demonstrate that American nationalism had to undergo a significant transformation in order to honor the ideals the nation asks its people to cherish. Based on a sociological field study, I also maintain that an investigation of opponents' fears and concerns reveals that marriage equality served as a projection for people's hopes and fears – feelings that at their core had nothing to do with same-sex marriage per se. Rather, socioeconomic struggles, a rapidly changing society, declining community cohesion, as well as a feeling of alienation from the contemporary American nation in which they felt voiceless were at the core of their anti-gay attitude. In chapter VI, I elaborate upon the high degree of politicization of the American marriage and argue that the debate over same-sex marriage was particularly prone to serving as a proxy war over negotiations of American nationalism as marriage, family, and nation are inextricably linked in the United States.

Since notions of nationalism are determined by forces of normalism and normativity, these are surveyed at the beginning of chapter VII in order to allow for an engagement with the normalizing and normativizing influences on the positioning of homosexual people within the American nation. The chapter is devoted to discussing the ideas of American nationalism that evolved as a result of the increasing voice and agency of gay Americans. I review Puar's theories on homonationalism and follow her invitation to develop them further in order to explore the intersection between queer studies and everyday nationalism studies. Thereby, I enable a perspective on homonationalism, which allows for an analysis of this phenomenon as a bottom-up process, and which sheds new light on the gay rights discourse's impact on inner-American nationalism. In order to acknowledge that marriage equality has not resulted in a greater inclusion of all gay and queer subjects into contemporary ideas of American nationalism, I also examine the drawbacks of same-sex marriage and homonationalism and maintain that new manifestations of marginalization and discrimination have emerged as a result of the redistribution of power and sociocultural capital in the wake of *Obergefell*.

In the conclusion, I recapitulate this research project on current notions of American everyday nationalism and situate this study within larger developments and transformations in American culture and society. *Renegotiating American Nationalism: The Proxy War over Marriage Equality through the Lens of Un-Americanism* concludes with a call for scholars to pursue a stronger focus of American studies in the interconnected field of nationalism studies and queer studies.

Chapter I

I 'Un-American' as Analytical Tool

Accusations of un-Americanism are frequent in the marriage equality debate in the United States and are highly popular with both its supporters and opponents. The term 'un-American' is rhetorically successful for a number of reasons. The word's appeal lies chiefly in its enormous firepower; however, this is not the only criterion which makes charges of un-Americanism so attractive in sociopolitical discourse. In his monograph *Political Communication in American Campaigns,* Joseph S. Tuman notes: "Before we can talk about a politically persuasive speech message itself, we must initially understand what and who the audience is. . ." (61). It is obvious who the audience in the dispute over marriage equality is: the American people.

The usage of the term 'un-American' in political and sociocultural discourse is an effective strategy since it appeals to all individuals who are American citizens or otherwise consider themselves American. There is no comparable rhetoric with which one could collectively address a group as diverse as Americans. When aiming at winning over an audience, finding common ground, such as Americanism or un-Americanism, is an essential oratorical strategy (Tuman 63). Despite the many competing interpretations of this term, the concept of Americanism[21] serves to

21 Michael Kazin provides one of the most frequently cited definitions of Americanism in the *Princeton Encyclopedia of American Political History* (see footnote 6). Unfortunately, his definition fails to provide details on what is actually distinctive about the United States and what its core values and ideals are. However, this would have been the most interesting aspect of adducing a definition of Americanism since this question poses the fiercest point of contestation for Americans. Kazin is quick to point out to the paradox that "Americans have always fought more over how to define and apply the national ideals than about the merits of their language or cuisine" (Kazin et al. 26) in contrast to many other nation states. The problem that arises from the concept of Americanism deriving itself mostly from political values and ideals is that "the resulting battles to define Americanism have alternately divided the nation and unified it, producing both internal strife and solidarity against foreign enemies," Kazin and McCartin note (2). They claim that "Americanism's propensity to generate both conflict and cohesion continues

unite the United States to a degree as it is not seen in any other nation (Kazin et al. 26). Everyone has an idea of what is meant by un-Americanism, namely, something that clashes with American ideals and values. Individual interpretations of the term 'un-American' can differ vastly. Speakers of interest groups rarely provide a definition of un-Americanism before relying on this rhetoric, since leaving it open means that the audience can assign their own meaning to the word, thereby allowing someone to reach as broad an audience as possible. Supporters and opponents of marriage equality adhere to competing interpretations of 'American/un-American,' but within the respective interest groups, references to Americanism tend to unite the members. Ideally, this argumentative strategy can even persuade former rivals to join one's fight.

A well-chosen appeal to emotion has a major impact on the persuasive power of one's oratory, and the term 'un-American' is a perfect choice to achieve this effect. Emotion looms large in the marriage equality controversy; the topic per se is highly emotional and cannot be discussed on a purely impersonal level. Americans have a tendency not to engage in political conversations in order to avoid potential social exclusion or having to deal with cognitive dissonance (Berry and Sobieraj 127; 130–31). However, everyone seems to have an opinion on gay marriage, even those Americans who usually show no interest in political debates. The decisive difference to purely political disputes is that the debate on marriage equality is about American self-definition as well as everyday experiences of nationhood, and this is a topic which concerns every American. Consequently, allusions to Americanism or core American events and values lend additional force to one's argumentation.[22]

into the early twenty-first century . . . when Americanism is fought about nearly everywhere" (2). As a result of the vagueness and contentious nature of Americanism, devoting further effort to figuring out a universal understanding of this idea at a time when it is so contested is not hugely beneficial to research on un-Americanism. Countless works have been published on Americanism which, firstly, is an enormous research area of its own and, secondly, did nothing to consolidate a commonly accepted definition of Americanism which is more specific than Kazin's suggestion. However, what is uncontested is that both Americanism and un-Americanism raise questions about inclusion and exclusion as well as discourses and practices of American everyday nationalism.

22 Joseph S. Tuman gave the example of San Francisco Mayor Gavin Newsom, who prominently favored marriage equality and raised his voice for the cause.

Of course, references to uniting themes of Americanism are more suitable for convincing one's opponents than accusing them of un-Americanism. However, both approaches fall into the same category of reaching the audience on an emotional level and through their self-identification as Americans in order to instigate them to act or act differently. When interest groups mutually accuse each other of un-Americanism, it is intentionally provocative, even offensive. As a result, it is not always beneficial to the conflict. Nevertheless, using the term 'un-American' is perceived as an oratorically successful strategy, since it helps achieve one important goal: appealing to the audience's emotions via their self-concept as Americans.

Accusations of un-Americanism have become widely popular in diverse areas of the national sociopolitical discourse, and it is conspicuous that they are the method of choice for minority interest groups who are looking to put pressure on lawmakers and increase support within the larger public.[23] Interestingly, in the debate on marriage equality, it is dif-

In a plea to his fellow Americans, the mayor did not only make references to Americanism in general but also reminded his audience of the struggles of the civil rights movement in order to root his claims in the nation's history (67). In doing so, he was not only trying to connect with Americans who already support this cause. He also attempted to reach those who had a different opinion on same-sex marriage by emphasizing a shared national history. Tuman explains this strategy as follows: "Newsom's analogy may have been logically connected to the theme of equality, but the first way it hit many in the audience was emotionally, with the memory of fighting racial discrimination still present in public consciousness" (67).

23 This phenomenon could, for instance, also be observed in the debate over the 2010 Patient Protection and Affordable Care Act (Obamacare). Opponents of this massive regulatory overhaul of the United States' health care system denounced the law as well as the Obama administration as un-American. Rick Santorum, senator from Pennsylvania and candidate for the Republican presidential nomination in 2012, is one of the most vocal opponents of the Affordable Care Act and expressed his aversion towards the reform at multiple occasions. He accused Obamacare supporters of un-Americanism and of not understanding how this nation works: "It is un-American. It's not how America functions well. It's not how we got to the greatest country in the history of the world. . . . It goes against the grain of who we are" (Santorum). Santorum was afraid that the implementation of a law such as the Affordable Care Act would change the United States forever: "It is the biggest fundamental shift in American history of the relationship between the government and the people. This is a disaster."

ficult to determine who the minority is. On the one hand, same-sex couples are a minority on a demographic level (Jones).[24] On the other hand, at this point in time, they enjoy overwhelming support from marriage equality advocates of every sexual orientation and the approval rate of same-sex marriage among the general population is now well above 50 per cent (McCarthy, "U.S. Support"). As a result, one could now argue that those who oppose a change in law have supplanted advocates of marriage equality as the "traditional" minority since opponents are now fewer in number. Therefore, the trend of minority groups employing charges of un-Americanism more frequently than those in the majority is not as obvious in the marriage equality controversy, as the majority-minority relationship in this culture war debate was subject to change. In states which had not legalized equal marriage before *Obergefell v. Hodges*, supporters of marriage equality were the minority that was contesting established law. Consequently, they relied heavily on accusations of un-Americanism in order to enforce their arguments. This radical rhetoric is often chosen if an interest group is concerned that their arguments will otherwise not be heard. It creates polarization which helps bring the issue onto the current political agenda and the table of national discourse.

From Rhetorical Weapon to Analytical Tool

The Swiss linguist Ferdinand de Saussure described the relationship between the signifier and the signified as arbitrary because there is no clear and sometimes not even a logical connection between the two (Storey 87).[25] Therefore, this relationship can only be understood in discourse

24 In the United States, 3.1% of Americans identify as bisexual, 1.4% as gay, 0.7% as lesbian and 0.6% as transgender according to the latest numbers published by the public opinion institute Gallup in 2021. LGBT identification is far more likely among young adults with one in six from the Generation Z (those aged 18 to 23 in 2020) considering themselves as non-heterosexual. That growth is expected to continue (Jones).

25 Saussure developed the model of the linguistic sign in order to illustrate which components words consist of. The linguistic sign (e.g., a word) consists of two parts which are inseparable from one another: the signifier (e.g., a sound or written word) on the level of expression and the signified concept on the level of meaning. This relationship between the two components of the linguistic sign is reciprocal since signifier and signified are mutually dependent,

if there is some shared understanding of what the signified could be. This is easy with physical objects (such as an apple or a book) but can turn into a challenge if the signified is an abstract and continuously changing concept such as un-Americanism. This lack of a clear signifier-signified relationship is often problematized because it complicates discourse and is a potential source of conflict (357); however, it can also be seen as an opportunity for research.

While there is little disagreement about what an apple is, the term 'un-American' is, at its center, a competition between various definitions which are as diverse as the American people themselves. Meaning is always created in context which involves the speaker's environment at a particular point in time, previous events and experiences, and cultural practices, among other factors (Brock et al. 29–30). How the term 'un-American' is understood depends heavily on the individual and their worldview, mindset, and sociocultural environment. This is what makes the term 'un-American' so interesting for research. The analysis of speech acts that include the term 'un-American' suggests that there must be more to accusations of un-Americanism than it only being an oratorical strategy. It also allows for an insight into people's way of thinking. Accusations of un-Americanism and the term 'un-American' itself are just the tip of the iceberg in the marriage equality debate. The high level of emotionality and personal involvement in accusations of un-Americanism can reveal more about the debate on marriage equality and those involved than just how the conflict is structured discursively.

The charge of un-Americanism is a powerful rhetoric. It is utilized to make one's voice heard in culture war debates that often determine the direction which the United States as a nation is heading. Participating in the process of shaping the national definition of what constitutes Americanism or un-Americanism also means being in a position to influence which morals and values dominate the national self-concept. However, at the same time, the term 'un-American' has become a substitute expression for thoughts, fears, and insecurities that people struggle to verbalize outside of accusations of un-Americanism. In several of the accusations, 'un-American' is a linguistic auxiliary construction through which Americans try to express their point of view. Chapter VI will demonstrate that

but, at the same time, this relationship between the two components is arbitrary because which signifier is used for which signified concept is based on the respective agreement of the speech community (Kortmann 16).

the reasons for insulting someone by calling them un-American often stem from social and socioeconomic anxieties. It is the fear of deteriorating values or a complete loss of morality in the United States. People are afraid of new concepts of family and society and that the world surrounding them is changing too fast and too intensely. Such a perceived instability in society often results in a longing for consistency and security, as well as desperate attempts to avert further changes.

When an accusation of un-Americanism is leveled, it is not merely an expression that the accused's attitude conflicts the accuser's subjective notion of American nationalism. Rather, it betrays the underlying perception of the other's behavior to be a threat to their collective identity as Americans, which is also a threat to their identity as an individual. Charges of un-Americanism are deeply personal and far from a purely political strategy. The term 'un-American' is difficult to grasp and highly contested in nature. However, it is connected to the culture and history of the United States in a unique way because it provides the American people with the language necessary to talk about the core of who they are as a nation.

Despite its uncertainty and controversy, or indeed even because of these factors, the term 'un-American' bears an enormous potential for research. In recent years, there has been some scholarly analysis of the competing notions of un-Americanism, but the term 'un-American' has so far only been treated as the object of study. Based on the insight into people's mindset this rhetoric allows for, I argue that the term 'un-American' has a far greater potential than only being the object of study and suggest taking research on un-Americanism one step further by developing the term 'un-American' into an analytical lens. Thereby, the term 'un-American' can evolve from a sole research object to a research tool through which we can gain a deeper insight into American culture wars and controversies. The term functions both as an indicator of conflicts involving American national identity but, more importantly, as a lens that uncovers the true or obscured motivations behind a dispute. This operationalizing of the term 'un-American' as an analytical tool allows us to dive deeper into the conflict and investigate people's fears and concerns. The term 'un-American' as an analytical tool enables scholars to not be fooled by the tip of the iceberg and to look at what lies under the surface. The marriage equality debate is a perfect example of a conflict which at the surface might be about the contested issue, in this case same-sex marriage, but the actual conflict hidden under the surface is about the meaning and experiences of American everyday nationalism. As subsequent chapters will illuminate, this change in law is about so much more than equal marriage rights for homosexual Americans, and, sometimes, it is not about same-sex marriage at all. The analysis of accusations of un-Americanism in which the term 'un-American' is the object of study examines why this lexical choice is made and what role these accusations play in the dispute over marriage equality. Employing the term 'un-American' as an analytical tool is an approach which takes a second step to facilitate a more profound understanding of how the American nation and its people handle the challenges posed by an increasingly diverse society and the continuous change to which it is consequently subject.

How Does the Term 'Un-American' as an Analytical Tool Work?

In order to utilize the term 'un-American' as an analytical tool to gain a deeper understanding of the construction of American nationalism through national debates and proxy wars, one first needs to identify accusations of un-Americanism in the debate being investigated. The amount of speech acts which can be found depends on the longevity and intensity of a controversy and on whether the debate was sufficiently covered by the media, as they document such accusations. The approach described above is not a well-defined method but much rather an analytical lens. As a result, there is no specific data-gathering procedure for this approach. The mode of procedure depends on the object of study and the samples which are available. As for the exploration of charges of un-Americanism in the marriage equality debate, the prime objective is to provide a sampling which is both wide-ranging and characteristic of the nature of the dispute over same-sex marriage.

The most important step in operationalizing the term 'un-American' for methodological purposes is to contextualize the respective accusations of un-Americanism. The interplay between the rhetorical means (accusations of un-Americanism) and the context of the utterance is what helps reveal nine-tenths of the iceberg submerged under the water surface. Only when the sociopolitical and cultural setting of the charge is unveiled, can the term 'un-American' be made use of as an analytical lens.

When trying to situate this analytical approach within the larger context, 'un-American' as a tool relates to the structures of critical discourse analysis (CDA) which focuses on discourse as "social practice" and as a key agent in the process of identity formation (Fairclough and Wodak

258). Wodak and Meyer define CDA "as being fundamentally interested in analyzing opaque as well as transparent structural relationships of dominance, discrimination, power and control as manifested in language" (10).[26] Although this is not the main focus of this study on American nationalism, these structural relationships play a significant role in the debate on marriage equality and accusations of un-Americanism.

One of the strengths of critical discourse analysis is its diversity and adaptability (Wodak and Meyer 32). CDA is not a singular method but rather an umbrella for a large variety of theoretical positions and methodological approaches[27]; however, the following definition of 'discourse,' coined by the critical discourse analysts Fairclough and Wodak, has become widely accepted among researchers and commonly defines the understanding of 'discourse' within this methodological tradition:

> CDA sees discourse – language use in speech and writing – as a form of 'social practice.' Describing discourse as social practice implies a dialectical relationship between a particular discursive event and the situation(s), institution(s) and social structure(s), which frame it: The discursive event is shaped by them, but it also shapes them. That is, discourse is socially constitutive as well as socially conditioned – it constitutes situations, objects of knowledge, and the social identities of and relationships between people and groups of people. It is constitutive both in the sense that it helps to sustain and reproduce the social status quo, and in the sense

26 A number of approaches in discourse analysis were informed by the theories of Michel Foucault who devoted a significant amount of his work to the relationship between power and knowledge in discourse by conducting theoretical and empirical analyses of power. The first volume of his work *The History of Sexuality* had a great influence on discourse theorists who explore structures of discrimination and power through language.

27 Critical Discourse Analysis as a highly interdisciplinary approach and field of research unites theories and methods from linguistics, anthropology, political science, philosophy, and cognitive science among many others. CDA research strategies range from deductive and more general perspectives (e.g., Fairclough's dialectical-relation approach or van Dijk's sociocognitive approach) to rather inductive approaches which prefer to employ detailed case studies (e.g., Wodak and Reisigl's discourse-historical approach). The respective focus of these diverse approaches of CDA mostly depend on the theoretical background which informs them (for an overview of CDA research strategies, see Wodak and Meyer, "Critical Discourse Analysis: History, Agenda, Theory and Methodology," p. 20).

> that it contributes to transforming it. Since discourse is so socially consequential, it gives rise to important issues of power. Discursive practices may have major ideological effects – that is, they can help produce and reproduce unequal power relations between (for instance) social classes, women and men, and ethnic/cultural majorities and minorities through the ways in which they represent things and position people. (258)

Fairclough and Wodak's foregoing description of discourse as "social practice" (258) provides the definition of 'discourse' which will be drawn upon in this study in the course of illustrating how accusations of un-Americanism are intertwined with their respective context and with the status quo of American everyday nationalism at the time of the discursive event.

Many CDA protagonists follow Teun A. van Dijk in his claim that "the study of discourse triangulates between society/culture/situation, cognition, and discourse/language," as Wodak and Meyer phrase it (14). Van Dijk emphasizes the same fundamental principle as Fairclough and Wodak, namely that language cannot exist without society/culture/situation and the latter cannot exist without the former (220). To this interplay, he adds a third component, 'cognition,' which directs the focus to the language user. Language and discourse are never independent of mental models and general social representations such as ideologies, attitudes, morals and values, memories, or the knowledge of the interlocuter. 'Cognition' is the component of the triangle which reflects the influence of these factors on discourse (190–92). This triangularity as proposed by van Dijk needs to be kept in mind in the investigation of charges of un-Americanism in the marriage equality debate. Thereby, the term 'un-American' constitutes the tool for this endeavor. Meyer and Wodak suggest that "[d]escription and interpretation should be kept apart, thus enabling transparency and retroduction of the respective analysis" (33). This recommendation should also be followed in this research project. Consequently, the chapters on supporters' and opponents' mutual accusations of un-Americanism are rather descriptive in nature whereas the subsequent chapters see the interpretation of the previous results as well as an in-depth analysis of cognition with the help of the analytical lens that the operationalization of the term 'un-American' offers.

Uniqueness of This Analytical Tool

The operationalization of the term 'un-American' into an analytical tool shows considerable advantages over other methods of analysis in the field of American studies. Many of these advantages stem from the term's deep rootedness in American history, culture, and national discourse. The term 'un-American' as an analytical lens is more tailored to investigate disputes over the American national self-concept than critical discourse analysis alone since the former has a strong focus on what drives the American people to go to a discursive war over these issues. This analytical tool is not only applicable for the analysis of this study's example, the same-sex marriage debate, but for a large variety of discourses, as long as one can find a sufficient number of mutual accusations of un-Americanism. Due to the enormous popularity of this insult both in the everyday discourse of the American people as well as in political debates, finding other debates worth investigating under this rubric should not prove difficult.[28]

The culture wars[29] carried out in the United States, may it be over same-sex marriage or any other topic, are ultimately wars over what constitutes good American character and American national identity. Accusations of un-Americanism have become one of the weapons in these wars, and they have enormous firepower. Utilizing the term 'un-American' as an analytical lens allows us to examine what drives the pulse of the American nation at a particular time in history. As Brian Steele put it:

28 Since accusations of un-Americanism are most popular in debates which revolve around American values, morals, character, and national identity, discourses which entail some of these elements are particularly prone to function as proxy wars for debates over American nationalism. Consequently, the term 'un-American' as a research lens would serve as a valuable tool for insight into, for instance, the debate over health care in the United States, immigration reforms and President Trump's travel bans, as well as gun laws and the ongoing discussion over the interpretation of the Second Amendment to the U.S. Constitution.

29 It is disputed whether the United States is still experiencing a culture war and whether some debates, e. g., over marriage equality, can be described as a culture war conflict (see chapter VI.A. for an inquiry into the history of the culture war hypothesis as well as an assessment of research in this field of study). Based on Prothero's "four key features" (*Liberals* 10), which he describes as characteristic for the culture war phenomenon, I decided to speak of a culture war in regard to the debate over marriage equality (see Prothero, *Liberals*, p. 10 and chapter VI.A).

> [I]t gives us a map toward exploring American self-conception and representation – what Americans have thought they were like and were willing to go to the mat to defend or to call out as un-American – through history. And because embedded in any invocation of the "un-American" is certain to be a set of positive assertions about American identity, wherever Americans have called out the "un-American" for exposure becomes a site for the exploration of the discourse of American identity itself. (894)

In other words, the term 'un-American' gives scholars a map which allows them to explore the American sociocultural terrain in regard to a certain issue or discourse. Accusations of un-Americanism help us understand what the cultural capital was at a specific point in time. They also reveal which Americans had the cultural capital to lead the discursive construction of the nation.

Everyday nationalism studies put special emphasis on how the nation is constructed by the everyday people in their everyday lives and on the ideas of nationalism which people form. The term 'un-American' as an analytical tool pairs perfectly with the approach of everyday nationalism studies since it is a linguistic choice made in the discourse of the American people at large. Treaties, laws, policies, and bills provide insight into what influences American national identity. However, the examination of such documents, while revealing of which topics and interests dominated American politics, do not shed light on why some Americans were willing to go the mat in order to defend their position regarding marriage equality. An analysis of charges of un-Americanism in sociocultural debates with the help of the term 'un-American' as a lens discloses exactly that. The potential of this analytical approach is enormous, especially in the field of everyday nationalism studies because this new approach of nationalism studies sometimes still lacks suitable methods for analysis (Fox and van Ginderachter 550). In his essay "The Edges of the Nation: A Research Agenda for Uncovering the Taken-for-Granted Foundations of Everyday Nationhood" where Fox tries to "turn unselfconscious suppositions about the nation into explicit articulations of the nation" (27), he calls this the "evidence problem" (27) of everyday nationalism studies. The term 'un-American' as an analytical lens has the potential to make everyday nationalism and the negotiation process over nationalism, which is sometimes overshadowed by loud and overt culture war conflicts, visible and available for research.

'Un-American' has always played a huge role in designating insiders from outsiders and in controlling which idea of American identity should prevail, not least of all during the heyday of the House Un-American Activities Committee. In the 20th century, the competing concepts of Americanism and un-Americanism were "designed for purposes of social organization and ordering" (Goodall 928). Brian Steele adds that "the concept of the 'un-American' – though it has long been used to identify domestic enemies – also has, in certain formulations, a kind of redemptive power to demand self-evaluation and call Americans back to first principles" (e. g., the principles of the Declaration of Independence) (897). Not much has changed about un-Americanism's role in ordering and social organizing since the turn to the 21st century. What indeed has changed are the people or institutions that use this term for the purpose of control. Especially during the time of the investigative committees of the 1930s until the 1950s, committees and their representatives were the ones who mainly raised accusations of un-Americanism, not the general American population. Ever since, a significant transformation has taken place in regard to who labels someone as un-American. It is no longer officials or committees' representatives who rely on this rhetoric for the purpose of controlling society, but it has become "an internal policing mechanism among citizens" (Steele 888), which means that those raising the charge are mainly ordinary Americans not acting in any official capacity. It is everyday Americans monitoring and criticizing each other's opinions and behavior according to their own definition of good Americanism and American national identity. This societal function of the term 'un-American' as an "internal policing mechanism" (888) is another aspect which makes the term 'un-American' as an analytical tool so valuable for research. This term, which is utilized as an attempt to regulate and bring society into line, can help reveal the social order of the nation. We learn about people's sociocultural maps of orientation and who dominates the discourses and practices of nationalism. This policing mechanism unveils what is deemed proper American thought or behavior at a certain in time by a certain group of people and also how this changes throughout history.

The term 'un-American' as rhetoric and as a research tool traces and discloses development, process, and change through American history down to the present day. 'Un-American' shows the evolution of ideas and concepts such as identity, equality, nationalism, and also marriage in the United States throughout time. The term 'un-American' brings to light how people understand themselves as Americans and whom they are willing to include in their definition of true representatives of American nationalism at a certain point in time. The conflict over marriage equality marked one such tremendous change in what was regarded as un-American. During the witch-hunt of the Cold War days, homosexual Americans were prosecuted by the House Un-American Activities Committee for un-Americanism on the basis of their sexual orientation (D. K. Johnson 8–9). From there, several decades would pass before same-sex marriage even became part of the national discourse. In the early days of the fight for marriage equality, when same-sex couples gained their first victories in the states of Vermont and Massachusetts, the majority of Americans still concurred that this was deeply un-American. Proposition 8 in California demonstrated that even one of the most progressive and liberal states in the country was not ready for such a significant change to marriage laws in 2008. It took several more years and court victories for the tide to turn and until it was no longer gay marriage that was un-American. As soon as the majority of the people supported marriage equality, this also changed what the majority of the American nation thought of to be un-American. Increasingly, the refusal to grant the same marriage rights to all American regardless of their sexual orientation was deemed un-American. This is just one example of how the term 'un-American' as a research tool can track and disclose how the perception of American values and concepts evolves over time. Relying on a term which is closely connected to American culture and at the same time persists in some discourses for decades allows scholars to investigate and uncover development and change in American national self-perception and everyday nationalism.

Transforming the term 'un-American' from a research object into an analytical tool helps us understand how the American nation addresses and copes with the challenges posed by diversity and minorities' claims for equality. 'Un-American' is especially tailored for such questions and issues since it is itself concerned with who and what are regarded as American according to the majority of Americans. Both in the term's definition and in its function as a policing mechanism, 'un-American' regulates inclusion and exclusion from the prevailing notion of American nationalism. Therefore, this category is of particular interest when it comes to minorities, as these groups are those who struggle for equality, cultural capital, and, ultimately, for full membership in the American community. Investigating which agents use accusations of un-Americanism and in which context gives profound insight into how diversity is handled in the discourses and practices of everyday nationalism. The marriage equality debate is just one example of a discourse where the term 'un-American' employed as an analytical tool uncovers the gradual inclusion of a minority group and their interests into the majority's conception of what constitutes American nationalism and American identity. This analytical lens leads scholars to the core of the controversy and points out the factors that influence how American nationalism is formed in a nation which needs to include this minority in regard to marriage rights.

Accusations of Un-Americanism: A Quantitative Analysis

A closer look at the national discourse on marriage equality shows that accusations of un-Americanism are most frequent when the debate heats up and the participants become increasingly concerned that their understanding of American national identity may not emerge victorious. The more worried Americans become over how certain culture war debates affect the state of their nation, the more are they willing to employ insults of un-Americanism. Fox and Miller-Idriss explain that the nation becomes a salient frame in everyday discourse when a nation is in a state of unrest or disorder (540). They call for the 'nation' to be seen as "a culturally available schema that can be discursively deployed to make sense of other topics of talk, explain predicaments and order social difference" (540). Accusations of un-Americanism are part of that process in which the nation is directly or indirectly used discursively as a mechanism intended to dissolve social difference and bring back order. Consequently, I argue that the frequency of the usage of the term 'un-American' serves as an indicator for the political climate in the nation. The more popular accusations of un-Americanism become in sociocultural and political discourse, the more are Americans worried about American identity and potential societal changes (Gage). These changes can possibly include a perceived loss of morals and values, a shift along the political spectrum, or any other transformation which would affect people's mental maps too quickly or too severely.

The correlation between the frequency of the usage of the term 'un-American' and the conflicts that cause situations of unrest, disorder, or social difference can be witnessed in a number of debates, as for instance in the controversies over marriage equality, health care, or immigration. This phenomenon has so far only been investigated via qualitative methods of analysis; however, the correlation described above can also be quantified. Since this book is a qualitative research project and due to the limitations of this study, a profound quantitative analysis cannot be conducted. However, a glimpse into a quantitative approach will be presented in order to point towards possibilities for future research which could be based on quantitative methods or could strive for a combination of both research methods.

This very brief quantitative analysis for the term 'un-American' was conducted with the help of *Google Trends,* which analyses the popularity of search terms. The years 2014 to 2016 were chosen as examples since they cover a period starting one year before *Obergefell v. Hodges* and ending in the year after the Supreme Court decision. Since accusations of un-Americanism are popular in multiple debates and controversies as the examples given in the following will illustrate, surges in the use of the term 'un-American' at a particular point in time are consequently the result of its presence in a variety of discourses. Therefore, working with *Google Trends* can only give an idea of the correlation between the frequency of the use of accusations of un-Americanism and the salience of a certain issue. Furthermore, this *Google* tool can only indicate trends; an in-depth quantitative analysis would require the use of quantitative research tools which offer more precise and stable results. In addition to that, the use of linguistic corpora also produces interesting results, particularly when exploring debates or contexts in which accusations of un-Americanism are especially common and how such trends can shift over time.

For the first five months of 2014, *Google Trends* shows an overall high popularity of the term 'un-American.' The year started with a federal judge in Oklahoma ruling that its ban on same-sex marriage violates the U.S. Constitution. This was described as "the latest in a string of legal victories for gay rights and one that occurred in the heart of the Bible Belt" (Eckholm, "Federal Judge") and most certainly one that was not a welcome beginning to the new year for marriage equality opponents. Only two months later, a federal judge in Michigan argued along the same lines and secured another victory for the equal protection of same-sex couples in the United States (Eckholm, "Michigan's Ban"). These are just two examples of decisive victories scored by marriage equality supporters in 2014. In May 2014, Oregon and Pennsylvania legalized gay marriage (Wolf). Whereas the frequency of accusations of un-Americanism was rather low during the summer months, it surged again during the months of October and November. While there were several controversies that contributed to this rise in the usage of the term 'un-American,' the ongoing winning streak of marriage equality supporters was certainly one of them when another sixteen states opened marriage to same-sex couples in October and November 2014. Among these new additions were many states in the heartland of the United States and the Bible Belt where support for gay rights was not as easy to gain as in states in the Northeast or at the Pacific Coast (Wolf).

The decisive year for marriage equality in the United States was in 2015. Although two thirds of the states had already legalized same-sex marriage prior to *Obergefell v. Hodges*, fifteen states were still holding on to their bans on same-sex marriage at the beginning of the year. In January, same-sex couples in Florida started to marry after a stay on an August 2014 decision, in which Florida's ban on marriage was ruled unconstitutional in the federal case *Brenner v. Scott*, expired (Wallshein). At the same time, the fight over marriage equality in Alabama was also in full swing.[30] The battle over same-sex marriage was far from over at the beginning of 2015, and the intensification of this debate was reflected in a rising number of accusations of un-Americanism. Additionally, the United States Supreme Court had decided at the beginning of the year that they would hear the cases of the plaintiffs which were consolidated in the case *Obergefell v. Hodges* (Barnes). The hearing took place in April 2015 at a time when *Google Trends* showed a high popularity of the term 'un-American.' The accusations of un-Americanism decreased during the summer months and even at the time of the Supreme Court ruling, but then saw another sudden rise in August 2015. This period coincided with the refusal of the Kentucky Country clerk Kim Davis to comply with the federal law mandating the issuing of marriage licenses to same-sex couples. This was extensively covered by the mass media for weeks, especially after she was jailed for contempt of court (Felton). The popularity of 'un-American' remained high during the rest of 2015, decreasing only slightly towards the end of the year. However, the consistent usage of the term in the last quarter of the year was likely due to other controversies, not least the presidential primaries, which kept the nation in a state of ongoing turmoil.

30 A federal judge in Alabama struck down the state's ban on same-sex marriage but blocked the ruling from taking effect in February 2015. Consequently, marriage equality should have been possible; however, it was immediately blocked by Alabama's Supreme Court. The state petitioned for an appeal, but this appeal was not granted (Wolf).

The popularity of the term 'un-American' reached its high point in the three-year period analyzed for this study in 2016. Although this year was dominated by the presidential election, some concurrent developments in LGBT rights certainly contributed to this peak. As marriage equality had become the law of the land, gay rights opponents were looking for new battles. Since overturning *Obergefell v. Hodges* was not an option, those who still wanted to wage this war had to turn to other areas where they could halt the increasing normalization of LGBT life in the United States. Especially in the South, a number of anti-LGBT bills were passed in spring of 2016. With homosexual Americans benefitting from a growing acceptance within American society, the focus of opponents also turned towards transgender Americans who were even less protected than LGB Americans (Lewis et al. 862).[31] The most notable anti-LGBT bills passed were a bill in Mississippi which allowed private and public businesses to refuse service to same-sex couples on the basis of religious or moral beliefs (Bixby), Tennessee's anti-LGBT counselling bill which allowed therapists and counselors to reject patients based on personal belief (Fang), and, the most controversial, North Carolina's "bathroom bill." The House Bill 2, or Public Facilities Privacy & Security Act as it was officially called, prevented transgender individuals from using a bathroom that did not correspond to their biological sex as stated on their birth certificate (Tan). North Carolina's bathroom bill controversy left its people so divided that North Carolina was even said to have "a crisis of identity" (Teague and Kasperkevic). The conflict soon affected the whole nation so intensely that major American companies considered leaving the state in protest and economists estimated that this could cost North Carolina $3.76 billion in lost business in the years to come (Teague and Kasperkevic). Given the scope of this controversy, the high frequency of uses of the term 'un-American' corresponded with the impact this bill had on the national

31 In their comprehensive study of acceptance towards the different segments of the LGBT community, Lewis et al. found that "attitudes towards sexual orientation minorities are significantly more positive than attitudes towards transgender people" (862). Furthermore, respondents in their survey were less likely to support discrimination protection for transgender individuals than for LGB people (871). Lewis et al. allocate some of their findings to the fact that people are far less likely to know a transgender person than a gay/lesbian person and that information on transgender persons is rather limited in comparison to information on sexual orientation minorities who enjoy a greater visibility (862–63).

debate over whether the American people understood themselves as a nation which was willing to integrate LGBT Americans into their national self-concept. American national identity was again heavily challenged with the election of Donald Trump as the new president in November 2016, which corresponds to the second highest popularity of the term 'un-American' from 2014 to 2016.

The usage of the term 'un-American' "gives us a map toward exploring American self-conception and representation" and teaches us a lot about which issues the American people "are willing to go to the mat" for, as Steele explained (894). The quantitative approach to an analysis of un-Americanism as exemplified above is not only useful to support hypotheses about correlations between charges of un-Americanism and a certain issue. Applying these tools of quantitative research and using 'un-American' as a search term also presents a means through which one can examine a specific time period and ascertain which issues were so important for Americans in regard to their American identity that they would level the charge of un-Americanism against their ideological opponents. More concretely, if the research goal is to determine the debates in which people most frequently accused their fellow Americans of un-Americanism or which discourses shaped American everyday nationalism, searching for the term 'un-American' in *Google Trends* or with comparable tracking tools uncovers these debates.

In order to exemplify this, a brief analysis with the goal to find out which debates were most relevant was conducted for the year 2017, the first year of the Trump administration. In 2017, Trump's so-called "travel bans" were thought to be highly un-American (Weigel and O'Keefe). No other issue saw such a sudden and intense increase of accusations of un-Americanism than these three executive orders which restricted citizens from several countries from entering the United States. Six of the eight countries that were affected by the bans were predominately Muslim, which left no doubt as to who the target of these discriminatory bans was (Almasy and Simon).[32] These executive orders were widely regarded as un-American, and Trump was even derided as "the most un-Ameri-

[32] While the White House tried to deny that the "travel ban" was a "Muslim ban," which would be unconstitutional, President Trump's campaign website indicated the contrary: "Donald J. Trump is calling for a total and complete shutdown of Muslims entering the United States until our country's representatives can figure out what is going on" (qtd. in Barbash). After a reporter

can president in living history" (Wolffe). What makes this issue so prone to accusations of un-Americanism is its discursive proximity to disputes over immigration and citizenship. The question of who is worthy of being an American and who should be excluded for being un-American has been thematically linked to questions of immigration and integration since the beginning of the republic. Consequently, it does not come as a surprise that the frequency of the term 'un-American' rose every time a new executive order was released. In addition to the travel ban, another move of the Trump administration led to repeated accusations of un-Americanism: attempts to replace the Patient Protection and Affordable Care Act (ACA), also known as Obamacare (Wright). This provoked a high prevalence of charges of un-Americanism for several weeks in spring 2017. However, the national dispute about whether Obamacare was compatible with core American ideals and American national self-concept was not a phenomenon exclusive to the Trump Era; it was also a hallmark of the discussions surrounding the drafting and passing of the ACA during the Obama presidency (Sensenbrenner). Yet another event which prompted Americans to bring the topic of American nationalism and (un-)Americanism back on the table were the riots in Charlottesville, Virginia after white-nationalist groups marched through the University of Virginia's Emancipation Park. The situation between white nationalists and counter-protestors escalated to such an extent that the Governor of Virginia declared a state of emergency. A few hours later, a woman was killed and several others were injured when a vehicle was intentionally driven into a crowd of counter-protestors (Herald). Democrats as well as Republicans condemned the demonstrations of the "Unite the Right" white-nationalist protestors and characterized them as "un-American" (Herald).

The results of this brief quantitative analysis demonstrate that charges of un-Americanism and competing concepts thereof serve as a schema of discourse which is employed when the American nation is unsettled by events and debates which bring along (the threat of) a reconceptualization of American nationalism and the discourses and practices of nationhood. The nation becomes a salient frame in times which require a renegotiation of everyday nationalism due to recent developments and sociocultural conflicts. Thereby, debates and controversies function as discursive platforms for these processes of change in regard to American

asked the White House press secretary about the statement, the text disappeared from the website shortly after (Barbash).

national identity. Due to the correlation between a rise in accusations of un-Americanism and situations of unrest, disorder, or social difference, the term 'un-American' also works as a crisis indicator for conflicts regarding American national self-conception. A quantitative analysis of the term 'un-American' and its concomitant utilization as an analytical lens shows the development of these debates over American identity, and it helps uncover what lies at the heart of these conflicts. Although the quantitative analysis provided in this study only offers a brief glimpse into the benefits of this approach, it is safe to say that quantitative methods have a contributive effect on research into un-Americanism and American nationalism. Quantitative or mixed-methods approaches could provide new insights and support the results of this qualitative analysis.

Conclusion

The operationalization of the term 'un-American' from an object of research into an analytical tool allows scholars to uncover the hidden part of the iceberg which lies below the surface of a respective conflict. The term 'un-American' as an analytical lens points to the actual core of a debate and reveals that issues such as marriage equality often function as platforms for the discursive negotiation of American everyday nationalism. Although this analytical approach can be situated within the larger field of critical discourse analysis, the term 'un-American' as an analytical tool shows several advantages over other methods of analysis in the field of American studies. The tool has the potential to reveal the underlying fears and concerns of Americans when they engage in mutual accusations of un-Americanism over a certain issue that relates to their self-concept as Americans.

In accordance with the theories of everyday nationalism studies, this approach aims to explore how the nation is discursively constructed by Americans at large. In the course of this process of reconstruction, Americans decide who should be included in their idea of American national identity while they attempt to order and socially organize their nation with the help of charges of un-Americanism as an "internal policing mechanism" (Steele 888). Since the nation itself is a continuous process (Skey 12), ideas of what constitutes contemporary American nationalism, and its people are continuously changing and evolving. Utilizing the term 'un-American' as an analytical lens allows researchers to reveal and track development, progress, and change in American self-perception and culture. 'Un-American' as a tool can disclose how 'un-American' as rhetoric experienced several semantic as well as ideological shifts and transformations over time as the context in which this term was employed changed and fluctuated. At the time of the House Un-American Activities Committee, gay Americans were ostracized for their un-American behavior if they were involved in homosexual conduct; by contrast, it is now opponents of LGBT rights who are widely regarded as un-American. This about-face is just one example in which the term 'un-American' can unveil the transformation of a concept and thereby elucidates how the American nation handles the challenges posed by diversity and minorities' claims for equality.

Chapter II

II Everyday Nationalism

Michael Billig is not a scholar of nationalism, but he has made a single and all the more impactful publication in nationalism studies. It was his inquiry into the public perception of the British royal family through which he was coincidentally confronted with nationalism. Billig has conducted research primarily in the field of social psychology with a special focus on rhetoric, ideology, and language (Skey and Antonsich 1). However, it was exactly this background which allowed him to have a different access to nationalism, resulting in a new approach which he presented in *Banal Nationalism*.[33] In his investigation of nationalism, Billig's socio-psychological background remains at the forefront. He pays special attention to rhetoric and language (*Banal* 8), which makes the turn that he initiated in nationalism studies so interesting for an analysis of American nationalism and the discursive negotiation of American national identity via charges of un-Americanism. With its strong focus on the banal reproductions of nationalism as the research object, Billig's theories laid the foundation for the later emergence of everyday nationalism studies.

Banal Nationalism

In his groundbreaking monograph *Banal Nationalism*, Billig bemoans that "there is something misleading about this accepted use of the word 'nationalism.' It always seems to locate nationalism on the periphery. . . . In consequence, those in established nations – at the centre of things – are led to see nationalism as the property of others, not of 'us'" (*Banal* 5).

33 Although Billig never returned to this area of research, the influence he had on nationalism studies was enormous, and his work remains one of the most frequently cited in the field. Michael Skey and Marco Antonsich, both scholars of everyday nationalism studies, cannot emphasize strongly enough how "*Banal Nationalism* changed the kind of questions that were asked about the nation" (2).

Billig insists that there must be more to nationalism than a fringe concept with little involvement from ordinary citizens. Billig criticizes:

> In general, liberal Western academics today find it easier to recognize nationalism in 'others' than in themselves. Nationalists can be identified as extremists who, impelled by a violently emotional psychology, seek irrational ends; or they can be painted as heroic figures who, in particular are to be found overseas, battling against repressive colonialists. (15)

He demands that "[i]f nationalism is a widespread ideology, then a different perspective is in order" (15). Nations and nationalism are reproduced on a daily basis in the form of beliefs, debates, habits, routines, myths, assumptions, and many more. He "insists on stretching the term 'nationalism,' so that it covers the ideological means by which nation-states are reproduced" (6). Therefore, he coined the term 'banal nationalism.' Billig's aim was to shift the focus of nationalism studies towards the banal and less visible forms of it which can be found in citizens' everyday lives rather than on the stage of international politics. He intended banal nationalism "to cover the ideological habits which enable the established nations of the West to be reproduced. It is argued that these habits are not removed from everyday life, as some observers have supposed. Daily, the nation is indicated, or 'flagged,' in the lives of its citizenry" (6). As an example, he names the constant presence of flags in the United States which are clearly visible yet easily overlooked due to their omnipresence. Billig explains that "[n]ational identity embraces all these forgotten reminders. Consequently, an identity is to be found in the embodied habits of social life. Such habits include those of thinking and using language. To have a national identity is to possess a way of talking about nationhood" (8). Discourse, rhetoric, and language play a major role in this continuous reproduction of the nation. The discursive engagement with nationalism fosters a common national identity and a sense of unity. As a result, the reproduction of nationalism on a daily basis is such an important process because "we are noticing something about ourselves. We are noticing the depths and mechanisms of our identity, embedded in routines of social life. These rhetorical episodes remind us that we are 'us'. . ." (175).

In order to provide some differentiation between daily banal nationalism and international matters, Billig distinguishes between the banal and the hot forms of nationalism. Whereas he identifies the hot form of nationalism as aligning with traditional nationalism studies, addressing concerns of world politics often detached from the lives of citizens, banal nationalism refers to subconscious everyday forms of nationalism as they can be identified in political debates, the media, or public rituals (*Banal* 43–44). What constitutes and upholds nationalism from within state borders is the constant reproduction of elements of national identity. This is where the attention of banal nationalism should be drawn, from the world of the inhabitants of a nation and how they are affected by practices of nationalism: "Having a national identity . . . means being situated within a homeland, which itself is situated within the worlds of nations. And only if people believe they have national identities, will such homelands, and the world of national homelands, be reproduced" (8). Without the American people, their traditions, routines, values and morals, cultural practices, and, most importantly, self-concepts as Americans, the nation state would have no raison d'être. Cultural practices and language in particular play an essential role in the process of upholding American nationalism. Only through a continuous reproduction of national identity via debates on what is American and un-American is nationalism created and upheld in the United States.

Billig wrote *Banal Nationalism* at a time when proper internet access was rare and people's agency was consequently much more limited than it is in today's highly-connected world. Billig admits in an edited volume on everyday nationalism that his 1995 monograph contains several oversimplifications and weaknesses ("Banal Nationalism and the Imagining of Politics" 307). One example he mentions is his assumption that a distinction between hot and banal nationalism can be made, without acknowledging that gradations between these two forms would better reflect reality (314). Billig hopes other researchers will enrich his, at times, simplified observations with nuance and empirical research (313), especially since nationalism studies are more important than ever in his eyes (308).[34]

34 However, he warns against seeing banal nationalism and the comparatively new approach of everyday nationalism as competing theories:

> In my view, analysts of nationalism do not need to choose between taking one approach or the other, as if there is a theoretical zero-sum game at work. . . . [I]t is possible to combine creatively the study of everyday actions that reproduce and reimagine the nation, with an awareness of how that reimagined nation can also be reproduced banally. Investigators, therefore, should try to avoid assuming that the reality of 'banal nationalism' must reflect the sorts of simplifications to be found in the book of the

Theoretical considerations: Everyday Nationalism Studies

Everyday nationalism "draws from the same intellectual well" as banal nationalism, as J. Paul Goode phrased it (974), but its scholars attribute a larger role to the agency of the people, regarding them as active negotiators and constructors of nationalism (Knott). However, since everyday nationalism is a rather young approach to nationalism studies and since it is of "increasing thematic scope and diversity of research" (Goode 974), it is not yet as well defined as more traditional understandings of nationalism. For instance, regarding the question what the 'everyday' entails, opinions are diverging. As Edensor explains, "the problem in defining the everyday is that it is too apparent" (18).

For Billig, the everyday is the banal, the overlooked routines and cultural practices, the habits and national traditions which have mostly been ignored by orthodox studies of nationalism. Scholars of everyday nationalism, for example Jones and Merriman, by contrast, believe that the everyday can entail the banal and the hot forms of nationalism since the everyday is what people are confronted with in their day to day lives and these tend to be both. Jones and Merriman propose to forget about such artificial boundaries and investigate all influences on people's concepts of national identity by blurring the imaginary line between the banal and the hot everyday experiences (Jones and Merriman 165).

Goode prefers to follow a very general definition which regards the everyday "as an ensemble of characteristics concerning the nature of agents, the context in which agency is exercised, and the scale of observations and measurement" because this "not only enables a clearer demarcation of banal nationalism and everyday nationalism as approaches but facilitates their broader comparison with more episodic, contentious forms of nationalisms, as well as the official nationalisms promoted by states and regime actors" (974–75). Goode's approach is exemplary for those in everyday nationalism

> same name and that anything more complex should be taken as evidence for the non-existence of banal nationalism. (315)

With this comment, Billig addresses a valid point since many researchers of everyday nationalism indeed attempt to distinguish between the earliest theories of banal nationalism and the newer concept of everyday nationalism without acknowledging that they need to be viewed as products of a specific time. Instead, they should be placed on a continuum of nationalism studies with everyday nationalism building on the turn initiated by Billig.

studies who opt for a very broad understanding of nationalism, involving different influences from different sources which shape national identity.

For Edensor, the everyday is both the static and dynamic of the life which surrounds us every day. He critiques that the everyday is often only regarded as the boring, low-key, ordinary, unexciting, static, and uninteresting parts of life. By contrast, he argues that "the everyday is far more dynamic than this complacent view suggests, whilst at the same time it also contains enduring consistencies through which identity is grounded" (18). Much rather, a "contemporary dynamism of national identity is embedded in everyday life, changing subtly as well as dramatically" (23). A similar idea is presented by Marta Bivand Erdal who explores how young people in Norway handle diversity within in the nation. She asserts that the everyday is so diverse that it is impossible to find a clear-cut definition of what it entails, not least since it is subject to constant change as her interview of young Norwegians demonstrated. She concurs with Edensor that nationalism is not static, but "a nationalism of everyday life foregrounds the dynamic and processual 'who' dimension of the nation, which are malleable, and apt to deal with demographic change over time" (46).

It is disputed what the everyday of everyday nationalism studies should entail and consequently acknowledge as research object. Recent approaches in everyday nationalism studies opt for a broadening of the everyday by investigating all the possible influences on people's concepts of nationalism which they encounter in their day to day lives, thereby following the idea that the individuals and their environment are interdependent. This understanding of the everyday also informs this study on the renegotiation of American nationalism through charges of un-Americanism.

In an attempt to systematize the research on everyday nationalism studies, Eleanor Knott describes everyday nationalism as a subfield of nationalism studies which takes particular interest in directing "attention on the 'masses' and human agency within nationalism studies to consider the role and relevance of the everyday, and relevance of the lived experience of nationalism." Furthermore, she explains that everyday nationalism "focuses, in particular, on the agency of ordinary people, as opposed to elites, as the co-constituents, participants and consumers of national symbols, rituals and identities." This definition contains two aspects which need to be clarified for the purpose of this study.

First, it is of interest who these "ordinary people" are and if a demarcation from the elite as the contrasting group is possible. This problem was addressed by Anthony Smith in his critique of Fox and Miller-Idriss' hypotheses on everyday nationalism in which he also draws attention to the limits of this new approach. Fox and Miller-Idriss repeatedly emphasize that everyday nationalism studies are about "ordinary people" (e.g., 539, 554). Smith laments that the two authors provide "little clue about the non-elite segment of 'the people' that is being studied, and how it relates to wider issues of nationhood and nationalism" (565). In addition to Smith's critique, one should add that a differentiation between elites and non-elites tends to be difficult, in particular in a debate over culture war issues were even the elites are driven by personal convictions, motivations, or sentiments. In the conflict over marriage equality, which is at its core a conflict over morals and values and a conflict in which people tend to be driven by their emotions and not pure politics, even those who are considered policymakers and representatives of the political elite tend to act as private persons. As a result, for the purpose of this study, I suggest refraining from drawing an artificial line between elites and non-elites to incorporate all voices which are participating in the continuous renegotiation of American nationalism and to follow the premise of a broad interpretation of the everyday.

Second, the focus on human agency is one of the core elements of everyday nationalism studies since its scholars think of nationalism as a bottom-up phenomenon and not primarily as a top-down force (Knott). As noted in the comment on the ordinariness of the people who are involved in the renegotiation of American nationalism, in the case of marriage equality, this was certainly a process which was initiated from the bottom up. It was gay couples and grassroots movements who brought the issue to the table of national discourse. It was people acting as private persons who mostly shaped the discourse over whether gay marriage should become the law of the land. One might argue that this study has its limitations since analyzing the Supreme Court rulings in *United States v. Windsor* and *Obergefell v. Hodges* (see chapter 5) could be regarded as a study of the elite discourse and since a certain amount of the accusations of un-Americanism (as investigated in chapter 4) comes from movement representatives, politicians, or journalists. However, I argue that in the debate over marriage equality, Supreme Court rulings and accusations of un-Americanism which were published in newspapers etc. represent the voices of a bottom-up reconceptualization of American nationalism. Those politicians, representatives and others at the top only acted as the mouthpiece of everyday Americans, or they spoke in no official capacity but as everyday Americans. Supreme Court rulings on marriage equality were only the last stage of a process which started at the very bottom in lower courts at a regional level.

Marriage equality might be a special topic to analyze against the backdrop of everyday nationalism since it is a dispute which is inherently characterized by a bottom-up dynamic and a discourse in which almost everyone speaks as an ordinary American. Thereby, the everyday includes the everything which is surrounding those involved or involving themselves in this discourse. Nevertheless, I want to point out to recent theories in everyday nationalism studies which warn against keeping bottom-up and top-down processes apart for reasons of analysis. This is problematic insofar as those 'ordinary people,' who are in the center of analysis, are not only shaped by bottom-up phenomena or non-elite discourses but also by top-down forces and the debates at an elite level. Even if ordinary Americans may not actively participate at negotiations at an elite level, they are still its recipients (e. g., via media outlets). In an attempt to stimulate new ways of acknowledging elite and non-elite forces, Hearn and Antonsich write:

> [W]e would like to caution against the possible risk of keeping macro-structural approaches separated from micro investigation of everyday life. . . . [A]gency should be studied in relation to social organisational contexts. Any nation is not and cannot be only the product of myriad individuals attributing sense to the nation itself, but an emergent property of complexly organised behaviour. Thus, joining the debate between Smith (2008) and Fox and Miller-Idriss (2008b), we would call for further empirical research which could bridge the apparent divide between 'macro' (structure) and 'micro' (individual agency) in nationalism studies. . . . (602–603)

A similar approach was presented by Eric Kaufmann in his essay "Complexity and nationalism" when he also calls for an equal consideration of the horizontal (i. e., bottom-up) dynamics, peer-to-peer influences, and top-down forces (6).

Everyday Nationalism: Fox and Miller-Idriss' Approach

Fox and Miller-Idriss' reflections on the daily contestation of nationalism provide an approach to nationalism with a special emphasis on what they call "talking the nation" (537) which they define as "the discursive construction of the nation" (537). This makes their theories particularly relevant for an analysis of the term 'un-American' as an oratorical choice in national discourse. Fox and Miller-Idriss direct attention to the implications of the continuous construction and deconstruction of nationalism and national identity via the debates and rhetorical choices of people in their everyday lives. They argue that citizens are much more than mere recipients of nationalism discourses. In the construction of everyday nationalism, citizens are active agents as voters, consumers, participants in political debates, or as representatives of various concepts of national identity (537). This emphasis on people's agency attempts to solve the problem which Fox and Miller-Idriss see in earlier studies of nationalism which focus exclusively on the macro-structural processes of nation-building:

> Nationalism has been examined as a political ideology holding that each state should have its nation and each nation its state; as the historically contingent outcome of modernizing and industrializing economic forces that bring the state into alignment with the nation; as a cultural construct of collective belonging realized and legitimated through institutional and discursive practices; and as a site for material and symbolic struggles over the definition of national inclusion and exclusion. The targets of these endeavours are the people themselves: to make the nation is to make people national. . . . The focus on the political, economic and cultural determinants of popular nationalism has not systematically accounted for the popularity of nationalism. Rather, the people in whose names nations are being made are simply assumed to be attuned to the national content of their self-appointed nationalist messengers. Nationhood from this perspective resonates evenly and unwaveringly among the people; the nation is a *fait accompli*. (536–37)

As current discourses on un-Americanism and the active renegotiation of national identity which this process entails demonstrate, the American nation is anything but a nation "*fait accompli*" (537). Fox and Miller-Idriss' critique accounts for the current changes in American nationalism which have been evoked from the bottom up in the wake of *Obergefell*. The discontent and dissent expressed through charges of un-Americanism are not the result of macro-structural forces which the elite try to impose on people. Those at the top are often much more interested in upholding the unity of the nation and avoiding contentious topics such as un-Americanism. The salience of discourses on national identity within the United States' population at large shows that questions of nationalism are a concern present in the everyday lives of the average citizen. "Findings reveal that these people's representations of the nation do not simply mimic those variants traded in elite discourse, but more often resonate with the currents and rhythms of their everyday concerns and predicaments" (539). Just as studies of "[u]n-Americanism . . . serve to reflect the most pressing concerns of contemporaneous American life" (Lewis 876), studies on everyday nationalism reveal what shapes and influences national discourse at specific periods of time.

In order to do justice to the multifacetedness of everyday nationalism, Fox and Miller-Idriss propose to analyze it from four different angles through which the nation is produced and constructed in everyday life: (1) "talking the nation," which investigates the discursive elements of the nation, (2) "choosing the nation," which entails having a look at people's everyday choices in regard to national identity, (3) "performing the nation," which includes rituals, traditions, and national symbols, and (4) "consuming the nation," which focuses on citizens as consumers (537–38). Although the examination of nationalism via all four perspectives would most certainly provide a comprehensive picture of a phenomenon, not all four of them constitute a suitable method for each research objective. Since this research project investigates how American nationalism is negotiated via charges of un-Americanism in proxy wars, the focus will primarily be on the first perspective, "talking the nation" (537).

The nation and the national identity of its people are the products of their own discursive engagement with ideas of nationalism, and in the case of the United States, competing definitions of un-Americanism are a significant part of this process. "These discursive acts are not simply descriptive of social reality," but rather "they are simultaneously constitutive of that reality" (538). According to Fox and Miller-Idriss, nationhood is "the practical accomplishment of ordinary people giving concrete expression to their understanding of the nation. Nationhood does not only define their talk; it is defined by their talk" (539). Fox and Miller-Idriss attribute equal importance to the context of discursive acts as Siegfried Jäger, a scholar of critical discourse analysis, does in his work. Discourse is not the same as language.[35] The latter is a tool with the help of which people assign meaning to objects, events, etc., whereas discourse

[35] By referring to Jürgen Link, Jäger understands discourse as a societal manner of speaking, which is institutionalized, which follows certain rules (although those can be subject to change), and which has a certain amount of power because it is able to affect people's behavior (170).

transports knowledge. Discourse tells us how the form and the content of utterances can be understood in their respective social context (Jäger 170).[36] Jäger believes that the speech act is influenced by the context and vice versa (170). This interplay is pertinent to the analysis of charges of un-Americanism insofar as context and personal reasons cause people to utilize the term 'un-American.' Fox and Miller-Idriss also call for these contexts that influence people's experiences of everyday nationalism to be defined in order to understand the interplay between people's environment and their perception of the world (541). Nationalism is the context which acts as an influencer but at the same time is shaped and influenced by those involved in the discourse on national identity.[37]

In their considerations about the interplay between people and nationhood, Fox and Miller-Idriss not only question what the nation is but also ask: "[W]hen is the nation? When – in what situations – does the category of the nation become a salient frame for routine talk and interaction?" (540). The two scholars admit while the nation is an influential factor in people's expression of everyday nationalism, it is usually not the object of discourse. It is more commonly experienced as a frame for other types of debates that while affected by nationalism are not governed by it. At times, however, the nation and national identity become the center of national discourse and political debates. In conclusion, certain parameters must change in order to let the nation become the object of talk at a particular point in time. As possible contexts for specific articulations on nationalism, Fox and Miller-Idriss list national catastrophes, wars, and sporting events (540). In reference to Gamson, Fox and Miller-Idriss add that the nation "is not (only) a topic of talk, but also a culturally available schema that can be discursively deployed to make sense of other topics of talk, explain predicaments and order social difference" (540). Consequently, the parameters which need to change in order to make the nation

36 Jäger argues that discourses are not simply a mirror of reality, but they are active agents that constitute reality. They are a crucial part of subject formation, and they provide the templates and frameworks for individuals' and societies' behavior (170–71).

37 Jäger points out in his methodological work on critical discourse analysis that the individual's contribution to this context can vary vastly in terms of quantity and quality. Some individuals and groups will try to control a certain discourse, whereas others try to avoid any involvement in debates. Nevertheless, no one can fully escape this discursive context which consequently makes it the product of the sociocultural context of a whole society (35–37).

the center of discourse are on the one hand a national conflict or situation of war and on the other hand the need for a discursive schema which helps ease or settle a conflict. I argue that a comparable mechanism occurs with inner-American, non-military types of conflicts, namely culture wars such as the debate over marriage equality. The nation is not as obviously contested as in national catastrophes, sporting events, or wars; however, the discursive frame of the nation is made use of in this controversy, even though in a less explicit manner as in the possible contexts listed by Fox and Miller-Idriss. The proxy wars of negotiations of American nationalism in culture war debates, as for instance over marriage equality, health care, or immigration, occupy the middle ground between everyday routine talk in which the nation is seldomly talked about in a conscious manner and more overt types of national conflicts such as wars or catastrophes. When charges of un-Americanism were most prominent in the fight over marriage equality, the debate became more focused on what constitutes American identity as well as on the future direction of the United States as a nation. The actual subject for negotiation, i. e., if the Constitution of the United States grants same-sex couples the right to marry, gradually moved to the background of the debate although most people engaged in the conflict probably have not noticed this shift.

Skey's Five Dimensions of Everyday Nationalism

Whereas Fox and Miller-Idriss rely on different modalities of experiencing everyday nationalism, Michael Skey aims at analyzing this concept with the help of five different dimensions: "spatial," "temporal," "cultural," "political," and "self/other" (Skey 11–12). By relying on these five dimensions, Skey tries to offer a picture of everyday nationalism that is as comprehensive as possible by investigating differently structured areas of life (12). Skey's intention was to theorize the ongoing production of nationalism in a way which is flexible and dynamic enough to acknowledge a nation's past and present as a continuum as well as to illuminate both the macrostructural and the microstructural forces to which it is exposed (9). Only then can the large variety of factors that lead to the stabilization or destabilization of a nation be taken fully into account.[38] Like other

[38] Skey's approach is also interesting insofar as he locates these processes of stabilization and destabilization in sociocultural discourse. He attributes

scholars of everyday nationalism, Skey does not conceive the nation as a fixed entity and demands that the focus of research should be on "understanding the ways in which manifold practices, symbols, texts, objects, and utterances form part of a wider social *discourse* (10). Additionally, it is important for Skey to reveal "the contested and contingent nature of apparently timeless national forms . . . because it challenges the idea that people should be defined only in terms of narrowly circumscribed racial, ethnic, and national characteristics" (5).

Symbols and a stable framework provide an anchor in one's everyday life. This type of consistency is so essential for humans in order to grow and develop in other areas of life. Conservatism and a stable set of values and morals enjoy immense popularity since progress can be challenging and even overwhelming at times. As Skey put it, "the logic of national thinking is one key element in the contemporary era, that may enable us – as isolated and insignificant individuals – to categorise, make sense of and act in what otherwise might be seen as overwhelming, uncertain

immense importance to language, in particular to the "everyday forms of taken-for-granted language" (10). Accusations of un-Americanism have also become a form of taken-for-granted language. The growing presence of the term not only in political debates but in everyday conversations of Americans is striking. Additionally, the often unreflective and incautious use of the term 'un-American' also supports the hypothesis that it has become taken-for-granted language. Skey's approach to everyday nationalism is also noteworthy for this study due to his "particular focus on exploring the degree to which these processes of categorization and interpretation are largely taken for granted by certain groups, so that they are considered 'common sense'" (Skey 11). Categorizing gay Americans as un-American has been common sense for a long period of the country's history since gay people were regarded as the outsiders and at times even as national security threats (D. K. Johnson 8). A re-interpretation did not take place until the tide turned in favor of homosexual Americans and their fellow Americans started to reconsider whether this categorization, which had been taken for granted for so long, was justified. As soon as the majority of Americans started to support gay rights and especially after the landmark civil rights case *Obergefell v. Hodges*, it has been opponents of marriage equality who are categorized as un-American for their failure to endorse the American ideal of equality for all (Robinson). Since such processes of categorization invariably result in a situation of inclusion and exclusion, Skey also directs attention to "the range of subject positions that are discursively produced and the degree to which they may generate material/psychological benefits for some, while marginalising others" (11).

and sometimes frightening world" (6). However, such conservative social maps or frameworks for orientation often come at the expense of those whose interests they do not mirror. If a coexistence of different social maps is not possible, for example, because a policy can only favor one group of people, the consequence is often the marginalization and the disadvantage of other groups. Such a behavior results in some people being "'more equal' than others because they possess greater levels of national cultural capital" (Skey 67). This is the case with same-sex marriage since the state can either grant or deny this right.

Identity formation also takes place by distinguishing oneself from others, sometimes in a radical way when only the interest of one group can be accommodated. Accusations of un-Americanism reinforce this process of the exclusion of dissidents and the inclusion of like-minded people into one's idea of American nationalism. When charges of un-Americanism are raised, it is indicative of a fight over what Skey calls the "national cultural capital" (67). National cultural capital is the currency with which one can purchase inclusion in a community of people who share the same idea of American national identity. "Others," i. e., those with less or a different national cultural capital, need to be watched closely since they could easily disrupt one's social map of orientation. In his studies, Skey also looked at migration movements to Great Britain in relation to everyday nationalism. One might assume that migration would introduce a different dynamic than the one that is present in inner-national culture wars; however, this is not the case. The group dynamics are often the same. Skey explains that the respective 'other' "may represent a key source of ontological insecurity by challenging established norms or social relations, that majority groups take for granted and rely on to underpin their own sense of subjectivity and place" (70–71). This is as true for debates on migration as it is for the debate on marriage equality where two opposing camps fought over the future of American nationalism with the help of insults of un-Americanism. Skey elaborates on this as follows:

> [T]he line between an unthreatening 'other' and one that causes anxiety because it can no longer be managed appears to being breached at the present time. In these instances, previously taken-for-granted ways of making sense of and articulating social relations are coming under increasing scrutiny, and there is a concomitant need for many to try to reassert their own position within a familiar and hence, ontologically secure, national space. (72)

This national space does not necessarily have to be within defined borders of nation states. Taking into account that nations are much more a national discourse than a fixed entity, reassurance of one's place within a nation should be understood as getting a seat at the table of discourse and having one's voice heard rather than merely existing within the nation's geographical area. If a person is not granted this seat and feels excluded from this process, accusations of un-Americanism are one possible reaction in order to express anxiety over imminent changes to society one cannot accept or handle. In the debate on marriage equality, both camps were under pressure and needed to either reassure or claim their national space. Opponents were afraid that their conservative social map was under attack whereas supporters of same-sex marriage had to fight for their national space.

If a certain discourse becomes so established that it dominates the national self-definition of the majority of the nation, Skey speaks of "sedimentation" (14). He defines the concept of sedimentation as "the process whereby a particular discourse becomes to be seen as objective or natural rather than one possible way of making sense of the world" (14). Considering the passion and the fierceness with which the most dedicated members of both marriage equality supporters and opponents fight for their cause and the little understanding they show for the position of the other side, one can confirm that sedimentation has taken place within these groups. However, as Skey explains, "even the most established social meanings, institutions, and relations are part of an ongoing and contingent process that are subject to contradictions and resistance" (35), and this is the moment when established structures begin to de-sediment. The gay rights movement is one of these contradictions and forms of resistance that gradually ablate the sediment. New elements are incorporated into the former sediment and thereby replace the structures that are no longer considered to be part of the sediment of American nationalism.

Skey proposes to analyze the social discourse of a nation by investigating it in five different dimensions. The spatial dimension refers to the concept of territory and is probably most closely connected to an orthodox understanding of nation, which sees the nation as an object. With the help of this perspective, Skey wants to ensure that the discourse of nation is not intermingled with discourses on ethnicity or race (11). In the temporal dimension, "the past is articulated in national terms and the present embodied through daily and mass 'national' rituals, thus enabling a (relatively) secure future to be envisaged" (Skey 11). Seeing national discourse as a continuum is beneficial to an analysis of everyday nationalism since the present can always only be the result of the past. A development such as destabilization can only be fully comprehended if the forces that eventually led to such a change are also recognized.

Regarding the cultural dimension, Skey looks at symbolic systems of everyday life, including social norms and values, which work as guidelines for people. He sees the significance of modern nationhood in the "notion of ontological security" that ideas of nationalism can provide (23). Despite struggles between social groups in society, Skey argues that "where a dominant system becomes established and part of what most people know, it is likely to act as a powerful framework for orientating them in the world" (11).[39] Skey sees "the role of established discursive frameworks in providing an ongoing and (relatively) secure sense of both place and subjectivity in what might otherwise be seen as a complex and threatening world" (21). If the stability of a discourse is no longer guaranteed or if a discourse is completely uprooted, the feeling of safety and stability associated with a formerly established discourse subsequently crumbles.

When a stable map for everyday orientation is too tight and inflexible to accommodate the needs of Americans' whose interests collide with the existing framework, social movements become effective. Whereas the cultural dimension of everyday nationalism is particularly useful for the analysis of the perspective of the opponents, the influence of supporters of marriage equality becomes most relevant in the political dimension of everyday nationalism, which is the fourth component of Skey's theoretical approach. With this dimension, Skey "emphasizes the importance of political organisations in mobilising and sustaining national movements" (12). Although he acknowledges that the state tends to be the "primary institutional apparatus for legitimising national discourse," he underlines that the state is not the nation, although the terms tend to be used inter-

[39] This cultural dimension of everyday nationalism could explain why some opponents of marriage equality were in disbelief when five U.S. Supreme Court judges ruled that same-sex marriage would become the law of the land. For some, this change to their idea of what constituted core American values and norms was too fast and too intense. If one considers that the landmark decision destroyed a framework which had provided them with orientation prior to the Supreme Court decision, the impact it had on them becomes tangible.

changeably in public discourse (12). While the state is something that can be conceived as a singular entity, the nation is a conglomerate of various entities, concepts, and discourses. The state is an actor in the conceptualization of the nation and people's everyday nationalism, but it is far from being the only or the most important one (12). As a result, Skey points to a long list of other parties and organizations involved in the discursive construction of national discourse and who are in a cultural, political, and ideological competition over who defines the nation. This fourth dimension draws attention to the role of interest groups and social movements as decisive forces in the process of how the nation is negotiated, experienced, expressed (12).[40] For Skey, such struggles "confirm the significance of the nation as a resonant category which is used to justify the (sometimes violent) activities of competing political interests" (12). Guibernau adds that "national movements bring light to problems central to more structurally complex societies: they raise questions about the need for new rights for all members of the community, particularly the right to be different" (74).

The fifth dimension is closely linked to question of identity in everyday nationalism, which has already been partly addressed by the cultural and the political dimension. With reference to Wodak, Skey explains that "[t]he final dimension – self/other – points to the critical role that people, and the different traits and values they are seen to embody, have in realizing and concretising the image of a nation in a world of nations" (12). This dimension tries to connect the everyday nationalism of one nation with the rest of the world and their concepts thereof. Consequently, it is the dimension which is closest to an orthodox and traditional understanding of nationalism studies. Trying to integrate a traditional component into more contemporary approaches to nationalism, such as everyday na-

40 The marriage equality movement emerged from the gay rights movement and quickly developed into a powerful voice which found supporters across society and became omnipresent in political debates. The state itself did not shape much of the national discourse on marriage equality; social movements and interest groups on both sides of the culture war were the actors dominating the national debate. The state only reacted to forces and voices from within the nation since state legislation never actively propelled any change. Consequently, the battlefield in this culture war was largely left to non-state institutions, organizations, and movements of both camps, fighting over whose worldview and framework was best for the future of the United States.

tionalism, would add value to a respective analysis. In addition to this aspect, the fifth dimension addresses the role of values and morals in the process of constructing and deconstructing nationalism and national identity. Above that, Skey stresses the importance of people's agency and their active contribution to the nation-building process, which is one of the core theories of everyday nationalism studies (12).

Everyday Nationalism and Identity Formation

Studies on everyday nationalism show that the nation plays a crucial role in the identity formation of its people.[41] Due to this immense importance of nationalism in the process of an individual's identity construction and the importance of everyday nationalism as a category for identification, the concept of everyday nationalism should receive special attention by scholars. The value and significance of nationalism as a category of iden-

[41] In their essay "Beyond 'identity,'" Brubaker and Cooper point out that it is impossible to fully grasp the concept of identity, but they nevertheless try to differentiate between various uses of the term (6–8). One interpretation they suggest is reading identity as a "*collective* phenomenon," whereby a "fundamental and consequential *sameness* among members of a group or category" is at the core of this concept (7). This sameness is expressed through shared characteristics, beliefs, or worldviews. Since the identity of the individual moves to the background for the benefit of the collective, this identity concept is prevalent in discourses on social movements, gender, or nationalism (7). Although there are multiple and competing definitions of American national identity, it is, in the end, a collective phenomenon that is indicative of a desire to unite the American people to one national family. Identity can also be the "product of social or political action" and thereby be apprehended as a consequence of a social movement or as the starting point of collective action (7–8). This interpretation of identity is reminiscent of Skey's 'political dimension' of everyday nationalism, since social movements play a major role in this analytical category of nationalism. Another approach to identity studies, which Brubaker and Cooper propose in their essay, can be regarded as a contrast to the former: identity as a "fundamental condition of social being" (7). In this context, "'identity' is invoked to point to something allegedly *deep, basic, abiding or foundational*" about a person" (7). This understanding is relevant for research on accusations of un-Americanism in the marriage equality debate insofar as Americans' stance on this issue is usually based on deeply held beliefs and sets of values.

tification for the individual cannot be overestimated. Guibernau holds that nationalism is "one of the major sources of identity for contemporary individuals" (46). This is the case not only in a political setting but also in a sociocultural context, such as in the marriage equality debate or other culture war debates which have had a tremendous impact on the national self-perception of Americans. National identity provides individuals with a place in society and a map for orientation. No one has the time or energy to continuously reconceptualize their own American identity in relation to others. National identity comes with a set of values, beliefs, morals, definitions, and interpretations. Guibernau emphasizes "the force of nationalism springs not from rational thought alone, but from the irrational power of emotions that stem from the feelings of belonging to a particular group" (76). This explains why national identity is inseparable from questions of inclusion and exclusion. It also accounts for the irrational or questionable decisions that can result from certain conceptualizations of American nationalism. The insult of un-Americanism is based on conflicting ideas of American everyday nationalism and is an attempt of one party to identify the other as the outgroup. The opposition to a particular issue, e.g., same-sex marriage, cannot always be rationally explained, but it is deeply connected to one's self-concept as American. Therefore, phrasing one's opinion with the help of the term 'un-American' is a strategy that is often chosen.

The work of De Cillia, Reisigl, and Wodak on nations and national identity is a vital resource for the present project due to its commentary and analysis on the discursive construction of national identities. They "assume that national identities – conceived as specific forms of social identities – are *discursively*, by means of language and other semiotic systems, *produced*, *reproduced*, *transformed* and *destructed*" (153). Consequently, national identity and the accompanying idea of nationalism are in a continuous flux; these ideas are constantly being built, broken apart, reassembled, and restructured with new components being added, whereas others are discarded. De Cillia, Reisigl, and Wodak also address the conflict of sameness and difference. They notice that "the discursive construction of nations and national identities runs hand in hand with the construction of difference/distinctiveness and uniqueness" (153): "As soon as [the discursive construction] is elevated to an imaginary collective level, both the construction of sameness and the construction of difference violate pluralistic and democratic variety and multiplicity by group-internal homogenization (of in-groups as well as out-groups)" (DeCillia et al. 153–54). Beliefs over what is considered American and un-American are turned into weapons that help secure the homogeneity as well as superiority of one's group. Accusations of un-Americanism help defend one's idea of national identity in addition to one's status within the nation. Acceptance of a rivalrous definition of (un-)Americanism is rather exceptional in the construction of national identity since this process of mutual insults of un-Americanism is also a struggle for power (P. King 615).

De Cillia et al. point out:

> [T]here is *no such thing as the one and only national identity* in an essentializing sense, but rather that different identities are discursively constructed according to context, that is according to the social field, the situational setting of the discursive act and the topic being discussed. In other words, national identities are not completely consistent, stable and immutable. (154)

For example, national identities can unite both liberal and conservative views, depending on the context, or they transform over time due to changing circumstances or new experiences. It is not uncommon for Americans who once had a very conservative stance on marriage equality to change their opinion in regard to this issue as soon as they have a close friend or family member who is gay.[42]

Extensive research has been done on the intersections of gender and nation especially since Nira Yuval-Davis' 1997 publication *Gender and Nation* in which she analyzes how these discourses mutually affect each

42 In a study on public attitudes towards the LGBT community, Lewis et al. were able to show that interpersonal contact often reduces a negative stance towards LGBT people and increases empathy towards them (862). A very prominent example in American politics is Senator Rob Portman of Ohio who no longer opposed same-sex marriage after he learned that his son was gay. In 2013, this made him the only Republican senator who publicly spoke out in favor or gay rights and marriage equality (Peters). Senator Portman nevertheless supported the Republican cause and was proud of his conservative American national identity. This identity concept did not keep him from allowing for some flexibility in order to be supportive of his son. Having a gay son caused Portman to reconstruct his self-concept (Peters). Consequently, his national self-concept as a conservative American was also no longer the same. As a result, he joined the side of the marriage equality supporters in the discursive construction of the nation. His identity as the father of a gay son shaped his understanding of which groups American nationalism could comprise.

other. Her work laid the foundation for various research on the interconnectedness between gender and nation which followed. In *Gender Ironies of Nationalism: Sexing the Nation*, Tamar Mayer brings the concept of sexuality into the interplay of dual discourses and thereby extends the intersection to three intertwined discourses. Whereas Yuval-Davis' work focuses strongly on the relations between feminism and nationalism, Mayer tries to broaden research in that field by explicitly adding the social construct of 'sexuality.' On the interplay between nationalism and identity, she writes that one must understand "that my 'ego' is often inseparable from the 'ego' of the nation to which I belong and which helps to define my identity" (6). What she describes here is a reciprocal process by which the nation shapes its people and the people shape their nation. Power structures are a key aspect of this process since "[t]he empowerment of one gender, one nation or one sexuality virtually always occurs at the expense and disempowerment of another" (Mayer 1). The nation is a stage where the principle of "survival of the fittest" applies. Minorities have little chance for a full inclusion into concepts of American nationalism and having their needs acknowledged until they win over a significant part of the nation's people and construct their national identity in a way that it is compatible with the dominant idea of everyday nationalism. "In order to survive and to justify its existence, the nation must preserve its uniqueness," Mayer argues, and "it does so by constructing myths about national creation and by defining 'proper behaviors' for members of the nation and for the nation itself" (9–10). The traditional concept of marriage was for most of United States' history an essential part of this 'proper behavior' that helped sustain the nation (Tocqueville 242; Yamin 5–6). The House Un-American Activities Committee defined proper behavior also in this regard by condemning homosexuality as un-American (D. K. Johnson 8–9). Nation, gender, and sexuality are intersecting discourses and "the interplay among nation, gender and sexuality often pressures people to negotiate their identities in complex ways" (Mayer 1). However, the increasing political and sociocultural power of gay subjects has intensified the discussion on the influence of sexuality on nationalism. This interconnectedness also plays a role in the analysis of the discursive linkage between marriage equality and discourses and practices of nationalism because the gay rights movement redefines what is considered acceptable and proper behavior regarding American nationalism.

Conclusion

After Michael Billig initiated a turn in nationalism studies with his work *Banal Nationalism*, scholars of everyday nationalism took his theories one step further and shifted the focus of attention to nationalism as a bottom-up force. In everyday nationalism studies, people are seen as active agents in the process of the construction and deconstruction of nationalism and not merely as passive recipients on which a certain idea of nationalism is imposed. Through the engagement with the nation, national identity and nationalism are negotiated in sociocultural discourse which can involve accusations of un-Americanism.

Nationalism as an everyday phenomenon is experienced in multiple ways. Therefore, the methodological approach by Fox and Miller-Idriss proposes four perspectives for analyzing everyday nationalism (talking, choosing, performing, and consuming the nation). Fox and Miller-Idriss' category of "talking the nation" (537) is particularly of interest for this study since debates over marriage equality, in which charges of un-Americanism are raised, are ultimately discursive negotiations of American nationalism. In a different approach to everyday nationalism studies, Skey proposes five dimensions (spatial, temporal, cultural, political, and self/other) through which nationalism can be explored (11–12).

Skey dedicates a large part of his study of everyday nationalism to explaining why people rely heavily on sociocultural maps of orientation and why places of security are important in the engagement with American nationalism and its ongoing transformation. He repeatedly emphasizes that "even the most established social meanings, institutions, and relations are part of an ongoing and contingent process that are subject to contradictions and resistance" (35). As a result, it is understandable why conservatism and stability are appealing to people. Many people struggle to handle ontological insecurity and consequently resist progress and change because they fear that too frequent and too intense alterations to their sociocultural map could unroot them. One possible manifestation of this fear are charges of un-Americanism. Furthermore, nationalism is an essential source of identity, and concepts thereof are in a continuous flux. With nationalism playing such an important part in people's everyday lives, it comes as no surprise that competing concepts of un-Americanism are turned into weapons in order to either challenge the existing form of nationalism or to fight for its preservation.

Chapter III

III History of Un-Americanism

What characterizes someone or something as un-American? What is this un-Americanism? This word is fascinating because it seems to be so simple, but at the same time it is impossible to find a single, precise definition for it. The prefix 'un-' suggests that the term 'un-American' refers to someone or something that is either the opposite of American or just not American. Since the word 'American,' used either as noun or adjective, denotes people from the United States, one might conclude that the un-American is anyone not having a U.S. citizenship. A look at the term's history shows examples of people being accused of un-American behavior coinciding with their status as foreign citizens in the 19th century. However, this is typically denoted by the term 'non-American' in modern usage and not the context in which the term 'un-American' has been used for most of the country's history. Furthermore, being 'un-American' also does not imply anti-American actions or sentiments, that is, having a hostile attitude towards the United States and its people.

The term 'un-American' is highly complex and what is considered un-American is subject to constant change. What all uses of the term 'un-American' have in common is a reference to the American ideology whose standards or criteria the un-American fails to meet. Un-Americanism is most prominently associated with the House Un-American Activities Committee; however, solely focusing on this single and comparatively short period of time would not do justice to the term's rich and perplexing history. Although this chapter does not aim at providing a comprehensive history of the term 'un-American,' a brief overview of how it developed over the years should nevertheless be given. To fully understand the term's impact on the process of American national self-identification and its significance in today's national discourse, it is beneficial to trace its development throughout history, starting in the Revolutionary era.

The Jeffersonian Principles

Thomas Jefferson initiated the binary opposition of American and un-American in the process of drafting the Declaration of Independence long before the term 'un-Americanism' was associated with the House Un-American Activities Committee (Steele 881–82). Brian Steele claims:

> No writer is more closely bound up with our deepest sense of the meaning of the "American" than Thomas Jefferson and it is difficult to imagine America's national purpose without some reference to his work. Yet Jefferson's projection of American identity also assumed and even constituted, of necessity, the un-American and it is in this sense that the un-American provided the necessary contours of what became the "American." (881)

Although the Declaration of Independence was primarily the pronouncement of separation of the newly founded United States of America, for Jefferson, the writing of the Declaration was much more than that. It was an act of self-reflection and a first attempt at the self-definition of a new nation and its people: "[T]he Declaration moves beyond an anticolonial statement of independence and toward the assertion of a national character and identity oriented around the embrace of natural-rights liberalism" (Steele 883–84). Jefferson's idea of Americanism is deeply consistent with what he constituted in his draft. "Americans would recognize each other – not by language and appearance, not by ethnicity or religion – but by their common adherence" to the premises of the Declaration of Independence (Steele 886). This founding document expressed how Americans defined themselves around 1776 and thereby gives an excellent record on an early idea of un-Americanism: "The Declaration would explain their distinctive character and moral commitments – principles that Jefferson would continue to uphold if they were to continue as a people" (Steele 886).

At that time, being American was first and foremost understood as the opposite to being British. Jefferson also included the friends of England in his draft "precisely because they demonstrated to Americans just how different their own character had become from that of the 'unfeeling brethren' they were leaving behind" (Steele 884). This process of demarcation also initiated the process of national self-discovery. According to the Declaration, Americans believed that every person was created equal and that every American was granted the right to life, liberty, and the pursuit of happiness. This God-given right was self-evident and deeply rooted in the self-perception of this young nation. "[T]rue Americans would be distinguished by what they believed, by what drove their heart's pulsations" (887). Therefore, by this rubric, it was easier to be regarded as a true American in Jefferson's time than it would be today, when constant arguing about un-Americanism creates an environment in which "being American" is an amorphous ideal that one can aspire to but never fully achieve in the eyes of everyone. In the 18th century, the un-American enemy came from outside the American community in the form of those people who would not grant this newly found union of states their desired independence. Today's alleged un-Americans, by contrast, are part of the intranational community, and they have become impossible to define or to distinguish since the differentiating criteria are arbitrary, due to the countless interpretations of the term. Jefferson's definition of un-Americanism is noteworthy since he did not directly link being American to a certain race, ethnicity, or religion. However, this does not mean that his definition was all-inclusive. He only included those Americans who were willing to be part of his idea of "one people" and consented to his principles.

Jefferson's definition is still of great relevance for today's citizens. References to the Jeffersonian principles shape many of America's current debates that revolve around the acquisition of equal rights for a minority group. The Declaration of Independence is likely to be evoked in culture wars by competing parties to assert their Americanness in contrast to the opponents' un-American policies (Hall, "Americanism" 1111–12). These frequent appeals to one's own Americanness from diverse and often polarizing sides has its side-effects. Among them are accusations of un-Americanism as well as intense fights over American nationalism and the inference that it is impossible to unite all people under the flag of Americanism. Steele explains part of the conflict over (un-)Americanism as follows:

> [A]ll the uses of the un-American are nationalist almost by definition, and American struggles of over the concept in civic life will continue to revolve around the story of their peoplehood and the claims about their character embedded in the Declaration of Independence which first articulated the un-American and which continually pushes them to read their practice against its claims. (902)

The Declaration of Independence is an 18th century document, but it has not lost any of its significance. It constituted the beginning of what is today the United States of America, and it continues to impress with its liberal and timeless values.[43] As a consequence, referring to the Jeffersonian ideals is still popular when people strive for equal rights and opportunities. The majority of today's citizens do not exclude certain people from the privilege of enjoying the nation's core values of life, liberty, and the pursuit of happiness out of malice; however, how those three rights can or should be achieved is very much up for interpretation. According to Steele, the problem is the following:

> Because nearly every successful claim about American character runs back through some route to the assertions that Jefferson made in the Declaration, America has at its core a transcendental set of ideals that remain almost unrealizable in practice – in the sense that they are both lofty and always susceptible to divergent interpretations and manipulable by partisans. (894)

If a concept is as undefined as 'Americanism' and 'un-Americanism', it is, consequently, also prone to battles over its "correct" interpretation.

Un-Americanism from the 1830s till the 1930s

Before the first official usage by the "House Special Committee on Un-American Activities Authorized to Investigate Nazi Propaganda and Certain Other Propaganda Activities," a forerunner of the later House Un-American Activities Committee better known as the McCormack-Dickstein Committee, the term 'un-American' had not been used in such a distinctive context as during the time of the investigative committees. A short analysis conducted in order to gain an impression of the respective contexts of the term's appearance in various newspapers starting in 1830s led to the conclusion that until un-Americanism became associated with the McCormack-Dickstein Committee in 1934, the term had only been

43 For instance, the Declaration of Independence was evoked by both Justice Scalia and Justice Thomas in the landmark civil rights case *Obergefell v. Hodges*. They discuss the concepts of liberty (Scalia, "*Obergefell*" 2) and human dignity (Thomas, "*Obergefell*" 2) in their respective dissents to the decision of the majority opinion. Both argue that a ruling in favor of marriage equality based on the principles as outlined in the Declaration is not justified.

used infrequently and without a specific connotation. A few examples of un-Americanism will be given in the following section in order to provide an overview of what was considered un-American at certain times.

One of the earliest accounts on the usage of the term 'un-American' in newspaper articles is in an issue of the *Daily National Intelligencer* in 1832. In an article titled "Congressional," a speech of Mr. Wilde of Georgia is printed in which he addressed a bill on the issue of duties on imports in front of the House of Representatives. He reports on a visit to Philadelphia where the meat manufacturers had heard that colleagues in other states in the U.S. imposed tariffs on their produce. Consequently, manufacturers in Philadelphia demanded the same protection for their meat. Wilde depicts the scene as follows: "They demanded *protection* against the ruinous influx of foreign beef, veal, lamb and mutton, from New Jersey and elsewhere, deprecated the un-patriotic, un-American traffic carried on by the friends of free trade. . ." (Wilde qtd. in "Congressional"). What is interesting in this article is that the American states of New Jersey and Pennsylvania, although united under the American flag, did not approve of the idea of an inner-American free trade. In fact, not having tariffs that protected the manufacturers of each state was regarded as un-American. This example demonstrates that although the idea of one American nation was not so prevalent at the time, people had an idea of what was un-American.

A whole newspaper dedicating itself to fighting un-American sentiments and tendencies was founded in Philadelphia in 1839. *The North American* saw itself as the defender of patriotism and Americanism: "The reason why it commands such an extraordinary popularity is because the North American stands alone out of 245 daily newspapers in Pennsylvania, New Jersey and Delaware in its fearless antagonism to everything unpatriotic and un-American" ("The Reason Why"). This was a message they successfully communicated to their audience, as a letter to the editor from Abraham S. Schropp proves: "A large number of persons who think themselves patriots are subscribers for The North American just because they believe it is the most patriotic in the State. It is just because The North American is unchangeably opposed to everything un-patriotic and un-American." *The North American* made ample use of the term 'un-American' not only in its self-description but also in its articles. Fighting un-Americanism seemed to be the spirit of this newspaper. Regarding a bill, which would have prohibited the display of foreign flags, they defended Governor Flower who vetoed the bill in 1894: "One of the reasons why he assigns for doing so is that the bill is un-American. Was there ever such a combination of impudence and mendacity! Un-American to stand by the flag and to declare that it alone shall receive official recognition within in the borders of the Republic!" ("A Shameful Veto"). *The North American* also thought the term 'un-American' to be suitable for expressing their aversion to the Democratic Party, which they call an "un-American party" and denounced Democrats and other "encroachments of un-American sectarian effort" as a threat to Americanism ("A Reply to Wm. James"). Another target of their attacks was the American Protective Association, a late 19th-century anti-Catholic organization, whose policy and principles they disdained for being "illiberal, unwise, un-patriotic, un-democratic and un-American" ("Voorhees and Turpee Endorsed"). As these examples illustrate, the writers of *The North American* had a very clear idea of what constituted good Americanism and which un-American tendencies needed to be kept under control to prevent their spread.

The 19th century also saw several articles which dealt with the un-American practices and behavior of immigrants if they were not willing to fully assimilate. In 1838, German Americans in the state of Ohio agitated fellow Americans when the Governor of Ohio proposed that German schools should be encouraged, and official and legal documents should also be in German. As recorded in an article in the *New-York Spectator*, the Governor's fondness of Germans was not shared by everyone in Ohio: "This recommendation is not only un-American, but ridiculous. The Germans came here to become Americans. Let their language be English" ("Ohio"). This is a quote from an article in which the foreigner or less American of the Americans became the center of attention regarding accusations of un-Americanism. The new nation and its people were struggling with the question of who a proper American was ("Ohio"). In its core, the question does not deviate much from what is at stake today. However, the important difference is that the un-American is often the recent immigrant or the American who still has strong ties to their former home country. Such incidents as in Ohio sparked a debate about whether the first immigrant families were more American than recent immigrants, and if yes, were "new Americans" un-American if they failed to immediately break all ties with their native countries. In the article "Evil of Native-ism" published in the *Emancipator and Weekly Chronicle* in 1844, an anonymous author denounced such a mindset as "evil":

> Beginning with the wrong unconstitutional, un-Republican, un-American assumption that a naturalized American is therefore less an American than one who had the good luck to be born here, they soon come to regard them not as citizens but as aliens; then as persons who have no business to be here, and who are here only by sufferance and not by right; then to feel as if they were enemies, only under a truce, but to be watched, and kept in their place, and prevented from doing any thing by concert to defend their own rights, or advance their own interests, or propagate their own sentiments, as the rest of us may lawfully do. ("Evil")

The author bemoaned that naturalized Americans were not even given a chance by native-born Americans. Everything naturalized Americans did was considered offensive and declared un-American. However, the idea of un-Americanism, which the author presented in this article, was different. He understood Americanism as distinctive of a culture which welcomed all those who wished to become part of it. What he considered un-American was forgetting how this nation started, namely as a nation of immigrants ("Evil").

During the Civil War, there was an increase in the usage of the term 'un-American' in debates over slavery and the secession of the South. In an article celebrating the 88th anniversary of the American Independence, a writer of San Francisco's *Daily Evening Bulletin* could not get around addressing the issue of slavery which was endangering American unity:

> It is the essential health of American principles, which, like a firm, strong constitution throwing off a malarious poison by a burning fever, is now in these terrible pangs and throes, as if of dissolution, casting off forever, that hateful, undemocratic, un-American, unchristian thing, that so long haunted, and rode us like a night mare – Negro Slavery. ("Independence Day in San Francisco")

The author was clear in his ascription. It was slavery that was un-American since it conflicted with all noble American principles. In an article published a few months after the end of the Civil War, a contributor to the *Daily National Intelligencer* also relied on this wording when he speaks of the "obstinate, un-American, warring faction" which needed to be obstructed in order to never again let such a war happen ("Multiple Editorial Items"). In his eyes, a true American would always advocate for the union of the North and the South. Provoking the secession of a part of the American nation was un-American and needed to have consequences.

In July 1881, a piece in *The New York Times* entitled "Is it Un-American?" engaged with the question of what is American (and what is not) in relation to the hotly debated Civil Service Reform which aimed to change the method of selecting civil servants. Typically, winners of elections handed government offices to their supporters, which meant that those chosen were not necessarily the most suitable for the position. Senator Ingalls from Kansas was one of the most outspoken opponents of the reform. He declared that "the theory of civil service reform is un-American and not in accord with the theory of the Government" (Ingalls qtd. in "Is it Un-American?"). The author of the article comments that Senator Ingalls stance is surprising since he should know that the old procedure of appointment fostered corruption and nepotism; however, Ingalls' stance on this issue is the "opinion of all men who look at politics and public life from a stand-point similar to his. If the un-American idea they so much deprecate were enforced they might be out of politics all together . . ." ("Is It Un-American?"). The author of the article is in favor of such a reform because he believed it was most un-American to expose American citizens to the high level of corruption which resulted from the existing civil servant appointment practice.

Tariffs seemed to be a topic in which accusations of un-Americanism were popular throughout the 19th century. An article from 1892 titled "Un-American" discussed a comment published by the *Bulletin* of the American Iron and Steel Association in regard to a decision of Judge Colt of the United States Circuit Court on tariff provisions. The association was enraged because the judge's decision on duty on common goat hair was not favorable towards the American industry and its workers: "The foreigner and not the employer of American labor, has their sympathy every time. . . . [This is] the latest manifestation of this un-American spirit by a United States Judge" ("Un-American"). This use of the term 'un-American' was reminiscent of Jefferson and his idea of un-Americanism in connection to foreigners. Being American is closely associated with always having the United States' best interest in mind. This situation was not unlike the aforementioned discussion regarding tariffs that took place in Philadelphia sixty years earlier. However, the decisive difference was that, as of the 1890s, tariffs were supposed to protect the whole of the United States against foreign competition. The term 'un-American' was then used to defend a united American front of industry and manufacturers.

An article from 1886 again made the un-Americanness of immigrants the subject of discussion. The author of the opinion piece, "Our Un-American Citizens," complained about the nuisance caused by strikers and labor union protest but primarily focused on the un-American attitude of recent immigrants who were participating in the strikes:

> It is a very common comment upon the labor troubles throughout the country that they are 'un-American,' and it is as true as it is frequent. . . . [One can see] in the minds of the strikers the inability to comprehend the equal rights of all men to life, liberty, and the pursuit of happiness. This is not a rhetorical flourish on the part of the author of the Declaration of Independence. It is a statement of a cardinal American doctrine. . . . This is not the result of reasoning. It is in the air of the country, and everybody native to it or who has acquired his ways of thinking in it holds it unconsciously as if it were an instinct. ("Our Un-American Citizens")

What is noteworthy about this article is that its author equates being un-American with a lack of citizenship or a citizenship of such short duration that the individual has not incorporated the American mentality. The use of the term in such a context is not comparable to today when accusations of un-Americanism are usually found in debates among Americans who overwhelmingly do not address American citizenship. German and Irish people caused the author's dismay with their un-American behavior ("Our Un-American Citizens"). According to his choice of words, the new immigrants were not very likely to assimilate or integrate because Americanism cannot be acquired by reasoning or an individual's effort, but rather it had to be inborn. Americanness could not be learned by a foreigner no matter how hard they tried to understand what it meant to be an American citizen: "Different as the methods of the various strikers and boycotters are, they have this in common, that they are entirely un-American, and show that those who employ them have no real conception of what American citizenship is or implies" ("Our Un-American Citizens"). The usage of the term 'un-American' differed considerably from today's, not only because it was used to refer to people who were literally not American but also because it provided a more defined concept of who the un-American actually was. In this case, it was the immigrant who did not share the same values and work ethic as the American who was either native-born or who had absorbed Americanness in their mind and soul ("Our Un-American Citizens"). This idea of the un-American as a foreigner or a stranger partly continued into the early 20th century.

Before New Mexico was admitted to the Union as the 47th state in 1912, it was despised as the "[m]ost un-American [p]art of the United

States" in an eponymous article from August 1905 in which Gilson Willets explained why it was impossible to allow this territory to become a part of the Union. Its inhabitants were more sympathetic with Mexico than the U.S. and most of the children had never heard "The Star-Spangled Banner," Willets bemoans. Although an American flag was hoisted up at a courthouse, during his visit, Willets witnessed a state that was solely governed by Mexicans with little to no understanding of the English language and much less the American mentality:

> [T]his Territory, where in half of the towns it is useless to ask one's way in English; where an American visitor meets conditions under the American flag that make him feel, despite himself, that he is in a foreign land; where, indeed, the Americans are actually regarded by the Mexicans as foreigners and usurpers; where the local authorities in many towns are Mexicans speaking a foreign tongue, and in no wise in sympathy with the American social customs or American industrial progress . . . where an American cannot secure justice in his own courts because tried by Mexicans who stand by one another, right or wrong. (Willets)

Frustrated as well as shocked by his investigations, Willets recommended postponing New Mexico's admission to the United States. He preferred to "wait until this most un-American part of our country [was] Americanized" (Willets). The interpretation of un-Americanism was unambiguous in this comment because the Mexicans were explicitly labeled as un-Americans for their lack of understanding of the English language and the American mindset. The Americanization, which was necessary for a later admission to the United States, required that the people of New Mexico sacrifice their Mexican lifestyle and heritage to become an American (Willets).

The un-Americanism rhetoric changed and shifted closer towards today's usage when President Theodore Roosevelt was publicly declared to be the most un-American president and placed on the same level as socialists by Rev. Dr. Jefferson in 1908 ("Plea for Big Navy Scored by Pastor"). The reverend criticized Roosevelt for his militarism as it was not in line with the ideals of the Founding Fathers. This article exemplified a shift in who was considered to be un-American. It is no longer the German immigrant or Mexican(-American) living on U.S. territory. Suddenly, the center of the accusations of un-Americanism was an American, in this case it was even the President of the United States, and no longer a foreigner or immigrant. This shows a development regarding who the target of the accusation of un-Americanism can be and regarding the motivation behind the charge. Being un-American became tantamount to not respecting the ideals of the Founding Fathers as well as core American values of liberty, equality, and freedom.

This shift was also evident in the discussion over immigration. In an article from April 1916, the Burnett Immigration Bill was addressed which aimed at the exclusion of un-educated aliens by making a literacy test a requirement for citizenship. The bill would not only reduce the wave of immigrants but also allow for a selection of immigrants according to their educational status. In contrast to earlier debates over immigration in which the foreigner or recent immigrant, who was not assimilating quickly enough, was unanimously regarded as un-American, Americans seem to have become more tolerant towards new immigrants. The Burnett Immigration Bill was heavily criticized because it would lead to an exclusion of Italian, Eastern-European, and Jewish immigrants. One of the speakers at a mass meeting in the Bronx reportedly insisted that "the exclusion of any oppressed aliens [was] un-American" and "contrary to the fundamental principles upon which the nation [had been] founded" ("Citizens Fight Bill to Bar Uneducated"). Judge Scanlon, another speaker at the mass protest, declared: "What we want here is the good people of other countries. They are not the people of literary ability, but rather the people of honor, of purpose, and of character" (Scanlon qtd. in "Citizens Fight Bill to Bar Uneducated"). A comparable article from 1921, "Un-American and Un-Christian," covered the growing protest against anti-Semitism in the United States and reported on a list of support signed by a large number of high-ranking officials including the President. The journalist responsible for the article commented on the prevailing sentiment in the country as follows:

> There is no place in this country for deliberately propagated race prejudices and hatreds. To the Jews in America, who have enough serious problems of their own, it must be especially gratifying that the right hand of democratic fellowship and confidence has thus been held out to them by distinguished and fair-minded men of their blood. In this the fundamental and typical American attitude is truly represented. ("Un-American and Un-Christian")

Once again, it was no longer the alien or the immigrant who was denounced for being un-American, but the accusation was directed at Americans by their fellow countrymen. Those who discriminated against Jews were considered un-American because they failed to understand that the United States offered life, liberty, and the pursuit of happiness to all who sought to build a new life on its soil regardless of where they were coming from or how educated they were.

In the 1930s, newspaper articles still showed evidence of an ongoing debate on the question of American identity and the nature of the American people. However, the years before the foundation of the McCormack-Dickstein Committee also saw the beginning of a wider use of the term 'un-American' in a large variety of contexts which were not necessarily political in nature. One example of an interpretation of un-Americanism in the early 1930s was a letter to the editor from a reader of *The New York Times* published in 1933. In her letter titled, "Victorian Era Not so Golden. Nostalgia for It Found Unjustified and Also Un-American," Justine Mansfield states that she believed that yearning for the Victorian Era might be fine for older generations but for young Americans "a more forward-looking attitude [was] sound" and referred to a previous article which promoted a nostalgic view of the Victorian Era (Mansfield). Convinced that nostalgia was un-American, she concluded: "This is a young country and need not yet stroke its beard and get its joy of living from the past. . . . It should look backward for guidance and forward for its hopes" (Mansfield). The article still dealt with the American mindset, however, the term 'un-American' was not as limited to the discourse about American qualities as it had been in the early 20th century. This tendency was also noticeable in an "Art in Review" piece from 1934, in which watercolors by Joseph Pennell shown at the Grand Central Galleries in New York City were a reason for concern. "[S]trikingly un-American in feeling" was the description of Pennell's work given in the review (K.G.S.). The art critic adduced why he could not help but label Pennell's work "un-American": "The small scale, the delicate, almost precious touch, the tonal palette, as well as the low horizon and panoramic sweep, recall English watercolor of the eighteenth century and naturally, the Dutch" (K.G.S). The urge to find a common American style had reached the arts as well, where ignoring the trend of the day resulted in being accused of un-Americanism. This article was one of the last that demonstrated the wide range of contexts in which the term 'un-American' was used.

Articles published in the year 1934 and after show a radical change in the term's usage due to the newly founded House Special Committee on Un-American Activities Authorized to Investigate Nazi Propaganda and

Certain Other Propaganda Activities (also called McCormack-Dickstein Committee). Although accusations of un-American beliefs or behavior were already present in a variety of different contexts, they had not yet arisen in connection with communism or homosexual conduct. This phenomenon did not start until committee members launched their crusade against alleged enemies inside of the United States whom they believed to be a security threat in the mid-1930s. Alex Goodall referred to the 1930s as the "critical years of development" for ideas of un-Americanism because he believes this decade gave contours to the term (941).

The Era of the Investigative Committees

Today, the term 'un-American' in its historical context is most commonly associated with the House Un-American Activities Committee (HUAC), an investigative committee established in 1938 by the House of Representatives. This committee was not the first congressional investigation of its kind, but the successor of comparable investigative bodies which had already dealt with other potential threats to the nation. Congressional investigations became increasingly popular after the First World War when the Senate was concerned about Bolshevik and German propaganda in the United States (Goodman 4–5). Notable precursors to the HUAC are the Lusk Committee (1919) which investigated the aforementioned, the Fish Committee (1930) targeting mainly communists and their supporters, and the McCormack-Dickstein Committee (1934–1935) (Goodman 5–10).[44]

[44] Subversive activities were at the focus of congressional investigators every now and then during the First World War, but it was not until February 1919 that the United States Senate made an actual effort to investigate into communist doctrines. The rise of Bolshevism in Russia and two pro-Soviet rallies in Washington D.C. led to the beginning of congressional investigations into such activities and the foundation of the Lusk Committee (Goodman 5). However, in contrast to later committees, the Lusk Committee still had little authority and was mainly established as "a beacon to Communist-hounders still unweaned" (5). After the stock market crash in 1929, the House of Representatives decided that bolshevist influence in the United States should receive the attention of a proper committee: the Fish Committee, named after Hamilton Fish of New York, who was the original sponsor of the resolution. Fish's proposal suggested the establishment of a committee going after communist propaganda, American Communists, and "all entities, groups, or indi-

The McCormack-Dickstein Committee was the first investigative body that officially sought to pursue un-American propaganda or behavior. Dickstein's resolution initially lacked support when it came to the floor of the House of Representatives because it not only allowed the investigation of Nazis but of anyone deemed un-American (Goodman 14). When Representative Johnson of Minnesota asked, "What is meant by un-American activities?" (Johnson qtd. in Goodman 14) his very important question was ignored, and he never got an answer. No one was able to come up with a clear definition of the term, even at a time when being un-American became a criminal offense as Dickstein eventually succeeded in persuading the House of Representatives to establish the suggested committee in March 1934 (Hawkins 35). However, the McCormack-Dickstein Committee only existed for a year as Congress seemed to have lost interest in the committee's work after Dickstein submitted its report in February 1935 (Hawkins 35).

The House Un-American Activities Committee, also known as the Dies Committee after its chairman Democrat Martin Dies Jr. of Texas, was established in 1938 (Goodman 21). It was not a direct successor of the McCormack-Dickstein Committee and did not include the limiting descriptions of "Nazi" and "propaganda" but was comparable in jurisdiction. When Dies appeared before the House of Representatives in order to defend his initiative, he was confronted with the same opposition as Dickstein. Representative Maverick warned that Dies' resolution gave "blanket powers to investigate, humiliate, and meddle with anything and everything" (qtd. in Goodman 22). When the question what un-Americanism actually is came up on the House floor, Maverick exclaimed:

viduals who are alleged to advise, teach or advocate the overthrow by force or violence of the Government of the United States, or attempt to undermine our republican form of government by inciting riots, sabotage or revolutionary disorders" (Goodman 6). This vague choice of words, which enabled the investigation of basically everyone if the investigators wished to do so, was highly problematic. However, the Fish Committee was by far not as powerful as the later House Un-American Activities Committee and mainly stayed with its original aim, the investigation into communist organizations (8–9). Its successor, the McCormack Dickstein-Committee, was the result of the rise of Adolf Hitler. As a consequence, the House Representative Samuel Dickstein urged to investigate Nazi activities in the United States. John McCormack was also appointed as chairman to the committee since Dickstein wanted a non-Jew to conduct the investigations.

"Un-American! Un-American is simply something that somebody else does not agree to" (qtd. in Goodman 22). Given the history of the HUAC and its controversial hearings, Maverick ended up being right.

The chairman Martin Dies initially attempted to provide more clarity to the definition of un-Americanism and therefore sought the help of the American Legion, the Veterans of Foreign Wars, and the Daughters of the American Revolution (Lewis, "Amorphous Code" 973). All three organizations were on the conservative right and strove to "assume the mantle of guardians of Americanism and, therefore, to identify themselves as the definers and diviners of un-Americanism" (973). Interestingly, liberal organizations were not considered in Dies' efforts to define un-Americanism: "Despite continued protestors from liberal organizations that they, too, were wholly American in character and outlook, their voices went largely unheard in Washington and they remained liminal to the central debates over un-Americanism" (973). Unfortunately, there are no records on whether turning to conservative organizations helped Dies in his efforts to define un-Americanism. The impression is created that Dies' consulting of conservative organizations did not result in the consolidation of a specific interpretation of un-Americanism. Although the HUAC never cultivated a singular image or definition of un-Americanism, a certain pattern does emerge. Their understanding of un-Americanism always seemed to coincide with the ideas of the conservative right. The committee refrained from conducting investigations into activities of conservative organizations but investigated civil rights activism whenever they pleased (974).[45] Regarding the chairmen of the committee, Kaplan not only speaks of conservatives but claims the officials were "right-wingers" and "racists" (66).[46]

The HUAC operated without a definition of un-Americanism. The committee's officials formed their own subjective definition of the concept and adopted it according to whom they planned to expose and who

[45] Liberals occasionally joined the committee in an attempt to realign its conservative political orientation but gave up shortly after without exception (Goodman 24).

[46] The committee supposedly investigated un-American activities and, according to Kaplan, for many Americans this should also have included the ideology of the Ku Klux Klan. However, the committee rather seemed to protect the KKK than inquire into their activities (66). Kaplan claims that the chairman, Martin Dies, who represented a district in Mississippi, had close connections to the Klan which was in control of two states in the South and had significant influence in most other Southern states as well as in some Northern States (66).

was considered the threat of the day. The HUAC notoriously abused its unlimited power as a House committee and tried to indoctrinate the American citizens with their concept of true Americanness: "HUAC attempted to instil [sic!] a public fear of insidious 'un-American' by casting itself as the Constitutional protector of Americanism's core values" (R. Martin 1044). The committee's understanding of Americanism was extremely subjective and arbitrary. This increased fear in society and aroused suspicion towards people who did not conform with the committee's idea of the true American citizen. The HUAC was officially designed to monitor people or organizations engaged in communist and other subversive activities which posed a threat to the internal security of the United States. However, the House Resolution 282 did not provide the committee with clear guidelines but just gave it the temporary authorization to investigate:

> (1) the extent, character, and objects of un-American propaganda activities in the United States, (2) the diffusion within the United States of subversive and un-American propaganda that is instigated from foreign countries or of a domestic origin and attacks the principle of the form of government as guaranteed by our Constitution, and (3) all other questions in relation thereto that would aid Congress in any necessary remedial legislation. (United States. Congress. House. Special Committee on Un-American Activities)

This vague choice of words gave the investigators the broadest possible scope of action and legislative freedom to probe un-Americans and un-American activities according to their own arbitrary definitions:

> Neither of the key words 'subversive' or 'un-American' has a generally accepted common meaning or an established definition in law. In common parlance they are used interchangeably as political epithets to designate what the user disapproves. . . . The term 'un-American' does not appear in any other legislative enactments, and it has not been judicially defined. ("Constitutional" 419)

The work of the committee is the best proof that it itself had no clear idea of its authority or what it was actually supposed to look into since they investigated an astounding variety of topics, people, and organizations and thereby exploited their unlimited powers (418; 422–23).[47] As

[47] Among the organizations investigated by the HUAC, the Columbia Law Review lists the "American Civil Liberties Union, the C.I.O., the National

Congressman Ranking rightly noticed, the HUAC presented itself as the "grand jury . . . in session to investigate un-American activities at all times" (qtd. in "Constitutional" 418). In an article from 1947, the authors of the *Columbia Law Review* warned:

> Unlimited power in the hands of a congressional committee may mean drastic curtailment for the civil liberties of those who dissent from prevailing political opinion. . . . A congressional investigation completely unlimited in scope may itself be called 'un-American' and is too dangerous to be continued. ("Constitutional" 430–31)

The House Un-American Activities Committee was originally established as a temporary committee for "investigating alleged disloyalty and subversive activities by public employees, private citizens and organizations" (R. Martin 1043). However, the HUAC quickly developed from a temporary investigative body to a permanent instrument for the surveillance of citizens who did not follow the standard dictated by this government committee. Its mandate was renewed each year until it became a standing committee in 1945 ("Constitutional" 417).[48] "Rooting out un-Americanism became a way of life" (Donner 12). The new standing committee became a nightmare for everyone who did not conform to the arbitrary understanding of Americanism dictated by the committee or who held beliefs that were not popular at that time. Frank J. Donner illustrated the problematic situation which was caused by the nebulous formulation of the resolution on which the body's mandate was based:

Catholic Welfare Conference, the American League for Peace and Democracy, the Farmer-Labor party, sitdown strikes, the Federal Theatre Project, consumers' organizations, the Union for Democratic Action, the magazine Time, the Daily Worker, the Joint Anti-Fascist Refugee Committee, the National Federation for Constitutional Liberties, and the Nation of American-Soviet Friendship" ("Constitutional" 418).

48 The HUAC was the only investigative committee to ever receive the status of a standing committee. Additionally, it was the first committee which was equipped with the permanent power to force people to testify and submit required documentation. The authors of the *Columbia Law Review* profess that the HUAC "occupies a unique place in Congressional history" ("Constitutional" 417).

> [T]he permanent committee was born, fully equipped with all of the basic components of the exposure system: (1) it was functionally independent of the body which created it, because (2) it lacked legislative responsibilities; (3) its investigative power was shaped to inquisitorial ends and conferred upon it by (4) a charter to probe speech and ideas so broad and vague as to impose no meaningful restraints upon it. (22)

In addition, the rights as guaranteed by the Constitution provided little protection in a hearing held by the House Un-American Activities Committee. Courts ruled that pleading the First Amendment was not legitimate in an HUAC hearing and pleading the Fifth Amendment was not a helpful strategy either as calling on one's right not to incriminate oneself was interpreted as guilt by inference (Donner 6).[49] If witnesses denied all accusations and the committee did not believe them or simply wanted to destroy their un-American lives, the witnesses were accused of perjury (6–7). In his book *The Un-Americans*, Frank J. Donner describes the situation of such a witness as follows:

> He knows that the Committee demands his physical presence in the hearing room for no other reason than to make him a target of its hostility, to have him photographed, exhibited and branded. Most of all, he is tormented by the awareness that he is being punished without valid cause, and deprived, by manipulated justice, of his fundamental rights as an American. (68)

The basic rights protecting every American citizen in a courtroom were useless in a HUAC hearing in which the goal was to expose and disgrace the witness.

The Lavender Scare

The House Un-American Activities Committee was supposedly investigating communism; however, what was considered un-American and a threat to the United States' internal security was inconsistent and open for interpretation. In the 1950s, a surveillance and exposure instrument

[49] The United States Supreme Court has ruled out that one can be guilty by inference. However, in a HUAC hearing, everything was possible, and the chairmen operated in a legal vacuum (Donner 6).

such as the House Un-American Activities Committee proved to be very useful for everyone who wished to persecute homosexuals as those were commonly seen as sexual perverts at that time (Eaklor 87). During the McCarthy Era, homosexuals were regarded as even more un-American and more dangerous than communists, especially if they worked in government positions and in foreign service (D. K. Johnson 2).[50] The so-called Lavender Scare "sparked a moral panic within mainstream American culture" (9) because homosexual conduct was suddenly the incarnation of un-Americanism and often considered to be even worse than the communist threat in the 1950s (2). Since gay Americans were "[v]iewed as emotionally unstable, of weak moral fibre, and vulnerable to blackmail, homosexuals were cast as a serious threat to the moral health and security of the United States . . ." (Hall, "Americanism" 1110). Investigating homosexuality soon became as important for the HUAC as the fight against communism. However, the boundaries were not always clear since alleged homosexuals were often additionally accused of communism. Many investigators believed that one evil must relate to the other (Eaklor 87–88). As a result, the public began to see both threats as indistinguishable, as rumors began to rise that the communists propagated homosexuality (D. K. Johnson 31). The tabloid journalist Arthur Guy Matthews called homosexuality "Stalin's Atom Bomb" because he was convinced that the communists encouraged homophile behavior in the U.S. to weaken the nation (qtd. in D. K. Johnson 37). "Homosexuality, McCarthy asserted, was the psychological maladjustment that led people towards communism" (D. K. Johnson 16). Although several different offenses were classified as security risks, during the time of the Lavender Scare, the term 'security risk' usually implied a potential threat caused by a homosexual (8).[51] The only way to counteract the threat posed by

50 In February 1950, Senator Joseph McCarthy claimed in a speech in Wheeling, West Virginia that 205 communists were working for the State Department. In the same month, Deputy Undersecretary John Peurifoy denied that any communists were working for the State Department in an appearance before a congressional committee. However, he admitted that a number of employees were dismissed for being security risks and that 91 of them were homosexuals. D. K. Johnson claims that this was the beginning of the Lavender Scare (1).

51 A lot of the newspaper coverage of the controversies during the Lavender Scare was not very explicit and language stayed rather vague. Gay Americans were often not directly referred to as "homosexuals" or "sexual per-

homosexuals was to dismiss them from federal government, expose them in hearings, and to disgrace them publicly for un-American behavior. Approximately one thousand employees were expelled from the Department of State for real or alleged homosexuality under the guise of being deemed a "security risk" (76). As this was just the number for the State Department, the total number of dismissals by the U.S. Civil Service Commission was much higher.[52] The legal basis for these dismissals was provided by President Truman's Executive Order 9835, "the Federal Employee Loyalty Program, which established review boards to work within all government agencies in order to fire any employee or not hire any job applicant suspected of being in any way 'disloyal' to the United States" (Faderman 17). When the Democratic President Truman was running for reelection in 1948, he knew he had "to be as good a Cold War Warrior as any conservative Republican or Southern Democrat" (17) and therefore decided to sign this executive order. Many Americans hoped it would bring stability to the country while they were facing the threat of communism.

At times of uncertainty, such as during the Cold War, safety could be found within the traditional family home, an image which the homosexual community was not able to uphold in the eyes of heteronormative, conservative America. "Heterosexual Americans, by contrast, . . . became emblematic of what it meant to be American. The American home, populated by the heterosexual couple and their family became, symbolically and literally, a fortress against the anxieties provoked by the Cold War" (Herbst Lewis 4). The traditional family and their home were the safe havens for which the Daughters of the American Revolution had been advocating and which were endangered by un-American enemies from without and within (Wendt 943–44; 949). The HUAC was a welcome

verts" but also as "moral weaklings," "sexual misfits," "undesirables," or people with "unusual morals" (D.K. Johnson 7). These unclear descriptions have made the chronicling and scholarly investigation of the Lavender Scare rather difficult. Consequently, the lack of scholarship on the time of the Lavender Scare is partly due to the complicated circumstances researchers are confronted with (5–7).

52 Through the late 1960s, officials had to appear before the congressional appropriations committee each year and reveal the number of homosexuals who were fired in the previous year. In public opinion, the State Department had become closely connected to the problem of homosexual subversion (D.K. Johnson 76).

instrument to ruin the lives of homosexuals as the inside enemies who, in the eyes of many Americans, despised the morals and values that constituted their nation and were responsible for its decline (D. K. Johnson 38). The connection between the communist threat and homosexuality, and consequently between homosexuals and un-Americanism, was instilled so deeply in the mindset of the Cold War generation that it would influence Americans' opinion of the gay community for decades. Those Americans were more than willing to adopt the rhetoric of un-Americanism as introduced by the House Un-American Activities Committee because they felt threatened by homosexual citizens. Due to this stigma, the gay community was motivated to affirm not only their Americanism but their patriotism to their critics (Hall, "Americanism" 1109). From the 1930s, accusations of un-Americanism were primarily employed by conservatives and Americans on the right of the political spectrum; however, starting in the 1960s, this language was increasingly adopted by the gay rights movement although they were still reluctant to use the term 'un-American' at the beginning (1114; 1118).

The Decline of the HUAC

The House Un-American Activities Committee's reputation suffered massively in the late 1950s when their dubious methods became public and protest movements against such investigatory bodies gained influence all over the country. The most notable of these protests took place in May 1960, when students from the University of California revolted against HUAC hearings in San Francisco (Donner 2–3). President Truman had already denounced the HUAC "as the most un-American thing" in 1959 (Truman qtd. in Donner 3). In 1965, the committee tried to return to former glory through investigations into the activities of the Ku Klux Klan and by blacklisting members of the left-wing organization "Students for a Democratic Society" (Lewis, "Amorphous Code" 974). However, their attempt failed since they had already lost credibility in the 1950s. Especially the HUAC's investigation into the KKK came as a surprise because "the Klan [had been] publicly declared to be an avowedly '100% American' organization'" (975) at the height of the House Un-American Activities Committee in the 1940 and early 1950s. "[B]y 1965 even the jaundiced eye of HUAC was openly proclaiming it to be the personification of contemporary un-Americanism"

(Lewis, “Amorphous Code” 975). This development was not just an “epochal shift in the history of un-Americanism” (986). It was a sign of the inconsistency and despotism of the House Un-American Activities Committee. The HUAC decided to drop the “un-American” in its name by changing it to Internal Security Committee in 1969 before being defunded by the 94th Congress in 1975 (Zirkle 284–85). Although the committee had almost been forgotten in its final years, its influence in shaping the history of un-Americanism must not be underestimated. In 2016, former House Speaker and Trump supporter Newt Gingrich called for the creation of a new House Committee on Un-American Activities, invoking the infamous “‘Red Scare’-era congressional body as a blueprint for weeding out American ISIS adherents and sympathizers” (Krieg). Given the history of the original House Un-American Activities Committee, his words raised immense concern among the Muslim American community and their allies (Krieg).

The Historical Connection Between Assertions of (Un-)Americanism and the Gay Rights Movement

The question of what is American and what is un-American has been closely linked to the gay rights movement from its inception, which occurred during the height of the HUAC’s investigations against homosexuals. “[A]ctivists in the early gay rights movement worked hard to affirm their patriotism and appealed frequently to the nation’s founding ideals of liberty and equality. At times, they also characterized those who discriminated against them as ‘un-American’” (Hall, “Americanism” 1109). The discrimination which homosexual Americans had to face during the Lavender Scare encouraged the founding of the first gay rights organization in California in 1951 and increased professionally organized efforts to fight against unequal and discriminatory practices in Washington D.C. in the 1960s (D.K. Johnson 13). A leading example of the early gay rights movement was the Mattachine Society of Washington, an organization where “[p]atriotism and the invocation of Americanism (appeals to the Declaration of Independence; the American Dream, and the nation’s founding principles of freedom, liberty and equality) were at the heart of the group’s rhetorical approach” (Hall, “Americanism” 1112). One of its founding members, Franklin Kameny, was a victim of the Lavender Scare since the astronomer was dismissed from the United States Army Map

Service and banned from future government employment by the U.S. Civil Service Commission for being gay in 1957 (Faderman 129–30). Reciprocal accusations of un-Americanism were just the consequence of the group's claim to represent true Americanism, especially since many of its members had been dedicated American civil service employees before they became the victims of McCarthy's witch hunt. They appealed to their rights as enshrined in the nation's defining documents and were convinced that their patriotism was the best possible tactic for supporters of the gay rights movement at a time when prospects for success were extremely low.

During the 1980s, the singing of the Black rights movement protest song, "We Shall Overcome," and the Civil War song, "Battle Hymn of the Republic," as well as allusions to the American Dream and Martin Luther King became increasingly popular among gay rights advocates as a means to substantiate their demands and to fight against accusations of un-American practices (Hall, *American Patriotism* 1–2; "Americanism" 1112–13). By choosing this form of protest, gay Americans rooted themselves in the history of their country and made clear that American blood was also running through their veins: "Numerous organizations and activists placed their demands for gay and lesbian equality within the broader tradition of America's revolutionary heritage and invoked the Republic's egalitarian rhetoric in fashioning a language of protest" (Hall, *American Patriotism* 50). The gay rights movement has always drawn heavily on the rhetoric of Americanism but since the 1980s, "the language of un-Americanism has operated alongside that of Americanism to a far more noticeable degree" than in the early days of the movement (Hall, "Americanism" 1118). Though gay rights advocates were continuously accused of un-Americanism, in their eyes, the situation was reversed. It was Americans denying equal rights to their fellow compatriots who did not understand the true mentality of the United States of America and who were the most un-American of all. The HUAC hearings during the Lavender Scare had laid the foundation for the later presence of the un-Americanism rhetoric in the marriage equality movement on both sides of the battleground. As supporters of this movement have been employing a wide range of allusions to American history from its outset, present debates about gay rights cannot be fully understood without looking at the early days of the movement and, in particular, at the role of un-Americanism, its varied and mutable interpretations, and the repercussions of being labeled as such (Hall, *American Patriotism* 27).

Conclusion

In exploring the history of the term 'un-American,' one does not see a linear development but rather a path that is characterized by disruptions, semantic shifts, and multiple contexts of use. The term's semantic development through American history as well as its complexity and vagueness make it impossible to come up with a single definition for 'un-American' which would ever adequately reflect its multifacetedness. Moreover, defining a term creates boundaries that might not be beneficial. Such an attempt would limit the multiplicity of possible understandings of un-Americanism and thereby close the doors to the unique chances that come with such an undefined term. "Attempting to find a single definition of 'un-American' is fraught with difficulties, but also to a great extent misconstrues the often complex nature of the term's importance and appeal" (Lewis, "Introduction" 872). Since the contexts in which someone is accused of acting un-American are as diverse as the nation itself, it makes little sense to focus on one interpretation of this term. Viewing this as an opportunity rather than a problem allows for the term to change accordingly when a certain development in the United States or a redefinition of American everyday nationalism requires such a semantic progression.

The obscure and ever-changing nature of a concept such as un-Americanism is certainly a challenge, but, even more so, it is a tremendous asset for research. "Un-Americanism has been understood in different ways and has carried different connotations at different times, many of which serve to reflect the most pressing concerns of contemporaneous American life" (Lewis, "Introduction" 876). A study of un-Americanism and especially of the term 'un-American' in sociocultural debates discloses what mattered to a certain group of people at a particular point in time. The discourse on un-Americanism reveals how Americans define themselves and which character traits are regarded as honorable and desirable. Thereby, the term 'un-American' functions as an analytical lens which allows for the investigation of American national identity and American nationalism. As Brian Steele confirms:

> [T]he "un-American" can revitalize our study of American identity, not by leading us to worry whether American practices are normative and exceptionalist, but by forcing us to think through the ways the various manifestations of this concept throughout American history demonstrate precisely what is at stake in such debates. (898–99)

Chapter IV

IV Charges of Un-Americanism in the Debate on Marriage Equality

A The Road to Marriage Equality

The road to marriage equality in the United States has been long and bumpy with countless setbacks and confusion about the right direction. "Love is love"[53] was not the prevailing position for most of the country's history as some relationships were deemed to be worthy of the institution of marriage while others were not. Prior to June 2015, marriage was not only about two loving partners, a mutual pledge, and a lifetime commitment, but also about the exclusion of some citizens from an act which many Americans consider to be an integral element of community building and citizenship. In 1967, the United States Supreme Court ruled in the landmark case *Loving v. Virginia* that bans on interracial marriage were a violation of the Equal Protection Clause[54] as part of the Fourteenth

53 Since the gay rights movement's focus on discrimination and equality often did not raise the attention of straight people, advocates' idea was to change the core message to "love" since this is the reason for which both same-sex and straight couples get married. Beam explains:

> [T]he past marriage campaigns' primary hindrance was that it was built by and for LGBT people, using a message that felt real to many queer people: that it was unfair to privilege one form of family and shower that form with benefits. This 'love pivot' ushered in a campaign geared towards straight people, one that mobilized fantasies of the American dream where love is depoliticized and private. (55)

The result of this change in strategy were slogans as, for instance, "Love Wins" or "Love is Love."

54 The Equal Protection Clause can be found at the end of Section 1 of the Fourteenth Amendment to the United States Constitution:

> All persons born or naturalized in the United States, and subject to the jurisdiction thereof, are citizens of the United States and of the state wherein

Amendment to the United States Constitution (United States, Supreme Court, "*Loving*" 12). In his opinion of the court, Chief Justice Earl Warren declared: "The freedom to marry has long been recognized as one of the vital personal rights essential to the orderly pursuit of happiness by free men. Marriage is one of the 'basic civil rights of man,' fundamental to our very existence and survival" (12). In this civil rights case, the court made clear that marriage was a personal decision in which no other party was permitted to interfere since it was inextricably linked with a person's pursuit of happiness, one of the three unalienable rights given to every American "by their Creator" according to the Declaration of Independence ("Declaration").[55] In all other marriage-related cases that followed thereafter, the Supreme Court affirmed its initial ruling that marriage was a fundamental right and a personal decision.[56] However, there was one stipulation: the plaintiffs had to be an opposite-sex couple.

The first known case in which a gay couple pursued a marriage license was in Minnesota in 1970 (United States, Supreme Court, "*Baker*" 4). When their request was denied, the couple filed a lawsuit since they believed that this denial constituted a discriminative treatment of same-sex couples and was therefore a violation of the First, Eighth, Ninth and Fourteenth Amendments to the United States Constitution (5). In *Baker v. Nelson,* the Supreme Court of Minnesota dismissed the plaintiffs' claims because they failed to prove a parallel with *Loving v. Virginia*:

> they reside. No state shall make or enforce any law which shall abridge the privileges or immunities of citizens of the United States; nor shall any state deprive any person of life, liberty, or property, without due process of law; nor deny to any person within its jurisdiction the *equal protection of the laws*. (emphasis added; United States, Constitution, "Fourteenth Amendment")

55 These rights are enshrined in the Declaration of Independence as follows: "We hold these truths to be self-evident, that all men are created equal, that they are endowed by their Creator with certain unalienable Rights, that among these are Life, Liberty and the pursuit of Happiness" ("Declaration").

56 Since 1888, the United States Supreme Court has established in 16 rulings that marriage is a fundamental right of all individuals in the United States. Besides *United States v. Windsor* and *Obergefell v. Hodges*, notable court cases were *Maynard v. Hill* (1888) as the first to address marriage in the United States, *Meyer v. Nebraska* (1923), *Griswold v. Connecticut* (1965), *Loving v. Virginia* (1967), *Zablocki v. Redhail* (1978), *Turner v. Safley* (1987), and *Lawrence v. Texas* (2003) ("14 Supreme Court Cases").

"Loving does indicate that not all state restrictions upon the right to marry are beyond reach of the Fourteenth Amendment. But in commonsense and in a constitutional sense, there is a clear distinction between a marital restriction based merely upon race and one based upon the fundamental difference in sex" (4). Since the plaintiffs Baker and McConnell appealed, the case was forwarded to the United States Supreme Court which dismissed the appeal as it did not constitute a substantial federal question. Thereby, the Supreme Court endorsed the decision of the Minnesota Supreme Court (United States, Supreme Court, "*Baker*" Appeal 3). Three years later, the *Yale Law Journal* published a legal opinion in which an anonymous author argues in favor of the plaintiffs in *Baker v. Nelson* and makes a strong case for same-sex marriage being protected by the Equal Protection Clause of the Fourteenth Amendment ("Legality of Homosexual Marriage" 573). The author urges the justices responsible to interpret the law accurately and not to decide on the basis of personal or societal constraints: "[T]he Court should not avoid granting full relief from discriminatory legislation simply because that legislation is based on deeply held beliefs" (589). Taking a very progressive stance, the author recommends a compromise, however, not without emphasizing that this would not be the solution he desires: "A quasi-marital status might satisfy many of the interests of homosexuals in gaining marriage licenses, but it would inevitably fall short of fully normalizing their relationships. A legislative stigma of deviance would remain" (589).

Another attempt in the quest for marriage equality was made in Hawaii in 1990 when four same-sex couples applied for marriage licenses at the Hawaii Department of Health. Again, their application was denied on the basis of them being same-sex couples, which ultimately motivated them to initiate their lawsuit *Baehr v. Lewin* (which was later changed to *Baehr v. Miike*) (Frank 91–95). To the applicants' disappointment, both the American Civil Liberties Union and the LGBT civil rights organization Lambda Legal refused to represent the plaintiffs in this lawsuit. The civil liberties groups did not want to invest their limited resources in a case with a rather small prospect of success (93–94). Furthermore, their respective representatives believed that the right time for such a bold move had not yet come; it was simply too soon. In the early 1990s, marriage was not a priority on the gay rights agenda as the community was still struggling with other day-to-day problems which made marriage seem out of reach. Furthermore, the community itself lacked unity on the importance and desirability of marriage equality (92–94). Nevertheless, the case was made possible thanks to an arrangement with the civil rights attorney Dan Foley (94–95). Since the trial court dismissed the lawsuit, the case went to the Supreme Court of Hawaii which ruled that a denial of marriage licenses to the plaintiffs violated the State of Hawaii's Equal Protection Clause and was therefore a discrimination based on sex (Hawaii State, Supreme Court of Hawaii, "*Baehr*" 17). The case was then sent back to a trial court in 1993 in order to determine whether the state's ban on same-sex marriage was unconstitutional.

Gay rights found its way onto the national political agenda also due to the presidential election in 1992 and Republicans' decision to fight a culture war against all progressive influences. In the course of the 1992 presidential election, Patrick Buchanan gave his famous "culture war speech" at the Republican National Convention in Houston, Texas. He encouraged his fellow Americans, and Republicans in particular, to not remain silent but to fight for the conservative cause. This "struggle for the soul of America," as he phrased it, included silencing the voice of the gay community and their supporters: "Bill Clinton and Al Gore represent the most pro-lesbian and pro-gay ticket in history. . . . [W]e stand with him [President George G.H. Bush] against the amoral idea that gay and lesbian couples should have the same standing in law as married men and women" (Buchanan). Bill Clinton had probably not planned on becoming a supporter of gay rights, but Buchanan was so effective with this strategy that Clinton could not help but accept this assigned position and make the best of it. "Clinton campaigned on a promise to end the military's exclusion of gay troops, to oppose anti-gay discrimination, and to step up in the fight against AIDS. That November, Clinton took the White House with the crucial help of gay dollars and votes" (Frank 96).

Depending on the individual's expectations, the Clinton presidency was either a win or a disappointment for gay Americans. One of Clinton's campaign promises, to let gays and lesbians serve openly in the military, could only be fulfilled partially. The new president's ambitious plan to end the absolute ban of gays serving in the military was blocked by Congress since many high-ranking officials were afraid of an infiltration of the military with immoral homosexuals (Frank 96). "The end results were the 'don't ask, don't tell' policy, a weakened Clinton, and a demonstration of strength of the religious right" (96). As a result, one could probably call the "Don't Ask, Don't Tell"-policy[57] a partial suc-

[57] "Don't Ask, Don't Tell" was a compromise which was achieved in 1993 in the debate over whether homosexuals should be able to serve in the U.S. mili-

cess, especially given the fierce opposition Clinton had to face in order to at least achieve a compromise. Consequently, Clinton's relationship with the gay community was characterized by mutual respect. However, this changed when he decided to support the Defense of Marriage Act.

The Defense of Marriage Act (DOMA), signed into law by President Clinton in 1996, was a major setback for the gay community because this law defined marriage as the union of a man and a woman for federal purposes.[58] This allowed the federal government and the states to refuse to recognize same-sex marriages even if they were legal in some states (United States, Congress, "*Defense of Marriage Act*"). DOMA was the conservative reaction to the lawsuit *Baehr v. Lewin* which was still pending in Hawaiian courts and which had been decided in favor of the plaintiffs in a first decision by the Supreme Court of Hawaii on the basis of the state's Equal Protection Clause (Hawaii State, Supreme Court of Hawaii, "Baehr" 17). Such an unexpected move by a U.S. court was conservatives' worst nightmare because they were highly afraid of a snowball effect:

> Social conservatives were enraged by the Hawaii court ruling. What they feared was . . . that a single court ruling in America's fiftieth state could be used as a tool to spread marriage equality nationwide, as couples married in Hawaii, then traveled or returned home expecting the other forty-nine states to recognize their legal unions. In their effort to block that possibility, they would find willing partners in national Republicans who saw in anti-gay initiatives an irresistible opportunity to increase support from the religious right and put Democrats on the defensive. (Frank 102)

tary service. The policy held that homosexual service members are allowed to serve as long as they remain discreet about their sexuality. Service members are not permitted to discuss their sexual orientation, nor are they to be asked about it. The commonly held belief was that the presence of homosexual service members in the U.S. military service would create a substantial risk to the moral, unit cohesion, and discipline of the soldiers (Davis vii).

58 The definition of marriage in DOMA Section 3 reads as follows:

> In determining the meaning of any Act of Congress, or of any ruling, regulation, or interpretation of the various administrative bureaus and agencies of the United States, the word 'marriage' means only a legal union between one man and one woman as husband and wife, and the word 'spouse' refers only to a person of the opposite sex who is a husband or a wife. (United States, Congress, "*Defense of Marriage Act*")

Adam notes that "the speed and success of the passage of this law and the 'mini-DOMAs' at the state level show many of the earmarks of a moral panic, especially when swept into law through referenda" (259). Despite the efforts of gay rights advocates, the success remained on the conservatives' side and marriage equality was soon off the table. In 1998, it became clear that same-sex marriage was not yet supported by the majority of Hawaiians when they passed a constitutional amendment that allowed state legislation to limit the right of marriage to opposite-sex couples (Lincoln).

The first real change to the legal standing of homosexual couples came in Vermont in 1999 with the lawsuit *Baker v. Vermont,* in which the Vermont Supreme Court ruled that refusing to grant marriage rights to homosexual citizens was inconsistent with the Vermont Constitution (Vermont State, Supreme Court of Vermont, "*Baker*").[59] It was the legislature's obligation to establish same-sex marriage or an equivalent legal status. The people of Vermont were still highly divided on the issue of same-sex marriage. The court's decision led to public backlash with an enormous wave of protest and the formation of the anti-gay group "Take Vermont Back" (Harrison 242). Subsequently, legislators did not dare to bestow homosexual couples with full marriage rights.[60] Nevertheless,

59 In *Baker v. Vermont*, the Vermont Supreme Court held:

> While many have noted the symbolic or spiritual significance of the marital relation, it is plaintiffs' claim to the secular benefits and protections of a singularly human relationship that, in our view, characterizes this case. The State's interest in extending official recognition and legal protection to the professed commitment of two individuals to a lasting relationship of mutual affection is predicated on the belief that legal support of a couple's commitment provides stability for the individuals, their family, and the broader community. (Vermont State, Supreme Court of Vermont, "*Baker*")

60 The Vermont Supreme Court only ruled that same-sex couples must be granted the same rights, benefits, and protections as opposite-sex couples. However, it did not hold that same-sex couples must be granted marriage and that Vermont legislators could not come up with a comparable solution (e. g., civil unions):

> Although plaintiffs sought injunctive and declaratory relief designed to secure a marriage license, their claims and arguments here have focused primarily upon the consequences of official exclusion from the statuto-

bound by the outcome of *Baker v. Vermont*, the legislators opted for the possibility of creating an equivalent to marriage and proposed the idea of civil unions. The establishment of civil unions was groundbreaking for those concerned since civil unions guaranteed equal benefits to all couples regardless of their sexual orientation (Goldberg). The only significant difference was in the name: The term 'marriage' was still sacrosanct and therefore reserved for "traditional" couples.

Encouraged by their success in Vermont, gay rights activists looked for another state where they could continue their fight for equal marital rights. Without much ado, they decided to file a similar lawsuit in Massachusetts since the state had always been favorable towards homosexual couples and had extensive equal protection and anti-discrimination clauses in their Constitution ("Paying" 11). On behalf of seven same-sex couples as plaintiffs, the organization Gay and Lesbian Advocates and Defenders sued the Massachusetts Department of Health in *Goodridge v. Department of Public Health* in 2001 (Frank 131). This lawsuit was another landslide victory. The Court concluded that "barring an individual from the protections, benefits, and obligations of civil marriage solely because that person would marry a person of the same sex violates the Massachusetts Constitution" (Massachusetts State, Massachusetts Supreme Judicial Court, "*Goodridge*" 344). Furthermore, an important point of contention

ry benefits, protections, and security incident to marriage under Vermont law. While some future case may attempt to establish that – notwithstanding equal benefits and protections under Vermont law – the denial of a marriage license operates per se to deny constitutionally-protected rights, that is not the claim we address today. We hold only that plaintiffs are entitled under Chapter I, Article 7, of the Vermont Constitution to obtain the same benefits and protections afforded by Vermont law to married opposite-sex couples. We do not purport to infringe upon the prerogatives of the Legislature to craft an appropriate means of addressing this constitutional mandate, other than to note that the record here refers to a number of potentially constitutional statutory schemes from other jurisdictions. These include what are typically referred to as "domestic partnership" or "registered partnership" acts, which generally establish an alternative legal status to marriage for same-sex couples, impose similar formal requirements and limitations, create a parallel licensing or registration scheme, and extend all or most of the same rights and obligations provided by the law to married partners. (Vermont State, Supreme Court of Vermont "*Baker*") in *Goodridge* was the question whether marriage and procreation were inextricably linked with each other, an argument which had often led to the denial of marriage to same-sex couples in the past. However, the majority opinion in the Massachusetts Supreme Judicial Court held that "General Laws c. 207 contains no requirement that the applicants for a marriage license attest to their ability or intention to conceive children by coitus. Fertility is not a condition of marriage, nor is it grounds for divorce" (331). In addition, this was the first time a court acknowledged that gay couples raise children as well, of which the plaintiffs' families were proof (314–15; 334–35). Similar to the case in Vermont, the court left it open to the legislature which legal status they grant to same-sex couples that would give them equal benefits. Massachusetts was the first state to establish full marriage equality for all citizens in 2004 (Hay).

To the disappointment of those celebrating these first decisive victories for gay couples, the court rulings in Vermont and Massachusetts resulted in a backlash:

> [T]he court rulings and the subsequent outcry by social conservatives, which often vilified gay people and their relationships, eroded national support for marriage equality, reflecting and perpetuating a public backlash, just as some gay advocates had worried. Polls also showed a stark drop in those supporting civil unions or even the very legality of same-sex relations. (Frank 164)

To the surprise of most Americans, California began issuing marriage licenses to gay couples in February 2004. However, this apparent success turned into another disappointment when California's Supreme Court decided a mere four weeks later that all of these marriages were void until a court resolves the question of the constitutionality of same-sex marriage in California (Younge). In June 2008, the California Supreme Court ruled that barring same-sex couples from the right to marriage is a violation of the California Constitution. The ruling went into effect immediately and an estimated 18,000 homosexual couples got married thereafter. However, the California Constitution enables constitutional change through three mechanisms, with a petition followed by a direct majority vote being one of them. This is what marriage equality opponents pursued right after the ruling. With enough voter signatures on their petition, they were able to place Proposition 8 on the ballot of the November 2008 presidential election. Proposition 8 suggested an amendment to the California Constitution which restricted marriage to the union between a man and a woman.

In the election, 52% of Californians supported the constitutional change (Eskridge 1236–37).[61] The debate over Proposition 8, including all lawsuits attached to it and its consequences, is too extensive to be included in this brief walk through the history of marriage equality. The most important aspect that could be derived from the proposition's passing was that the majority of Californians in 2008 were convinced that marriage should be restricted to heterosexual couples: "[G]ays and lesbians throughout the country felt the strange, bittersweet sensation of shedding tears of joy at the election of the first African American president and, on the same day, tears of rejection as the 'bluest of blue states' yanked away their right to marry" (Frank 182). Retrospectively, such a defeat may have been more beneficial to the gay rights movement than another victory:

> It was not only new LGBTQ energy that infused the battle following the Proposition 8 ballot loss. Many straight people, for the first time, became fully aware of the genuine, profound, and consequential inequality resulting from the denial of marriage rights to gays and lesbians they knew, and it angered them. For some, the election result and the heightened focus it brought to gay rights marketed the beginning of a new understanding of that unfairness and a commitment to working against it. (190)

The fight over Proposition 8 resulted in a new culmination of mutual charges of an un-American position on this issue. For instance, the actor Tom Hanks called Mormon supporters of Prop. 8 "un-American" (Hanks qtd. in Leonard).

Among the most prominent voices of marriage equality advocates was Ted Olson, solicitor general under George W. Bush and a devoted Republican. To the astonishment of conservatives and liberals alike, the American Foundation for Equal Rights appointed him, together with Davis Bois, his former adversary in *Bush v. Gore*, as lead counsel in the Proposition 8 case *Perry v. Schwarzenegger* (Geidner). In an opinion piece published in 2010, he argues that marriage equality is a conservative idea and, most importantly, a quintessential American value:

[61] Until the famous constitutional amendment Proposition 8 was on the ballot in 2008, California's former governor, Arnold Schwarzenegger, had vetoed same-sex marriage twice (Frank 174).

> [S]ame-sex unions promote the values conservatives prize. . . . The fact that individuals who happen to be gay want to share in this vital social institution is evidence that conservative ideals enjoy widespread acceptance. Conservatives should celebrate this, rather than lament it. Legalizing same-sex marriage would also be a recognition of basic American principles, and would represent the culmination of our nation's commitment to equal rights. It is, some have said, the last major civil-rights milestone yet to be surpassed in our two-century struggle to attain the goals we set for this nation at its formation. . . . Americans who believe in the words of the Declaration of Independence, in Lincoln's Gettysburg Address, in the 14th Amendment, and in the Constitution's guarantees of equal protection and equal dignity before the law cannot sit by while this wrong continues. This is not a conservative or liberal issue; it is an American one, and it is time that we, as Americans, embraced it. (Olson, "The Conservative Case")

When Proposition 8 was finally declared to be unconstitutional in 2012 and when same-sex marriage became legal in California in 2013, Olson reaffirmed his beliefs and stated: "This case is about equality and freedom and dignity and fairness and decency . . . . It is about us. It is about every one of us . . . . Today we are more American because of this decision" (Olson qtd. in "Prop 8"). The road to marriage equality was a long one, characterized by a back and forth of victories and backlashes. After Massachusetts in 2004 and before California in 2013, nine other states and the District of Columbia (2010) had decided to offer marriage rights to same-sex couples: Connecticut (2008), Iowa (2009), Vermont (2009), New Hampshire (2010), New York (2011), Washington (2012), Maine (2012), and Maryland (2013) (Wolf).

Despite the successes in some states, gay Americans who already enjoyed the privilege of marriage, were still struggling with legal obstacles. The Defense of Marriage Act was a serious problem, also for married same-sex couples, and led to protests denouncing this law as fundamentally un-American (Hall, "Americanism" 1120). One prominent case was the Air-Force veteran Marvin Burrows who was forced to move out of his home after his partner of fifty years died. Burrows was denied the rights and benefits that a heterosexual widower would have received. Enraged by this unequal treatment, he stated in a personal testimony before the Committee on the Judiciary of the United States Senate in 2011:

> It is unfair, and it is un-American that I should be left this way by our country. This is what DOMA does to people. It shatters their lives at a time when they need stability and comfort the most. It makes people, including me, feel like less of a person – like an outcast not worthy of full equality. ("Statement of Marvin Burrows")

Motivated by Burrows' powerful speech, gay rights advocates adopted his un-Americanism rhetoric and continued the fight for equal rights in his name.

An important landmark case on the road to marriage equality, *United States v. Windsor* (2013), had a propelling effect on the gay rights movement. Edie Windsor sued the United States government in 2010 because, due to Section 3 of DOMA, she was not eligible for the federal estate tax exemption for surviving spouses which she wanted to claim after the death of her wife Thea Spyer. Section 3 of the Defense of Marriage Act reserved the term 'spouse' to opposite-sex couples, which meant that Windsor would have been required to pay estate tax for the property she inherited from Spyer, as though they had never been married (United States, Supreme Court, Syllabus "*Windsor*" 1). In what was a decisive victory for the gay rights movement, the Supreme Court held in 2013 that this was unconstitutional (3–4). In the *Windsor* hearing, Justice Ruth Bader Ginsburg described the situation as intolerable: "So there are two kinds of marriages, the full marriage and then this sort of skim milk marriage" (Ginsburg qtd. in Faderman 628). The court put an end to this "skim milk marriage" (628) in *United States v. Windsor* and thereby made Edie Windsor a spouse in the eyes of federal law. In a statement released shortly after the court's ruling, President Obama congratulated the gay community on this remarkable success:

> This was discrimination enshrined in law. It treated loving, committed gay and lesbian couples as a separate and lesser class of people. The Supreme Court has righted that wrong, and our country is better off for it. We are a people who declared that we are all created equal – and the love we commit to one another must be equal as well. . . . The laws of our land are catching up to the fundamental truth that millions of Americans hold in our hearts: when all Americans are treated as equal, no matter who they are or whom they love, we are all more free. (qtd. in Raghavan)

This statement came as a surprise to many gay rights advocates because they had often been disappointed by Obama and his failure to step up for their cause, in spite of the campaign promises he had made to them (Eleveld 255–58).

Millions of Americans were advocating for marriage equality while their president could not bring himself to announce his public support for a change in law. "It was becoming increasingly awkward for Obama, the nation's first biracial president, a stalwart liberal, an intellectual, and someone who had favored same-sex marriage on a questionnaire in the 1990s, to tell his gay and lesbian supporters and the pesky mainstream press that he did not support the freedom to marry" (Frank 269). In 2006, Obama declared himself in favor of gay marriage when asked about his opinion on that matter, recalling the story of his black father and white mother whose marriage was not honored in eighteen states at the time they got married in 1961 before *Loving v. Virginia* (Faderman 610). However, as soon as he became a presidential candidate, he was suddenly less outspoken about gay rights. In the following years, Obama was in a conflict because he needed both the conservative and religious voters on his side as well as marriage equality advocates. Consequently, he spoke out in favor of some gay rights, such as the repeal of "Don't Ask, Don't Tell," but was not yet ready to publicly support gay marriage. This allowed him to keep both groups of voters. By opposing the freedom to marry, he was able to please its opponents, but by making concessions to its advocates, he could keep them hoping that he would eventually come out in support of them (McKinley).

Vice President Joe Biden was not willing to wait until Obama finally came around and supported the cause. Therefore, he decided to go over Obama's head by declaring: "Things are changing so rapidly, it's going to become a political liability in the near term for an individual to say, 'I oppose gay marriage.' Mark my words" (Biden qtd. in Stern, "Biden's True Legacy"). Biden's sudden, unexpected move coming out in favor of the cause made the president appear even more backwards and cowardly than before. The day every gay marriage advocate had been waiting for since the 2008 presidential election finally came on May 9th, 2012 during an interview with *ABC News*' Robin Roberts. When asked "Mr. President, are you still opposed to same-sex marriage?" Obama was finally brave enough to admit that he does, indeed, support marriage equality and explained:

> I've been going through an evolution on this issue. I've always been adamant that -- gay and lesbian -- Americans should be treated fairly and equally. . . . I've stood on the side of broader equality for -- the L.G.B.T. community. And I had hesitated on gay marriage -- in part, because I thought civil unions would be sufficient. . . . But I have to tell you that over the course of -- several years, as I talk to friends and family and neighbors. When I think about -- members of my own staff who are incredibly committed, in monogamous relationships, same-sex relationships, who are raising kids together. When I think about -- those soldiers or airmen or marines or -- sailors who are out there fighting on my behalf -- and yet, feel constrained, even now that Don't Ask, Don't Tell is gone, because – they're not able to -- commit themselves in a marriage. At a certain point, I've just concluded that -- for me personally, it is important for me to go ahead and affirm that -- I think same-sex couples should be able to get married. (Obama in interview with Roberts)

Obama finally committed himself to marriage equality and to doing justice to all the gay rights advocates who had voted for and donated to him in his two presidential campaigns. "The president's announcement had an enormous impact on both gay and straight Americans. In one reflection of this, a number of affluent gay advocates announced they would max out contributions to Obama's reelection campaign" (Frank 273).

President Obama's coming out in favor of marriage equality was a powerful move. Gay rights advocates and journalists such as Kerry Eleveld had been working for years towards such a statement by tenaciously pursuing the president to clarify his position. Additionally, Obama's affirmation helped pave the way for what was to come in spring of 2015, when the Supreme Court decided to argue the case *Obergefell v. Hodges* (Barnes). Prior to this ruling, the ban on same-sex marriage had already been repealed in 36 states, the U.S. territory of Guam, and the District of Columbia, which meant that most Americans were already living in a place that had equal marriage rights, and that supporters of marriage equality had gained enormous ground (Wolf). In a *CNN* poll from February 2015, 63% of Americans said that same-sex couples should have the constitutional right to marry (Agiesta). The U.S. Supreme Court was set to decide on the issue of gay marriage in June and chances were good for supporters to gain a victory since the Supreme Court had ruled in favor of same-sex couples in the landmark case *United States v. Windsor* in 2013. On June 26, 2015, the United States Supreme Court held in a 5–4 decision that the United States would grant same-sex couples equal marriage rights on the basis of the Equal Protection Clause of the Fourteenth Amendment to the United States Constitution and its Due Process Clause[62] (United States, Supreme Court, "*Obergefell*" 4).

In order to understand how accusations of un-Americanism shaped the debate on marriage equality before the ruling in *Obergefell* and how this relates to disputes over national identity and everyday nationalism in the United States, these reciprocal accusations will be analyzed in the following chapter. This investigation will give profound insight into how this rhetoric is utilized by both supporters and opponents of marriage equality to gain ground and increase their cultural capital in this controversy which raised fundamental questions about what constitutes the American nation and its people. In accordance with Wodak and Meyer's recommendation to keep description and interpretation apart for reasons of transparency (33), the following analysis of the speech acts containing the term 'un-American' is predominantly descriptive and has a strong focus on the context of the respective utterance. The specific context of a speech act needs to be closely examined because it situates the accusation of un-Americanism in the larger context of disputes over the nature of American nationalism.

[62] Just as the Equal Protection Clause, the Due Process Clause can be found at the end of Section 1 of the Fourteenth Amendment to the United States Constitution:

> All persons born or naturalized in the United States, and subject to the jurisdiction thereof, are citizens of the United States and of the state wherein they reside. No state shall make or enforce any law which shall abridge the privileges or immunities of citizens of the United States; nor shall any state deprive any person of life, liberty, or property, *without due process of law*; nor deny to any person within its jurisdiction the equal protection of the laws. (emphasis added; United States, Constitution, "Fourteenth Amendment")

This promise made in the United States Constitution assures that all levels of government must guarantee fair procedures and legality to its people.

B Supporters' Arguments for Charges of Un-Americanism

A couple of months before the United States Supreme Court was set to decide on the case *Obergefell v. Hodges*, Supreme Court Justice Ruth Bader Ginsburg took the opportunity to share her observations on the country's evolvement regarding the issue of marriage equality. In an interview with the news agency *Bloomberg*, Justice Bader Ginsburg revealed that she was not worried about same-sex marriage becoming the law of the land and some Americans not tolerating such a change in law: "I think it is doubtful that it wouldn't be accepted. The change in people's attitudes on that issue has been enormous" (in interview with Stohr and Winkler). Bader Ginsburg's decision to speak up publicly in favor of marriage equality was not received well by some Americans. They considered it to be inappropriate for her as a Supreme Court justice to voice her opinion before the court officially heard the case and reached a decision. However, her stance on that issue had always been clear (Stohr and Winkler). In June 2013, she joined the majority opinion in *United States v. Windsor*, a landmark decision which can be regarded as a successful forerunner of *Obergefell v. Hodges* because it struck down Section 3 of the Defense of Marriage Act. In the same year, Bader Ginsburg became the first Supreme Court Justice to preside at a gay wedding when she officiated for Kennedy Center for Performing Arts President Michael Kaiser and his husband, the economist John Roberts (Joynt). In May 2015, just a month before *Obergefell v. Hodges,* she officiated at a same-sex wedding for the third time where she pronounced the two grooms married by the powers vested in her by the Constitution of the United States. Wedding guests noted that she put a special emphasis on the word 'Constitution' as if she wanted to indicate the potential outcome of a later decision of the United States Supreme Court (Dowd). In the *Bloomberg* interview, Bader Ginsburg also showed herself confident that the Supreme Court would reach an outcome in favor of marriage equality. She was not only convinced that people's change of hearts on that issue had been enormous but also that a change in law "would not take a large adjustment" for the American people (in interview with Stohr and Winkler).

The fierce culture war battles fought before the landmark decision and the occasional backlash which followed are proof that, contrary to Bader Ginsburg's prediction, it was a significant adjustment for some Americans. Whereas the larger part of the country was celebrating this historical civil rights victory enabled by the 5–4 majority in the Supreme Court, another part of the country saw this day as a further detrimental liberalization of the country. Although some Americans had changed their opinion over the years, this was not true for everyone. An analysis of the public debates on marriage equality in the United States during President Obama's second term illustrates that both sides fought hard to gain ground and establish their beliefs on this issue as the prevailing opinion in the country. The use of the term 'un-American' is a common phenomenon in these debates between advocates and opponents of marriage equality. Both camps are driven by sociocultural motives as well as their personal fears and ideals when it comes to fighting for what they believe is right.

Before inquiring into these determinants and exploring the impact of the term 'un-American' on sociocultural discourse and ideas of everyday nationalism in the United States, it is vital to have a close look at the debate itself. Several statements of marriage equality advocates employing the term 'un-American' will be presented and contextualized in the following section in order to illustrate the term's usage on the side of marriage equality supporters. This will aid in the understanding of how charges of un-American behavior or thought determine the debate on marriage equality and the meaning and practices of American nationhood.

Equal Rights for All Americans

First, I inquire into the line of argument which stated that the fight for same-sex marriage was based on the American principle of equal rights for every citizen. Same-sex marriage advocates pleaded that denying some citizens the right to marry their partner bereaved them of their fundamental rights which were codified in the United States Constitution and the Declaration of Independence. The right to life, liberty, and the pursuit of happiness can only be achieved if all Americans are treated equally in the eyes of the law. Although the terms 'marriage equality,' 'same-sex marriage,' and 'gay marriage' are used interchangeably, its supporters mostly rely on the term 'marriage equality' because it emphasized what they were fighting for: Equality for all Americans as promised by the Fourteenth Amendment, regardless of sexual orientation. As equality has been promised to Americans in their most cherished documents, this was the most prominent and weightiest argument utilized by marriage equality supporters.

When the United States Supreme Court decided in January 2015 to hear marriage equality plaintiffs in that year's session, the president of the judicial advocacy group Alliance for Justice, Nan Aron, released a statement in which she emphasized the importance of this step: "Now the Supreme Court has the chance to make absolutely clear that denying marriage equality is unconstitutional – and un-American" ("Alliance"). In collaboration with several organizations promoting gay rights and equality rights in general, Alliance for Justice has long been an avid supporter of cases and initiatives that aided the federal judiciary in expediting equality and ending un-American practices of discrimination against minorities ("Alliance"). The denial of marriage equality, according to Aron as the spokesperson for Alliance for Justice, was unconstitutional and needed to be reconsidered as it was against United States law. Calling such attitude unconstitutional and un-American at the same time is a common choice. This combination emphasized how incompatible unequal marriage rights were with the American national self-concept in regard to both American values and American law. Representing the liberal voice of the legal system, Aron insisted in her official statement that "[d]enying the freedom to marry is abhorrent to the American values embedded in our Constitution." Same-sex marriage opponents believed that American values would suffer tremendously if gay and lesbian couples get the right to marry; however, Aron insists that the reverse is true.

January 2015 was also a critical month for same-sex marriage advocates in the state of Florida. As a growing number of state legislators decided to change their marriage laws and grant equal rights to same-sex couples, the pressure on Florida lawmakers to join this national trend increased immensely. Traditionally a swing state, Florida is dominated by both progressives and conservatives alike, which aggravated the divide caused by this issue among Floridians. The U.S. House Representative of Florida's 23rd district Debbie Wassermann Schultz was one of the first to accuse marriage equality opponents of un-American behavior (Wassermann Schulz in interview with C. Johnson). Her accusation was a response to 2012 Republican presidential candidate Rick Santorum who gave his voters a campaign promise of instating a federal marriage amendment which would reverse and invalidate already existing same-sex marriages (C. Johnson). In an interview with the *Washington Blade*, Debbie Wassermann Schulz expressed her concern over Santorum's plans and warned that such a federal marriage amendment "would be un-American, undemocratic and entirely inappropriate and unacceptable"

(Wassermann Schulz in interview with C. Johnson). By calling the federal marriage amendment un-American, Wassermann Schulz emphasized that this question was not a partisan issue. She thereby demonstrated that American nationhood was at stake in this debate.

At the height of the marriage equality debate, Utah was not a progressive state regarding the protection of LGBT Americans. State politics in Utah were (and still are) dominated by the influential and conservative Church of Latter-day Saints movement, which fiercely opposes any form of acknowledgement of same-sex relationships ("Same-Sex Marriage"). However, support for marriage equality came from actor and founder of Utah's annual Sundance Film Festival, Robert Redford, who was invited to the Equality Utah "Allies Dinner" as a keynote speaker (Thorpe). Redford used this platform to advocate for a change of the discriminatory laws which still prevailed in Utah and relied on the oratorical strategy of calling these laws and those who upheld them "un-American": "There is no room in our society for discrimination. None. I think it is un-American" (Redford qtd. in Thorpe). Furthermore, Redford explained that he did not see the point in sticking to laws which were patently outdated, evidenced by people all over the country who were changing their minds and wanted to move forward: "Utah is changing. There are good people in Utah. More people want to change the discriminatory laws than want to keep them. People should be able to marry whomever they love" (Redford qtd. in Thorpe). His bluntness and use of the accusation of an un-American attitude offended some Utahns. His phrasing implied that those opposing same-sex marriage and stronger anti-discrimination laws could not be good Americans and were also not among the "good people in Utah" (Redford qtd. in Thorpe).

Many advocates of marriage equality did not only believe that it was un-American to deny equal rights to some Americans, but they were also convinced that such discriminatory attitudes clashed with their state's principles and values. Therefore, the defense of the traditional concept of marriage was also condemned as un-Kentuckian or un-Minnesotan. This demonstrates that taking pride in defending one's state's reputation can become as important as standing up for ideals which are upheld by the nation as a whole. Accordingly, in their publication *Kentucky Kernel*, students of University of Kentucky appealed to their readers to support "equality for all Kentuckians and Americans" because they were convinced that Kentucky could not allow itself to stagnate when change was at the state's doorstep ("Students"). Although it seemed like a large and daunting transformation, sometimes such changes ultimately improve the lives of all Americans. The writers of the *Kentucky Kernel* believed that marriage equality would allow their state to come closer to their nation's promises and make them better Americans and better Kentuckians. They urged fellow students to "follow in [their] parents' footsteps by changing the definition of marriage once more" and therefore reminded them of the change in law that had been achieved in 1967 when interracial marriages were finally legalized ("Students"). The staff of the *Kentucky Kernel* insisted that "[t]here is no constitutional justification for inequality. The Supreme Court has held that all rights enjoyed by the majority must be given to every minority. Marriage Equality is one of those Constitutionally-protected rights" ("Students"). According to the publication's editors, there was no "good reason to ban same-sex marriage, just as there was no good reason to ban interracial ones. Inequality is un-American, and it is not Kentuckian" ("Students").

Students in Kentucky were not the only Americans who believed that refusing equal marriage rights to same-sex couples was not only un-American but also went against their self-definition as citizens of their states. When Minnesota Republicans tried to defend traditional marriage by implementing a constitutional amendment banning marriage equality in their state, Minnesotan Governor Mark Dayton and Senator Al Franken spoke out against such plans. As the Minnesota House decision on this ban drew closer, Franken voiced his concerns: "This amendment would do nothing more than write discrimination into our state's constitution and add to the barriers same-sex couples already face to the full recognition of their families" (Franken qtd. in Andrew). Governor Dayton did not hesitate to join Franken and appealed to his fellow Minnesotans: "The path of social progress in this country has been to include everyone fully and equally. This path of social progress, of human compassion and understanding, would be tragically reversed by this amendment. Minnesota is better than this. Minnesotans are better than this" (Dayton qtd. in Andrew). As the situation did not look promising for supporters of marriage equality, Dayton decided to adopt a sharper tone by stating that Minnesotans must "reject this mean-spirited, divisive, un-Minnesotan, and un-American amendment" (Dayton qtd. in Andrew). Calling the amendment "un-American" seemed to be a last resort for Dayton, as he could no longer think of a subtler strategy to protect Minnesota from becoming an un-American state. However, this sharp rhetoric did not prevent the amendment from passing in 2012 as Republicans were in the majority in the Minnesota House and Senate and both were split along party lines with only a handful of exceptions (Andrew).

In Arkansas, where same-sex marriage was not legal until all bans were struck down by the U.S. Supreme Court, a bill was proposed just a few months prior to *Obergefell v. Hodges* which was a detrimental setback for the LGBT movement. This bill would prohibit cities and counties from passing laws to protect citizens from discrimination based on sexual orientation if this protection had not yet been guaranteed by state law (Gill). The director of the Human Rights Campaign Arkansas, highly indignant at such an injustice, said that this proposed bill "[was] an attack on liberty and democracy, pure and simple" (Johnson qtd. in Gill). Even if gay Americans lived in cities or counties protecting its citizens, state legislation could interfere with their local sovereignty and prevent such progress (Gill). Human Rights Campaign Arkansas' state director Johnson called this practice "un-American" because it did not only prohibit self-governance on a local level but also discriminated against fellow Arkansans: "It's crystal clear that the motivation for this bill is to stifle local efforts to advance equality for LGBT Arkansans. Not only is this wrong, this explicit attempt at legislative overreach is discriminatory, dangerous and fundamentally un-American" (Johnson qtd. in Gill). Struggling to find words which could adequately reflect his anger, he called the bill "un-American" because the adjectives 'discriminatory' and 'dangerous' were insufficient to describe the full impact of such a law.

The Connection Between the Gay Rights Movement and the Civil Rights Movement

Since the very first days of the gay rights movement, references to racial discrimination and the civil rights movement have been employed frequently by gay rights advocates. Both minorities know what it means to be treated as second-class citizens and as less American than their fellow compatriots. Both movements pursue their claims based on the American ideal of equality. The civil rights movement set the standard for the gay rights movement and its later subchapter, the marriage equality movement (Hall, "Americanism" 1112). The connection between these two movements is most clearly seen in their appeals to the Fourteenth Amendment. However, throughout American history, minorities had to fight for their rights as guaranteed to them by the Fourteenth Amendment.

The Fourteenth Amendment along with the Thirteenth and Fifteenth Amendment were already passed in 1865 during the Reconstruction era after the Civil War (Neuborne 115). Nevertheless, it took 100 years before the protections of the Fifteenth Amendment were finally granted to Black Americans with the passage of the 1965 Voting Rights Act (116). The Fourteenth Amendment, guaranteeing equal protection of the laws and no deprivation of life, liberty, and property without due process, has a long "history of judicial failure" since the Supreme Court "failed to enforce" the amendment "well into the 20th century," "[r]eflecting a national lack of will" (Neuborne 119). The activism of the civil rights movement was the prerequisite for today's enforcement of the Fourteenth Amendment and the possibility to extend this discrimination protection to other minorities. Inspired by the civil rights movement, marriage equality advocates demanded same-sex marriage based on their conviction that the Equal Protection Clause of the Fourteenth Amendment is granting equal marriage rights to same-sex couples.[63]

The two non-profit organizations National Association for the Advancement of Colored People (NAACP) and the Gay & Lesbian Alliance Against Defamation (GLAAD) were among the forerunners of equality advocacy in the United States. GLAAD was pleased to hear that NAACP's board of directors had decided to officially endorse marriage equality. In a statement released in May 2012, NAACP president Benjamin Todd Jealous affirmed: "Civil marriage is a civil right and a matter of civil law. . . . The NAACP's support for marriage equality is deeply rooted in the Fourteenth Amendment of the United States Constitution and equal protection of all people." (Jealous qtd. in Wallsten). This statement was a milestone because the most influential black civil rights organization in the country was paving the way for equality for another minority. Furthermore, such a remarkable move might have come as a surprise for many since the African American community has historically been divided over the question of marriage equality becoming the law of the land. A joint poll conducted a few months earlier by *The Washington Post* and the Kaiser Family Foundation reported that almost 60 percent of African Americans found same-sex marriage to be "unacceptable" (Wallsten). The predominantly conservative African Amer-

63 For the interconnection between (un-)Americanism, the civil rights movement, and the gay rights movement, see: Hall, Simon. "The American Gay Rights Movement and Patriotic Protest." *Journal of the History of Sexuality*, vol. 19, no. 3, 2010, p. 536–62. *JSTOR*, doi: 10.1353/sex.2010.0011.

ican churches' influence was very strong in the matter, and they tended to dominate the respective discourse on gay rights in the communities.[64] However, there had been a shift in this pattern, and the official statement by the NAACP gave hope to many Black gays that times were about to change. GLAAD President Herndon Graddick welcomed the NAACP's strive for greater equality and their continued fight against discrimination:

> We applaud President Ben Jealous and the NAACP Board of Directors for their leadership on this issue. Across races, faith traditions, and political persuasions, a majority of our culture recognizes that denying gay couples the chance at happiness that comes with being married is unfair and un-American. (Graddick qtd. in Wallsten)

Graddick's designation of the denial of marriage equality as un-American came mere months before the 2012 presidential election during which the African American Presidential Candidate Barack Obama remained hesitant to take position in this debate. He needed the support from both the African American community and the gay community but struggled to unite them (McKinley).

In a 2014 op-ed piece for *The New York Times*' Sunday Review, Frank Bruni commented on the link between racism and the denial of equal marriage rights, as well as the remarkable shift in attitude that had taken place in people's minds. Although people's awareness of the similarities between these types of discrimination had grown over time, it was a long way until a majority of Americans regarded the Equal Protection Clause of the Fourteenth Amendment a valid basis for allowing same-sex marriage.[65] "Increasingly, opposition to gay marriage is being

64 The rather negative attitude of the African American community has a detrimental impact on gay African Americans in particular. They struggle with this hostility to a higher degree than their non-black counterparts as they need to unite their ethnic minority status with their sexual orientation minority status. For more, see: Walsh, Clare F. "It Really Is Not Just Gay, but African American Gay: The Impact of Community and Church on the Experiences of Black Lesbians Living in North Central Florida." *Journal of Homosexuality*, vol. 63, no. 9, 2016, p. 1236–52, doi: 10.1080/00918369.2016.1151694; Johnson, E. Patrick. *Sweet Tea: Black Gay Men of the South*. North Carolina UP, 2008; Stewart-Winter, Timothy. *Queer Clout: Chicago and the Rise of Gay Politics*. Pennsylvania UP, 2015.

65 The United States Supreme Court was highly conflicted whether the Fourteenth Amendment to the United States Constitution requires all states to

equated with racism – as indefensible, un-American," he wrote, using the term 'un-American' for opposition of both the civil rights movement and the gay rights movement. Bruni also denounced opposition to marriage equality as "un-American" not only because it conflicted with his idea of a good nation, but because it was also diametrically opposed to his understanding of basic human rights. He welcomed the development that "in a great many circles, endorsement of same-sex marriage has rather suddenly become nonnegotiable. Expected. Assumed. Proof of a baseline level of enlightenment and humanity. Akin to the understanding that all people, regardless of race or color, warrant the same rights and respect" (Bruni).

The former legal doctrine "separate but equal," according to which racial segregation did not violate the Fourteenth Amendment to the United States Constitution until it was struck down in 1964, was frequently cited in the debate on marriage equality. Supporters adopted this phrase from the civil rights movement because it expressed the exact situation which many gay couples faced when some states started allowing civil unions but not full marriage rights. This was also the case in Illinois, where "after a year-long legislative showdown that invoked the Bible, the civil rights movement and competing definitions of what constitutes a family in America" (McDermott), the state finally decided to pave the way for greater equality for all Americans by introducing a bill which would enable same-sex marriage. Reactions to the House passage of the bill SB 10[66] differed widely, both within the legislature as well as among the people of Illinois. Even among Democrats, which constituted the majority of the legislature, members were split since some were influenced by a rather conservative African American background or were representing more rural areas of Illinois (McDermott). The bill's sponsor, Repre-

perform and recognize marriages of same-sex couples. While the majority opinion in *Obergefell* held that the amendment does require all states to do so (United States, Supreme Court, "*Obergefell*" 4), the dissenting judges strongly disagreed (Roberts, "*Obergefell*" 23–24; Thomas, "*Obergefell*" 3; Scalia, "*Obergefell*" 3; Alito, "*Obergefell*" 2).

66 SB 10 amended Illinois state law insofar as it defined marriage as a union between two individuals (and no longer restricted it to a union between a man and a woman). Additionally, legal benefits, rights, and protections were extended to individuals of all marriages and their children. At the same time, it was enshrined in state law that churches, synagogues, mosques and comparable religious institutions cannot be required to solemnize or provide facilities for marriages ("SB 10").

sentative Greg Harris, D-Chicago, referencing breakthroughs in the civil rights movement and the women's rights movement, declared: "We find ourselves at another one of those moments today" (Harris qtd. in McDermott). By contrast, Representative Jeanne M. Ives, R-Wheaton was afraid that "conservative people of faith will lose religious rights" and that the new bill was sending wrong signals because the "country was built on freedom of religion, not freedom *from* religion" (Ives qtd. in McDermott). Many representatives did not see the point in this bill because same-sex couples already had the possibility of having their partnership recognized as civil union. As this statute gave them the same legal rights as married couples, there was no need to fight for something that effectively granted them the same rights under a different name (McDermott). Representative Jehan A. Gordon-Booth, D-Peoria got right to the heart of the problem when he urged the fellow representatives to remember: "Separate but equal in Illinois and in this land is un-American" (qtd. in Sudo). The term 'un-American' in combination with the "separate but equal" doctrine was supposed to remind the legislators that the American people had already established that unequal treatment as in "separate but equal" is in conflict with the legal and ideological principles of the United States.

In her article "The Supreme Court's New Gay Marriage Case Tests MLK's Dream of True Equality," the civil rights lawyer Lisa Bloom began with directing the readers' attention to the fact that the Supreme Court justices had decided on accepting the case *Obergefell v. Hodges* right before Martin Luther King Jr. weekend in 2015. Bloom explained that, in theory, the United States could be a union guaranteeing perfect equality to all its people, thereby making Martin Luther King's Jr. dreams come true. The promise of equality turned out to be broken on several occasions:

> On paper, we Americans make sweeping pronouncements about equality, from the Declaration of Independence's promise that 'all men are created equal' to our constitution's 14th Amendment guarantee that all persons are entitled to the 'equal protection' of the laws. Yet it's up to the courts to bring those texts to life. (Bloom)

It is the latter where the nation lags behind. Lisa Bloom argued that this "[s]econd class citizenship demeans the LGBT community – and all of us for tolerating such an un-American state of affairs." It was important for Bloom to address the un-American nature of second-class citizenship caused through discrimination and also through the denial of certain rights which are guaranteed to everyone but a minority of Americans. The nation can only be thoroughly American if all people are treated equally.

Marriage Equality and Religion

A county clerk from Rowan County in Kentucky hit global media headlines in summer 2015 when she refused to issue marriage licenses to same-sex couples after she was ordered to do so as a consequence of the U.S. Supreme Court ruling in *Obergefell v. Hodges*. The clerk, Kim Davis, denied a marriage license to the couple David Ermold and David Moore due to moral objections, asserting that such an act would violate her deeply held Christian beliefs as a member of the Apostolic Christian Church (Blinder and Perez-Peña). Stating that she was acting "[u]nder God's authority" (Davis qtd. in Blinder and Perez-Peña), Davis refused to comply with federal law and stopped issuing marriage licenses to all couples regardless of sexual orientation in order to avoid having to grant them to same-sex couples. Kim Davis was not intimidated by the potential consequences of her behavior and became one of the fiercest and most resistant opponents of same-sex marriage, even spending five days in jail for contempt of court (Blinder and Perez-Peña).[67] She was unrelenting in her defense of religious

67 The six couples to whom she denied marriage licenses sued her in her official capacity as the country clerk of Rowan County by filing the federal lawsuit *Miller v. Davis*. The case first went to the United States District Court for the Eastern District of Kentucky where the judge responsible for the case decided in favor of the plaintiffs ("*Miller v. Davis*"). Judge Bunning ruled Kim Davis would suffer no harm if her name was on marriage licenses of same-sex couples, and it would not interfere with her religious liberty as guaranteed by the First Amendment. Still, Davis refused to accept defeat and appealed the ruling to the United States Court of Appeals for the Sixth Circuit, even turning to the U.S. Supreme Court for a stay ("*Miller v. Davis*"). However, none of her efforts were successful. Since she still declined to comply with the federal court order requiring her to issue marriage licenses to all couples, she opted to go to jail (Felton). Davis was not the only county clerk who refused to acknowledge the change of law. However, most of her colleagues relented their positions, especially as soon as they faced legal consequences (Blinder and Perez-Peña). In a statement published by her lawyers, Davis declared: "To issue a marriage license which conflicts with God's definition of marriage, with my name affixed to the certificate, would violate my conscience. . . . To me this has never been

liberties of public employees and private citizens that she believed were protected by the First Amendment (Blinder and Perez-Peña).

Given the vehemence which marked the debate in the case of Kim Davis, it is unsurprising that accusations of un-American behavior or attitudes were raised by marriage equality advocates. They could not believe that even after an unequivocal ruling by the United States Supreme Court, some Americans would still actively resist complying with the new law and go to such lengths in their opposition. The outrage of same-sex marriage advocates was, for example, visible in a comment on the events in Kentucky, titled "That's Me in the Corner, Losing My Religion," published by the blogger Domenick Scudera in the online newspaper *The Huffington Post*. "I am disgusted by the un-American, hypocritical, mean-spirited rallies and shows of support for Kim Davis," he wrote in the blog post. He was especially furious that some Americans believed that the First Amendment to the United States Constitution gave them the right to use their religion as an excuse for ignoring other laws that might conflict with their personal beliefs: "Practicing your religion does not give you free reign to do whatever the hell you want, laws be damned. We live in a diverse country. Assuming your religion trumps our core civil laws is arrogant, ugly, and un-American" (Scudera). Like many other Americans using this insult, Scudera put the term 'un-American' last in a tricolon, thereby assigning it the most rhetorical weight in his sentence. Insults of un-Americanism are the ultimate weapon. Consequently, the term is typically used at the point of a line of argument on which the audience will put their focus.

Clerks like Kim Davis were not the only Americans who refused to accept the Supreme Court decision in 2015. Conservative bakers, florists, and wedding photographers were suddenly at the center of the conflict between religious liberty and discriminatory behavior toward minorities. Opponents of same-sex marriage portrayed these business owners as victims of America's judiciary system which put its progressive idea

a gay or lesbian issue. It is about marriage and God's word" (Davis qtd. in Maitland). The name-giving plaintiff of the case, April Miller, admitted she does understand Davis' motives to a certain extent: "She's standing up for her beliefs, as we're standing up for our beliefs, and we understand how hard that is" (Miller qtd. in Blinder and Perez-Peña). However, for Miller, this still does not justify Davis letting her personal religious beliefs interfere with her profession: "But we also believe that we do have the right to get married and that as a clerk in a county government office, she should be issuing the license. It's her job" (Miller qtd. in Blinder and Perez-Peña).

of marriage above the personal freedom of religious citizens (Holmes). Same-sex marriage became an imminent existential threat to conservative America since it was now these bakers, florists, or clerks who were suffering from discrimination and a lack of minority protection because they were not willing to support such a progressive idea of marriage. The question emerging from this conflict was who needed protection through law and whose rights could be abridged for the benefit of the rights of others. This was the issue addressed by Dave Holmes in an opinion piece on the behavior of Kim Davis and those who followed her example in boycotting the new status quo. Holmes had a strong stance on the question of who the actual victims of discrimination were: "'We don't serve your kind' is discrimination, pure and simple. It's un-American. We know that. Kim Davis knows that." For Holmes, the discrimination was unidirectional, i.e. from those refusing to serve same-sex couples, and thereby treating them unequally. There were no other words for unequal discriminatory behavior than calling it "un-American" (Holmes).

In Indiana, the Senate was to decide whether to pass the so-called Religious Freedom Restoration Acts.[68] The proposals for the Senate Bills 101 and 568 were drafted with the intention to provide religious citizens with in-

[68] The Indiana Bill 101 established the standard of "compelling governmental interest" which means that laws and governmental practices would first have to be evaluated in regard to whether they would create a substantial burden on a person's free exercise of religion (Indiana State, Senate, "Senate Enrolled Act 101" 3). The Senate Bill 568 is very similar to Senate Bill 101 as it reads:

> Religious Freedom Restoration Act. Provides that a state or local government action may not substantially burden a person's right to the exercise of religion unless it is demonstrated that applying the burden to the person's exercise of religion is: (1) essential to further a compelling governmental interest; and (2) the least restrictive means of furthering the compelling governmental interest. Provides that a person whose exercise of religion has been substantially burdened, or is likely to be substantially burdened, by a state or local government action may assert the burden as a claim or defense in a judicial proceeding, regardless of whether the state or a political subdivision of the state is a party to the judicial proceeding. Allows a person who asserts a burden as a claim or defense to obtain appropriate relief, including: (1) injunctive relief; (2) declaratory relief; (3) compensatory damages; and (4) recovery of court costs and reasonable attorney's fees. ("Senate Bill 568")

The Freedom Restoration Acts were ultimately signed into law.

creased protection from being forced to violate their religious beliefs (Metz). As a consequence, Jane Hanegar, executive director for the American Civil Liberties Union of Indiana, was worried what these laws could mean for the state of Indiana: "The bills create a widespread and negative perception of Indiana by appearing to invite the use of religion to discriminate, including on the basis of sexual orientation and gender identity" (Hanegar qtd. in Metz). The Religious Freedom Restoration Acts immediately sparked a discussion at the University of Indiana where Doug Bauder from the university's LGBT Support Services endorsed Hanegar's reproach by stating: "I guess if people want to discriminate, they're going to do it. But it just seems to me to allow that to happen by law is pretty un-American" (Bauder qtd. in Metz). However, Bauder also acknowledged what drove people to act in such an un-American way: "It's sort of their last chance to make their values known. . . . It's pandering to a certain group of constituents, and they feel like their rights have been violated, and they're doing their best to find some way to make their moral values heard because they're on the losing side at this point" (Bauder qtd. in Metz). Although Bauder knew opponents of the Senate bills were losing ground, he nevertheless relied on strong political rhetoric, calling such behavior "un-American."

In a letter to the editor published in a local Georgian newspaper, its author Corey Briley reminded her fellow Americans that the United States was still a democracy in which church and state were separated in order to avoid a conflict of interest. "A country consisting of diverse citizens, each unique in his or her own beliefs, desires and needs cannot afford to sacrifice its protected personal freedoms by kneeling at an altar of theocracy," she argued in her writing. "Such separations provide benefits to the familial unit, current U.S. tax system and protect the right to lead a life free from oppression and bondage" (Briley).[69] In order to fully make her

[69] Interestingly, the United States are militarily involved in Middle Eastern countries where a separation of church and state is not guaranteed, and one of their purported missions in these areas is to bring democratic principles to these theocracies. Although there is a large difference in the degree of oppression resulting from such a lack of separation of church and state in the United States compared to Iran or Saudi Arabia, the principles that are fought for are nevertheless the same. In her letter to the editor, Briley described opposition to same-sex marriage with the term "fanatical," which in current usage most commonly evokes religious fanaticism: "The sole argument against the acceptance of same-sex marriage is a fanatical and blindly ignorant position."

point clear, she also went on to call it "un-American" since such a mindset was not consistent with the nation's image of itself:

> To deny homosexuals state-sanctioned marriages is oppressive and un-American. To disregard the guarantee of equal rights to all citizens of the United States as protected in our Constitution is appalling. It is shameful that opposition even exists in allowing free citizens of the United States to exercise the right to a peaceful and happy existence. (Briley)

Progressive Christians, no longer willing to turn a blind eye on the discriminatory behavior of fellow religious Americans, increasingly began raising their voices in Christian newspapers and other media formats. Brandan Robertson, a Christian writer declaring his support for the gay rights movement, has commented frequently on the hostile attitude of some American Christians toward the LGBT community in the United States. In a statement on the Ethics and Religious Liberty Commission (ERLC) of the Southern Baptist Convention's legislative agenda for 2015, he was appalled by the commission's religious justification of their objections toward marriage equality. Marriage equality was a civil rights issue and not a religious one since it concerned marriage granted by the state. In his article, Robertson quotes the resolutions of the commission as follows: "When we tamper with God's design, we fundamentally disorder creation and open up pandoras (sic!) box of immorality. When we allow marriage to be redefined, families are dismantled, society is infected, and our values are undermined." Robertson was outraged that, as a Supreme Court ruling in favor of marriage equality became more likely, Christians were becoming more creative in finding ways to exclude homosexual Americans from public life. The justification for such measures was that people should never interfere with God's order of the world because this would lead to the downfall of society and leave the world in disarray. Robertson clearly distanced himself from Christians opposing such progress: "This 'agenda' item of the ERLC [is] fundamentally un-American and un-Christian. Denying dignity and equality to any individual for any reason is an affront to the Kingdom of God and I am deeply troubled to see my fellow followers of Jesus continually working as a force for injustice and inequality." Robertson used accusations of un-Americanism in order to admonish some denominations to reconsider their stance toward LGBT Americans. For him, charity, which is one of the core values of the Christian faith, does not entail the exclusion of a minority based on their sexual orientation.

How easily accusations of un-Americanism can be perceived as offensive became obvious when the actor and producer Tom Hanks had to apologize publicly for insulting Mormon supporters of California's Proposition 8 against marriage equality in the state. In his initial remark on the Church of Latter-Day Saints' role in the Proposition 8 debate he said: "The truth is this takes place in Utah, the truth is these people are some bizarre offshoot of the Mormon Church, and the truth is a lot of Mormons gave a lot of money to the church to make Prop-8 happen. . . . There are a lot of people who feel that is un-American, and I am one of them" (Hanks qtd. in McKay). As the previous examples have shown, Tom Hanks was far from the only person to denounce church members as un-American. However, his utterance may have received special focus since he was the producer of the controversial *HBO* television series, "Big Love," which was about polygamy in a Mormon sect (McKay). Some people claimed that he wanted to offend members of the Church of Latter-Day Saints by labelling them as un-American for supporting the politics of their choice (McKay). Leaders of the church quickly picked up on his rhetoric and issued statements in response to his claims. Kim Farah, a spokesperson for the denomination that was the subject of "Big Love," responded that "[e]xpressing an opinion in a free and democratic society is as American as it gets" (Farah qtd. in McKay). Thereby, she managed to circumvent using the term which caused the outcry and argued for the values and ideals which were usually championed by the advocates of the marriage equality debate. Bill McKeever, a representative for the Mormonism Research Ministry, commented on the situation as follows: "Personally, I find it un-American to tell people that they shouldn't vote their conscience. Hanks' comment shows that he very much believes in discriminating against people with whom he disagrees" (McKeever qtd. in McKay). This conflict was a disaster for marriage equality advocates since Hanks' rhetorical choice backfired. This example showed that while the strategic use of the term 'un-American' in political controversies can be a powerful choice, it can just as easily turn the situation around, making those using this wording an aggressor to be blamed. Tom Hanks quickly realized that he had crossed boundaries with his statement and offered an apology to those who felt offended. "I believe Proposition 8 is counter to the promise of our Constitution; it is codified discrimination. . . . [but] everyone has a right to vote their conscience – nothing could be more American" (Hanks qtd. in Leonard). Furthermore, he admitted that such rhetoric "creates more division when the time calls for respectful disagreement" and that "[n]o one should use 'un-American' lightly or in haste" (Hanks qtd. in Leonard).

Not Just Un-American but Also Un-Republican

One of the first Republicans who campaigned for marriage equality and who condemned marriage equality bans as un-American was Meghan McCain, daughter of the Senator and former presidential nominee John McCain. In 2009, she wrote an open letter to New York Republicans urging them to choose the right path as conservatives and more importantly as Americans. McCain acknowledged that in the ongoing battle on gay rights, it was "easy for many to get distracted by the politics and rhetoric on this issue and lose sight of what is really at its heart: the equality of freedom" (McCain). Reminding fellow Republicans of the Jeffersonian principles, McCain asked her fellow Americans if they believed that those rights enshrined in the nation's most cherished documents were only guaranteed to some of them or to all Americans. Failing to guarantee these principles to all Americans was, in her eyes, inconsistent with being a Republican and an American: "People may always have a difference of opinion . . . but championing a position that wants to treat people unequally isn't just un-Republican. At its fundamental core, it's un-American." Being called un-Republican as well as un-American was a severe blow for many opponents of gay marriage because it attacked their self-concept as Americans and as conservatives. Meghan McCain continued her argumentation by refuting typical allegations of opponents: "When a committed gay couple seeks to declare their love for one another and get married, the whole community benefits from the added stability and strength of that family. On top of that, we don't give up anything by sharing responsibilities and protections with those whom we love. . . ." Meghan McCain's open letter was particularly noteworthy because she addressed the worries of fellow Republicans rather than simply accusing them of being un-American and un-Republican.

It made headlines when one of the top Republican consultants, Steve Schmidt, publicly declared that he considered it disrespectful to not let gay people marry if they wished to do so. Schmidt held several high-ranking positions during the Bush administration and was co-responsible for the nomination of two conservative candidates for the U.S. Supreme Court, Chief Justice John Roberts and Justice Samuel Alito (Vesoulis).

Shortly after Meghan McCain's statement on marriage equality, Schmidt announced in front of his fellow Republicans: "It cannot be argued that marriage between people of the same sex is un-American or threatens the rights of others" (Schmidt qtd. in George). Schmidt did not use the term un-American as an accusation toward marriage equality opponents but condemned their repeated usage of this rhetoric. Therefore, he portrayed them as the aggressors who relied on language which was not appropriate for the cause.

In 2012, almost 80 high-ranking Republicans signed a legal brief in which they argued that same-sex couples had the constitutional right to marry. In addition, they endorsed the repeal of any laws that prohibited gay marriage (Stolberg).[70] In March 2015, more than 300 Republicans signed a similar amicus brief urging the Supreme Court to rule in favor of marriage equality in June 2015 (Miller). This was a milestone because among those who signed were former and current members of the House of Representatives and the Senate who stated that marriage equality was consistent with Republican values. The brief was evidence for the sweeping change that took place among conservatives in the United States, demonstrating that even people within more conservative circles increasingly believed that a ban on same-sex marriage conflicted with the American self-concept.[71] The amicus brief was drafted by the former Republican National Committee Chairman Ken Mehlman whose efforts contributed to overturning California's Proposition 8 (Miller). Amicus

[70] The brief declared that "same-sex marriage promotes family values by allowing children of gay couples to grow-up in two-parent homes, and that it advances conservative values of 'limited government and maximizing individual freedom'" (Stolberg).

[71] The Republicans declared in the amicus brief:

> Although amici hold a broad spectrum of socially and politically conservative, moderate, and libertarian views, amici share the view that laws that bar same-sex couples from the institution of civil marriage, with all its attendant profoundly important rights and responsibilities, are inconsistent with the United States Constitution's dual promises of equal protection and due process. (qtd. in Miller)

In their brief, the amici adduced the constitutional principles which later became the decisive legal basis for opening marriage for all Americans regardless of their sexual orientation: the right to equal protection and due process as guaranteed by the Fourteenth Amendment to the United States Constitution.

briefs, as the one composed by Ken Mehlman, demonstrated that marriage equality was not a purely liberal issue but found advocates on both ends of the political spectrum. Conservatives who signed this amicus brief knew "there are regional as well as generational divisions, with opposition especially strong in the South" (Feeherey qtd. in Stolberg). However, as more and more Republicans openly supported equal protection of all Americans regardless of their own or others' sexuality, the easier it became to convince those holding conservative views.

Legal Uncertainty and the Lack of Federal Protection

In the United States, a large number of benefits and protections for couples and families are still bound to the institution of marriage. Unmarried couples miss out on more than one thousand benefits and usually do not have the protective hand of the state over them (Caiazza). "While families with means might be able to withstand the costs of extra taxation or the unfair denial of Social Security benefits, for a family already struggling, these financial penalties can mean the difference between getting by and getting evicted," Caiazza warns. Laura E. Durso from Center for American Progress added that the financial disadvantages were "just a couple of the added costs that are harming the economic security of LGBT people across the country. It is unfair and un-American that LGBT people are penalized because of who they are, and it has real and profound effects on their ability to stay out of poverty and provide for their families" (Durso qtd. in Caiazza). As long as gay marriage was not legal in all states, same-sex couples and their families suffered disproportionately from a lack of equal rights, benefits, and protections. Through this unequal treatment and denial of the right to marry, same-sex couples and their families were given the status of second-class citizens. The disrespect of the American ideal of equality, which was an inherent result of such unequal treatment, and the far-reaching consequences for same-sex couples were what marriage equality supporters deemed un-American.

Despite the victories that have been achieved, one cannot ignore that discrimination against the LGBT community persists in various forms. The option of marriage for same-sex couples does not necessarily protect them from other patterns of discrimination. Pennsylvania State Representative Dan Frankel, who is the co-chair of the legislature's LGBT Equality Caucus, warned his fellow citizens:

> We must not lose sight that it remains legal to deny our family, friends and neighbors jobs, housing or a public accommodation such as a restaurant table because of who they are. That is wrong, is un-American, and about 70 percent of Pennsylvanians have agreed for years that we need laws against that type of discrimination. (Frankel qtd. in Tabachnick et al.)

Frankel wanted to be sure that every American understood the urgency of his statement as he reinforced his argument by using the term 'un-American.'

After winning the 2013 landmark civil rights case *United States v. Windsor*, Roberta Kaplan, the lawyer who argued the case before the Supreme Court and succeeded in overturning Section 3 of the Defense of Marriage Act, appeared to be optimistic that the nation had become far more accepting regarding the issue. She did not deny, however, that there was still a long way to go for LGBT Americans until they could achieve full acceptance and equality. When asked which struggles and challenges still needed to be addressed by the LGBT movement, she named serious problems such as adoption laws, income inequality and homelessness, as well as the precarious circumstances for transsexual people (Krantz). Nevertheless, Kaplan still had faith that the majority of Americans did not wish to disadvantage their fellow Americans or treat them unequally: "No American really believes it's OK to treat someone differently and discriminate against them simply because of who they are. Simply because it's un-American" (Kaplan qtd. in Krantz).

In January 2012, the bipartisan coalition Mayors for the Freedom to Marry was launched by mayors from all over the United States who wished to showcase support for marriage equality. The coalition had representatives from all geographical areas, and the mayors themselves were a highly diverse group (Parker et al.). They not only believed that marriage equality was a human right which needed to be defended, but they also saw the enormous potential such a change in law would entail: "Our support for marriage is not just a matter of principle. It is also a matter of prosperity. Cities that cultivate diversity are the places where creativity and ideas thrive. They are the places where today's entrepreneurs are most likely to build the businesses of tomorrow" (Parker et al.). Enraged by how such a discriminatory practice could still be upheld in most states in 2012, the five chairs of the group publicly declared that such "treatment is unacceptable, and it is un-American. . . . Ending marriage discrimination against gay and lesbian couples is just one more step on that steady march toward a more perfect union" (Parker et al.). Along with many other public figures who voiced their support for same-sex marriage, the Mayors for the Freedom to Marry relied on charges of un-Americanism in order to demonstrate the severity of this injustice toward their fellow Americans.

What motivated many marriage equality activists to fight for this cause was their wish for gay couples and families to be officially recognized. In the run-up to the Supreme Court case *United States v. Windsor*, several LGBT leaders and advocacy organizations met in Florida to discuss the potential impact of either a positive or negative ruling in this case. Present at the event was CJ Ortuno, the Executive Director of nonprofit organization SAVE Dade, a LGBT advocacy organization in Florida. Ortuno explained that for him, his wife, and children, it was very easy to be recognized as a family since they represented what one could call the traditional family concept (Ortuno qtd. in "Tonight"). What drove him to fight for marriage equality was that he believed every American deserved to have that right: "Marriage is the way in which government, society, and its people recognize and honor committed relationships. When I introduce my wife, people understand who this person is and what she means to me in relation to my being. Asking anyone to even consider less is truly un-American" (Ortuno qtd. in "Tonight"). In his statement, Ortuno commented on two aspects of identity: One was the personal identity of every individual, which included being recognized in relation to one's nuclear family. The second aspect concerns one's national identity as an American. If marriage was denied to homosexual Americans, they could not fully live up to both aspects. Society did not recognize their relationships and families, and they were afforded fewer rights, making them second-class citizens, which Ortuno despised as un-American.

C Opponents' Arguments for Charges of Un-Americanism

While marriage equality advocates were able to celebrate a number of important victories in courts in the years before *Obergefell*, in particular in 2014, more than 100 anti-equality bills were introduced into state legislatures in order to stem the spread of gay rights in the United States and to avoid the inclusion of gay subjects into contemporary notions of American nationalism.[72] Many of these measures were meant to protect religious liberty, but the target of these bills and the motivation of their initiators was clear ("Who is Weaponizing"). This legal battle against same-sex marriage started long before *Obergefell* because marriage equality opponents had already sensed the imminent threat of a redefinition of marriage. This fear was incited by activist groups of the religious right. Among its forerunners are the American Family Association, the Family Research Council, and the Concerned Women for America. All of them claim to be non-profit organizations, conducting research on topics such as family, education, and society in the United States and providing education on how to enhance public well-being. The Family Research Council (FRC) published the following self-description on its website:

> Founded in 1983, Family Research Council is a nonprofit research and educational organization dedicated to articulating and advancing a family-centered philosophy of public life. In addition to providing policy research and analysis for the legislative, executive, and judicial branches of the federal government, FRC seeks to inform the news media, the academic community, business leaders, and the general public about family issues that affect the nation from a biblical worldview. Our vision is a prevailing culture in which all human life is valued, families flourish, and religious liberty thrives. ("About")

Their intentions might sound honorable; however, how the FRC and similar organizations define family is very exclusivist as it does not in-

[72] More than 100 anti-LGBT legislative proposals were introduced in 29 different states with many of them being Religious Freedom Restoration Acts. Indiana's Religious Freedom Restoration Act, as discussed in the previous chapter, was one of the most prominent examples. The proposed bills attack LGBT rights in several areas of life, for example health care, adoption and foster care, discrimination protection, marriage rights, or student groups on campus (Montgomery).

corporate any concept of family besides its traditional understanding. In the end, these organizations are, as some insist, fundamentalist activist groups of the religious right which aim at combating gay rights at all costs ("Who is Weaponizing").

Their preoccupation with homosexuality becomes obvious when analyzing their websites. According to the mission statement of FRC, topics concerning family and their well-being should be most prominent. However, a content analysis of their websites by searching for the frequency of keywords created a different impression. The website of the Family Research Council showed 4720 results on 'homosexuality' and 5261 results on 'same-sex marriage.' When looking for other topics which are common concerns for families in the United States, there were significantly fewer search results. 'Community' had 1488 results, 'domestic violence' a mere 775, and even the keyword 'parent' with 4835 hits had fewer search results than 'same-sex marriage.' A look at the website of the American Family Association showed the same pattern. 'Homosexuality' was referred to 712 times and 'gay marriage' 816 times. By contrast, topics such as 'education' (324 results), 'poverty' (155 results), 'domestic violence' (20 results) or 'parent' (693 results) were not as frequently discussed in website articles than topics related to homosexuality. Considering that these organizations claim to focus on family issues and that homosexuality is a topic that concerns only a very small number of American families directly, the preponderant number of articles that contain the term 'homosexuality' or 'same-sex marriage' is astonishing. Therefore, the search results support the earlier claim that the primary goal of these organizations is to fight the gay rights movement and not to secure overall advancements for families and education as they commonly profess.

The rise of these anti-gay organizations is symptomatic of a growing fear among conservatives that the increasing influence of the gay rights movement in the United States in several areas of life is a threat to a conservative American nationhood. As the accusations of un-Americanism discussed in the following will demonstrate, marriage equality opponents are terrified that the continuous victories of gay rights advocates in court rooms and on ballots accelerate the loss of American values and morals. For some, this development will ultimately lead to the decline of the American nation, even to a social apocalypse, as some of the examples investigated in the following illustrate. This line of thought is especially popular with same-sex marriage opponents who reject same-sex marriage based on their religious beliefs but also with politicians who like to foment panic. Consequently, much of the debate among opponents also centers around the possible infringement of their First Amendment rights and the supposition that gay-friendly judges make rulings and facilitate legislation which do not represent the American people. This development is what marriage equality opponents commonly denounce as un-American because it is diametrically opposed to their identity as Americans.

Loss of Morals and Values

Although the Republican and former Speaker of the House of Representatives, Paul Ryan, did not raise charges of un-Americanism, his statement is nevertheless included in this analysis since he addressed what many opponents felt about same-sex marriage. In the course of the 2016 presidential election campaign, Ryan did not hesitate to share his idea of good American values. In response to an audience member's question at a rally in Cincinnati, he explained: "The things you talk about like traditional marriage and family and entrepreneurship . . . these are American values, these are universal human values" (Ryan qtd. in "Paul Ryan says"). With this statement, Paul Ryan, who is a fierce opponent of gay rights, indicated that marriage equality was neither an American nor a human right in his eyes. In order to prevent damaging the American nation, changes in the concepts of marriage and family must be adamantly resisted. Former House Representative Allen West chimed in with support for Ryan's belief that gay marriage would have detrimental consequences on society. West called gay marriage an "oxymoron" since "marriage is a union and a bond between a man and a woman to do one thing: the furtherance of society by procreation, through creating new life" (West qtd. in Tashman, "West"). If marriage were opened to same-sex couples, it would be "a matter of time before we [didn't] have society" (West qtd. in Tashman, "West"). West dramatized the consequences of marriage equality in order to appeal to his ultra-conservative electorate. For him and like-minded opponents, the prosperity and future of the American nation was inextricably linked with living according to God's word or at least their interpretation thereof. Marriage equality would lead to chaos and destroy society beyond repair.

In October 2014, a highly controversial statement by the American Family Association's Director of Issues Analysis, Bryan Fischer, sparked a public outcry. He stated that same-sex marriage was "as morally bankrupt and indefensible as the institution of slavery. . . . For this sexual debauchery to be normalized by the highest court in the land is a sign of a nation plunging headlong into a bottomless moral abyss" (Fischer qtd. in Hooper). His statement was the consequence of the Supreme Court decision to repel marriage equality appeals from the states of Indiana, Oklahoma, Utah, Virginia, and Wisconsin (Liptak).[73] To Fischer, preserving and defending family values only included the heterosexual family and was not open to alternative conceptions which deviated from the conservative image, as such a reconceptualization would result in a degeneration of the American nation. Comparing same-sex marriage to slavery was a provocative move because alluding to the African American civil rights movement was usually a strategy of marriage equality supporters. Supporters employed this tactic in order to emphasize that African Americans and LGBT Americans shared comparable histories of discrimination and struggles for equal rights. Part of the controversy surrounding Fischer's statement was that he attempted to pit both minorities against each other and showed compassion for the first while attacking the latter. Although Fischer got the attention he was aiming at, he nevertheless realized that opponents need to improve and intensify their efforts in order to not lose on all ends in the battle over American everyday nationalism: "It's going to be virtually impossible to stop this press and this push toward nationalizing, imposing on every state in the union, marriage that is based on the infamous crime against nature" (Fischer qtd. in Wong, "SCOTUS"). As a consequence, Fischer continued his offensive comment, declaring that marriage equality was not only "un-constitutional" but also "un-American": "Yesterday the Supreme court did something unconscionable, unconstitutional and un-American. It cannot stand and in the end it will not stand" (Fischer qtd. in Hooper). Fischer is an extreme example since he went far beyond expressing his concerns about the possibility of marriage equality

[73] With the Supreme Court accepting appeals court rulings that allow same-sex marriages in Indiana, Oklahoma, Utah, Virginia, and Wisconsin, same-sex couples in those states were able to get married right after this decision. As a result, the number of states which allowed same-sex marriage rose from 19 to 24 states and the District of Columbia. Thereby, almost two-thirds of all gay and lesbian couples lived in states where marriage was legal for them. 2014 was a particularly successful year for the marriage equality movement, which increased fear among marriage equality opponents that this development could no longer be halted.

being permitted by deliberately offending gay Americans in multiple ways. He did not resort to accusations of un-Americanism in order to substantiate his claims, but generally adopted a radical rhetoric in order to convey his opinion. This example demonstrates that the degree of offensiveness of insults of un-Americanism depends greatly on the context of the utterance, the intention of the speaker, and the other content of the speech act.

For Fischer, the debate on marriage equality and the un-Americanism rhetoric went hand in hand. This is clearly demonstrated in an opinion piece which he published a few years after the previously discussed statement. In his article "First, It's Unthinkable. Then, It's Permitted. Then, It's Mandatory," Fischer explained that gay rights advocates not only want marriage equality. Moreover, they were striving for a liberal takeover of the whole American nation: They "have a simple strategy for taking control of all of American society, one segment at a time. . . . They are not interested in equality, they are interested in supremacy." Fischer was concerned about the future of conservatives and their interests and rights within the American nation because "if you don't embrace the LGBT agenda, you will get fined, fired, or worse. This sin went from being a crime to becoming a mandatory national virtue." He was correct that an increasing acceptance of gay rights in society made marriage equality opponents the minority. However, the scenario that Fischer constructed for conservatives was still unrealistic. Nevertheless, he was convinced his hypotheses were likely since "homosexual activists convinced gullible Americans and even the Supreme Court that such prohibitions [laws disadvantaging homosexuals] were hateful, homophobic, and un-American." In this case, Fischer did not use the term 'un-American' to attack marriage equality supporters but to describe "homosexual activists'" (Fischer) perception of prohibitions against same-sex marriage. In his opinion, the efforts of liberals to lure Supreme Court judges to their side was decidedly un-American. As a consequence, these two discourses, marriage equality and un-Americanism, were intertwined in his eyes.

In 2011, the fast food restaurant chain Chick-fil-A was sponsoring an anti-marriage-equality conference ("Chick-fil-A Sponsors"). This was not a singular event since over the years the company had donated millions of dollars to homophobic organizations (K. Taylor). In 2012, the company's COO, Dan Cathy, stated on Ken Coleman's radio show in regard to same-sex marriage: "As it relates to society in general, I think we are inviting

God's judgment on our nation when we shake our fist at him" (Cathy qtd. in "What Dan Cathy said"). In 2012, the Chick-fil-A controversy was one of the settings where marriage equality supporters and opponents antagonized each other. Advocates even found support among mayors from cities such as Chicago, Boston, and San Francisco. For instance, Chicago Mayor Rahm Emanuel declared that he did not want any Chick-fil-A restaurants in his city (O'Reilly). As a result, opponents of marriage equality were furious about the way liberals treated this company which was only standing up for traditional marriage. They believed such an act should not result in punishment by consumers in the United States. Bill O'Reilly commented on this as follows: "[T]he attacks on Chick-fil-A are un-American, and here's why. Gay marriage is not a civil right in the USA, and until the Supreme Court rules that it is, there is no bias case to be made against those who, in good conscience, oppose it." It would be interesting to know how Bill O'Reilly would have argued if gay marriage had already been a civil right in the United States in 2012. However, his agitation over the White House being lit in rainbow colors after the 2015 Supreme Court decision in *Obergefell v. Hodges* indicated that a constitutionally granted right to same-sex marriage did not change his stance (Gilman). In his statement as outlined above, he closely connected the American legal framework of marriage as a defining factor for what he considers un-American.

A surprising development in the Chick-fil-A controversy came when the company received support from an unexpected direction. R. Clarke Cooper, the executive director of the LGBT Republican organization Log Cabin Republicans, published an opinion piece in the *Huffington Post* in which he warned gay rights supporters that they should not become "the thought police, willing and able to use the power of the state to impose our will on oppressed social conservatives." Cooper believed that this behavior only played in the hands of those who wanted to portray Chick-fil-A as a martyr for traditional marriage and religious freedom. Cooper was especially disappointed by agents of government, for example mayors from various cities, because he disapproved of them discriminating against a company due to their political convictions. He wrote that driving the company out of business was "un-American, and when fellow conservatives are finally standing up and speaking out for marriage equality as consistent with the sober values of responsibility and commitment, splashing a popular American company with metaphorical chicken blood in protest is nothing less than friendly fire." The term 'un-American' was used by Cooper to draw a line between what was acceptable behavior in the quest for marriage equality and what crossed that line.

The debate on marriage equality also reached another segment of everyday nationalism and popular culture: the National Football League (NFL). Ahead of the 2012 presidential election, marriage equality became one of the fiercely debated issues in the election campaigns. There was scarcely a public figure, regardless of whether they were in politics, sports, or the entertainment industry, who did not announce their personal opinion on same-sex marriage and the option of a nationwide legalization. The NFL player Matt Birk from the Baltimore Ravens brought the conversation onto the football field with a comment published in the *Minneapolis Star-Tribune*. Worried about the long-term effects of gay marriage on society and the wellbeing of American children, he wrote: "The effects of no-fault divorce, adultery, and the nonchalant attitude toward marriage by some have done great harm to this sacred institution. . . . Marriage redefinition will affect the broader well-being of children and the welfare of society" (Birk qtd. in Hallowell). For Birk, children could only grow up to live happy and fulfilled lives if they had the chance to experience the love and care of both a mother and a father. Additionally, Birk also emphasized in his writing that he occasionally felt offended by marriage equality supporters since he believed that he was not allowed to freely express his opinion without being attacking in return. Therefore, he called such behavior "un-American" (Birk qtd. in Hallowell) since he had the impression that his right to free speech was often violated in this debate.

A few months before the *Obergefell v. Hodges* ruling, people in Utah were afraid that they would no longer be able to express their disapproval of marriage equality freely. Bill Duncan, Director of the Sutherland Institute's Center for Family and Society, was furious that supporters of the traditional definition of marriage were expected to just shut up and accept whatever the U.S. Supreme Court would decide was best for the nation: "That's really kind of a fundamentally un-American way of seeing the world. We think that everyone, regardless of whether the government ever agrees with their view, ought to be able to express that" (Duncan qtd. in Roche). As a consequence, the institute started a petition supporting traditional marriage that garnered more than 18.600 signatures and was then handed to Utah Governor Gary Herbert's office. The petition was the result of the U.S. Supreme Court taking the state's appeal of lower court rulings that struck down a Utah constitutional amendment restricting marriage to the union between a man and a woman (Roche). The emotions surrounding the debate were further exacerbated by former Governor Jon Huntsman Jr. declaring that marriage equality will most likely become the nation's reality in all states (Roche). As a consequence, the fear among gay marriage opponents grew that they would soon have to accept a new reality and integrate a more diverse idea of marriage into their concept of American nationalism increased in the highly conservative and religious state of Utah. The frequency with which people invoked the First Amendment to the Constitution and called gay marriage supporters un-American showed that opponents were becoming more and more desperate. Although freedom of speech was not infringed by a SCOTUS decision in favor of marriage equality, opponents felt threatened by the consequences, whether real or imagined, that would result from it.[74]

The future of freedom of speech and freedom of religion after a legalization of same-sex marriage concerned many opponents. The Family Research Council was one of the most popular anti-gay religious-fundamentalist activist groups whose members saw religious rights as endangered if the rights and protections for homosexual Americans were extended (Moreau). In order to prevent this from happening, Peter Sprigg, a senior fellow with the Family Research Council, wanted to outlaw homosexual behavior in the United States: "I think that the Supreme Court decision in Lawrence v. Texas which overturned the sodomy laws in this country was wrongly decided. I think there would be a place for criminal sanctions against homosexual behavior" (Sprigg qtd. in Mantyla). In an interview on a bill in Mississippi that would allow business owners to refuse service to people on the basis of their sexual orientation, Sprigg was very open about what he thought of gay Americans and their supporters. He repeatedly denounced gay rights activists as "un-American" because they wanted to punish people for holding traditional moral views and in regard to traditional moral views, those activists believed that the government should "do everything it can to wipe those views out of existence"

[74] In his dissent to the ruling in *Obergefell v. Hodges*, Justice Alito brought forward this fear of marriage equality opponents when he claimed that marriage equality becoming the law of the land could lead to a marginalization of conservative Americans: "I assume that those who cling to old beliefs will be able to whisper their thoughts in the recesses of their homes, but if they repeat those views in public, they will risk being labeled as bigots and treated as such by governments, employers, and schools" ("*Obergefell*" 6–7).

(Sprigg qtd. in Blue). Sprigg also objected to a bill which would allow gay Americans to unite with their foreign partners since he "would much prefer to export homosexuals from the United States than to import them into the United States" (Sprigg qtd. in Blue). Based on his radical comments, Sprigg was one of the most controversial fellows of the Family Research Council. He did not shy away from expressing his aversion to gay Americans, and he was fond of phrasing this antipathy in insults of un-Americanism. He concluded the interview with imputing to gay rights activists a crusade against Americans with traditional moral beliefs, in the course of which they did not refrain from discriminating against those who were in their way. "That's basically the point of view of the LGBT movement at this point in history," Sprigg declared. "It's shocking and it's un-American, it's contrary to our traditions, which are to protect the views of all people, including the people who agree with you and the people who disagree with you" (Sprigg qtd. in Blue). In regard to Sprigg's offensive language and his use of the term 'un-American,' the statements quoted above speak for themselves. Sprigg did not care about marriage equality or a potential redefinition of marriage as a single issue. He used this discourse as a platform to display a homophobic stance wrapped in rhetoric of concerns over the future of the American nation.

Legislation without Representation

In the aftermath of controversial civil rights cases such as *Obergefell v. Hodges*, Supreme Court judges increasingly faced accusations of being an activist court because they contributed to propelling progress for gay rights in the country with their rulings. Critics of the decision charged the judges with overstepping their jurisdiction by acting as policymakers who made decisions based on their personal moral convictions. As a consequence, opponents claimed that the court force-fed Americans certain cultural and social values and presented changes in traditional concepts of marriage and family as progress. Opponents insisted that marriage equality was only made possible through the so-called judicial activism of the majority opinion and not because a legal interpretation of the Fourteenth Amendment unequivocally granted that right.[75]

[75] In *Baker v. Vermont*, the majority opinion admitted that, despite deciding at the best of their knowledge, judges cannot always offer the best solution to an issue:

November 2003, Massachusetts: The ruling in *Goodridge v. Dept. of Public Health* was the first by a U.S. state court to hold that same-sex couples had the right to marry. Mary Bonauto, a lawyer working for the legal rights organization Gay & Lesbian Advocates & Defenders, argued the case on behalf of the plaintiffs before Massachusetts' Supreme Judicial Court. When the marriage equality debate was an issue all over the country in 2014, Bonauto was still the target of criticism from gay marriage opponents (T. Smith). One of her most vocal critics was Kris Mineau, president emeritus of the Massachusetts Family Institute. He accused Bonauto of not only adducing questionable legal arguments but also of employing on unfair practices during the trial: "She pressed forward on obviously a soft spot in the Massachusetts court and exploited it" (Mineau qtd. in T. Smith). According to Mineau, opening the institution of marriage to same-sex couples in Massachusetts was not the will of the people but a strategic combination of Bonauto's line of argument and the judges' inability to see that her arguments lacked merit. In Mineau's eyes, the ruling in *Goodridge v. Dept. of Public Health* was a perfect example of judicial legislation without representation (T. Smith). "With her creative genius, she was the catalyst that began this process, and now it's running willy-nilly through our nation, and I believe it's un-American," Mineau claimed (qtd. in T. Smith). "This is not the way that we live in a pluralistic society, where one side is absolutely shut down and marginalized" (Mineau qtd. in T. Smith). Mineau used the term 'un-American' in order to describe a process which had completely spiraled out of control since the plaintiffs' victory in Massachusetts. After outlining why Bonauto's practices were unacceptable, he concluded with the accusation that what happened in Massachusetts and afterwards was "un-American." Moreover, he expressed his consternation that the former majority in the debate, i. e., the opponents of marriage equality, had become the oppressed

> When a democracy is in moral flux, courts may not have the best or the final answers. Judicial answers may be wrong. They may be counterproductive even if they are right. Courts do best by proceeding in a way that is catalytic rather than preclusive, and that is closely attuned to the fact that courts are participants in the system of democratic deliberation.

This problem opens the doors to accusations of judicial activism (i. e., judges exercise a certain amount of judicial review and do not follow the words of the Constitution literally because they believe the interpretation of law needs to take societal changes into account).

and the new marginalized minority. He pointed to the United States' pluralistic society for which freedom of speech was fundamental (T. Smith). Thereby, he relied on the same line of argumentation that the gay rights movement had been utilizing in their fight for equality since the earliest days of the movement. As a result, Mineau accused Bonauto of un-Americanism because he needed a strong wording to make his increasingly marginalized voice heard (Mineau qtd. in T. Smith).

'Un-American' and 'un-constitutional' are two terms which became more frequently used in conjunction with one another by opponents after the ruling in favor of marriage equality. The constitutionality of the majority opinion was repeatedly questioned since some opponents could not believe that the traditional definition of marriage had now become a thing of the past. Disapproval of this development was also voiced by the former veteran Jerry McConnell in an opinion piece titled, "Five Grossly Un-American Supreme Court Justices Have Ruled Against Traditional Marriages." "The word 'family' as we and others around the world know it, will soon disappear from the daily lexicon of human beings. . . . At my age I have to wonder how soon this country will implode and wither away into a vast nothingness," he wrote. McConnell regarded the five judges of the majority opinion as unprofessional due to their unconstitutional ruling and judicial activism. If these were to become characteristic of the Supreme Court's work ethic, then *Obergefell v. Hodges* was only the first sign of the country's impending downward spiral in the eyes of McConnell. He repeatedly lashed out at these five Supreme Court judges and at one point even labeled them as the "un-Americans": "Already there is great turmoil and dissatisfaction in America over these five un-Americans who now welcome un-constitutional conduct favored by socio-communists around the world." McConnell not only labeled their behavior or thought as "un-American" but gave them the name "these five un-Americans." Furthermore, he drew parallels between their "un-constitutional conduct" and communism, which is extremely rare in today's usage of the term 'un-American' and is reminiscent of the investigations of the House Un-American Activities Committee.

Another uncommon usage of 'un-American' can be found in David Lampo's monograph *A Fundamental Freedom: Why Republicans, Conservatives, and Libertarians Should Support Gay Rights.* Although he was a vivid supporter of marriage equality and held that opponents' attitude needed to change with changing times, he was nevertheless critical about how this fight for greater equality was proceeding. In his book, Lampo argued that although conservatives needed to move on from the marriage equality debate along with the rest of the country, they might need more time to accept that society was transforming. Therefore, Lampo asked fellow gay rights supporters to be more patient with those who were struggling to acknowledge that American everyday nationalism was changing. Such a process would be long and strenuous and demanded extraordinary compassion and understanding on both sides (Lampo). Thus, he warned that "[t]rying to force-feed certain cultural and religious values to the American public, through legal sanctions and preferences, is both destined to fail and distinctly un-American." He condemned judicial activism as seen in *Obergefell* as the wrong approach. Real change would not come if it did not take place in people's hearts and minds but was forced upon them through court rulings (Lampo). Lampo believed that legislation without an overwhelming representation was more un-American than continuing to deny a minority of Americans the right to marry their loved one. Having a gay rights supporter who criticized the court ruling and described this legal victory for gay Americans as un-American was an extreme rarity.

When President Trump nominated Jeff Sessions as his Attorney General in 2017, supporters of gay rights were alarmed (Thompson). Described as an "outwardly racist, xenophobic, homophobic misogynist" (Stern, "Attorney General"), it was feared that Sessions' time as the head of the Department of Justice might turn into a nightmare for LGBT Americans. During his time as an attorney in Alabama, Jeff Sessions reportedly denounced the National Association for the Advancement of Colored People (NAACP) and the American Civil Liberties Union (ACLU) as "un-American" and "Communist-inspired" (Sessions qtd. in Wildman). According to a Justice Department employee who testified against him, Sessions allegedly stated that these nonprofit organizations "forced civil rights down the throats of people," and he degraded them as "un-American" since "they involve themselves in promoting un-American positions" (Session qtd. in Wildman). Jeff Sessions used the term 'un-American' extensively, especially when expressing his opinion of minorities, for whom he regularly demonstrated a lack of respect and even contempt. Furthermore, Sessions critiqued these nonprofit organizations for not acting in favor of, what he believed, was the interest of the majority (Wildman). The activism and influence of such organizations leads to legislation without representation, which could be seen in previous landmark civil rights cases. *Brown v. Board of Education* or *Roe v. Wade* were just two examples in which conservatives accused courts of judicial activism and judicial legislation without representation (Deming 272). Sessions was also known for accusing a white civil rights lawyer of being a "disgrace to his race" and for calling the Voting Rights Act a "piece of intrusive legislation" (Sessions qtd. in Wildman). With such statements in mind, Sessions' extensive use of the term 'un-American' was more drastic and offensive than examples by other marriage equality opponents. He did not shy away from expressing a highly controversial opinion, and the term 'un-American' was a rhetorical tool used to add even more scorn to his claims. Therefore, Sessions is a perfect example for how the context of the utterance and the speaker dramatically influence the usage of the term, both in regard to the offensiveness and the severity of the accusation.

Tony Perkins, president of the conservative organization Family Research Council was alarmed by the success of same-sex couples in courts in 2013. In an interview on *CBS* "Face the Nation," he warned against the judicial activism that played a crucial role in U.S. Supreme Court's decision on the appeal in the case *Hollingsworth v. Perry*: "Many Americans are upset with the activism of this court. Essentially what the court has done is that . . . they've dragged 'We the People' from behind the wheel of this republic and they've carjacked the nation and this never ends up good. . . . This is not good for our republic" (Perkins). Perkins compared the court's ruling in favor of gay couples in *Hollingsworth v. Perry* to the violent crime of carjacking in order to stress how helpless the named appellant, the conservative California Senate Member Dennis Hollingsworth, and his like-minded supporters felt after the U.S. Supreme Court decided to pave the way for a future redefinition of marriage. For Perkins, legislation without representation in important civil rights cases, as for instance *Hollingsworth v. Perry*, posed a serious threat to the prosperity of the nation. "Same-sex marriage [was] a pandora's box" and constituted an attack on the "natural definition of a man and a woman" (Perkins). This coerced the American people into living with inestimable consequences of a future redefinition of marriage and the redefinition of American values that came with it. When asked if he could elaborate further on the implications of this ruling on opponents of same-sex marriage, he referred to cases of private businesses being forced to act against their personal set of values and beliefs: "We're already seeing bakers and florists and photographers forced to participate in same-sex marriages under the threat of law and in some cases even jail. I can't think of anything that's more un-American than that" (Perkins). America touts itself as the land of the free; therefore, it was highly un-American to force people to act against their beliefs under penalty of legal consequences. This was especially relevant in regard to religious beliefs since these are prominently protected by the Freedom of Religion clause of the First Amendment to the United States Constitution. If it was a question of whether an anti-discrimination act or whether the First Amendment should prevail, the answer was obvious for opponents of marriage equality. As a result, any court decision infringing upon First Amendment rights was un-American, unconstitutional, and an act of judicial activism of liberal judges in the eyes of marriage equality opponents.

Religious Objections and First Amendment Rights

As the nationwide legalization of same-sex marriage became more and more likely over the years, especially after the Supreme Court ruling *United States v. Windsor* in 2013, evangelical churches and organizations of the Christian right increased their efforts in their fight against marriage equality. According to a study conducted by the Pew Research Center in 2013, Americans were less accepting of homosexuality than other Western countries. The fact that half of the Americans consider religion as very important to their lives was one of the weightiest reasons for that (Horowitz). In a survey from 2003, the Pew Research Center found out that 82% of religious Americans said gay marriage went against their religious beliefs and more than half of them said the same about civil unions although those would grant same-sex couples some legal rights without redefining marriage ("Religious Beliefs"). Furthermore, polls found that if clergy addressed the topic of homosexuality, their congregation was more likely to have unfavorable views of homosexuals in general ("Religious Beliefs"). Americans with strong religious beliefs were the fiercest opponents of same-sex marriage advocates, and they were also least open to persuasion. Religious Americans feared that their First Amendment rights would clash with the interests of same-sex couples, which increasingly caused them to accuse supporters of un-Americanism.[76]

[76] Mark Movsesian, Professor of Contract Law and the Director of the Center for Law and Religion at St. John's University School of Law, was highly concerned about the evolution of these conflicts between freedom of religion and the protection of minority interests in the United States. When looking

Among those calling same-sex marriage un-American was Roy Moore, then Chief Justice of the Alabama Supreme Court (Ashtari). Moore is one of the most controversial figures in Alabama's judiciary and politics. During his time as the Chief Justice, he was removed from office in 2003 for installing a Ten Commandments monument that he had designed in the state courthouse. In 2016, he was suspended for ordering Alabama's probate judges not to comply with federal court orders on same-sex marriage (Ashtari; C. Robertson). The former Chief Justice frequently gave speeches on the correct interpretation of the United States Constitution and considered himself an expert in this field. However, many of his remarks demonstrate that he fails to understand that the separation of church and state is one of the cornerstones of the American legal philosophy and democracy. In a speech from May 2014, he advocated for a new constitution which would reflect the "reverent morality" of "God's institution" (Moore qtd. in Ashtari). If Americans did not start to realize that they were violating God's plan for them with their un-American behavior of granting gay couples rights, the American nation was destined to fail. He was convinced that same-sex marriage was "not about two men getting married or two women, it's about destroying an institution ordained of God" (Moore qtd. in Ashtari). Outspoken marriage equality opponents were celebrated for such claims by likeminded Americans. "We need more like him" (@SamCoyle1), was one of the responses on *Twitter* after Moore's state-

at polls on the approval rate of the *Obergefell* decision, they turned out to be less positive than the celebrations of the decision across the United States might suggest. He quoted two polls, one from *Associated Press* and the other from *The Washington Post.* They showed a disapproval rate of 41 percent and 44 percent respectively (Movesian). In the polls published by *Associated Press*, Movsesian also noticed that religious reasons played a substantial role in the objection to marriage equality because religious Americans were worried that the free exercise of religion might be restricted or at least affected. In addition, the polls revealed an alarming partisan divide. Democrats prioritize gay rights over religious freedom whereas Republicans do the opposite (Movsesian). Movsesian hypothesized that the "political consensus on the value of religion is breaking down" which could lead to an increase in partisan divide in the United States. He described this as "a clear trend: Religious freedom is becoming a partisan issue." As a professor working at the interface between law and religion, he was troubled by this development: "That's a very bad thing for America. You might even say it's un-American" (Movsesian).

ment was published by news media. This rhetoric was characteristic of anti-marriage equality statements given in a religious context. In the course of this argumentation, the political right ignored that separation of church and state was also an American ideal. If liberals uttered their concerns in this regard, the religious right tended to dismiss their claims "as anti-God, and thus un-American" (Friedman and Lithwick).

Religious Americans feared that they would have to pay the price for the liberalization trend in the country which led to an increasing number of states allowing same-sex marriage. The case of Masterpiece Cakeshop in Colorado,[77] in which the owner was forced to bake a wedding cake for a gay couple, was exemplary of the situation that Tony Perkins described as "un-American" because religious Americans were forced to act against their beliefs (Perkins). Perkins was not the only one who relied on this lexical choice in order to express his dissent in regard to how Christian Americans were treated in the United States as the marriage equality movement continued to gain momentum. Nicolle Martin, lawyer for the Christian baker and cakeshop owner Jack Phillips, was in disbelief over how the state's Civil Rights Commission could rule that her client could not refuse to bake a cake for a homosexual couple (Blair). In regard to the wedding cake, she explained that a wedding cake was "special, it's an iconic symbol of marriage and it has been for several hundred years, and because it says something, it's protected under the First Amendment" (Martin qtd. in Blair). This line of argumentation is debatable. However, Martin had no doubt that the majority of Americans agreed with her reasoning:

> Indeed, I believe we can all agree that the First Amendment is the very cornerstone to our freedoms as Americans. It is part of who we are in our fabric, and for the government and the state of Colorado to come in and

[77] This conflict ultimately resulted in the United States Supreme Court case *Masterpiece Cakeshop v. Colorado Civil Rights Commission*. The court ruled in a 7–2 decision in favor of the owner of Masterpiece Cakeshop and held that in its treatment of the plaintiff, the Colorado Civil Rights Commission "violated the State's duty under the First Amendment not to base laws or regulations on hostility to a religion or religious viewpoint" (United States, Supreme Court, "*Masterpiece*" 16). The Colorado Civil Rights Commission had originally found that the bakery had discriminated against the couple concerned under the Colorado's anti-discrimination law (United States, Supreme Court, Syllabus "*Masterpiece*" 1).

> demand that Jack create expression for something that conflicts with his deeply held beliefs – it's offensive and it's un-American. (Martin qtd. in Blair)

In her usage of the term 'un-American,' Martin drew a connection between an opposition to marriage equality, which was based on her client's deeply held religious beliefs, and the legal basis given by the First Amendment which she believed protected and supported her client's decision to refuse the gay couple's order. For Martin, being American was equitable to respecting religious values and respecting the First Amendment's promise of freedom of religion and religious expression.

In an opinion piece, Damon Linker, senior correspondent at *The Week*, worried about religious freedom in the United States after *Obergefell* and called for a "parallel movement [that] must accompany the continued struggle for gay rights." Linker suggests: "Every proposed expansion of state and federal anti-discrimination law to cover homosexuality must include explicit carveouts regarding same-sex marriage for churches and religiously affiliated institutions, as well as for small businesses owned by conservative Christians." Linker's writing stood out from those of other opponents of same-sex marriage. He was not even a fierce opponent of gay rights and marriage equality, and he was happy to celebrate the legal success of his gay friends. In a balanced introduction, he congratulated advocates on their victory in front of the United States Supreme Court but at the same time raised his concerns about the future of religious freedom:

> Either it's a glorious triumph for equality and an irrefutable demonstration that the arc of history does indeed bend toward justice – or else it's a galling example of judicial overreach, the end of public Christianity in America, and the start of an era that will be marked by unprecedented persecution of traditionalist Christians. Why can't it be both?

Linker tried to understand arguments and worries on both sides of the debate, which protected him from the accusation of not listening to the other party or being unreflecting. Despite all the insight and sympathy for marriage equality supporters, he nevertheless had one concern he was adamant about: measures to protect religious freedom without having to cry for a repeal of *Obergefell v. Hodges*. What he had in mind were situations where Christians were forced to act against their deeply held beliefs despite there being many other businesses available that would not have objected to making a cake for a same-sex ceremony. In order to make his point comprehensible, he gave his readers an example:

> Think of a Muslim woman forced to remove her hijab in all public places – or an Orthodox Jew compelled to open his shop on the Sabbath. Instead of the historic American norm of allowing broad leeway for religious free exercise, conservative religious believers would, in effect, be forced to withdraw into their homes and churches, coerced into keeping their faith cordoned off in those purely private spaces. To call this un-American is the least that one could say about it. (Linker)

As many others before him, Damon Linker used the term 'un-American' to describe a form of behavior he simply could not agree with because he believed it contradicted the values the American nation was built upon. However, his opinion piece was an example of how the verbal framing of one's personal opinion tremendously affected the degree to which this rhetoric was perceived as offensive. Accordingly, Linker tried to look at this problem from various angles, demonstrating to supporters as well as opponents of marriage equality that his opinion was the result of careful deliberation and an attempt to find a compromise acceptable to both sides.

The case of the county clerk Kim Davis, who refused to comply with federal law and accept the implications of *Obergefell v. Hodges*, has already been analyzed from the perspective of marriage equality supporters who called her behavior un-American. However, opponents of same-sex marriage used the same choice of words to make their opinion on this dilemma heard. Congressman Thomas Massie, Republican Representative for Kentucky, was one conservative politician who was quick to jump to her defense:

> The spurious and un-American way in which the law, and therefore her job description, abruptly changed mid-term gives Mrs. Davis a moral, if not legal, defense for her actions until her next election and until a legitimate rewriting of Kentucky's marriage laws occurs during a legislative session with elected officials. (Massie qtd. in Shesgreen)

Senator and former presidential candidate Ted Cruz also stood up for Kim Davis and was outraged by Davis being jailed for defying court orders: "Today, judicial lawlessness crossed into judicial tyranny. . . . Today, for the first time ever, the government arrested a Christian woman for living according to her faith. This is wrong. This is not America" (Cruz qtd. in Chalfant). Both Massie and Cruz did not believe in the legality of the ruling in *Obergefell v. Hodges* with Cruz even calling the consequences of the ruling “judicial tyranny” (Cruz qtd. in Chalfant). Although Cruz did not explicitly use the term ‘un-American,’ this was nevertheless what was understood by him calling the situation “not America” (Cruz qtd. in Chalfant). The headline of the article written about his comments was “Ted Cruz Blasts Jailing of Christian Kentucky Clerk as Un-American” (Chalfant). Cruz’ choice to claim that this was “not America” was automatically rephrased with the word ‘un-American.’

Among opponents of a change in law regarding marriage, the topic of slavery was a prominent point brought up in debates on marriage equality. Pastor Holliday from the Victory Baptist Church explained why he believed the civil rights movement could not be likened to the fight for marriage equality: “We all know that the 14th Amendment was made because Black folk were considered as property. Gays have never been considered as property” (Holliday qtd. in Tashman, “Anti-Gay Pastor”). Although he was correct in his argument that homosexual Americans were never treated as property, gay rights supporters nevertheless struggled to understand how this line of argument could justify a ban on marriage equality (Tashman, “Anti-Gay Pastor”). Like Bryan Fischer, Bishop Samuel Smith of the Apostolic World Christian Fellowship feared the end of American society and prosperity if marriage equality became accepted in the United States: “Every once in a while, the homosexual agenda makes an effort to redefine morality, but history tells us, that every culture that has embraced a homosexual culture has suffered decadence, depravity, and decline” (Smith qtd. in Tashman, “Anti-Gay Pastor”). The fear that the American people would be doomed if marriage equality continued its triumph in state after state was instilled in many opponents’ system of beliefs. The accusations published by Pastor Holliday and Pastor Smith were part of a larger initiative of a nonprofit public interest law firm and several African American Christian leaders. United by a common interest, they filed an amicus brief in order to influence upcoming court rulings on same-sex marriage (“A Game Changer”). Richard Thompson, President and Chief Counsel of the Thomas More Law Center, explained their ambition as follows: “In its briefs, the Law Center reflects the voice of a majority of African-Americans that discrimination because of one’s sexual preference is not the same thing as racial discrimination and that tradition and morality should not be discarded as a basis of the law” (Thompson qtd. in “A Game Changer”). This example proves that legal interpretations of the Fourteenth Amendment and its Equal Protection Clause were as varied as positions on marriage equality. Sharing a history of discrimination and lack of equal rights did not result in all African Americans supporting or even tolerating the gay rights movement's quest for marriage equality. Much rather, the African American community, which has a large percentage of frequent congregants, tended to present itself as hostile and, at times, homophobic towards gay Americans (Wallsten). The efforts of same-sex marriage supporters to win African Americans' voice due to their shared history of discrimination was often in vain. Although the amicus brief first and foremost addressed African American parishioners, the African American religious community also realized that they needed to speak to a broader audience. Consequently, Pastor Moss tried to appeal to all Americans regardless of race when he added to the brief: "The American Revolution had taxation without representation and we're going to have marriage legislation without representation. It's un-American and all Americans should stand up against it" (Moss qtd. in "A Game Changer"). With their amicus brief, the pastors attempted to reach their audience by framing their accusations of un-Americanism around several contexts: the doom of the American people, a lack of representation due to judicial activism, and the religious feelings of many Americans ("A Game Changer").

D Conclusion

The road to marriage equality in the United States required a great deal of persistence and stamina since the first decades were marked by disappointments and setbacks. *Baker v. Vermont* and *Goodridge v. Department of Public Health* were the beginning of a step-by-step reconceptualization of American everyday nationalism. Gradually, the gay rights movement gained a foothold in the United States and became a force to be reckoned with at the table of national sociocultural discourse.

In the debate over marriage equality ahead of *Obergefell*, supporters often clashed with conservative Americans over what was considered un-American. Goldman and Brewer see one of the many problems in the discourse over equal marriage rights in the very different framing of the parties' respective claims. For example, marriage equality opponents frame their argumentation on egalitarian principles and frequently appeal to the nation's founding ideal of equality (105). However, the problem is, Goldman and Brewer argue, that "many – perhaps most – Americans do not see it as an equality issue. They simply do not make the connection between the principle, which they cherish, and the policy. Instead, they see gay marriage as an issue that has to do with their moral beliefs and their feelings towards gays" (120). Gay marriage opponents tend to rely strongly on the frame of morality and tradition in their argumentation. Although the number of Americans seeing same-sex marriage as an equality issue has most certainly increased enormously since Goldman and Brewer's study in 2006, the problem they describe nevertheless still applies to a significant number of marriage equality opponents.

Charges of un-Americanism are a powerful oratorical device which grabs attention and helps people secure their claims, as in the case of marriage equality supporters. The term 'un-American' is a highly popular lexical choice when force needs to be added to a statement and when the speaker would otherwise struggle to be heard. As charges of un-Americanism are not only a powerful but also a confrontational tactic, it is usually an effective means of attracting public attention to one's argument. In addition to the power of such accusations, the term 'un-American' is deeply rooted within American history and discourse, and its use underlines that the point of contestation is ultimately an American issue that entails a negotiation over American nationalism. However, the choice to include the term 'un-American' in one's speech act can be highly problematic, in particular due to the rhetoric's extreme firepower. At times, the blast radius of such accusations can go beyond their intended target and have unexpected repercussions. The usage of the term 'un-American,' which differentiates between insiders and outsiders, often severely complicates the process of finding a solution or a compromise as fronts harden. As Simon Hall warns, the insult of un-Americanism can turn issues "into fundamental questions about the nature, character and meaning of the republic itself. Raising the political and rhetorical stakes in this way makes compromise and pragmatism more difficult, and perhaps encourages a more divisive (and at times bad-tempered) political culture" ("Americanism" 1126). Consequently, the usage of charges of un-Americanism should be considered carefully, especially in conflicts which revolve around such highly volatile topics as American nationalism and national identity.

Chapter V

V Marriage Equality in Court

A Legislation without Representation

Opinions of federal and state courts and the respective dissents do usually not receive much attention from the public at large. However, an in-depth analysis of *United States v. Windsor* and *Obergefell v. Hodges* is revealing of the interconnectedness of the marriage equality discourse with ideas of nationalism. It discloses what causes marriage equality supporters and opponents to rely on the rhetoric of un-Americanism in order to express their dissent of the other party's stance on that issue. Furthermore, examining the judges' concerns and reasoning provides insight into the nature of this debate and how it was deliberated not only inside the courtroom but also by the public at large. The argumentation of the minority and the majority mirrored the concerns and ideological lines of the American people outside of the Supreme Court. Whereas the public at large often struggled to precisely conceptualize and formulate their line of argument and therefore easily fell back on substitute expressions such as 'un-American,' the Supreme Court judges were more experienced at getting to the heart of a point of difference and explicitly verbalizing it. Consequently, a study of the dissenting opinions reveals the problems and moot points of the ruling which eventually led to insults of un-Americanism. However, before such an analysis of the opinion of the court and the accompanying dissenting opinions is possible, the phenomenon of 'judicial activism' needs to be addressed in order to allow for a full understanding of the argumentation raised in the judicial opinions in *Windsor* and *Obergefell*. The accusation that the majority opinion did not shy away from judicial activism can be found in all of the dissenting opinions and was also frequently raised by marriage equality opponents as the analysis in chapter IV.C demonstrated.

Judicial activism, legislation without representation, or five un-American judges were just some of the reproaches that were used by marriage equality opponents after the United States Supreme Court ruled in favor of same-sex couples in the two aforementioned landmark rulings (e. g., McConnell, Wildman, Perkins). After in particular *Obergefell*, many opponents were left in disbelief that a 5–4 majority in the Supreme Court could suddenly and radically change the definition of marriage in this country. They had been full of hope that Judge Kennedy, who was often the swing vote in civil rights cases, would decide to uphold the traditional idea of marriage and not join Justices Bader Ginsburg, Sotomayor, Breyer, and Kagan in their liberal stance on this issue. As a result, conservative politicians, commentators, and advocacy groups were quick to condemn the ruling of the United States Supreme Court and demanded that *Obergefell v. Hodges* be repealed immediately since it was un-American and unconstitutional to its core (Hooper, Flory). Those who raised the charge of judicial activism did not believe that marriage equality was rooted in the United States Constitution. Consequently, they claimed that such a decision was the act of liberal judges who wished to impose their personal moral convictions on the public at large (Perkins). In the eyes of marriage equality opponents, those judges showed no respect for the history and tradition of marriage. By acting not only as legal interpreters but as policymakers in the form of an activist court, opponents believed that the majority opinion had clearly overstepped their jurisdiction. Tremendous changes such as redefining marriage need to be considered in all their bearings and should be a decision made by the whole American nation, not just five individuals who made their ruling according to the conviction that the Constitution grants same-sex couples the right to marry due to their liberal and progressive viewpoint (McConnell). Therefore, making marriage equality the law of the land should have been in the hands of the American people or at least their elected legislators. For many marriage equality opponents, the ruling in favor of same-sex couples was an example of judicial activism.

Definition, History, and Conflict

'Judicial activism' is a term as contested, uncertain, and ever-changing as the term 'un-American.' "Some scholars have suggested that in its present state, 'judicial activism' is virtually an empty term. They rightly point out that by itself, the label carries little more than a pejorative term" (Kmiec 144). *Black's Law Dictionary*, the leading American law dictionary which is cited in U.S. Supreme Court cases, defines judicial activism as "a philosophy of judicial decision-making whereby judges allow their personal views about public policy, among other factors, to guide their decisions, usually with the suggestion that adherents of this philosophy tend to find constitutional violations and are willing to ignore precedent" (Garner 850). The decisive components of this definition are that the judges concerned give enormous weight to personal convictions, and, as a result, they are willing to ignore legal precedents.[78] This was exactly the charge that was raised against the majority opinion in *Obergefell v. Hodges*. Critics claimed that Judges Kennedy, Bader Ginsburg, Kagan, Sotomayor, and Breyer acted on the basis of their personal views about public policy. If true, this landmark court case would be an example of judicial activism. However, a conclusion should not be drawn so easily since the debate needs to be assessed from various perspectives in order to reach a well-conceived judgment of the situation.[79] Judicial activism has always been approached from various perspectives and many scholars have tried to coin a commonly accepted definition over the years. However, interpretations of the term are as diverse as the legal schools and trends trying to influence the prevailing understanding of judicial activism. The fact that this term is not only widely used in a scholarly or professional legal context but also by the public at large has only contributed to the ambiguity of the term. Just as the accusation of un-Americanism, the charge of judicial activism has become a self-enhancing and fast-selling rhetoric in American public discourse.

Textualism vs. judicial review, formalism vs. realism, judicial restraint vs. judicial activism: all these antagonisms describe the same conflict between two approaches of judicial behavior which are diametrically opposed to one another. Of course, there is also a grey area, and many judges

78 Whether this is actually true is subject to interpretation. With a document as old as the United States Constitution, there are undeniably benefits of a certain level of judicial review or even judicial activism. In many cases, the interpretation of law must change with changing times since society has evolved over decades. Among defenders of a literal reading of the Constitution, the overall attitude towards judicial activism tends to be sceptical.

79 Although *Black's Law Dictionary* might be the leading law dictionary in the United States, it is not the only source that offers a definition of the term 'judicial activism.' This makes an evaluation of the term even more challenging, as Keenan D. Kmiec points out in his article "The Origin and Current Meanings of 'Judicial Activism'": "Ironically, as the term has become more commonplace, its meaning has become increasingly unclear. This is so because 'judicial activism' is defined in a number of disparate, even contradictory, ways; scholars and justices recognize this problem, yet persist in speaking about the concept without defining it" (1443).

would rather position themselves somewhere along this continuum than on either end of it. Defenders of judicial activism argue that in many cases, it is a legitimate form of judicial review, and that the interpretation of the law must change with changing times. In order to understand the conflict between judicial activism and judicial restraint, it is important to examine the latter, although it is plagued by as much uncertainty and confusion as the former. Richard A. Posner calls the term judicial self-restraint a "chameleon" (520) but tries to narrow it down by listing three aspects which can define it:

> (1) [J]udges apply law, they don't make it . . . ; (2) judges defer to a very great extent to decisions by other officials – appellate judges defer to trial judges and administrative agencies, and all judges to legislative and executive decisions . . . ; (3) judges are *highly* reluctant to declare legislative or executive action unconstitutional. . . . (521)

Posner himself is an advocate of judicial restraint. Nevertheless, he acknowledges that some judicial review is necessary because judicial decision making is a highly complex process:

> Justices usually are competent lawyers, but rarely more; judicial decisions can be rich in unintended consequences; the scope of the Constitution is vast and the Justices operate on limited information; because there are no sensible algorithmic methods of deciding difficult cases, most constitutional decisions have only weak claims to objective validity; the parts of the Constitution that generate litigation at the Supreme Court level general to be directive; the issues presented in constitutional cases tend to be both emotional and momentous and the decisions resolving them inescapably reflect the Justices' personal values, psychology, background, peer pressures, political anxieties, professional experiences, ideological inclinations, and other non-legalistic factors, often operating unconsciously; unrestrained courts produce unrestrained backlash. (553–54)

Posner admits that the aspects leading to court rulings are countless and often not even within the realm of consciousness of these judges. Though it is impossible to be completely objective, judicial restraint should be heeded especially in landmark court cases since "unrestrained courts produce unrestrained backlash" (554).

The late United States Supreme Court Justice Antonin Scalia, one of the nine judges in *Windsor* and *Obergefell*, was one of the fiercest defenders of judicial restraint and even textualism at times. In his 2012 book *Reading Law: The Interpretation of Legal Texts*, Scalia assails judicial activism and what he and his co-author Bryan A. Garner describe as "the judiciary incrementally tak[ing] control of larger and larger swaths of territory that ought to be settled legislatively. It used to be said that judges do not make law – they simply apply it" (Scalia and Garner 5). Critics of the decision in *Obergefell* claim that the opinion of the court is the result of activist judges who overstepped their jurisdiction and thereby contributed to the propulsion of progress in the country with their liberal ruling.[80] It comes as no surprise that one of these five judges, Ruth Bader Ginsburg, assessed the situation in a completely different manner. In her opinion, the court was merely following the change that had already taken place in society, not vice versa. Furthermore, in an August 2013 interview with *The New York Times*, Justice Ruth Bader Ginsburg also invoked judicial activism, speaking of the current court and its rather conservative leanings: "If it's measured in terms of read-

80 One of the most prominent points of criticism towards the United States Supreme Court and its judges is that this court is an elitist court and, in particular when it comes to civil rights cases such as *Obergefell*, many critics claim that the judges are so removed from the day-to-day lives of ordinary American citizens that it is beyond their capabilities to decide on such far-reaching issues. Michael J. Klarman elaborated on this problem as follows:

> [J]udges may occasionally misread public opinion because they are better educated and more affluent than the average American. Their elite socioeconomic status predisposes judges to hold views on certain cultural issues that are more liberal than those of the mainstream. Judges are part not only of the cultural elite but of a distinctive subculture – the legal elite – which tends to be even more liberal than the general public on issues such as gender equality and gay equality. (*Closet* 170)

Attitudes on same-sex marriage and gay rights in general correlate strongly with people's education, social, and economic status. The more well-off Americans are in these categories, the more likely they are to be accepting and supportive of their fellow homosexual Americans. Of course, Supreme Court judges do extraordinary well in all of these categories. The fact that there was only a 5–4 majority in *Obergefell v. Hodges* was probably also because many in the minority opinion believed that the court should not even decide on that case since there is no basis for same-sex marriage in the Constitution or in precedents, regardless of if they personally would have supported marriage equality.

iness to overturn legislation, this is one of the most activist courts in history" (Bader Ginsburg, "Court"). In this quote, she was referring to her disillusionment regarding the ruling in the landmark United States Supreme Court case *Shelby County v. Holder* in which a conservative majority struck down the core of the Voting Rights Act of 1965 (United States, Supreme Court, "*Shelby County v. Holder*" 24). Whereas Justice Bader Ginsburg saw judicial activism on the side of the conservative wing of the court, critics of the ruling in *Obergefell v. Hodges* would most certainly not agree.

When attempting to discern what judicial activism entails or constitutes, Theodor Olson, solicitor general under George W. Bush and marriage equality advocate, also voiced his opinion on that subject. In an interview on *Fox News Sunday* about *Hollingsworth v. Perry*, a case for same-sex marriage he had successfully litigated, he was convinced that "most people use[d] the term 'judicial activism' to explain decisions that they [did]n't like" (Olson in interview with Wallace). Supreme Court Justice Anthony Kennedy agreed with Olson's assessment and claimed: "An activist court is a court that makes a decision you don't like" (Kennedy qtd. in Associated Press). Kennedy's definition of an activist court espouses the idea that such an accusation is often made by a minority opinion that cannot accept defeat. However, his wording also indicated that courts are confronted with this complaint after having heard cases which are controversial and are more likely to result in a ruling that parts of the American people struggle to accept.

Judicial Activism, Un-Americanism, and Everyday Nationalism

There are striking similarities between allegations of judicial activism and un-Americanism. As mentioned earlier, both terms are impossible to clearly define. They are equally controversial and contested, and interpretations of the terms are as varied as political perspectives. Both terms are primarily used in the context of power structures, when a certain interest group wishes to push their demands forward. Despite the changing and often competing interpretations that seem to lie in the nature of these terms, the intention behind its use tends to be the same. Accusations of un-Americanism and accusations of judicial activism are both reactions of dissent and opposition to social developments in the United States. They are a form of resistance to unpopular changes in law, especially changes which opponents believe alter the general course of American nationalism. Both charges function in the same manner in the discourse on marriage equality. Therefore, a look at allegations of judicial activism regarding the court cases concerned provides a better understanding of how insults of un-Americanism work in the proxy war of marriage equality.

Opponents who raised these charges often feel overwhelmed by how quickly the country was changing regarding gay rights and believed that marriage equality was a form of progress for which the nation was not yet ready. Consequently, this created the impression that the judges were engaging in forced identity formation. Therefore, opponents of the rulings in *Windsor* and *Obergefell* attacked the majority opinion for force-feeding the American people certain liberal morals and values (Lampo). Some felt that, as a result of the ruling, they were obligated to act against their personal beliefs, tolerate marriage equality, and, in the case of some civil servants or businesses, comply with a ruling which had resulted from this act of judicial activism (Linker). The motivations behind charges of judicial activism were often similar to those which led to accusations of un-Americanism. A feeling of powerlessness, of not having a voice in the conceptualization of American nationalism, and of not being heard without serious allegations against those in charge.

Real progress and change are hard to achieve if they do not take place in people's hearts and minds but are forced upon them through the ruling of an unelected court. Furthermore, Supreme Court rulings usually lead to an abrupt end of a debate (Roberts, "*Obergefell*" 27). As soon as the highest court in the country has decided on a case, there is little ordinary Americans can do if they wish to re-open a debate. Supreme Court judges walk a precariously fine line if they decide to hear a controversial civil rights case. "Despite the potential to act as a catalyst for social change, the Supreme Court takes a substantial risk whenever it does so. If it misjudges public opinion, it may take an action that attracts serious backlash" (Deming 297). If judicial activism is not a purely empty charge but has some truth to it, this could increase accusations of un-Americanism. As revealed by Fontana and Braman, controversial court cases can significantly contribute to polarization in the country (735). The higher the level of polarization, the more likely Americans are to condemn their opponents and their opponents' behavior as un-American. This insult is considered the ultimate weapon since it attacks Americans at the core of who they are and poses the question of who is worthy of being an American. It puts their national identity up for debate.

Judicial activism has an impact on concepts of everyday nationalism in the United States. It is irrelevant for this book on American nationalism if a ruling such as in *Obergefell* was de facto influenced by the judicial activism of the majority opinion. What matters is that people believed, mistakenly or not, that judicial activism was a deciding factor and that, as a direct result, they were confronted with the consequences of a decision they did not support.[81] The impact this has on opponents of a ruling regarding their self-concept as Americans and their (un)willingness to accept changes to American everyday nationalism should not be underestimated. Through *Windsor*, *Obergefell*, or comparable landmark civil rights cases, the United States Supreme Court as the highest representative of the country's legal branch shapes what American everyday nationalism will look like in the future. It decides on the sociocultural profile of the country and who is to be included in the prevailing concept of Americanism or un-Americanism. What makes judicial activism so problematic is that it provides a platform for more extreme nationalist groups to address the anger of the people who felt unheard. In the case of liberal and progressive rulings as in *Obergefell*, adamant opponents see their understanding of everyday nationalism better represented by groups of the

81 The criticism levelled against courts which rule on cases involving same-sex marriage and their judicial activism does not start with the rendition of judgement and some Americans probably not being content with the outcome of a case. The actual point of contestation, which is closely connected to the issue of judicial activism, is the question if courts should even accept such cases. "[T]here is widespread disagreement about whether courts can or should rule for same-sex marriage rights given their institutional limitations, their counter-majoritarian role, and the possibility of violent backlash, among other reasons" (Gerstmann 217). Many Americans, and some Supreme Court justices among them, argue that same-sex marriage does not lie within the jurisdiction of the court but needs to be addressed in a legislative manner. Such a decision must be made by the American people or their elected representatives and not by nine judges who happen to have been appointed to the Supreme Court by the President of the United States at the time of a vacancy. Courts may not create new law as they please. In addition, many critics argue that judicial activism is also not an appropriate method for dealing with legal uncertainties such as posed by the question of the constitutionality of same-sex marriage simply because there are no specific answers in the United States Constitution and American legal history lacks precedents. Therefore, such uncertainties need to be addressed by the legislative and not the judicial branch. Only then would the American democracy function in a healthy way, according to critics of judicial activism.

political right. This is not the case with all opponents; however, the election of President Trump and the rise of white-nationalist and right-wing groups in the United States suggests that such a correlation cannot be dismissed as inconsequential (Hawley 3).

B *United States v. Windsor*: An Analysis

When Thea Spyer proposed to Edie Windsor with a diamond brooch in 1967, the two women would never have thought that they would be able to marry one day. Similarly, they could not have anticipated that they would become key figures in the fight for marriage equality in the United States. The couple first met at a restaurant in New York City in 1963 (Gray). Before her relationship with Spyer, Windsor had married a man since homophobia was so ubiquitous in the 1950s that she wished to conform to societal standards in order to avoid being a target. However, the couple divorced within a year of marriage, after Windsor admitted to him that she longed to be with women (Gray). Thea Spyer was from a wealthy Dutch family that managed to escape the Holocaust just before the Nazis reached Amsterdam. Dr. Spyer was described as a dedicated psychologist, as well as an excellent violinist and dancer (Gray). After the engagement, the couple continued to remain silent about their relationship. Support for same-sex couples was practically non-existent at that time. Consequently, making their engagement public would have likely resulted in detrimental consequences for their careers as well as their private lives. However, over time, they became increasingly active in various gay rights organizations, first by supporting them financially and later as participating advocates (Gray). It was a step-by-step coming out process for the couple.

In 1977, their lives changed tremendously when Spyer was diagnosed with multiple sclerosis. Windsor, who was one of the first female senior systems programmers at the IT company IBM, left the firm to become a full-time caregiver for her fiancée and dedicated more of her time to gay rights activism (McFadden). In 1996, the Clinton administration signed the Defense of Marriage Act (DOMA) which in Section 3 defined marriage as a union between a man and a woman for federal purposes (United States, Congress, "*Defense of Marriage Act*").[82] Back then, it did not have a substantial effect on same-sex couples, since marriage had

[82] The definition of marriage in DOMA Section 3 reads as follows:

> In determining the meaning of any Act of Congress, or of any ruling, regulation, or interpretation of the various administrative bureaus and agencies of the United States, the word 'marriage' means only a legal union between one man and one woman as husband and wife, and the word

not been within reach. After Spyer suffered from a heart attack in 2002 and received a poor prognosis for her heart condition in 2007, the couple decided they would travel to Canada in order to get married there. Same-sex marriage was legalized in Canada in 2003, and their marriage was later recognized by the state of New York after a court decision. This trip to Toronto was an enormous challenge since Spyer's multiple sclerosis had left her quadriplegic; however, they eventually completed the journey with the help of friends (Frank 250). Their wedding was announced in *The New York Times*, a step which they would never have thought possible when they first met at a West Village Restaurant in 1965 ("Thea Spyer and Edith Windsor").

The Beginning of the Fight against DOMA

Thea Spyer died from her heart condition within two years after the wedding (Gray), which left her wife Edie Windsor with a $363,053 estate tax bill for the property she had inherited from Spyer. Since surviving spouses are exempt from federal estates tax, Windsor contacted the Internal Revenue Service (IRS) in order to claim a refund. Her claim was denied on the basis of Section 3 of DOMA (United States, Supreme Court, Syllabus "*Windsor*" 1). Windsor felt betrayed by her country, abandoned in her time of despair as she was treated as a second-class citizen and denied the same rights as fellow heterosexual Americans. Spyer and Windsor's relationship spanned five decades in which they were fully committed to each other with Windsor sacrificing her career to become her wife's full-time caretaker (Frank 250). Nevertheless, their country dared to discriminate against Windsor because of her sexual orientation and did not consider this relationship to be eligible for the rights and benefits given to married couples only because Spyer and Windsor were both women. Windsor's efforts to negotiate with the IRS were hopeless. The IRS argued that they did not recognize her marriage and could deny her claim on the basis of DOMA's Section 3 (United States, Supreme Court, Syllabus "*Windsor*" 1) which defines marriage as a union between a man and a woman for federal purposes (United States, Congress, "*Defense of Marriage Act*"). Windsor reached out to gay rights activist groups

'spouse' refers only to a person of the opposite sex who is a husband or a wife. (United States, Congress, "*Defense of Marriage Act*") such as Lambda Legal and the Human Rights Campaign of which the couple had been longtime supporters. However, both advocacy groups rebuffed her since they presumed the country was not yet ready for a lawsuit which would require a repeal of the Defense of Marriage Act (Frank 251). Windsor eventually contacted the civil rights litigator Roberta Kaplan who had experience arguing in favor of gay marriage in front of New York's Court of Appeals (a case she lost) and who believed that they had a real chance at winning Windsor's case. In the end, they were able to convince the legal advocacy organization American Civil Liberties Union (ACLU) to join their case in order to have some support of the gay rights movement (Frank 254).

In 2010, Kaplan and the ACLU on behalf of Windsor sued the federal government in the United States District Court for the Southern District of New York, contending that DOMA violated her equal protection rights as guaranteed by the Fifth Amendment to the United States Constitution (United States, Supreme Court, Syllabus "*Windsor*" 1). While the suit was still pending, the United States Attorney General Eric Holder, in agreement with President Obama, informed the Speaker of the House of Representatives that the Department of Justice would no longer defend DOMA in cases involving same-sex couples (1–2). This was an unexpected but welcome turn. In 2011, most Americans were in favor of marriage equality for the first time in the history of the United States, and the president decided to reflect that (Gray). Therefore, the chances for Windsor having the support of the public were better than ever. In addition, Obama and Holder's joint decision to no longer defend DOMA also meant that cases involving couples legally married under state law would be subject to heightened scrutiny and no longer just rational basis review (Frank 259).[83] This modification in level of scrutiny changed the legal standing of gay Americans for

[83] Whether *Windsor* was subject to heightened scrutiny in the end is much debated since some sources claim otherwise. Cary Franklin elaborates on this difference in opinion in an article for the *Virginia Law Review*:

> *United States v. Windsor* was (at least in part) an equal protection decision – about that, lower courts are in agreement. But when it comes to the formal doctrinal aspects of the holding, that is where the agreement ends. Some courts have concluded that the *Windsor* Court applied heightened scrutiny; others have found that it applied intermediate scrutiny. Still others have determined that the Court applied rational basis review – or

the better. It acknowledged that they had a history of discrimination, suffered from classification based on sexual orientation, and struggled with limited political power (259).[84] In contrast to the Department of Justice, the House of Representative's Bipartisan Legal Advisory Group (BLAG), represented by the former U.S. Solicitor General under President Bush and lawyer, Paul Clement, voted to defend the constitutionality of Section 3 of DOMA (United States, Supreme Court, "*Windsor*" 4). This motion was controversial. It was debatable if BLAG could even enter the suit because the United States was already represented by the Department of Justice. However, the District Court granted intervention by BLAG as an interested party (4). The first victory for Windsor was achieved in 2012, when the United States District Court for the Southern District of New York held that Section 3 of DOMA was unconstitutional and ordered the federal government to refund Windsor's property tax with interest (United States, Supreme Court, Syllabus "*Windsor*" 1). Additionally, the U.S. Court of Appeals for the Second Circuit affirmed the District Court's judgment. As a consequence, BLAG and the Department of Justice filed notices of appeal. Paradoxically, the United States Treasury did not comply with the ruling, and Windsor did not receive a refund. Although the Executive Branch had decided

perhaps the 'more searching form of rational basis review' known colloquially as rational basis with bite. (872)

84 When it comes to evaluating which level of scrutiny gay civil rights cases should be subject to, the increasing visibility and political power of this minority has a negative effect on their success rate. Strict or heightened scrutiny levels are only to be issued to minorities struggling to gain enough political influence to protect themselves without the help of the courts. However, without any political influence already achieved and without any lobbyism or high-profile legal support, a minority's case is not very likely at all to make it to the highest court of the country The process of scrutiny analysis is paradoxical, as David Schraub explained: "Since truly powerless groups do not typically receive judicial protections, a vulnerable social group must show political power in order to gain the attention of the courts. But, by showing this power, vulnerable groups simultaneously give the judiciary a doctrinal excuse to reject their claims" (1437). In assigning a standard of judicial review to a certain case, the respective judges often already indicate a case's likely outcome. Consequently, Schraub postulates that "the Equal Protection Clause should not focus on the relative power of the disfavored group" but rather on the existence of animus towards that group (1438).

to no longer defend Section 3, they continued to enforce DOMA by not refunding Windsor (1).[85] The Solicitor General filed a petition for certiorari,[86] which was granted by the United States Supreme Court before judgement (1). Although Windsor and Kaplan were fully aware that this case could have far-reaching consequences for same-sex couples all over the United States by establishing a precedent, they certainly had not expected it to proceed all the way to the Supreme Court where Windsor's case was heard in *United States v. Windsor*.

The main question that the nine judges of United States Supreme Court had to decide on was whether Section 3 of the Defense of Marriage Act was unconstitutional because it violated the Fifth Amendment's guarantee of equal protection for same-sex couples (United States, Supreme Court, Syllabus "*Windsor*" 2–3). In addition to that, the Court requested to argue two more questions: whether the United States Executive's agreement with Windsor's legal position and with the Second Circuit's ruling precluded an actual dispute since both represent the same interest (namely not defending DOMA Section 3), and whether BLAG could have a legal standing of its own and therefore appeal the case (Syllabus "*Windsor*" 2–4). Another question which was extensively debated in the hearing, although not part of the petition, was if DOMA violated principles of federalism in the United States (United States, Supreme Court, "*Windsor*" 18; Roberts, "*Windsor*" 2). The regulation of marriage is generally within the authority of the separate states. However, DOMA was a federal law

85 In *Windsor*, the Supreme Court describes the conflict which arises from the Executive's decision as follows:

> This case clearly presented a concrete disagreement between opposing parties that was suitable for judicial resolution in the District Court, but the Executive's decision not to defend §3's constitutionality in court while continuing to deny refunds and assess deficiencies introduces a complication. Given the Government's concession, *amicus* contends, once the District Court ordered the refund, the case should have ended and the appeal been dismissed. (United States, Supreme Court, Syllabus "*Windsor*" 1–2)

86 If a plaintiff loses in a lower court and is not automatically entitled to an appeal, the party can only appeal by filing a writ of certiorari. If the writ of certiorari is granted, as in the case of the Solicitor General, the party is allowed to appeal the decision to a higher court, in this case the United States Supreme Court ("Certiorari").

with such an enormous reach that it often caused conflicts between state law and federal law. Marriage laws are state laws and consequently vary between the different states; however, they must be consistent within the individual states (United States, Supreme Court, "*Windsor*" 18–19).[87]

United States v. Windsor: Opinion of the Court

The opinion of the court in *United States v. Windsor* was delivered by Justice Kennedy and joined by Justices Bader Ginsburg, Breyer, Sotomayor, and Kagan. The majority opinion held that "DOMA is unconstitutional as a deprivation of the equal liberty of persons that is protected by the Fifth Amendment" (United States, Supreme Court, Syllabus "*Windsor*" 2). Additionally, the judgment stated that DOMA ignored the principle of federalism insofar as it bereaved same-sex couples of the status and the protection which the State of New York guaranteed them. This was not tolerable since marriage rights traditionally lay within the realm of the state. Consequently, the majority opinion decided as follows:

> By seeking to injure the very class New York seeks to protect, DOMA violates basic due process and equal protection principles applicable to the Federal Government. The Constitution's guarantee of equality "must at the very least mean that a bare congressional desire to harm a politically unpopular group cannot" justify disparate treatment of that group. *Department of Agriculture v. Moreno*, 413 U.S. 528, 534–535. DOMA cannot survive under these principles. . . . DOMA's avowed purpose and practical effect are to impose a disadvantage, a separate status, and so a stigma upon all who enter into same-sex marriages made lawful by the unquestioned authority of the States. (United States, Supreme Court, Syllabus "*Windsor*" 3–4)

With the decision of the majority opinion, Section 3 of DOMA, which had previously excluded same-sex couples from the terms 'marriage' and 'spouse' by definition, was ruled unconstitutional. However, an analysis

[87] When DOMA passed both houses in 1996, this was not a problem because no state had marriage rights for same-sex couples at that time. However, as soon as the first states granted marriage equality, DOMA violated the principle of federalism in certain contexts, as it did in Edith Windsor's claim for estate tax exemption for surviving spouses.

of the opinion of the court in *United States v. Windsor* reveals that much more was at stake in this ruling than merely whether DOMA's Section 3 violated Fifth Amendment rights. Marriage is a highly politicized institution in the United States and regulations or policies regarding marriage rights are often reflective of current sociopolitical developments (Yamin 13). In 2013, *United States v. Windsor* provided a platform for Americans in order to engage in the continuous (re)construction of American nationalism in regard to how they, as a nation, wished to treat same-sex couples.

In their opinion of the court, the judges acknowledged that reaching the point where a majority of Americans would speak out in favor of marriage equality would not be an easy transformation for the American nation, especially since many Americans had never even considered two people of the same sex getting married to be a possibility (United States, Supreme Court, "*Windsor*" 13–14). However, Justice Kennedy believed that the American people simply had not realized that denying gay couples the right to marry could be an injustice, implying that he was convinced an American would never tolerate inequality as long as they were aware of it:

> After a statewide deliberative process that enabled its citizens to discuss and weigh arguments for and against same sex marriage, New York acted to enlarge the definition of marriage to correct what its citizens and elected representatives perceived to be an injustice that they had not earlier known or understood. (14)

His choice of words suggests that a good American, as soon as they become aware of an injustice or inequality towards fellow Americans, would immediately try to correct an unjust exclusion or unequal condition. Same-sex couples pursued the right to marry in order to strengthen their relationships and believed that this was in the best interest for their families, for their community, and for their nation. For the majority opinion, granting marriage rights to couples regardless of sexual orientation was about the American ideals of equality, liberty, and dignity. Kennedy praised the people of the State of New York for providing protection and equality to same-sex couples as they did to Edie Windsor and Thea Spyer[88]:

[88] New York was the sixth state to legalize same-sex marriage after New York lawmakers voted in favor of same-sex marriage in June 2011. The Senate

> This status is a far-reaching legal acknowledgment of the intimate relationship between two people, a relationship deemed by the State worthy of dignity in the community equal with all other marriages. It reflects both the community's considered perspective on the historical roots of the institution of marriage and its evolving understanding of the meaning of equality. (United States, Supreme Court, "*Windsor*" 20)

Accordingly, the people of New York had found the perfect balance. They honored the history of the institution of marriage but at the same time realized that excluding some Americans from the right of marriage was un-American.

While paying his respects to the people of New York, Kennedy also openly accused the members of Congress who had voted in favor of DOMA of willingly stigmatizing and disadvantaging gay Americans. The majority opinion was convinced that the Congress of 1996 was fully aware that they were discriminating against a minority with the Defense of Marriage Act. Marriage, as the title of the federal law suggests, was to be defended against un-American people and practices:

> The avowed purpose and practical effect of the law here in question are to impose a disadvantage, a separate status, and so a stigma upon all who enter into same-sex marriages made lawful by the unquestioned authority of the States. The history of DOMA's enactment and its own text demonstrate that interference with the equal dignity of same-sex marriages, a dignity conferred by the States in the exercise of their sovereign power, was more than an incidental effect of the federal statute. It was its essence. (United States, Supreme Court, "*Windsor*" 20)

According to the majority opinion, the members of Congress who endorsed DOMA could not pretend to have been unaware of the blatant discrimination inscribed in this federal law. The judges of the majority were joined in their assessment by other legal experts who also claimed that the title of the federal law alone was revelatory of its purpose. For instance, Dale Carpenter commented on the discrimination enshrined in DOMA as follows:

approved of a marriage bill in a 33 to 29 vote, with four members of the Republican majority joining the Democrats (Confessore and Barbaro).

> Beyond the sweeping text, the title of the law, the "Defense of Marriage Act," immediately raises three questions. First, against what or whom is the law a "defense"? What is the threat and how has it been generated? Second, assuming there is a hypothetical future invader armed with weaponry capable of bringing down the entire institution of marriage, why must the "defense" be a Great Wall running up and down the continent rather than a moat around a specific and vulnerable fortification? Third, since when is the Congress charged with "defending" marriage? That has been the states' responsibility, with Congress acting only interstitially or at the margins. (249)

The purpose of DOMA was to exclude American same-sex couples from being full and accepted members of the national family. The "national cultural capital" (Skey 67) of homosexual Americans in the mid-1990s was incredibly low. They did not have a voice at the table where the discursive construction of national identity and American everyday nationalism was taking place. The Defense of Marriage Act infringed on same-sex couples' "freedom and choice," treated their marriages and unions as "second-class marriages for the purpose of federal law," "DOMA [wrote] inequality into the entire United States Code," and all of this "raise[d] a most serious question under the Constitution's Fifth Amendment" (United States, Supreme Court, "*Windsor*" 21–22). The majority opinion claimed that DOMA established "two contradictory marriage regimes" (United States, Supreme Court, Syllabus "*Windsor*" 4) and thereby emphasized that, as long as such inequality persisted, the nation and national identity of homosexual Americans was necessarily classified as different from that of heterosexual Americans. The humiliation same-sex couples and their families experienced as a consequence of "being in a second-tier marriage" was significant and had an enormous impact on their life choices (United States, Supreme Court, "*Windsor*" 23). In his concluding remarks, Justice Kennedy warned Congress not to impose their idea of American national identity on the whole of the American people and violate the Constitution because they wish to let their understanding of Americanism prevail: "The power the Constitution grants it also restrains. And though Congress has great authority to design laws to fit its own conception of sound national policy, it cannot deny the liberty protected by the Due Process Clause of the Fifth Amendment" (United States, Supreme Court, "*Windsor*" 25).

United States v. Windsor: Dissenting Opinions

Dissenting opinions in *United States v. Windsor* were presented by Justice Roberts, Justice Alito, and most extensively by Justice Scalia. Justice Roberts began his dissenting opinion by objecting to the allegation made by Justice Kennedy that Congress had overstepped its authority with their 1996 decision: "Interests in uniformity and stability amply justified Congress's decision to retain the definition of marriage that, at that point, had been adopted by every State in our Nation, and every nation in the world" (Roberts, "*Windsor*" 1). For Roberts, this made Congress' passing of DOMA an act in accordance with the Constitution. With his comment, Roberts, just as Kennedy, acknowledged that the concepts of marriage and nation were closely linked with each other. Whatever definition of marriage a nation chooses to adapt defines its self-understanding and the national identity of its people. Just as the majority opinion, the dissenting justices clearly understood that this landmark civil rights case was not solely about a section of a federal law, rather the whole debate was, as Justice Alito phrased it, "about the nature of the institution of marriage" (Alito, "*Windsor*" 1).

The dissenting judges spent a considerable amount of their writing on the question of whether *United States v. Windsor* constituted a proper case and, second, if the ruling of the majority opinion was the result of judicial activism. One could argue that this was the opponents' way of coping with losing the case as such allegations are most prominent when a ruling does not turn out as one had hoped (Olson in interview with Wallace). Justice Alito stated that the United States could not be a petitioner in *United States v. Windsor* since both the petitioner and the plaintiff held that Section 3 of DOMA was unconstitutional and should therefore no longer be defended ("*Windsor*" 2). The problem with this case was that a controversy is required in order to have a dispute which needs to be resolved by court. It is questionable that this was the case in *United States v. Windsor* (Scalia, "*Windsor*" 8). Though the Executive no longer defended Section 3 of DOMA, thereby agreeing with Windsor, the United States government failed to comply with earlier rulings which made the United States a proper petitioner. Justice Scalia did not agree with such reasoning and seemed annoyed about such basic misconceptions: The power of the judges was only "a power to decide not abstract questions but real, concrete 'Cases' and 'Controversies'" (2). "Yet the plaintiff and the Government agree entirely on what should happen in this lawsuit. They agree that the court below got it right; and they agreed in the court below that the court below that one got it right as well. What, then, are we *doing* here?", Scalia complained (2).

The three dissenting judges concurred with each other regarding what the court was doing there: they were overstepping their jurisdiction by deciding on a question which should have been in the hands of the American people or their elected representatives (Roberts, "*Windsor*" 1–4; Scalia, "*Windsor*" 1–3; Alito, "*Windsor*" 10). Justice Alito argued that the Constitution did not say anything about what defines marriage. This should have been reason enough for the judges of the Supreme Court to refrain from hearing such a case (Alito, "*Windsor*" 14). Justice Scalia, with whom Justice Roberts agreed that the "Court lack[ed] jurisdiction to review the decisions of the courts below" (Roberts, "*Windsor*" 1), elaborated at length on why he believed the ruling in *Windsor* was an example of judicial activism. Angered by the reckless behavior of his colleagues of the majority opinion, Scalia wrote: "That is jaw-dropping. It is an assertion of judicial supremacy over the people's Representatives in Congress and the Executive" (Scalia, "*Windsor*" 2). In Scalia's opinion, the judges of the majority were so fixated on expediting progress in regard to marriage rights for same-sex couples that they overstepped the power granted to the judiciary in the United States:

> This case is about power in several respects. It is about the power of our people to govern themselves, and the power of this Court to pronounce the law. Today's opinion aggrandizes the latter, with the predictable consequence of diminishing the former. We have no power to decide this case. And even if we did, we have no power under the Constitution to invalidate this democratically adopted legislation. The Court's errors on both points spring forth from the same diseased root: an exalted conception of the role of this institution in America. . . . The Court is eager – *hungry* – to tell everyone its view of the legal question at the heart of this case. (1)

This civil rights case was on the surface about the injustice Edie Windsor had suffered and how this injustice would be righted. However, *Windsor* was about much more than the individual case of a person who was denied estate tax exemption for surviving spouses. It was about the power structures which discourses on the institution of American marriage and American nationhood entail. In Scalia's eyes, the majority opinion abused their power because they wanted to propel progress in regard to the rights of gay Americans. By doing this, they influenced the natural development of these discourses in a way that was outside of the realm of their jurisdiction. Justice Alito remarked that the institution of marriage has always been in a process of change and transformation: "[T]he process by which such consequences come about is complex, involving the interaction of numerous factors, and tends to occur over an extended period of time. We can expect something similar to take place if same-sex marriage becomes widely accepted" ("*Windsor*" 8). Alito believed that the American people would have eventually reached the point when all states had established marriage equality and acceptance had become so widespread that the intervention of the Supreme Court would not have been necessary. He lamented that by bringing cases such as *Windsor* to court, this natural transformation of the institution of marriage was expedited at the cost of those Americans who needed more time to accept marriage equality as part of the American self-definition.[89] While this argument has valid points, it would have required Edie Windsor to accept her injury simply because the nation was not yet ready for her and others like her to be treated equally. "Family structure reveals the characteristics of a civilization," Justice Alito noted ("*Windsor*" 8). The second-class marriage of same-sex couples reflected an American nation that was not yet willing to fully include gay Americans in their American everyday nationalism.

A further point of criticism, which all dissenting judges agreed on, was that the opinion of the court lacked profound legal merit (Roberts, "*Windsor*" 3–4; Alito, "*Windsor*" 10; Scalia, "*Windsor*" 15–18). Gay rights cases tend to be based on the Equal Protection Clause of the Fourteenth Amendment or the Due Process Clause of the Fifth and Fourteenth Amendment. However, the legal interpretation of these clauses is often highly controversial and contested since the Equal Protection Clause and the Due Process Clause protect vague concepts and rights, such as 'liberty' or 'equality,' whose definitions depend on one's personal understanding of these terms. In *United States v. Windsor*, the majority's legal interpretation of the Fifth Amendment's Due Process Clause infuriated

89 David Lampo argues along the same lines in his monograph *A Fundamental Freedom: Why Republicans, Conservatives, and Libertarians Should Support Gay Rights,* when he asks gay rights advocates to be more patient with those how cannot adapt so easily to the changes they are confronted with when same-sex marriage becomes an integral part of American everyday nationalism. Lampo warned that "[t]rying to force-feed certain cultural and religious values to the American public, through legal sanctions and preferences, is both destined to fail and distinctly un-American."

Justice Scalia so much that he could not refrain from verbally lashing out at the majority opinion: "There are many remarkable things about the majority's merits holding. The first is how rootless and shifting its justifications are," he wrote ("*Windsor*" 15). At a later point, he again questioned the majority's legal competence. He claimed that although they desperately tried to construct a coherent legal argumentation, they ultimately failed to do so: "The sum of all the Court's nonspecific hand-waving is that this law is invalid (maybe on equal-protection grounds, maybe on substantive-due-process grounds, and perhaps with some amorphous federalism component playing a role)" (18). In addition, Justice Alito lamented that "because they cannot show that same-sex marriage is a fundamental right under our Constitution, Windsor and the United States couch their arguments in equal protection terms" ("*Windsor*" 10). With this comment, Alito exposed the problem of basing a ruling on the Equal Protection Clause. The broad and unspecific formulation of the clause provokes accusations of dubious legal merit. Furthermore, it creates a loophole for the justification of rulings that otherwise have only a weak legal basis. Scalia attacked the majority on this ground. Clearly frustrated by their inability to write an ironclad ruling, Scalia criticized that "if this is meant to be an equal-protection opinion, it is a confusing one. The opinion does not resolve and indeed does not even mention what had been the central question in this litigation" ("*Windsor*" 16–17). With this comment, Scalia blatantly accused the "black-robed Supremacy" (3) of judicial activism and of overstepping their jurisdiction by changing the law and attempting to implement their progressive worldview on the rest of the nation.

Scalia, who had a history of dissenting in gay rights cases,[90] was afraid of what could follow since "the majority has declared open season on any law that (in the opinion of law's opponents and any panel of like-minded federal judges) can be characterized as mean-spirited" (19). He seemed to fear that the situation was spiraling out of control. The problem started with the first gay rights case that was decided in favor of gay Americans. According to Scalia, the case *Lawrence v. Texas*, in which the United States Supreme Court struck down sodomy laws, was the starting shot

90 Justice Scalia consistently ruled against gay rights and consequently dissented in *Romer v. Evans* (1996), *Lawrence v. Texas* (2003), *United States v. Windsor* (2013), and in *Obergefell v. Hodges* (2015).

for all the cases that followed and which increased gay rights step by step through litigation:

> When the Court declared a constitutional right to homosexual sodomy, we were assured that the case had nothing, nothing at all to do with 'whether the government must give formal recognition to any relationship that homosexual persons seek to enter'. . . . Now we are told that DOMA is invalid. . . . with an accompanying citation of *Lawrence*. (22)

United States v. Windsor was the next steppingstone for the gradual inclusion of same-sex couples into how American nationalism is represented through everyday life. Indeed, Scalia was right in his assumption because the marriage equality case *Obergefell v. Hodges* was heard by the Supreme Court only two years later.

Edie Windsor: The Perfect Lesbian American Plaintiff?

After the ruling in *United States v. Windsor*, Edie Windsor was not only refunded $363,053 estate tax with interest. She had also become the new hero of the marriage equality movement (Obergefell). She was celebrated for her bravery to challenge Section 3 of the Defense of Marriage Act at a time when many gay rights organizations were still reluctant to take this step (McFadden). The nationwide interest this Supreme Court case sparked is indicative of the enormous impact this landmark civil rights case had on the American people at large. Not only did the ruling grant same-sex couples access to a wide range of federal benefits, privileges, and rights. The holding also addressed fundamental questions regarding the institution of marriage in the United States and the question of who was considered American or un-American. *United States v. Windsor* was a discursive renegotiation of who the American people were, who they wanted to be in the future, and how they would like to draft American nationalism and national identity at the advent of the 21st century. The opinion of the court as well as the dissenting opinions were reflective of the process in which a dominant system is challenged and "national cultural capital" (Skey 67) is redistributed.

At the beginning, there was concern among Windsor's team about whether she was the right plaintiff for such a historical legal battle. Mary Bonauto, who was the lead counsel in the case *Goodridge v. Department of Public Health* and one of the key strategists in the fight against

DOMA, had previously expressed concern that a wealthy woman having to pay a hefty estate tax might not be the most sympathetic plaintiff (Frank 254). Although most Americans would certainly be sorry for her personal loss, she was not in a dire financial situation since the tax burden did not pose an existential threat to her. James Esseks of the ACLU also did not think Windsor was the ideal plaintiff, capable of winning people's hearts (Frank 254). Windsor was a white, influential Upper East Side New Yorker who owned considerable property, had an expensive taste, and who had travelled the world with her wife (Gray). Although her case was ultimately successful and a milestone in the history of gay rights, the choice of Windsor as plaintiff provoked criticism among the gay rights movement. Many critics argued that the organizations supporting the fight against DOMA should have opted for someone who would have represented marginalization on a broader scale, which would have made the court victory an even greater victory for equality as an American ideal (Frank 255). Esseks, along with the rest of Windsor's legal team, was fully aware of that problem. As a result, they created a story "which fit nicely into the framework of what recent movement opinion research had found to be publicly resonant: focus on love and commitment when talking to the nation about same-sex marriage" (255). The enduring love of the two women was to become the center of the litigation and the estate tax issue was kept out of the spotlight. "Windsor was going to come across as a charming old lady who had stuck by her partner of forty-four years, through a period of considerable sickness, and was now being treated unfairly" (255). With this strategy, they tried to be louder than the critics who rightly insisted that Windsor's "legal victory hinged on a strategically constructed narrative of 'normalcy,' anti-tax politics, and the financial capability to employ skillful litigators and pursue her case all the way to the Supreme Court" (Long-Droppert 43). Ultimately, all of these points were necessary in order to make this lawsuit a success. The story of normalcy and tragic loss evoked compassion and helped gain support for Windsor's cause. However, her extensive financial means were the prerequisite for being able to pursue such a litigation and employ a team of attorneys who were experienced and skilled enough to argue a high-profile case in front of the United States Supreme Court.

The estate tax proved to be an advantage in the end. In addition to the humiliation and betrayal Windsor experienced by not being treated equally after the death of her wife, the injury which prompted her case was economic in nature. It was this financial injury of the state tax which secured Windsor bipartisan support, even among conservatives who had previously not cared about same-sex marriage. Long-Droppert explains this phenomenon as follows:

> The various tax cuts implemented by the Bush Administration were set to expire during Obama's first term, and there was a great deal of debate between Republicans and Democrats concerning which concessions would be extended, and how the federal tax structure debate would be altered. In this debate, the Republicans took particular exception to the estate tax, which they labelled as a "death tax" on unsuspecting widows. In this context, Windsor had the advantage of challenging DOMA for its perpetuation of the "death tax," an angle more likely to garner the support of the anti-tax Right. (50–51)

In the logic of the anti-tax right, Edie Windsor was one of these "unsuspecting widows" (51) who needed to be protected from the inhuman federal estate tax policy. For many gay rights advocates, this support came unexpectedly. One could argue that this endorsement was irrelevant since it had no influence on the judges of the United States Supreme Court. However, it was relevant insofar as this case was not only about the ruling and which judges constituted the majority. The sociocultural setting of the case was equally as important as its legal context since such landmark civil rights cases determine who garners a voice in the discursive drafting of the nation and who can decide what is American or un-American.

Windsor was not initially seen as the ideal plaintiff in the eyes of some civil rights organizations. They would have preferred someone who more fully represented the ideals of a civil rights struggle and equality for all Americans. However, Windsor's case is illustrative of the discourses and practices of American nationhood and national cultural capital. Homeownership and real estate property have always played a tremendous role in American national self-definition, and this turned out as an advantage for Windsor. Owning property is a part of being American, and Windsor was outstanding in this category. If it were not for the fact that they were a lesbian couple, Windsor and her wife could have represented the perfect couple, one that managed to live up to the ideal of the American Dream and who possessed enormous national cultural capital. They had both the financial means as well as the influence and connections to participate actively in shaping American everyday nationalism (Gray). They also did this to a certain extent by supporting gay rights organizations and, after

Spyer's death, by litigating for the repeal of the Defense of Marriage Act. In the end, it was the property ownership and the resulting estate tax which gave Windsor a voice to challenge Section 3 of DOMA and made her American enough to participate in the debate on what defines American national identity. Taking these aspects into consideration, Edie Windsor may have been the perfect plaintiff for this lawsuit, despite all criticism. At the time of the ruling, the American people opposing marriage equality might not have been ready for a plaintiff who was not only homosexual but who asked for equality in terms of class, race, or another category in addition to sexual orientation. Windsor as the plaintiff was successful in selling a picture of "normalcy." The ruling in *United States v. Windsor* challenged the dominant system of nationalism in regard to marriage. It was one step closer towards full and nationwide marriage equality which was to follow two years later. For many opponents of same-sex marriage, the *Windsor* ruling destabilized their concept of society and sociocultural order. This ruling and the sociocultural change it implied were difficult to accept.

"Hostes Humani Generis"

For Americans who firmly believe in the prevalence of the traditional concept of marriage in the United States, the holding in *Windsor* was a transformation with an enormous impact on American nationalism. Of course, some states had previously granted civil unions or marriage to same-sex couples; however, at the time of the ruling, only New York and eleven other states had decided to open marriage to gay citizens. Therefore, this was not yet the sweeping success that marriage equality would have after *Windsor* and the 2014 midterm elections, when state after state legalized same-sex marriage within a span of only months (Wolf). Before *Windsor*, same-sex marriage was not an overarching national phenomenon but rather the concept of marriage of supported by the people of a few progressive states. In the *Windsor* hearing as well as in his dissenting opinion, Justice Scalia was the voice of Americans who did not want American nationalism to take a progressive turn. The rhetoric and tone of his dissent suggest that his worldview was uprooted by the holding of the majority opinion. Ian Loveland, who analyzed Scalia's contribution to several sexual orientation cases, describes Scalia's writing in *Windsor* as "another hyperbolic, almost hysterical dissent" of "vitriolic nature" (77). An examination of Scalia's dissent supports Loveland's analysis. "Scalia does eschew in *Windsor* however the direct demonization of gay activists that he indulged in both in *Romer* and *Lawrence*" (Loveland 78); but this does not mean that he refrained from insulting the majority judges, managed to regulate his temperament, or exercised restraint in his use of sarcasm, as several examples outlined above demonstrate. His comments on the majority opinion's "jaw-dropping . . . assertion of judicial supremacy" (Scalia, "*Windsor*" 2) and their "non-specific hand-waving" (18) or his remark on the "*hostes humani generis*" (21) were only a sampling of his offensive choice of words. Loveland stated that "Scalia's opinions repeatedly mischaracterized the positions adopted by members of the court with whom he disagreed and invoked quite absurd analogies to sustain his own. It also lies in Scalia's repeatedly derogatory, almost demonizing portrayal, of the litigants and organizations seeking to promote the cause of sexual orientation equality" (61).

Scalia's problematic comments in *United States v. Windsor* were not isolated examples. In *Romer v. Evans*,[91] Scalia attracted attention with a comparison of same-sex marriage to murder, polygamy, and animal cruelty:

> The Court's opinion contains grim, disapproving hints that Coloradans have been guilty of "animus" or "animosity" toward homosexuality, as though that has been established as Unamerican. Of course it is our moral heritage that one should not hate any human being or class of human beings. But I had thought that one could consider certain conduct reprehensible – murder, for example, or polygamy, or cruelty to animals – and could exhibit even "animus" toward such conduct. Surely that is the only sort of "animus" at issue here: moral disapproval of homosexual conduct, the same sort of moral disapproval that produced the centuries-old criminal laws that we held constitutional in Bowers. ("*Romer*" 10)

Justice Scalia's use of the term 'un-American' in this context was an indicator that he considered the question over same-sex marriage to be closely intertwined with ideas of nationalism and American identity. He could have used a wide range of other adjectives in that context such as 'inappropriate' or 'inhuman.'[92]

91 In *Romer v. Evans*, a Colorado constitutional amendment that prohibited protected status for homosexuals or bisexuals under the law was struck down since it violated the Equal Protection Clause to the Fourteenth Amendment of the United States Constitution (United States. Supreme Court, "*Romer v. Evans*" 14).

92 Scalia never commented on this remark in the years before his passing in

Interestingly, Justice Scalia issued his remark in *Romer* just a few months before Congress passed the Defense of Marriage Act in 1996 and thereby defined marriage as a union between a man and a woman. Americans at that time seemed to feel threatened by same-sex couples, which resulted in the state taking measures to put a hold on gay Americans who started to become a voice to be reckoned with at the table of national discourse. However, the repeal of DOMA through the civil rights case *United States v. Windsor* showed that silencing of a minority group and excluding it from national discourse only works for a limited amount of time. In his "hyperbolic, almost hysterical dissent" (Loveland 77), in which he repeatedly warned that gay rights activists and their supporters would not stop fighting for their cause, Scalia cast himself as the protector of traditional marriage and conservative values. As a result, he was the voice for Americans who were also struggling with the massive transformations which the gay rights movement was having on their sociocultural concept of the nation. In her analysis of the new jurisprudence of gay rights, Franklin explains that courts can no longer "treat the marriage question as isolated or exceptional, but rather as embedded in a larger set of social, political, and legal changes. The invalidation of laws restricting marriage to different-sex couples is part of the dismantling of an entire social regime in which gays and lesbians rank as second-class citizens" (873). It is this "dismantling of an entire social regime" (873) which makes conservatives fear for their concept of American everyday nationalism since the dominant system is fundamentally challenged.

Windsor as a Door Opener to American Everyday Nationalism

When attempting to identify the point at which tensions surrounding the same-sex marriage debate began to escalate into a full-blown culture war, gay rights advocates' efforts to repeal the Defense of Marriage Act can be regarded as a decisive gunshot. DOMA was the conservative front's bastion against the threat of same-sex marriage. "DOMA was far from mere formal enshrinement of long-standing American values regarding the institution of marriage. Instead, this legislation was drafted to shore up 'traditional' marriage against a perceived, pending threat – same-sex marriage," Long-Droppert claims (45). In the mid-1990s, gay marriage was suddenly

2016. As a consequence, it is unknown if his attitude toward same-sex couples had evolved over time or if he still subscribed to the opinion in *Romer.*

seen as something so potentially threatening that basic principles of federalism were thrown overboard in order to protect the traditional American concept of marriage. DOMA was the rampart designed to protect traditional marriage from a future reconceptualization that could threaten the nation.[93]

In the case of DOMA, it was the U.S. Congress which presumed to have the liberty to restrict marriage to a union between a man and a woman. In the wake of *Windsor*, many critics asked how Congress could have ever believed that it lay within its power to regulate participation rights as well as inclusion or exclusion of one of the nation's most cherished rights, the right to marry, in such a profound way. By defining and restricting marriage to a certain group of citizens, Congress was also trying to instill into the American people their ideal of what was American and un-American. They deliberately singled out Americans, who according to their set of values, did not fulfill the criteria for an uncontested, full membership in the nationhood.[94] Same-sex marriage was regarded as un-American and therefore should not play a role in American nationalism.

93 In her essay "When Opposites Attract: The Rise and Fall of the Defense of Marriage Act within a Neoliberal Hegemonic Framework," Verity Long-Droppert analyzes the socio-legal history of DOMA and looks at how this federal law determined citizenship and national identity formation. Her work is particularly interesting as she understands the state not as a thing or a fixed object but as "a sum of cultural and political processes" (44). By putting her focus on the nation's "continual formation and re-formation in opposition to the forces with which it exists in tension – forces such as popular culture, civil rights and social justice movements, or subordinate groups" (44), Long-Droppert shares the same concept of nation and nationhood as scholars of everyday nationalism.

94 Almost fifteen years after DOMA was passed, many supporters of gay rights ask themselves how the American people could have agreed on Congress initiating such a law and how they could not have seen the blatant animus it contains. The debate on whether some laws or policies were created out of animus towards homosexuals is at the core of many cases which are reviewed for their constitutionality. It was the question in *Romer*, as Justice Scalia's remark as quoted above shows, and it also dominated the hearing in *Windsor* as it was argued that supporters of DOMA were motivated by animus towards same-sex couples. The problem with such cases is that it is extremely difficult to establish what animus is and when animus might have been the reason for discrimination. Carpenter explains that "the doctrine [of animus] is analytically empty, a conclusion clothed in argument. Another point of critique is that it calls for the kind of unprincipled judgment about subjective legislative motivation that has long been discredited in jurisprudence" (184–85). Due to

The systematic exclusion of homosexual Americans through acts of Congress is reminiscent of the time of the House Un-American Activities Committee which had also portrayed itself as the protector of Americanism's values and infringed the rights of those they deemed un-American (R. Martin 1044). Despite all efforts to cast same-sex couples as the un-American enemy and to exclude them from full participation in the American nation, *Windsor* is the striking proof that such a system cannot prevail forever, as it is not immune to social change and the power of social justice movements. Skey addresses the importance of such movements in acting as a corrective to exclusionary models of nationhood in the political dimension of everyday nationalism (Skey 12). Although the state is sometimes the "primary institutional apparatus for legitimising national discourse" (12), social movements and advocacy groups play an important role in challenging this power of the state by bringing marginalized or underrepresented groups of Americans to the stage where nationalism is debated and constructed. The prodigious role the concept of the nation had in *Windsor*, both the court case as well as the accompanying national debate, is another example which underlines the "significance of the nation as a resonant category" (12). This resonant category of the nation is most prominent on the national agenda if the national identity of people is undergoing tremendous change due to transformations around them. The nation then is "a culturally available schema that can be discursively deployed to make sense of other topics of talk, explain predicaments and order social difference" (Fox and Miller-Idriss 540).

The concept of the nation helped structure the controversial topic of same-sex marriage and, at the same time, was at the core of a transformative process which included a reconceptualization of American national-

this uncertainty and subjectivity of the legal protection from animus, accusations of judicial activism, as they were the case in *Windsor*, are easy to raise. Furthermore, some critics complain "that slapping the animus label on a law is an attempt to hush debate about deeply contested moral and legal controversies. On this view, it insults those who differ from the Court's majority, dismissing them as bigots – a form of constitutional name-calling" (Carpenter 185). The problem with animus is also that what is now commonly regarded as discrimination might have not been classified as a discriminatory practice or law at an earlier point in American history. The Defense of Marriage Act was passed in 1996 with overwhelming bipartisan support in Congress as well as by the public at large. Only 81 of 535 members voted against the law (Long-Droppert 44).

ism. In addition to proving that an exclusionary system such as the one created by DOMA would eventually disappear, *Windsor* also demonstrated that it is the discursive construction of the nation which most significantly shapes American everyday nationalism. In the end, it is not the state which determines what constitutes American national identity or who is to be accused of un-American values or behavior, but it is the people as active agents who "talk the nation" (Fox and Miller-Idriss 537) and thereby design their American everyday nationalism. Long-Droppert finds that "DOMA's socio-legal history is an exemplar of a 'cultural front,' in which both ordering and dissipating forces competed for ascendancy" (52). DOMA constituted the legal front at which a new idea of nationalism was fought for. This nationalism was ultimately challenged by *Windsor* and the persuasive force of social movements which demanded the full inclusion of formerly marginalized subjects.

Neoliberalism's Influence on Gay Rights

The passing of DOMA by Congress in 1996 coincided with the rise in popularity of the economic philosophy of neoliberalism in the United States. Accordingly, Long-Droppert situates the fight over same-sex marriage in the larger context of this rise of neoliberalism. This is an interesting approach for two reasons. First, this turn towards a laissez-faire liberalism implied a redesign of everyday nationalism, and second, neoliberalism's imperatives of liberty and minimal state intervention are contradictory to what DOMA entails. Neoliberalism is most commonly known as a marked-based policy which encourages privatization, deregulation, free markets and free trade, and especially minimal governmental intervention to the benefit of entrepreneurial freedom. DOMA did exactly the opposite, as Long-Droppert explains:

> In many ways, then, DOMA can be seen as distinctively at odds with the hegemonic framework in which it was enacted. The legislation's expansion of state power into the private lives of citizens and its impediment to economic participation were incommensurate with the neoliberal doctrines of limited government and individual liberty. (47)

However, Long-Droppert argues that one may not ignore the societal transformation which neoliberalism instigated. With the rise of neoliberalism, the image of the traditional American family with the man as the breadwinner sustaining his family resurged in people's ideas of American nationalism. The subtext of this image was that minimal support from the state was needed in the form of welfare or other subsidies. The concept of the traditional nuclear family was the goal of the neoliberalist nation (47).

Given this line of thought, opening marriage to same-sex couples should have been encouraged by the state because it would have strengthened poor gay couples financially and reduce their dependence on welfare. However, despite the emphasis on laissez-faire and private liberty, this was not what the state had in mind. In the neoliberalist tradition, the state was willing to loosen the reigns in the economic sector, but the opposite was true in the private domain. Hawkesworth argues that, in contrast to what neoliberalism promised, the aim of "the institutions and agencies of governance was to produce a micropolitics of domination" (168). She sees this as characteristic of the American nation since "the evidence from the United States suggests that the liberal state has been deeply involved not only in regulating the criteria of citizenship but also in using the law to produce particular mentalities and dispositions among its citizens" (168). DOMA was one of these laws regulating who was American enough in order to enjoy the right of marriage and who was deemed un-American for representing the wrong mentality or disposition. "Far from protecting the freedoms and respecting the inalienable rights of all, the allegedly *laissez-faire* state has selectively privileged certain citizens while harshly regulating others" (Hawkesworth 168).

While neoliberalism did not initially improve the situation of gay Americans and while DOMA seemed at odds with neoliberalist principles, this conflict gradually turned out to be beneficial to same-sex couples as "the entrenchment of neoliberal economic policy brought an increasing belief in its imperative to let the free-market naturally regulate the private lives of individuals" (Long-Droppert 49). As the American nation evolved over time in its attitude towards their fellow gay compatriots, neoliberalism as a concept also progressed, becoming more inclusive and more neoliberal. Long-Droppert explains this development in favor of same-sex couples as follows:

> The proliferation of neoliberalism re-ordered the forces competing for ascendency on the cultural front of marriage equality. Same-sex marriage was compatible with neoliberal hegemony, as it encouraged the production of family units and would result in the further withdrawal of state en-

> croachment on the private lives of citizens. By the same token, DOMA's practical operation became increasingly discordant with this framework, as it impeded individual participation in the free-market, denied the allocations of federal benefits to homosexual couples, and perpetuated tax schemes better suited to a welfare state. (53)

The transformation of neoliberalism went hand in hand with a more accepting stance towards same-sex couples in the United States. This redesign of nationalism was the prerequisite that eventually allowed for the victory of Edie Windsor in the landmark civil rights case *United States v. Windsor*. In this process of reconceptualizing American nationalism, the influence of the state was reduced while the agency of the people and, thereby, their impact on concepts of the nation rose.

C *Obergefell v. Hodges*: An Analysis

In the landmark civil rights case *Obergefell v. Hodges*, the United States Supreme Court was not only asked for judicial review in the case of the marriage of the plaintiff Jim Obergefell and his late husband John Arthur. *Obergefell* was the consolidation of six lower-court cases from the states of Michigan, Kentucky, Ohio, and Tennessee (United States, Supreme Court, "*Obergefell*" 2).[95] Therefore, it was pure chance that Jim Obergefell was the name-giving plaintiff. Per tradition, the suit with the lowest case number sets the name of the consolidated cases, and this was Obergefell's (Rosenwald). Obergefell is perhaps also better known than the other plaintiffs since his story was probably the most compelling. Jim Obergefell had only been married for three months and eleven days when he lost his husband to the motor neuron disease Amyotrophic Lateral Sclerosis (ALS). Although the marriage had lasted only a few months, their relationship had spanned two decades. In 2013, the health of John Arthur was declining rapidly, and same-sex marriage was not yet legal in their home state of Ohio. Nevertheless, Obergefell was determined to establish a legal basis for their relationship before Arthur eventually succumbed to his illness, so he arranged for a medical flight to Maryland with the help of their friends and family. The couple got married on the tarmac of Baltimore-Washington International Marshall Airport, where the wedding was officiated by Arthur's aunt, who had become ordained online to perform weddings in order to help make this endeavor possible (Rosenwald). What the newlyweds did not anticipate was that due to legal constraints in the state of Ohio, Obergefell was not listed as the surviving spouse on Arthur's death certificate. Although they were married by the law of the state of Maryland, after death, they remained legal strangers in Ohio (United States, Supreme Court, "*Obergefell*" 5). Obergefell's sto-

95 The cases all came from states which defined marriage as a union between a man and a woman. The petitioners, fourteen same-sex couples and two widowers, all filed suits in the district courts of their home states and those federal district courts ruled in their favor in each case. As officials of the states concerned did not comply with the rulings and appealed, the cases went to the United States Court of Appeals for the Sixth Circuit which consolidated them but reversed the rulings of the district courts. Consequently, the petitioners sought certiorari which the United States Supreme Court granted (United States, Supreme Court, "*Obergefell*" 2).

ry was considered highly tragic because he lost his partner of 20 years and was then deserted by his country. However, the cases of the other co-plaintiffs were of no less importance since they addressed several other problems that arose from the lack of nationwide marriage equality and the legal uncertainty it created for many same-sex couples and their families. The Supreme Court was to decide on whether the plaintiffs' Fourteenth Amendment rights were violated "by denying them the right to marry or to have marriages lawfully performed in another State given full recognition" (Syllabus, United States, Supreme Court, "*Obergefell*" 1).[96]

Obergefell v. Hodges: Opinion of the Court

The majority opinion decided that the concept of marriage, being fundamental under the United States Constitution, could not exclude same-sex couples based on four principles (United States, Supreme Court, "*Obergefell*" 4). The first principle was the right to individual autonomy and personal choice, which drew a connection between the concept of liberty and marriage. Second, the right to marry was fundamental because it bestowed special protection to two people who sought to form a union and live as committed individuals. Third, the institution of marriage provided safety and stability for families and children. And fourth, marriage was "a keystone of the Nation's social order" (4). In the eyes of the majority opinion, same-sex couples' right to marry was guaranteed to them by the Due Process Clause and the Equal Protection Clause of the Fourteenth Amendment, which were "connected in a profound way" (4). In his opinion of the majority, Justice Kennedy tried to refute all potential criticism and elucidated in detail what led him and the four joining judges to the decision that the United States Constitution as well as legal precedents granted same-sex couples the right to marry. In his reasoning, he invoked several precedents with similar legal circumstances, which provided the

96 On the basis of the cases from Michigan and Kentucky, the United States Supreme Court was to decide whether the Fourteenth Amendment to the United States Constitution requires a state to license a marriage of a same-sex couple. The second question arose from the cases in Kentucky, Tennessee, and Ohio. The Court was to decide whether the Fourteenth Amendment requires a state to recognize same-sex marriages performed in another state (United States, Supreme Court, "*Obergefell*" 2–3).

majority opinion with arguments supportive of their ruling that the Constitution could be interpreted in favor of same-sex couples. Among the most important precedents named by Justice Kennedy were *Loving v. Virginia* (1967), *Zablocki v. Redhail* (1978), *Turner v. Safley* (1987), *Goodridge v. Department of Public Health* (2003), and *United States v. Windsor* (2013) (United States, Supreme Court, "*Obergefell*" 9–11).[97] The majority opinion was eager to provide a broad legal basis in order to strengthen their decision since the critique of the dissenting judges, particularly in regard to their progressive interpretation of the Fourteenth Amendment's Due Process Clause, was unsparing and construed the ruling as controversial.[98]

Fully aware that a ruling in favor of marriage equality would provoke accusations of judicial activism, the majority opinion tried to invalidate such criticism beforehand: "While the Constitution contemplates that democracy is the appropriate process for change, individuals who are harmed need not await legislative action before asserting a fundamental right" (United States, Supreme Court, "*Obergefell*" 5). In his opinion of the court, which Justices Bader Ginsburg, Breyer, Sotomayor, and Kagan joined, Justice Kennedy explained why he believed that such a case required a certain degree of judicial review and why originalism was the wrong approach:

> History and tradition guide and discipline this inquiry but do not set its outer boundaries. . . . That method respects our history and learns from it without allowing the past alone to rule the present. The nature of injustice is that we may not always see it in our own times. The generations that wrote and ratified the Bill of Rights and the Fourteenth Amendment did not presume to know the extent of freedom in all of its dimensions, and so they entrusted to future generations a charter protecting the right of

97 *Loving v. Virginia* "invalidated bans on interracial unions" since "a unanimous Court held that marriage is 'one of the vital personal rights essential to the orderly pursuit of happiness by free men'" (United States, Supreme Court, "*Obergefell*" 11). In *Zablocki v. Redhail*, the court held that "the right to marry was burdened by a law prohibiting fathers who were behind on child support from marrying" (11). According to Justice Kennedy, the same principle was applied in *Turner v. Safley* "which held that the right to marry was unabridged by regulations limiting the privilege of prison inmates to marry" (11).

98 While the majority opinion held that denying marriage to same-sex couples violates their Fourteenth Amendment rights (United States, Supreme Court, "*Obergefell*" 4), the dissenting judges strongly disagreed (Roberts, "*Obergefell*" 23–24; Thomas, "*Obergefell*" 3; Scalia, "*Obergefell*" 3; Alito, "*Obergefell*" 2).

> all persons to enjoy liberty as we learn its meaning. When new insight reveals discord between the Constitution's central protections and a received legal stricture, a claim to liberty must be addressed. (United States, Supreme Court, "*Obergefell*" 2)

Furthermore, Justice Kennedy emphasized that the institution of marriage had changed previously and was still undergoing change because society continues to transform and evolve over time. When critics of same-sex marriage argued that a ruling in favor of marriage equality would alter the traditional concept of marriage, they seemed to have forgotten that the institution of marriage had already experienced tremendous changes. At one time, marriage used to be an arrangement between the couple's parents, who made their decision according to what was strategically beneficial for the family. The idea of love as the prime motivation for marriage is a comparatively modern concept and is still not prevalent in all parts of the world. Another major change that had been made to the institution of marriage was the legal role of women in marriage. The end of coverture[99] had an enormous impact on the concept of marriage and empowered women by granting them rights in marriage independent of their husband (Abrams 415–16). Kennedy affirmed that "these and other developments in the institution of marriage over the past centuries were not mere superficial changes. Rather, they worked deep transformations in its structure, affecting aspects of marriage long viewed by many as essential" (United States, Supreme Court, "*Obergefell*" 6–7). Retrospectively, most Americans could not even imagine that these aspects were once deemed essential. The majority opinion and their supporters hoped that the minds of Americans would advance in the same way as they had with previous marriage reconceptualizations.

"[C]hanged understandings of marriage are characteristic of a Nation where new dimensions of freedom become apparent to new generations," Justice Kennedy insisted in his writing (United States, Su-

[99] Under the law of coverture, a married woman had no legal status of her own but did everything under the protection and cover of her husband. As a result, she was referred to as a covered woman, which led to the term 'coverture.' A woman under coverture was not allowed to enter a contract, make a will, testify in court, work, or sue or be sued without her husband's approval. Coverture ended in the late 19th century when laws were enacted which gradually extended women's rights (Abrams 415–16).

preme Court, "*Obergefell*" 7). Thereby, Kennedy inextricably linked marriage and the nation. The debate on marriage equality could not be assessed separately from questions concerning the nation and American everyday nationalism. The debate on marriage equality was a discursive reconstruction of the American nation and American national identity. American everyday nationalism could not escape change in this process since transformations to the institution of marriage cannot take place without affecting the American national self-concept. By granting marriage to same-sex couples, the United States added its name to the list of nations supporting marriage equality.[100] This change in law influenced both how the American nation was perceived in an international context as well as how the American people saw themselves. A change to the institution of marriage implied a change to the nation. Justice Kennedy and the majority opinion also seemed to suggest that the American people could not avoid opening marriage to same-sex couples unless they wished to fully change their self-concept as a nation as one that unequivocally believes in freedom and progress. A nation that upholds a set of values like that of the United States must be open to transforming its understanding of marriage.

The majority opinion was aware of the fact that due to this interconnectedness of the discourses on marriage equality and nationalism, their ruling in *Obergefell* would affect Americans' identities, and depending on which side of the discursive war over marriage one stood, this change could be interpreted as one for the better or for the worse. The liberty promised to the American people by their Constitution "included certain specific rights that allow persons, with in a lawful realm, to define

[100] At the time of the ruling in *Obergefell*, same-sex marriage had already been legalized in a number of Western European countries (see Felter and Renwick): the Netherlands (2001), Belgium (2003), Spain (2005), Norway and Sweden (2009), Portugal and Iceland (2010), Denmark (2012), the United Kingdom (2013), and Luxembourg and Ireland (2015). Some countries, for instance Germany, had not yet legalized same-sex marriage but allowed civil unions as of 2001. In 2005, Canada was the first non-European country to legalize same-sex marriage. In South America, marriage equality became the law of the land in Argentina in 2010, in Brazil and Uruguay in 2013, and in Mexico in 2015. In Africa, only South Africa would allow same-sex marriage as of 2006. In comparison to other Western countries and even some countries in South America, the United States was comparatively late in its nationwide legalization of same-sex marriage.

and express their identity" (United States, Supreme Court, "*Obergefell*" 1–2). By interpreting the Constitution and thereby determining if it was within same-sex couples' liberty rights to marry, the majority opinion also determined who was able to define and express their identity, in what way they were able to express it, and if it was consistent with what they considered American national identity at that point in time. Since the Supreme Court decided in favor of marriage equality, it was primarily same-sex couples and their supporters whose self-concept as Americans aligned with the idea of nationalism of a nation that granted marriage equality.

The majority opinion delivered by Justice Kennedy gave the example of Army Reserve Sergeant First Class Ijpe DeKoe and his partner Thomas Kostura. The couple married in New York in 2012 and after DeKoe returned from his deployment to Afghanistan, the husbands settled in Tennessee where their marriage was not recognized. In the eyes of the majority opinion, this meant that "DeKoe, who served this Nation to preserve the freedom the Constitution protects, must endure substantial burden" (United States, Supreme Court, "*Obergefell*" 7). An American fighting to protect the freedom and the liberty the Constitution and the nation promised to him should not be deprived of exactly what he had served to protect merely on the grounds of his sexual orientation. As a result, Justice Kennedy concluded the opinion of the court with the following remarks in which he repeatedly affirmed that this ruling was based on principles of equality and dignity and was ultimately rooted in the text of the Constitution and the American nation itself:

> No union is more profound than marriage, for it embodies the highest ideals of love, fidelity, devotion, sacrifice, and family. In forming a marital union, two people become something greater than once they were. As some of the petitioners in these cases demonstrate, marriage embodies a love that may endure even past death. It would misunderstand these men and women to say they disrespect the idea of marriage. Their plea is that they do respect it, respect it so deeply that they seek to find its fulfillment for themselves. Their hope is not to be condemned to live in loneliness, excluded from one of civilization's oldest institutions. They ask for equal dignity in the eyes of the law. The Constitution grants them that right. (United States, Supreme Court, "*Obergefell*" 28).

With these closing words, marriage equality became the law of the land in the United States.

Dissenting Opinion: Justice Roberts

The focus of Justice Roberts' dissent was judicial activism because, in his opinion, the majority overstepped their jurisdiction when they ruled as though they were legitimated to decide on same-sex marriage. Roberts admitted at the beginning of his writing that the petitioners made incredibly strong arguments for their case (Roberts, "*Obergefell*" 1). Despite his understanding for the majority opinion's decision to consequently rule in favor of the plaintiffs, Roberts was unambiguous that he could not agree with how they fulfilled their judicial duties. The majority opinion's liberal and free interpretation of the law was his strongest point of concern that ultimately led to his dissent:

> [T]his court is not a legislature. Whether same-sex marriage is a good idea should be of no concern to us. Under the Constitution, judges have power to say what the law is, not what it should be. . . . The majority's decision is an act of will, not legal judgment. The right it announces has no basis in the Constitution or this Court's precedent. The majority expressly disclaims judicial "caution" and omits even a pretense of humility, openly relying on its desire to remake society according to its own "new insight" into the "nature of injustice". . . . As a result, the Court invalidates the marriage laws of more than half the States and orders the transformation of a social institution that has formed the basis of human society for millennia, for the Kalahari Bushmen and the Han Chinese, the Carthaginians and the Aztecs. Just who do we think we are? It can be tempting for judges to confuse our own preferences with the requirements of the law. (3)

Chief Justice John Roberts criticized the majority for ignoring history and tradition and completely discarding judicial restraint. Furthermore, he claimed that the five justices overrode the democratic process and exceeded their judicial authority. Roberts was convinced that the majority opinion decided without regard toward the American people and used the judiciary in a way for which it was not originally intended. This would come at a cost, and it was the public at large who would pay the price: "The Court's accumulation of power does not occur in a vacuum. It comes at the expense of the people. And they know it" (26). For Roberts, *Obergefell v. Hodges* was more about a jurisdictional issue than about the question of whether marriage equality was the right choice for the American people. It was an act of hubris to believe that they should expedite the process of marriage equality becoming the law of the land. "Nowhere is the majority's extravagant conception of judicial supremacy more evident than in its description – and dismissal – of the public debate regarding same-sex marriage," Roberts wrote (25). Chief Justice Roberts found it deeply problematic that the American people were not able to enact this change themselves and at the speed that such a change through legislation would have required. Roberts correctly warned that closing a debate often results in even greater opposition towards a contentious point:

> By deciding this question under the Constitution, the Court removes it from the realm of democratic decision. There will be consequences to shutting down the political process on an issue of such profound public significance. Closing debate tends to close minds. People denied a voice are less likely to accept the ruling of a court on an issue that does not seem to be the sort of thing courts usually decide. As a thoughtful commentator observed about another issue. . . . Indeed, however heartened the proponents of same-sex marriage might be on this day, it is worth acknowledging what they have lost, and lost forever: the opportunity to win the true acceptance that comes from persuading their fellow citizens of the justice of their cause. And they lose this just when the winds of change were freshening at their backs. (27)[101]

Chief Justice Roberts was right that progress, especially progress achieved via a court ruling and not through change in people's hearts and minds, often provokes opposition and fear. Transformations of the status-quo lead to a fear of a loss of stability, even more so when the alleged progress affects deeply held beliefs and leads to core changes in a society's framework and self-definition. Altered concepts of marriage and family were perceived as highly dangerous for the stability and integrity of the nation by some Americans, as they can be classified as core transformations. A change to the institution of marriage had implications on American national self-definition as the analysis of insults of un-Americanism in chapters IV.B and C illustrated. If people feel as

[101] This appears to be an aspect Roberts deeply cared about since he employed similar words at the beginning of his dissent when detailing the downside of the majority ruling: "Supporters of same-sex marriage have achieved considerable success persuading their fellow citizens – through the democratic process – to adopt their view. That ends today. Five lawyers have closed the debate and enacted their own vision of marriage as a matter of constitutional law" (Roberts, "*Obergefell*" 2).

if they have no say in a certain issue, they are much less likely to accept change or be open to new ideas. This is the point at which accusations of un-Americanism become the loudest and most prominent. Many opponents of marriage equality no longer saw the purpose in political debates as the debate had been closed.

Another controversial point at the center of the heated debate on same-sex marriage, which was also addressed by Roberts in his dissent, was the question of whether this ruling resulted in a redefinition of marriage. "The real question in these cases is what constitutes 'marriage,' or – more precisely – *who decides* what constitutes 'marriage'?" Roberts asked in his dissent (4). Roberts was engaging in two debates here: first, he reiterated his criticism of the fact that five judges decided on marriage equality and not the American people, and secondly, he took up the conflict on the definition of marriage. Were those who defined what was understood by marriage in American society also the those who ruled this conflict? Opponents of marriage equality claimed that gay rights advocates had no sense of history or tradition since they wanted to redefine marriage no matter the cost and without any consideration. By contrast, same-sex marriage advocates protested these accusations and maintained that they did not wish to redefine the core meaning of marriage. They only demanded equal rights for all Americans regardless of sexual orientation; the rights that were promised to them by the Fourteenth Amendment to the United States Constitution. Roberts argued that the majority opinion in *Obergefell v. Hodges* did in fact redefine marriage and their assertions to the contrary were based on a weak line of argumentation. Justices Bader Ginsburg, Breyer, Sotomayor, Kagan, and Kennedy based their argument that same-sex couples should have equal marriage rights primarily on three precedents. These precedents were *Loving v. Virginia*, which invalidated racial restrictions on marriage, *Zablocki v. Redhail*, where the Court invalidated a law barring fathers delinquent on child-support payments from marrying, and *Turner v. Safley*, which invalidated marriage restrictions on the basis of one's status as a prisoner (United States, Supreme Court, "*Obergefell*" 11). Roberts held that these three cases present completely different situations since "[n]one of the laws at issue in those cases purported to change the core definition of marriage as the union of a man and a woman" (16). Furthermore, he used the examples of *Loving v. Virginia* and *Brown v. Board of Education* in order to illustrate his point: "Removing racial barriers to marriage therefore did not change what a marriage was any more than integrating schools changed what a school was" (16). Roberts then continued his dissent by further explaining why he saw no legal basis for using these three cases as precedents supportive of the ruling in *Obergefell v. Hodges*: "In short, the 'right to marry' cases stand for the important but limited proposition that particular restrictions on access to marriage as *traditionally defined* violate due process. These precedents say nothing at all about a right to make a State change its definition of marriage. . ." (16). In this section of his dissent, Roberts mirrored the worries and concerns of same-sex marriage opponents who were convinced that extending the right to marriage to gay Americans entailed a redefinition of the concept of marriage as society had known it for centuries (Birk in Hallowell).

Some Americans perceived this ruling as a departure from American history and sensed that it would redefine the nation permanently. Chief Justice Roberts viewed the ruling as dangerous because it would cause the nation to move away from its founding principles which had made the United States a city upon a hill shining over all other nations. Marriage and the nation are closely intertwined.[102] Altering the common understanding of marriage so significantly as to move away from its conceptualization as a union between a man and a woman could have tremendous consequences for the integrity and stability of the nation. "This singular understanding of marriage has prevailed in the United States throughout our history. . . . To those who drafted and ratified the Constitution, this conception of marriage and family 'was a given: its structure, its stability, roles, and values accepted by all,'" Roberts reminded the court ("*Obergefell*" 5–6). Risking potential harm to the American nation in exchange for granting marriage rights to a minority group according to a highly controversial interpretation of the Constitution was not acceptable for dissenting Americans. What was at stake were the stability and the values that had made this nation successful.

Not only was Roberts critical of the precedents the majority opinion cited, he was also not convinced that marriage rights could be granted to same-sex couples on the basis of the Constitution's Fourteenth Amendment and its Equal Protection and Due Process Clause. Marriage equality supporters took it for granted that same-sex marriage was guaranteed by the Fourteenth Amendment. This point had been part of their rhetoric in the fight for same-sex marriage. However, the idea that marriage equality was

[102] For an investigation of the interconnectedness between the institution of marriage and nation in the United States, see chapter VI.B.

granted to same-sex couples by both the Due Process Clause and the Equal Protection Clause was not as obvious and uncontested as many advocates believed. Chief Justice Roberts failed to see any justification for marriage equality in the Fourteenth Amendment's Equal Protection Clause although it was frequently cited by the majority opinion, and he attacked the opinion of the court for this false interpretation of the law: "[T]he majority fails to provide even a single sentence explaining how the Equal Protection Clause supplies independent weight for its position, nor does it attempt to justify its gratuitous violation of the canon against unnecessarily resolving constitutional questions" ("*Obergefell*" 23–24). In his critique, Roberts expressed doubts about the judicial competences of the majority judges. He admitted that the five judges made an effort to justify their decision by adducing four principles in the Court's due process precedents but concluded that they had ultimately failed to convince due to their weak line of argumentation:

> [T]he majority's approach has no basis in principle or tradition, except for the unprincipled tradition of judicial policymaking. . . . Stripped of its shiny rhetorical gloss, the majority's argument is that the Due Process Clause gives same-sex couples a fundamental right to marry because it will be good for them and for society. If I were a legislator, I would certainly consider that view as a matter of social policy. But as a judge, I find the majority's position indefensible as a matter of constitutional law. (Roberts, "*Obergefell*" 10)

Roberts continued with the same point of criticism at a later point of his dissent in which he also addressed his concerns about the problematic future of this court if they failed to correctly interpret the law, if they had no respect for American history and tradition, and if they did not refrain from judicial activism:

> The majority's understanding of due process lays out a tantalizing vision of the future for Members of this Court: If an unvarying social institution enduring over all of recorded history cannot inhibit judicial policymaking, what can? But this approach is dangerous for the rule of law. The purpose of insisting that implied fundamental rights have roots in the history and tradition of our people is to ensure that when unelected judges strike down democratically enacted laws, they do so based on something more than their own beliefs. The Court today not only overlooks our country's entire history and tradition but actively repudiates it, preferring to live only in the heady days of the here and now. (Roberts, "*Obergefell*" 10)

Chief Justice Roberts was far from the only legal expert to heavily criticize the majority opinion for their interpretation of the Constitution's Fourteenth Amendment, its Equal Protect Clause, and especially its Due Process Clause. In his analysis of *Obergefell v. Hodges*, the constitutional law Professor Michael Stokes Paulsen claimed that "the Court's conclusion . . . has no basis in the text, structure, logic or history of the Constitution, and is contrary to all evidence of historical understandings at the time the amendment was adopted." Furthermore, Stokes Paulsen called the majority opinion's interpretation of the Constitution in favor of same-sex couples one of the most radical examples of judicial activism the Supreme Court had seen since *Roe v. Wade*: "For better or worse – for richer or poorer – the Court has married same-sex unions to the Constitution, and to an unabashedly activist and historically indefensible conception of judicial power." Both Stokes Paulsen and Chief Justice Roberts deemed this ruling an example of extreme judicial activism and were convinced that the Constitution did not grant same-sex couples the right to marry. Roberts concluded his dissent with the following remark: "If you are among the many Americans – of whatever sexual orientation – who favor expanding same-sex marriage, by all means celebrate today's decision. Celebrate the achievement of a desired goal. . . . But do not celebrate the Constitution. It had nothing to do with it" ("*Obergefell*" 29).

Dissenting Opinion: Justice Scalia

Justice Scalia's dissent was much shorter than Chief Justice Roberts' and for the most part he concentrated on one point of criticism: judicial activism. In contrast to Roberts, he did not make an effort to address various aspects of the majority ruling with which he could not agree. He set the tone of his dissent in the first paragraph and left no room for ambiguity regarding his thoughts about the majority opinion's behavior in this landmark civil rights case:

> I join THE CHIEF JUSTICE's opinion in full. I write separately to call attention to this Court's threat to American democracy. The substance of today's decree is not of immense personal importance to me. The law can recognize as marriage whatever sexual attachments and living arrangements it wishes, and can accord them favorable civil consequences, from

> tax treatment to rights of inheritance. Those civil consequences – and the public approval that conferring the name of marriage evidences – can perhaps have adverse social effects, but no more adverse than the effects of many other controversial laws. So it is not of special importance to me what the law says about marriage. It is of overwhelming importance, however, who it is that rules me. Today's decree says that my Ruler, and the Ruler of 320 million Americans coast-to-coast, is a majority of the nine lawyers on the Supreme Court. The opinion in these cases is the furthest extension in fact – and the furthest extension one can even imagine – of the Court's claimed power to create "liberties" that the Constitution and its Amendments neglect to mention. This practice of constitutional revision by an unelected committee of nine, always accompanied (as it is today) by extravagant praise of liberty, robs the People of the most important liberty they asserted in the Declaration of Independence and won in the Revolution of 1776: the freedom to govern themselves. (Scalia, "*Obergefell*" 1–2)

Immediately speaking of the "Court's threat to American democracy" (1), Scalia did not engage in a lengthy introduction to guide the reader towards his point of criticism. In calling the court a "threat to American democracy" (1), he left no room for speculation about his belief that the judicial activism of the court would harm the American nation. Scalia emphasized that he did not care if marriage equality became the law of the land and same-sex couples were granted additional rights and benefits. Furthermore, he acknowledged that many laws are hotly debated and controversial. Therefore, avoiding a change in law to prevent a potential backlash is not a viable option. However, for Scalia, the decisive difference lay in the process through which a law came to be. If a law was decided by democratic majoritarian means, i. e., the American people or their elected representatives voted on an issue, Justice Scalia would support that change in law even though some Americans could experience negative consequences as a result (2). He found it highly problematic that a majority of the nine unelected judges of the Supreme Court – a mere five people – could dictate laws to 320 million Americans while claiming to bring liberties and equality to them (1–2). What made the situation even worse was that the majority of these judges failed to realize that they were overstepping their jurisdiction by sanctioning same-sex marriage based on their interpretation of the Constitution:

> The strikingly unrepresentative character of the body voting on today's social upheaval would be irrelevant if they were functioning as *judges*, answering the legal question whether the American people had ever ratified a constitutional provision that was understood to proscribe the traditional definition of marriage. (Scalia, "*Obergefell*" 6)

In addition to using phrases such as "social upheaval" (6) and "threat to American democracy" (1) in his dissent, Scalia continued employing words with a similar sentiment as he repeatedly evoked the imagery of a violent and unlawful overthrow of the status quo: "But what astounds is the hubris reflected in today's judicial *Putsch*" (6; emphasis added). His choice of words was reflective of his fury over the judicial activism he witnessed in *Obergefell v. Hodges*, and he was not alone in the intensity of his outrage over the judicial activism that seemed to characterize the majority opinion's ruling in *Obergefell v. Hodges*.

Scalia acted as the voice of the many opponents of marriage equality whose concerns he was able to verbalize more precisely than most of them could. As marriage rights were extended to same-sex couples through a court ruling, many opponents who raised charges of un-Americanism felt that their voices never played a role in this whole process of marriage equality becoming the law of the land. Like Roberts, Scalia heavily criticized that this ruling effectively ended the debate on the constitutionality of same-sex marriage. This also meant that a healthy discussion among American citizens, something which could have been beneficial in the overall acceptance of gay Americans, was ended abruptly. Scalia lamented: "[T]he court ends this debate, in an opinion lacking even a thin veneer of law" ("*Obergefell*" 4). According to Scalia, such an undemocratic process does not extend the rights of people but much rather "robs the People of the . . . freedom to govern themselves" (2) as promised to them by their most cherished documents. By referring to the Declaration of Independence, Scalia named one of the same documents that gay rights supporters often referenced in their fight for personal liberty. This illustrates that, just as charges of un-Americanism were used by both sides of the debate, the founding documents were also mutually cited in both parties' argumentation. Furthermore, Scalia also dug deep into early American cultural history by raising allusions to the Boston Tea Party: "[T]o allow the policy question of same-sex marriage to be considered and resolved by a select, patrician, highly unrepresentative panel of nine is to violate a principle even more fundamental than no taxation without representation: no social transformation without representation" (6).[103] Here Scalia frames the alleged judicial activism in *Obergefell v. Hodges* as a judicial legislation "without representation" (6), which he regarded as worse than the revolutionary-precipitating event of the Boston Tea Party. The Declaration of Independence, which resulted from taxation without representation, was worthless for contemporary Americans if they were still not adequately heard and represented. As a consequence, it is unsurprising that many people called this ruling un-American since it went against who they were, or at least believed themselves to be, as Americans and against their idea of American everyday nationalism.

Dissenting Opinion: Justice Thomas

Justice Thomas engaged with this conflict over the core of American nationalism in his dissent on *Obergefell v. Hodges* when he wrote: "The Court's decision today is at odds not only with the Constitution, but with the principles upon which our Nation was built. . . . This distortion of our Constitution not only ignores the text, it inverts the relationship between the individual and the state in our Republic" (Thomas, "*Obergefell*" 2). As a consequence, the ruling would not only result in a redefinition of mar-

[103] In his dissent on *Obergefell v. Hodges*, Justice Scalia repeatedly lamented the severe lack of diversity among the justices of the Supreme Court:

> [T]his Court, which consists of only nine men and women, all of them successful lawyers who studied at Harvard or Yale Law School. Four of the nine are natives of New York City. Eight of them grew up in east- and west-coast States. Only one hails from the vast expanse in-between. Not a single South-westerner or even, to tell the truth, a genuine Westerner (California does not count). Not a single evangelical Christian (a group that comprises about one quarter of Americans), or even a Protestant of any denomination. The strikingly unrepresentative character of the body voting on today's social upheaval would be irrelevant if they were functioning as judges, answering the legal question whether the American people had ever ratified a constitutional provision that was understood to proscribe the traditional definition of marriage. ("*Obergefell*" 6)

The lack of diversity which Scalia describes is problematic when taken into consideration that it is mostly those Americans in the South or the American Midwest who did not feel heard in the hearings on the nationwide legalization of same-sex marriage.

riage but also in a redefinition of American democracy and the nation itself. Such a deep intrusion into people's concept of the American nation would lead to even greater fear of the potential consequences of marriage equality on American everyday nationalism. In addition, Justice Thomas discussed an aspect which he also regarded as problematic: the majority opinion's questionable stance on liberty. Justice Thomas wrote: "In the American legal tradition, liberty has long been understood as individual freedom *from* governmental action, and not as a right *to* a particular governmental entitlement" (7). Although the majority opinion intended to extend the liberty and freedom rights of Americans, freedom from governmental intervention or action had been threatened by their court ruling. "The majority's inversion of the original meaning of liberty will likely cause collateral damage to other aspects of our constitutional order that protect liberty. . . . The majority apparently disregards the political process as a protection for liberty" (13), Thomas continued. This claim that the majority opinion falsely construed or misunderstood the concept of liberty was closely connected to the charge that they willingly misinterpreted the Due Process Clause of the Fourteenth Amendment so that it would conform with their own personal convictions:

> Even if the doctrine of substantive due process were somehow defensible – it is not – petitioners still would not have a claim. To invoke the protection of the Due Process Clause at all – whether under a theory of "substantive" or "procedural" due process – a party must first identify a deprivation of "life, liberty, or property." The majority claims these state laws deprive petitioners of "liberty," but the concept of "liberty" it conjures up bears no resemblance to any plausible meaning of that word as it is used in the Due Process Clauses. (3)

This is a controversial issue that was already discussed at length by Chief Justice Roberts (Roberts, "*Obergefell*" 10–15). Justice Thomas joined him but put more emphasis on the majority opinion's incorrect understanding of the American concept of liberty.[104] Roberts, Thomas, and Scalia regard-

[104] The discussion of the idea of liberty was of such great importance to Thomas that he dedicated the whole conclusion of his dissent to this point of criticism. He once again explained:

> Our Constitution – like the Declaration of Independence before it – was predicated on a simple truth: One's liberty, not to mention one's dignity, was something to be shielded from – not provided by – the State. Today's decision casts that truth aside. In its haste to reach a desired result, the ma-

ed judicial activism as one of the most dangerous threats to the concept of liberty. Since five judges demonstrated that they could reinterpret or redefine liberty as they pleased to support a minority in its quest for equal rights, some Americans feared an actual reconceptualization of American nationalism, possibly resulting in a form of American identity with which they no longer were able to sympathize or identify.

Another concern of the public at large was religious liberty. The majority opinion did not elaborate on this concern but simply confirmed to those worried about religious freedom: "[T]he First Amendment ensures that religions, those who adhere to religious doctrines, and others have protection as they seek to teach the principles that are so fulfilling and so central to their lives and faiths" (United States, Supreme Court, "*Obergefell*" 5). However, many critics asked themselves if they could still rely on the liberties promised to them in the Constitution if the interpretation of the amendments had become questionable and some justices of the court had started to act as judicial legislators. Thomas was not the only dissenting judge who expressed his concern about the future of the First Amendment; however, he focused on this point to a much larger extent than Justices Roberts and Scalia. In his dissent, he wrote: "Aside from undermining the political processes that protect our liberty, the majority's decision threatens the religious liberty our Nation has long sought to protect" (Thomas, "*Obergefell*" 14). At a later point in his writing, he continued this line of argumentation by drawing a connection between marriage and the bleak prospects of religion in the United States:

> In our society, marriage is not simply a governmental institution; it is a religious institution as well. . . . Today's decision might change the former, but it cannot change the latter. It appears all but inevitable that the two will come into conflict, particularly as individuals and churches are confronted with demands to participate in and endorse civil marriages between same-sex couples. The majority appears unmoved by that inevitability. It makes only a weak gesture toward religious liberty in a single paragraph. (15)

> jority misapplies a clause focused on "due process" to afford substantive rights, disregards the most plausible understanding of the "liberty" protected by that clause, and distorts the principles on which this Nation was founded. Its decision will have inestimable consequences for our Constitution and our society. (Thomas, "*Obergefell*" 17–18)

This redefinition of marriage that took place through *Obergefell v. Hodges* would harm religion and religious liberty in the United States just as many opponents had warned for years. Thomas' statement, which emphasized that marriage was also a religious institution, addressed the fear among opponents of marriage equality that the religious aspect of marriage would further disappear in the future. Accusations of un-Americanism came most prominently from opponents who saw the possibility that marriage equality would negatively affect their religious identity and force them to act against their religious beliefs. By dedicating only one paragraph to the concerns of these Americans, the majority opinion reinforced the impression that they did not care about them or were dismissive towards their worries.

Dissenting Opinion: Justice Alito

Justice Alito mainly focused on two topics in his dissent: judicial legislation and the threat of reverse discrimination. Regarding the question if it was within the court's jurisdiction to decide on this case, he firmly advised against that:

> Until the federal courts intervened, the American people were engaged in a debate about whether their States should recognize same-sex marriage. The question in these cases, however, is not what States should do about same-sex marriage but whether the Constitution answers that question for them. It does not. The Constitution leaves that question to be decided by the people of each State. ("*Obergefell*" 1–2)

Justice Alito held that the only rightful way for the United States to decide on the matter of same-sex marriage was in the legislative process. It would have respected the right of the American people to govern themselves, a right that the majority opinion had taken away from them with their reckless judicial activism (Alito, "*Obergefell*" 6–8).

In the ruling, Alito saw a ruthless attack both on American tradition itself and on Americans supporting traditional ideas and values. He took the side of these Americans and endorsed their claims that this ruling was unconstitutional, and that the majority opinion's interpretation of the law had no secure foundation in the history or the legal framework of this country: "If a bare majority of Justices can invent a new right and impose that right on the rest of the country, the only real limit on what future majorities will be able to do is their own sense of what those with political power and cultural influence are willing to tolerate" ("*Obergefell*" 7). The most critical part of this statement was the formulation "invent a new right" (7). With his choice of words, Alito supported opponents of same-sex marriage in their allegations that same-sex marriage was not consistent with American law, history, and tradition. Therefore, it was not a part of the American national identity and self-definition, especially not if it was decided in an un-American act of judicial activism without regard for the right of the American people to self-govern.

Alito feared that *Obergefell v. Hodges* might lead to severe reverse discrimination. This Supreme Court ruling was the ultimate confirmation that it was no longer accepted to discriminate against same-sex couples when it came to marriage rights. As a result, Alito accused the majority opinion of willingly exposing opponents to potential discrimination and endangering national cohesion: "By imposing its own views on the entire country, the majority facilitates the marginalization of the many Americans who have traditional ideas" (*Obergefell* 7). Not only was this ruling an attack on people's rights to self-govern, but it also paved the way for the marginalization and discrimination of conservative Americans, as Alito claims:

> Today's decision usurps the constitutional right of the people to decide whether to keep or alter the traditional understanding of marriage. The decision will also have other important consequences. It will be used to vilify Americans who are unwilling to assent to the new orthodoxy. . . . Perhaps recognizing how its reasoning may be used, the majority attempts, toward the end of its opinion, to reassure those who oppose same-sex marriage that their rights of conscience will be protected. . . . We will soon see whether this proves to be true. I assume that those who cling to old beliefs will be able to whisper their thoughts in the recesses of their homes, but if they repeat those views in public, they will risk being labeled as bigots and treated as such by governments, employers, and schools. (6–7)

By raising this concern, Alito verbalized the worries of many opponents of marriage equality. With the overall acceptance of marriage quality growing in the United States, the tide had turned. Those who were once in the majority now increasingly found themselves in the minority. Additionally, this new minority status came with the side effect of needing to defend their disapproval of same-sex marriage. Alito's choice of words might sound dramatic and overstated; however, he was speaking for those who often relied on the rhetoric of un-Americanism because they either could not adequately express their worries or would no longer dare to do so out of fear of reverse discrimination. This societal change, which was perceived by many opponents as severe and threatening, reversed the power structure in the American society in regard to opinions on same-sex marriage.

D Backlash to Court Rulings

The Supreme Court rulings in *United States v. Windsor* and *Obergefell v. Hodges* were important steps in the gradual inclusion of gay Americans into people's contemporary notions of American nationalism. However, not every American agreed to the court's rulings and regarded them as progress. Controversial landmark civil rights cases, especially if they were subject to a certain degree of judicial activism, are disproportionally prone to backlash. "Courts are the most likely institution to inspire backlash simply because of their propensity to issue holdings that settle a matter for one side and against another, rather than reaching the type of political compromise usually sought by legislators" (Deming 288). In addition, cases like *Brown v. Board of Education*, *Roe v. Wade*, or *Obergefell v. Hodges* affect the lives of millions of Americans because they can change core American values and alter the prevailing understanding of what (un-)Americanism entails. To list *Obergefell v. Hodges* in the same breath as *Brown v. Board of Education* and *Roe v. Wade* in regard to its impact on American nationalism is not an overstatement. Considering the scope and the far-reaching consequences of this marriage equality ruling, it is vital to look at studies on public backlash after same-sex marriage cases. The reaction of the public to such a ruling is critical to understanding the trajectory of the further development of American nationalism. If the backlash is too severe, the inclusion of a minority group into the dominant concept of American everyday nationalism will not be successful despite the best efforts of the judiciary. In this context, backlash should be understood "as the mobilization of political opposition against an adverse court ruling, the effect of which is to undermine either the ruling's implementation or subsequent policy goals of the victor" (Deming 283). However, such a backlash does not have to be acute or immediate. Opposition can follow either directly after a ruling or with a certain delay, for instance, after a change in administration which gave rise to different voices as it was the case in the change of government from President Obama to President Trump. Even years after *Obergefell*, there is still the potentiality of a backlash. Parameters increasing the likelihood of a backlash could have changed in the meantime because the relevant voices of opposition have become louder or because they have received a platform for their opposition.

One of the first decisive judicial victories of marriage equality advocates was *Goodridge v. Department of Public Health* in 2003, in which the Massachusetts Supreme Court held that an individual may not be barred from protections and benefits of civil marriage on the grounds that the person was marrying someone of the same sex (Massachusetts State, Massachusetts Supreme Judicial Court, "*Goodridge*" 11).[105] Michael J. Klarman conducted extensive research on whether *Goodridge v. Department of Public Health* triggered a backlash from same-sex marriage opponents. To a certain extent, his findings diminish the victory that was achieved for gay rights: "Some evidence suggests that *Goodridge* temporarily halted or even reversed a liberalizing trend in favor of gay marriage; support did not rebound to previous levels until the summer of 2005. . . . Indeed, *Goodridge* may have caused a temporary resurgence in anti-gay sentiment, generally" (Klarman, *Closet* 98). Although Vermont had already debated same-sex marriage in court in 2000, which resulted in civil unions being introduced in the same year, the public and political attention generated by the Massachusetts case was significantly higher, not least because Massachusetts was the first state to grant marriage and not only civil unions to same-sex couples. In reaction to the ruling, thirteen states added provisions to their state marriage laws which defined marriage in the traditional sense as the union between a man and a woman (Klarman, "Brown" 466). This made marriage equality much harder to achieve for gay rights advocates because it limited the possibilities of both legislatures and judges in interpreting state constitutions in favor of homosexual Americans. These newly added provisions had the clear support of the majority of Americans living in these states since these measures passed by a wide margin (466).[106] Klarman argues that the backlash to *Goodridge v. Department of Public Health* was so severe in 2004 that it might have even contributed to the reelection of President George W.

[105] The question which the Massachusetts Supreme Judicial Court was to decide on in *Goodridge v. Department of Public Health* was whether government action that bars same-sex couples from civil marriage constitutes a legitimate exercise of the State's authority to regulate conduct, or whether, as the plaintiffs claimed, this categorical marriage exclusion violates the Massachusetts Constitution (Massachusetts State, Massachusetts Supreme Judicial Court, "*Goodridge*" 321). *Goodridge* was the first ruling in which a state court granted full marriage rights to same-sex couples (344).

[106] In most states, the opponents of gay rights won with a margin of approximately 75%. In the state of Mississippi, the provision even had the support of 86% of voters. Only in Michigan and Oregon were such initiatives less successful as they won less than 60% of the vote (Klarman, "Brown" 466).

Bush since African Americans, the elderly, and working-class Catholics voted for a Republican presidential candidate in unprecedented numbers (467): "[T]he backlash ignited by *Goodridge* possibly ensured the re-election of a president whose judicial appointments will almost certainly delay the legal recognition of same-sex marriage" (468). Furthermore, Robert Knight, director of the Culture and Family Institute of Concerned Women for America, was quoted as saying: "President Bush should send a bouquet of flowers to the members of the Massachusetts Supreme Judicial Court who wrote the decision legalizing same-sex marriage there" (Knight qtd in Latour 298).

There are two questions that arise from the aftermath of the Massachusetts ruling. First, what provokes backlash to such court rulings and, second, was the backlash after *Goodridge* a singular occurrence or was it indicative of a correlation between court rulings in favor of gay rights and negative repercussions for gay Americans resulting from the larger public's response? Klarman identifies three reasons why marriage equality court rulings tend to cause backlash: "They raise the salience of an issue, they incite anger over 'outside interference' or 'judicial activism,' and they alter the order in which social change would otherwise have occurred" ("Brown" 473). In regard to the latter indicator, Klarman agrees with previous scholars that "judicially mandated social reform may mobilize greater resistance than change accomplished through legislatures or with the acquiescence of other democratically operated institutions" (475). As a result of this "countermobilization" (Siegel 1746) in some parts of the American society, attempts of lower court judges to bolster gay rights sometimes resulted in citizens overturning their ruling through legislative actions.

Siegel observed that "a growing number of commentators began to argue that popular reaction to decisions recognizing the right of same-sex couples to marry demonstrated the impotence of courts to vindicate minority rights" (1735). The judiciary, even more than the legislature and the executive branch of government, is meant to be a counter-majoritarian balance in order to protect the interests and rights of minorities, especially in cases where the majority holds anti-minority preferences.[107] At the same time, we expect judges to be resistant to influence from trends,

[107] This is a concept that was first formally established in the so-called "Footnote Four" of the United States Supreme Court ruling in *United States v. Carolene Products Company*. In Footnote Four, the U.S. Supreme Court established a system of heightened scrutiny for any laws involving "discrete and insular mi-

public pressure, or potential backlash and to be guided by precedent and by the legal texts which serve as the foundation for their work. The independence of judges and their ruling in favor of minorities is the ideal, but this is not always the reality. Judges with lifetime appointments, like the United States Supreme Court judges, may be less prone to allowing themselves to be affected by ever-changing circumstances and sentiments in the country. However, at the state level where judges are subject to an electoral process by the public, the independence of the court is far more vulnerable. In such a case, being counter-majoritarian and supporting small or unpopular minorities might easily end a judge's career. An empirical evaluation of gay rights cases from 1981 to 2004 has shown that "on average, the probability of a judge casting a vote in favor of gay rights is reduced by nearly 16% in direct democracy states. . . . [J]udges in high impact direct democracy states are even less likely to cast a pro-gay rights vote than their counterparts in low impact direct democracy states" (Lewis et al. 378).

The question whether the backlash in the wake of *Goodridge v. Department of Public Health* was typical in same-sex marriage court cases is subject to heavy disagreement. Whereas Klarman's research provides evidence that backlash resulted from the Massachusetts case, Flores and Barclay's study on the effect of same-sex marriage policies on mass attitudes does not support the hypothesis that backlash or polarization result from such a change in law. In their study, the two scholars analyzed attitudes towards marriage equality and homosexual Americans after judicial action and policy implementation. Therefore, Flores and Barclay insist that their findings do not concur with Klarman's conclusion: "We find that attitudes change over time following policy changes. This supports the role that instilling new policy supportive of a minority group fosters greater approval or (at least) ambivalence toward that group" (52). However, it is important to note that Flores and Barclay's study analyzed attitudinal changes as a consequence of not only same-sex marriage litigation but also legislation. This is a decisive difference. As the research on judicial activism has shown, backlash is more likely if a change in law is the result of litigation. Additionally, this likelihood further increases if the court consists of unelected justices, as is the case with the United States Supreme Court. Flores and Barclay acknowledge this argument

norities" (United States, Supreme Court, "*United States v. Carolene Products Company*" 155).

but nevertheless adhere to their hypothesis that long-term backlash is unlikely: "States where same-sex marriage became legal with the Court decisions are likely the most susceptible to backlash. And yet, we fail to find the large and long-lasting negative reaction to these policies being introduced" (52).

Adam Deming supports the findings of Flores and Barclay on the consequences of the 2015 Supreme Court ruling in his article "Backlash Blunders: Obergefell and the Efficacy of Litigation to Achieve Social Change." He argues that it "has not caused and will not incite a major backlash" (274). His principal reasoning for this is based on what he calls the "unique road" of *Obergefell's* history of litigation which ultimately "had the effect of reducing future resistance to it" (274). Deming describes this "unique road" (274) as the "Supreme Court's strategy of moving alongside public opinion, neither falling too far behind nor stretching too far ahead of it, [which] seems to reflect institutional learning from previous landmark cases" (283). While backlash had indeed been a persisting problem, in particular in the early years of the long journey to marriage equality,[108] Deming believes that the nation had become much more accepting of same-sex marriage since *Goodridge* (274).

Fontana and Braman offer a different approach in backlash studies by looking at change through legislation and litigation separately. In their essay "Judicial Backlash or Just Backlash: Evidence from a National Experiment," they explain:

> We found that neither the Court nor Congress changes net support for the underlying constitutional issue it is deciding, but Court decisions polarize public sentiments on constitutional issues more than congressional acts. We also found that decisions by the Court shifted anticipated electoral turnout more than decisions by Congress. (735)

This means that the "Court, although generating no shift in the *balance* of public opinion, did generate significantly greater *polarization* than Congress" (735).

[108] For instance, backlash was an issue when the constitutional amendment suggested in Proposition 8 limited marriage to a union between a man and a woman. Furthermore, backlash followed when a ballot initiative overturned same-sex marriage legislation in Maine in 2009 and also when an Iowa Supreme Court judge, who had voted in favor of marriage equality in *Varnum v. Brien* (2009), was removed from office by Iowa voters (Deming 280).

Therefore, "[r]ather than changing the underlying beliefs about gay marriage. . . , action by Congress and the Court tended to make existing beliefs more extreme, thereby increasing cultural polarization" (747). Affirmation or denial of one's cultural worldview plays a tremendous role in the (perceived) intensity of the backlash and the cultural polarization resulting from an unpopular court decision:

> Because citizens with relatively egalitarian and communitarian values are generally supportive of gay rights, and those with relatively hierarchical and individualistic views are generally opposed, we hypothesize that legislative and judicial decisions affirming gay rights will drive egalitarian and communitarian citizens to further support the underlying position that marriage equality is protected by the Constitution. Conversely, relatively hierarchic and individualistic citizens will become even more adamant in their belief that there is no constitutional protection against marriage discrimination. (Fontana and Braman 749)

Fontana and Braman's findings provide an explanation for several phenomena. Their study supports Klarman's research which indicated that George W. Bush massively benefitted from the severe backlash to *Goodridge v. Department of Public Health* in the 2004 presidential election. Furthermore, Fontana and Braman's findings explain why backlash to same-sex marriage rulings are not always traceable in the fluctuations in the balance of public opinion but can still be experienced by the American people due to an increase in polarization, an intensification of people's stance on an issue, or an increase in minority discrimination and hate crimes. These effects make opposition to a court decision more noticeable and create the appearance of intense backlash although there is no significant change in the balance of public opinion.

With regard to the case *Obergefell v. Hodges*, Klarman, whose findings showed that there had been severe backlash to previous same-sex marriage cases, doubted that the 2015 ruling would ignite the same level of backlash. In an email interview with the *History News Network* of George Mason University, he listed a number of reasons why he believed *Obergefell* to be less controversial than the marriage equality rulings in Hawaii in 1993 or Massachusetts in 2003:

> [P]erhaps the most important factor in determining whether a court ruling generates backlash is whether it contravenes public opinion and, if so, how dramatically. In 1993, when the Hawaii supreme court [sic!] ruled tenta-

> tively in favor of gay marriage, Americans opposed it by a margin of at least three to one. When the Massachusetts supreme court [sic!] ruled squarely in favor of gay marriage in 2003, the country was still opposed by roughly two to one. However, according to recent opinion polls, roughly 60 percent of Americans now support gay marriage. . . . A second factor relevant to backlash is how directly a court decision impacts the lives of those who disagree with it. It is hard to imagine how opponents of same-sex marriage can experience it as affecting their lives as directly and powerfully as critics of Brown and Roe believed those rulings affected theirs. . . . [Third], opposition has not elicited anything like uniform support from the national Republican Party, as it would have only a few years ago. . . . A final factor relevant to predicting backlash is the ease with which a Court decision can be circumvented. . . . By contrast, circumventing a Supreme Court ruling in favor of gay marriage will prove nearly impossible. (Klarman in interview with Rick Shenkman)

Surveys confirm Klarman's argument that the attitude of Americans towards same-sex marriage and gay rights in general was significantly better in 2015 than ten years prior (McCarthy, "U.S. Support"). However, roughly two thirds of Americans in support of same-sex marriage also meant that one third was still opposed to it. While it is a minority, this number needs to be acknowledged, and Americans belonging to this number need to be heard in order to prevent a further intensification of opposition from this group. As to Klarman's second point, some same-sex marriage opponents did experience tangible negative consequences in the wake of the ruling, and they were usually quite vocal about it. It overwhelmingly affected people who were either state employees or business owners who suddenly had to comply with the ruling and were indignant that their religious liberty rights were being infringed. Notable court cases are *Masterpiece Cakeshop, Ltd. v. Colorado Civil Rights Commission* and several lawsuits aimed at Mississippi's Religious Liberty Accommodations Act (HB1523), which was approved in March 2016 and is deemed the most aggressive anti-LGBT law in the country (S. Kaplan). Although there is no longer a unanimous opposition to gay rights within the Republican Party as the analysis of charges of un-Americanism by pro-gay Republicans in chapter IV.B. has shown, the Trump administration has proven itself to be a persistent threat to LGBT rights in the United States. Considering that this interview with Klarman was given only a week after *Obergefell* was decided, developments, such as the long-term public response and the scope of the potential backlash, were not yet apparent. Consequently, Klarman was unable to foresee how the country would change in the years to come.

Although studies and surveys suggest that the overall situation of homosexual Americans has been improving in the United States and that the majority of the population is now in favor of marriage equality and ready to include gay Americans into American everyday nationalism, Siegel warns that this does not mean that backlash and efforts of countermobilization have waned: "Just as *Brown v. Board of Education* did not end debate over racial segregation, *Obergefell* has not ended debate over marriage but instead has channeled it into new forms. Proponents of same-sex marriage persisted in the face of loss, and so too will its opponents" (1745). As indicated in chapter II in the discussion of recent anti-LGBT bills, it did not take opponents long to find new battles in which they could fight the increasing acceptance of LGBT Americans and their inclusion into the common conceptualization of American nationalism. Particularly in conservative states, several anti-LGBT bills were passed which allowed private and public businesses to refuse service to same-sex couples on the basis of religious or moral beliefs. In addition, many gay rights advocates were frustrated when the United States Supreme Court affirmed that it was constitutional to refuse service on the basis of the First Amendment's clauses of free speech and free exercise of religion in *Masterpiece Cakeshop v. Colorado Civil Rights Commission* (United States, Supreme Court, "*Masterpiece Cakeshop*" 1–3). In the case, a Colorado bakery owned by a devout Christian refused to create a wedding cake for the marital celebration of a gay couple, which resulted in the couple filing a charge with the Colorado Civil Rights Commission (1). Due to opponents' ongoing efforts to limit or curtail gay Americans' growing power and influence, Siegel believes that "*Obergefell* is still bitterly contested. . . . New constitutional meanings are still being forged through backlash, as Americans arguing in *Obergefell*'s wake try to shape the decision's meaning for the next phase of conflict" (1759) It remains to be seen if the conflict will enter a next phase, as Siegel predicted (1759). President Donald Trump courted gay rights opponents when he selected the devout Christian Mike Pence as his vice president and did so again when he presented a list of conservative judges for his Supreme Court nominations. The ruling in *Obergefell* was decided in favor of same-sex marriage by a narrow 5–4 decision that was only made possible because Justice Kennedy, who was often the swing vote, believed in the constitutionality of same-sex marriage.[109]

109 With the passing of Justice Ruth Bader Ginsburg in September 2020, a liberal

One year after *Obergefell*, 57 percent of all voters supported same-sex marriage, whereas only 39 percent of Republicans did ("Campaign" 32). Until 2017, which was two years after the Supreme Court decision, the approval of same-sex marriage among all Americans was at its highest point in American history. A report by the Pew Research Center shows that 62 percent of the public was in favor of marriage equality and even 47 percent of Republicans had come out in favor of same-sex marriage, while 48 percent still opposed it ("Support" 1; 5). This was the first time that Republicans were evenly divided on the issue. This change was remarkable as a mere ten years earlier, only 20 percent of Republicans supported same-sex marriage ("Support" 5). As an increasing number of Republicans come out in favor of gay marriage, the more difficult it must be for conservatives who view this development as contrary to everything the United States stand for as a nation. As a result, it is not surprising that some of them feel the need to escalate their efforts and become even more adamant in expressing their dissent on this development. By 2019, the number of Republicans who supported same-sex marriage decreased to 44 percent ("Majority" 2).[110] While this is not a major difference in approval rates, it is not yet clear if this downward shift is only a temporary dip or if it is indicative of a prolonged trend.

judge left the United States Supreme Court during a Republican administration. Bader Ginsburg was replaced by the conservative Justice Amy Coney Barrett, which resulted in a majority situation that will be unfavorable for LGBT Americans in comparable court cases.

110 The development is surprising as one would rather expect approval rates for same-sex marriage to continue rising. A decline goes against the common trend of a growing support for gay rights. Additionally, the decline is also surprising as gay rights see a higher degree of support among the younger demographic in contrast to older Americans. With some older Americans having deceased and younger Americans becoming part of the polling group, one would have rather expected approval rates to rise as this growing support in the share of adults in favor of marriage equality is partly due to generational change.

E Conclusion

The inclusion of same-sex couples into contemporary notions of American nationalism was a gradual process. The transformation in Americans' attitude was the starting point for a more inclusive and tolerant nationalism, a development which was then accompanied by a state-induced nationalism when Obama embraced a more inclusive concept of marriage. This made the change the American nation was experiencing regarding the inclusion of homosexual Americans even more imminent and real.

The majority opinions and the dissents in *United States v. Windsor* and *Obergefell v. Hodges* reflected the sentiments and reactions of the American public in the national discourse over same-sex marriage. The core arguments of the judges mirrored the concerns of the American public at large, which is why an investigation of these legal opinions is vital for an understanding what motivates Americans to accuse one another of un-Americanism and how this reflects their reaction to transformations of American everyday nationalism. Edith Windsor and her supporters argued that imposing a separate status for same-sex spouses was not only unconstitutional but also un-American. This reasoning was acknowledged in the opinion of the court which held in *United States v. Windsor* that Section 3 of DOMA is unconstitutional. The landmark civil rights case *Obergefell v. Hodges* followed only two years later. All four justices of the dissenting opinions agreed that redefining marriage constituted such a fundamental change to the self-concept of the American nation that it should not be decided by the judiciary. Nonetheless, a majority of five judges held that the right to marry was guaranteed to same-sex couples by the Equal Protection Clause and the Due Process Clause of the Fourteenth Amendment to the United States Constitution.

United States v. Windsor and *Obergefell v. Hodges* were among the most prominent battlefields in the culture war over American marriage, and consequently, they had a profound impact on American national identity. Both cases were examples of how the American nation tried to address the challenges posed by a minority group's growing demand for equal representation and participation in the American nationhood and the concomitant transformations to American nationalism. Thereby, the United States Supreme Court and the landmark civil rights cases acted as a stage on which the discursive construction and renegotiation of American nationalism played out in front of the eyes of the American people. Depending on the person's stance on the issue, it was either an affirmation of one's concept of national identity or the endangerment of it. The main actors were the Supreme Court judges and the parties concerned in the cases, but also the American people played a significant role. After all, it was on their behalf that this battle was being fought, either for a more inclusionary idea of nationalism or for the continued defense of the traditional concept of marriage.

As Justice Scalia noted in his dissent, *United States v. Windsor* was about power (Scalia, "*Windsor*" 1). It was about the question whether the hitherto existing power structures which encompass the discourses of marriage and nationalism would be challenged or upheld. The majority of the court decided to stand on the side of marriage equality and challenge the dominant system. Of course, this did not mean that the previously established idea of marriage and the associated idea of American identity no longer found passionate supporters. As Justice Scalia warned, with this victory the majority opinion armed the supporters of marriage equality for the next fight. He expected that the fight over same-sex marriage would continue rather sooner than later. Indeed, he was right. As the renegotiation of Americanism, un-Americanism, and American nationalism is a continuous process, it remains to be seen whether same-sex marriage will crystalize as a true American right or whether it will be challenged in the near future.

Chapter VI

VI Polarization, American Values, and the Nation

A The Divided States of America

American everyday nationalism is the unfinished, continuous, and imperfect self-discovery process of people who try to come to grips with who they are or who they want to be as a national community. In this process, the American nation is discursively constructed and deconstructed by people who wish for this vague concept to represent their understanding of themselves and to mirror their ideas and hopes as well as the battles they are fighting in their everyday lives. Thereby, 'nation' functions as "a culturally available schema that can be discursively employed to make sense of" the world surrounding them and to handle the challenges they are confronted with when having to maneuver social difference and sociocultural change (Fox and Miller-Idriss 540). Thereby, a conflict over national identity is a reciprocal process. Adversarial parties shape the nature of the conflict, but the conflict also shapes their self-concept, both within the respective conflict and more broadly as individuals. Furthermore, it forces the parties involved to take a specific position, which in turn requires them to engage in a process of self-definition to demarcate themselves from their opponents. Smith and Windes argue in their study of the rhetorical war over sexuality that people's nature and identity are forged in combat (56). This is certainly true for conflicts such as the dispute over marriage equality where mutual accusations of un-Americanism shape both the debate itself as well as the self-concept of the American national identity of those involved in this renegotiation over American nationalism.

The American Culture War

Smith and Windes' proclamation leads to the question: what type of combat is it in which the American people engage and thereby forge their nature and identity? Their rhetoric of combat is reminiscent of James Davison Hunter's culture war theory. In his 1991 book *Culture Wars: The Struggle to Define America*, the sociologist Hunter proclaims that the nation is split into two camps and construes culture war or cultural conflict as "political and social hostility rooted in different systems of moral understanding. The end to which these hostilities tend is the domination of one cultural and moral ethos over all others" (42). The issues in dispute are connected to questions of identity, morality, and everyday nationalism. Hunter explains that "the divisions of political consequence today are . . . the result of differing worldviews. . . . [They revolve] around our most fundamental and cherished assumptions about how to order our lives and our lives together in this society" (42). Abortion, gay rights, affirmative action, public education, or funding for the arts are issues that are typically at stake in culture wars according to Hunter (42). "It is the commitment to different and opposing bases of moral authority and the world views that derive from them that creates the deep cleavages between antagonists in the contemporary culture war," he states (43).

Hunter describes a national split into the orthodox and the progressive camp. He defines progressivism as a "tendency to resymbolize historic faiths according to the prevailing assumptions of contemporary life" (44–45) and orthodoxy as characterized by a "consistent, unchangeable measure of value, purpose, goodness, and identity, both personal and collective" (44). Those supporting the orthodox group tend to be conservatives while those advocating for progressive values are usually liberals. However, Hunter warns that relying exclusively on political labels such as 'conservative' and 'liberal' increases the risk of forgetting that these conflicts are not political wars but cultural wars because they are centered on moral disagreements (46). Furthermore, he adds that although moral concepts are "at the heart of today's culture wars, these do not always take form in coherent, clearly articulated, sharply differentiated world views" (43). This is clearly illustrated in the debate on marriage equality. Opinions are buttressed by accusations of un-Americanism as auxiliaries since Americans struggle to adduce coherent arguments for these vague ideas.

A year after Hunter's publication, the politician and political commentator Patrick J. Buchanan delivered his "culture war speech" at the 1992 Republican National Convention in Houston, Texas in which he claimed: "It is about who we are. It is about what we believe. It is about what we stand for as Americans. . . . It is a cultural war, as critical to the kind of nation we will one day be as was the Cold War itself." Buchanan promoted the idea that the United States was divided by a culture war and encouraged his fellow Americans, and Republicans in particular, not to remain silent but to fight for the conservative cause. Buchanan understood culture war as "a struggle for the soul of America" and thereby emphasized that this war was about American national identity and American nationalism. Furthermore, it affected every American because it was about who they were, what they believed, and what they stood for as Americans (Buchanan). The election in 1992 was not simply a decision about whether George H.W. Bush or Bill Clinton would be the president for the next four years; it was about shaping the country's future for decades to come. Cultural issues such as abortion, homosexuality, feminism, religious education, and school choice were the defining topics of the 1992 presidential election. Buchanan urged voters to not allow for any change regarding these issues because this "is not the kind of change America needs. And it is not the kind of change we can tolerate in a nation that we still call God's country." Buchanan was determined not to allow liberals to take over the country because it would be detrimental to American values and morals. He pleaded that it was crucial to "take back our culture, and [to] take back our country." Republicans could no longer compromise and collaborate with the left. How momentous Buchanan's speech actually was, became clear two years later when the Republicans gained control of both legislative bodies and refused to collaborate with the Clinton administration on several occasions. Although Hunter introduced the concept of culture war in American sociological discourse, his theories were not widely known outside of a scholarly context. It was Buchanan's fiery and polarizing speech which ultimately popularized this idea in American society at large.

The Struggle for the American Soul in the 21st Century

Almost thirty years after Patrick Buchanan's infamous statement about a culture war raging in the United States, Americans still appear to be deeply divided over issues such as immigration, health care, and marriage equality. Especially in the aftermath of the 2016 presidential election, one would be hard-pressed to find someone who would argue that the rift in American society has begun to mend in the years since Hunter first proclaimed that the American nation was split into two camps by a bitter culture war. Hunter's monograph *Culture Wars: The Struggle to Define America* was published almost thirty years ago but many of his theories still sound strikingly familiar. Ever since its publication, his monograph has inspired lively debates among scholars from various disciplines trying to either defend or refute his arguments.

Morris P. Fiorina and his co-authors Samuel J. Abrams and Jeremy C. Pope dedicated their whole book *Culture War? The Myth of a Polarized America* to debunking the myth of the culture war by claiming that the ordinary electorate is strongly centrist and that only political elites are polarized. While there is widespread agreement that the political elite in the United States is divided or at least polarized in terms of cultural issues, there is no agreement if and to what scope this extends to the public at large.[111] Fiorina et al. as well as McAdam and Kloos[112] also found evidence of severe polarization at the elite level but emphasize that this phenomenon is not a top-down development (Fiorina et al. 9; McAdam and Kloos 11). Measuring voter behavior is a commonly used approach to assessing political polarization but even that did not deliver a clear answer because whether an opinion is considered centrist or extremist is often dependent on the researcher's interpretation. Alan I. Abramowitz and Kyle L. Saunders's article "Is Polarization a Myth?" is an approval of Hunter's general hypothesis of a divided nation and a critique of Fiorina et al. Although they question Hunter's assertion that Americans are "heading to the barricades to do battle over abortion, gay marriage, and other emo-

[111] Fiorina et al. argue that the electorate only appears to be in a culture war with each other because the political elite offer nothing but polarizing and dividing statements in political debates (9). However, when questioned on hot-button issues, the majority of the people take moderate or centrist views. "The simple truth is that there is no culture war in the United States – no battle for the soul of America rages, at least none that most Americans are aware of" (8), Fiorina et al. claim by referring to Buchanan's famous speech in which he called for a fight for the American soul.

[112] Doug McAdam and Karina Kloos find evidence of strong polarization at the elite level but emphasize that this is not the case with the American public at large. Although the American electorate has differing views on culture war issues, the majority of them opt for a moderate view (11). While the Obama presidency was often, probably prematurely, declared to be the end of culture wars in the United States, McAdam and Kloos are not convinced that electing Barack Obama for president had a reverse effect on the polarization in the United States: "Obama's presidency has done little to reduce the country's underlying racial, political, and economic division. . . . The country is more starkly divided in political terms than at any time since the end of the Reconstruction. . ." (3–4). Although McAdam and Kloos' research has shown that the partisan divide is not mirrored by the public, the division and the inequality they describe amongst Americans easily causes voters to believe that they are in a cultural war.

tionally charged issues" (543), as they phrase it. Abramowitz and Kyle are convinced that "there are large differences in outlook between Democrats and Republicans, between red state voters and blue state voters, and between religious voters and secular voters" (543).[113] In 2012, the journal *Canadian Review of American Studies* published a special issue on this topic, in which most of the contributors agreed that the American nation was still fighting a culture war.[114]

113 Abramowitz and Saunders refute the hypothesis supported by Fiorina et al. by presenting evidence against what they call "Fiorina's Five Claims" ("Moderation," "Partisan Polarization," "Geographical Polarization," "Social Cleavages," and "Voter Engagement and Participation") (543). None of those categories survived Abramowitz and Saunders' close analysis on the basis of data from the American National Election Studies and national exit polls. In addition, Abramowitz and Saunders' study of polarization showed that "[t]hese divisions are not confined to a small minority of elected officials and activists – they involve a large segment of the public and the deepest divisions are found among the most interested, informed, and active members of the public" (543). Although Abramowitz and Saunders also admit that the least informed and least active Americans tend to be moderate in their views, they proved that those "ordinary Americans" (Hunter 43) interested in politics are indeed deeply divided.

114 In his article "Crusade or Charade? The Religious Right and the Culture Wars," Graham G. Dodds claims that the Religious Right may have lost influence during the last years, which affected their battles on cultural issues' grounds, but this does not mean that the culture war is over. The Tea Party has taken over a central role in the fight over cultural issues in the United States as over one third of Americans sympathize with their party platform or at least some of their ideas (Dodds 284). John Dombrink agrees with Dodds in his article "After the Culture War? Shifts and Continuities in American Conservatism" by stating: [T]he American culture war seems destined to remain with us, resurgent and redefined, reconfigured for a new era" (317). The role of the media in culture wars was examined by David Grondin in his study "Understanding Culture Wars through Satirical/Political Infotainment TV: John Stewart and the *Daily Show*'s Critique as Mediated Re-enactment of the Culture War" in which he asserts that infotainment TV is the "medium and locus where the culture wars are waged" (347). Grondin points out to the fact that television is one of our most important news sources and if those are presented in a culture war style by "culture warriors" (350), such as John Stuart, Bill O'Reilly, or Glenn Beck, it does not come as a surprise that a large number of Americans believe that they are still in the midst of a fierce culture war (352).

When reviewing scholarship on the culture war hypothesis, the impression is created that much of the scholarly disagreement about the existence of a culture war in the United States can be explained by the problem that different scholars have different understandings of the terms 'culture' and 'culture war.' The scholarly war over whether there is a culture war raging in the United States is unlikely to be settled anytime soon due to diverging interpretations of the relevant concepts. However, the popularity of mutual accusations of un-Americanism in numerous national discourses support the persistent impression that Americans are still fighting a culture war, in particular since the American people are becoming more divided and more polarized over questions of what defines Americanism or un-Americanism. A study on political polarization in the American public, published in June 2016 by the nonpartisan fact tank Pew Research Center, indicates an increased polarization and partisanship in American society and thereby supports the hypothesis that a culture war is still raging in the United States ("Partisanship" 1). This process had already started during the Obama era when some Americans were increasingly convinced that their interests were not being represented in the discursive (re)construction of the nation. Despite popular claims, the rising polarization is not just a recent development resulting from President Trump's election in 2016.

In their study "Partisanship and Political Animosity in 2016," researchers at the Pew Research Center discovered that people's "views of the opposing party are now more negative than at any point in nearly a quarter of a century" because "[f]or the first time in surveys dating back to 1992, majorities in both parties express not just unfavorable but *very* unfavorable views of the other party" ("Partisanship" 1). In 2016, 55% of Democrats (up from 23% in 2000) and 58% of Republicans (up from 26% in 2000) have a very negative opinion of the opposite party (9). It is still true that those engaged in politics (frequent voters, volunteers, or donors) tend to be most hostile towards the other party; however, their degree of "coldness" towards political opponents as measured on the "feeling thermometer" only differs from that of less engaged Americans by 10–13% percent (14). When asked if someone's political view says something about their character, 70% of Democrats and 63% of Republicans agreed and 38% of both supporters of both parties stated that if they disagree with someone on political questions, they will generally not agree with them about other issues (30). Democrats as well as Republicans think members of the other party are close-minded (D: 52%,

R: 70%), unintelligent (D: 33%, R: 33%), or immoral (D: 35%, R: 47%), which makes clear an association between political views and negative character traits (31). Anger, frustration, or even fear towards the other political party is felt by 46–58% of the members of both parties (51). When asked if they perceive people of opposing political view as mean, Democrats give Republicans a rating of 31 on the "mean thermometer" and Democrats are given a rating of 29 by Republicans (2). This connection between political affiliation and a person's moral character is particularly troubling as it fortifies polarization and is a reason for people to remain in their sociocultural echo chambers. However, this connection explains why accusations of un-Americanism have become "taken-for-granted-language" (Skey 10) because someone who believes that a person's political stance correlates with their character traits will not hesitate to make a connection between political bent and the other person's (un-)Americanism. As a result, the disagreement between supporters of the two major U.S. parties does not seem to involve political decisions for which a compromise can be achieved. Conflicts over morals, values, and emotions, which are typical for culture wars, dominate the political as well as sociocultural discursive landscape. What everyday nationalism should look like or how Americans experience it differs depending on which end of the political spectrum they position themselves. Whereas liberal Americans are more willing to expand their understanding of American nationalism in order to include new groups of citizens, their conservative-leaning fellow Americans prefer to keep the existing boundaries between inclusion and exclusion by sticking to a more traditional viewpoint of who should be incorporated in the prevalent understanding of true Americanism.

In another study conducted by the Pew Research Center in 2016, 66% of (lean) Republicans stated that they believe their lives are worse compared to fifty years ago whereas only 19% believe that life in the United States has improved for people like them ("Campaign" 1). By contrast, (lean) Democrats were far more optimistic. Only 28% have the impression that their lives have worsened whereas almost half of them are convinced that their situation has improved over the last fifty years (1). This difference in the perception of conservatives and liberals might be a result of the Obama years fostering an increasing liberalization in laws and policies which were connected to culture war issues, such as the victory of gay rights supporters in *United States v. Windsor* and *Obergefell v. Hodges*. Liberal progress in the country was also seen in the areas of health care

(e. g., The Patient Protection and Affordable Care Act[115]) and immigration (e. g., the implementation of the DACA Act[116]), among others. During both Obama administrations, American nationalism was overwhelmingly constructed according to the preferences of liberal Americans, which was one reason that led conservatives to believe that their lives in the United States had worsened. Their interests regarding the nature of the American nation were not sufficiently reflected in public policy. The growing acceptance and integration of same-sex couples into the prevailing concept of American nationalism and the legal changes, which awarded this minority with equal marriage rights, were supported by two thirds of the country (McCarthy, "U.S. Support"). The remaining third wanted the nation to take a different path, either upholding the status quo before the extension of rights to same-sex couples or the adoption of a more conservative position about gay rights issues.

Culture War as an Opportunity for the American Nation

Stephen Prothero's monograph *Why Liberals Win the Culture Wars (Even When They Lose Elections): The Battles That Define America from Jefferson's Heresies to Gay Marriage* is one of the most recent publications on the American culture war and one of the few works that attempts to define 'culture war' by listing specific criteria. Prothero provides what he calls "four key features" (9) of the phenomenon 'culture war:'

[115] The Patient Protection and Affordable Care Act, commonly called "Obamacare" as it was signed into law by President Obama in 2010, is the most comprehensive regulatory overhaul of the United States' health care system since the introduction of Medicare and Medicaid in the 1960s. Reasons that prompted the enactment of this federal statute was that more than 40 million Americans did not have health insurance, and health care costs in the U.S. were spiraling out of control, for the individual Americans as well as for the state (E. J. Martin 407).

[116] In 2012, the Obama administration implemented the DACA (Deferred Action for Childhood Arrivals) immigration policy, which offered individuals with unlawful presence in the United States, who were brought into the country as minors, a two-year respite from deportation and the opportunity to become eligible for a U.S. work permit (Fathali 223).

- First, they are public disputes recorded in such sources as presidential speeches; the Congressional Record; and popular books, magazines, and newspapers.
- Second, they extend beyond economic questions of taxing and spending to moral, religious, and cultural concerns, which are typically less amenable to negotiation and compromise.
- Third, they give rise to normative questions about the meaning of *America* and who is and who is not a true *American*.
- Fourth, they are heated, fueled by rhetoric of war and driven by the conviction that one's enemies are also enemies of the nation. (*Liberals* 10)

Prothero's definition should be kept in mind because its key features are indeed characteristic of the present-day culture war in the United States. Regarding the culture warriors, he does not divide them into the orthodox and the progressive as Hunter did but eliminates the religious terminology of culture wars by simply calling them the "conservatives" and the "liberals" (*Liberals* 11). Prothero suggests for "cultural conservatism to be characterized by (a) anxiety over beloved forms of life that are passing away, (b) a commitment to restore what has been lost, and (c) an effort to exclude from full cultural citizenship whose who are responsible for this loss" (11). The term 'un-American' is used in culture wars to do exactly that, namely, to deprive some Americans of their full cultural citizenship. "Cultural conservatism," according to Prothero, is "centripetal" because it "posits a shared center in American culture and carefully enforces its boundaries" (12). By contrast, "cultural liberalism is centrifugal, forever spinning off new forms of culture and including them in the mix" (12). In an overwhelming majority of cases, it is conservatives that start a culture war, often when it has already been lost. This leads to intense and dramatic actions. Although conservatives are the initial instigators, it is almost always the liberal camp that makes the decisive strike in the end (16–17). However, this does not seem to discourage conservatives from waging further culture wars. On the contrary, "any given loss simply energizes them for the next conflict, not least because it confirms their status as martyrs. Having lost one culture war, they become even more convinced that American society is going to hell. So, they prepare themselves for the next battle" (20). Stephen Prothero calls this recurring phenomenon the "culture wars cycle" (18), and he does not see it coming to an end. In a *Washington Post* opinion piece, which was published along with his monograph in January 2016, Prothero explains:

> As a historian, I'm not optimistic that our culture wars will end anytime soon. These angry disputes about the meaning of America, and who is a true American, have been raging since the early days of our nation. We've lurched from one cultural conflict to the next. A loss in one battle further convinces culture warriors that our society is going to hell. So they cast about for another grievance – another "them" to blame for what is happening to "us." In this way, the culture wars are perpetually rising from the dead. ("Conservatives")

Prothero would not argue that culture wars are per se negative or problematic because he sees the many opportunities which can result from a profound and heartfelt negotiation about American national identity and self-definition (3). This stance is in clear disagreement with Irene Taviss Thomson's, who warns that a nation torn by culture war is dysfunctional (Thomson 12).[117] Prothero sees culture wars as a potential catalyst for

[117] In her monograph *Culture Wars and Enduring American Dilemmas*, Irene Taviss Thomson also makes a case against the culture war hypothesis. After her comprehensive analysis of 436 articles on typical culture war issues, published in the popular American magazines *National Review*, *Time*, *The New Republic*, and *The Nation* between 1980 and 2000, she concluded that the American people just appear to be divided by a culture war because political elites tend to present arguments that are situated on the extremes of the political spectrum (1–2). Supporting her hypothesis with the help of her research findings, she claims that "the arguments or culture war partisans are nuanced and riddled with internal disagreements" (2), that culture warriors are very heterogeneous in terms of race, gender, class, and age, and that they are inconsistent regarding the issues they are fighting for. (5). She attributes this phenomenon to what she describes as "the contradictory pattern of American values" (7). Furthermore, by referring to the World Values Surveys, Thomson explains that Americans show an extraordinary devotion to traditional values which is comparable to that of developing and low-income societies. At the same time, however, Americans pride themselves on values of personal liberty, freedom of expression, and self-reliance. Consequently, "it is no wonder that Americans may experience conflicts over culture war issues and may simultaneously embrace both sides of the debate" (Thomson 7). Although Thomson is confident that the United States is not divided by a culture war, she emphasizes that it is still important to discuss this matter because "[a] society experiencing a culture war would face grave difficulties. It would lack common standards and assumptions, and as a result, the ability to make public policy decisions would be severely compromised" (12).

changes that could lead to an improvement of the nation, for instance, through the strengthening of minority rights.

If American identity is forged in combat (Smith and Windes 56), the culture war as "a struggle for the soul of America" (Buchanan) can be the venue where this process of identity formation takes place. It is not the objective of this study to reach a definite conclusion on whether the United States was or is still torn by a culture war. However, the heated debate over marriage equality demonstrates that conflicts over American morals, values, and not least of all, American everyday nationalism are creating division among the American people, regardless of what this conflict is called. Hunter believes that a culture war is "ultimately a struggle over national identity – over the meaning of America, who we have been in the past, who we are now, and perhaps most important, who we, as a nation, will aspire to become" (50). In the current dispute over which direction American everyday nationalism should take, the last component of Hunter's definition has become of utmost importance. The marriage equality dispute and the concomitant accusations of un-Americanism were first and foremost a discursive negotiation over what American nationalism and the American self-concept should look like in the years to come. As Buchanan stated in his speech, culture wars are a battle over the "kind of nation we will one day be." Despite the negativity that the metaphor of the culture war suggests, it is important to remember that, per Prothero's remark, this process is not necessarily a detrimental development. In the case of same-sex marriage, a culture war situation provided an opportunity for a previously marginalized group to strengthen their position as equal Americans in the national community. In the course of this equalization process, it is interesting to observe how the American people are coping with the challenges this change in law brings and how they will integrate homosexual couples and their families into their notions of American nationalism as it is experienced everyday through discursive negotiation.

In the following subchapters, the reasons for charges of un-Americanism in the fight over of marriage equality will be assessed from a variety of angles in order to demonstrate that this conflict is ultimately a proxy war for disputes over American nationalism and American national identity. The arguments in the debate over same-sex marriage as analyzed in chapter IV are not necessarily congruent with the reasons that lie behind these accusations. The term 'un-American' predominately operates as a substitute expression for thoughts, fears, and insecurities that people struggle to verbalize by other means. Consequently, the true reasons for insulting someone with charges of un-Americanism must be revealed to understand how these conflicts over marriage equality and similar disputes function as discursive platforms for renegotiations of American nationalism. This is the submerged part of the iceberg which lies below the surface of a conflict. In addition, the following subchapters illustrate the close interconnectedness between family, marriage, and nation in the United States.

B The Politicization of Marriage in the United States

Most people would agree that marriage is a private affair, involving the couple, their families, and their loved ones. However, in April 2015 when the Supreme Court judges heard the oral arguments of the plaintiffs in the landmark civil rights case *Obergefell v. Hodges*, the personal became political. The personal as the political is a phrase which was frequently used during the period of second-wave feminism after Carol Hanisch's essay publication "The Personal is Political" in 1969. The slogan was spread to emphasize that certain times and circumstances require private matters to become topics of public relevance. The phrase was coined to raise awareness that the private experiences of women are connected to much larger sociocultural phenomena and systematic structures. In order to achieve the feminists' objectives, the private may no longer remain private but must be put on the public table of national discourse (Hanisch).[118] The same willingness to make one's private life public was required from the plaintiffs in the same-sex marriage court cases. Their relationships were publicly discussed for the purpose of fighting for the greater good and the ultimate goal of marriage equality. Once again, marriage was politicized.

American Politicization of Marriage

The politicization of marriage is a recurrent theme throughout American history. *Loving v. Virginia*, a 1976 U.S. Supreme Court ruling which struck down all laws prohibiting interracial marriage, is a prominent example of such a politicization. The ruling was preceded by years of debates on whether to permit interracial marriage and finally abolish anti-miscegenation laws that upheld so-called racial integrity. In addition to civil rights

[118] The theories of Hanisch's paper were the result of her battle against the women's causus of the Southern Conference Educational Found, a women's liberation group in the South. Hanisch claims that the group was occasionally willing to admit that women were oppressed and did not get equal pay: however, the SCEF was not ready to take the stories of women's oppression into the public but preferred to discuss these matters in private. Hanisch wrote her paper "The Personal is Political" in order to publicly fight against SCEF's attempts to silence more radical women's movements whose members dared to confront and expose male supremacy (Hanisch).

cases, marriage promotion through administrative regulations and recommendations has also been popular in the United States, particularly in the 1990s. One example was the 1996 Welfare Reform Act, officially called the Personal Responsibility and Work Opportunity Reconciliation Act (PRWORA), as initiated by the Clinton administration.[119] The program clearly advantaged married two-parent households and was intended to reduce the number of out-of-wedlock births and single-parents. The promotion of "family values" and the emphasis on the importance of marriage were core elements of the program.[120] Furthermore, the concern that marriage was under threat prompted the same administration to sign the Defense of Marriage Act (DOMA) into federal law. Until it was declared unconstitutional in 2013, Section 3 of DOMA defined marriage as the union between a man and a woman, and states were not required to recognize same-sex marriages even if they were granted under the laws of other states (United States, Congress, "*Defense of Marriage Act*"). The fact that the title of a federal law on marriage included the word 'defense' as if marriage were endangered and required vigorous defense by all available means, speaks to the political climate at that time. The marriage equality movement and the same-sex marriage case *Obergefell v. Hodges* were the consequential next steps in a long row of examples of the politicization of marriage. All in all, marriage often seems to be the concern of a political institution and not only a private matter in the United States.

Potential threats to marriage remain a hot button topic even though many other forms of partnership or cohabitation are generally accepted today. Research on marriage in the American society has revealed that "[m]arriage is more prevalent in the United States than in nearly all other developed Western nations. . . . Not only is marriage stronger demographically in the United States than in other developed countries, it also seems stronger as an ideal" (Cherlin 43–44).[121] In the opinion of the court in

[119] The Personal Responsibility and Work Opportunity Act, passed by U.S. Congress in 1996, replaced the cash welfare program Aid to Families with Dependent Children (AFDC) with the new Temporary Assistance to Needy Families (TANF) program which had a stronger focus on providing work incentives and imposed stricter limits on the length of time a recipient could receive welfare (Reintsma 2). The reform was heavily criticized for its focus on marriage promotion and abstinence education (3–4).

[120] In the opening preamble of the welfare reform, it was held that "marriage is the foundation of a successful society" (qtd. in Yamin 2).

[121] In a World Values Survey conducted between 1999 and 2001, respondents

Obergefell v. Hodges, Justice Kennedy quoted from Alexis de Tocqueville's *Democracy in America* when he explained that "marriage is a keystone of our social order" (United States, Supreme Court, "*Obergefell*" 16):

> There is certainly no country in the world where the tie of marriage is so much respected as in America. . . . [W]hen the American retires from the turmoil of public life to the bosom of his family, he finds in it the image of order and of peace. . . . [H]e afterwards carries [that image] with him into public affairs. (Tocqueville qtd. in United States, Supreme Court, "*Obergefell*" 16)

The turmoil and controversy provoked by the marriage equality movement is proof of that special status of marriage in the United States. In no other Western country has same-sex marriage caused such a continuous and fierce debate on values, morals, and national identity than in the U.S.[122] Although same-sex marriage only affects a tiny fraction of the American people directly, the impression was created as if this was a national life-or-death issue for some Americans. "Given the small percentage of the population that would opt for same-sex marriage, the practical effects of same-sex marriage would be minimal while maintaining that the cultural effect would be dramatic," Sadler notes (589). The frequent charges of un-Americanism from both camps in this culture war have demonstrated time and again that core ideas of American life and character were at stake. One might expect due to all this controversy over marriage and its promotion that marriage stability would be high in the country. By contrast, the opposite is the case. "[T]he relatively high value place on marriage in the United States coexists with an unmatched level of family instability and large numbers of single-parent families. This, too, is part of the American family cultural heritage" (Cherlin 50). This

were asked whether they agree that marriage is an outdated institution. With only 10 percent of Americans agreeing, the United States had the lowest number of any developed nation, except for Iceland. In Canada, 22% of the study participants agreed, in Great Britain the number was 26%, and 36% of the French agreed (Cherlin 44).

122 In no other Western country did same-sex marriage spark such a furor as in the United States. Apart from occasional rallies and protests, no European country saw the emergence of a continuous marriage equality movement or highly influential interest groups (Cherlin 48).

gap between Americans' ideals and their reality may account for their marriage promotion efforts as well as their aversion to further modification of this already fragile institution.

Whereas some may argue that same-sex marriage could strengthen the institution of marriage, not least by extending a national value to a larger group of Americans, conservatives mostly see instability in such an expansion. Conservative organizations, such as the Heritage Foundation or the Family Research Council, suggest that same-sex marriage would further weaken the institution of marriage and have negative effects on the wellbeing of children (Stevenson and Oliver 77). On its website, the Family Research Council states: "We oppose the vigorous efforts of homosexual activists to demand that homosexuality be accepted as equivalent to heterosexuality in law, in the media, and in schools. Attempts to join two men or two women in 'marriage' constitute a radical redefinition and falsification of the institution" ("Homosexuality"). Extending the right to marriage to a group of Americans who have been excluded from that right for the vast majority of the nation's history was downright un-American for many of them and also potentially dangerous. Additionally, Thomas Messner affirms in a statement for the Heritage Foundation: "The public has a strong interest in using law and policy to recognize, affirm, support, solidify, encourage, strengthen, and defend marriage as the cornerstone of the family and the building block of society." However, for the Heritage Foundation this refers solely to the marriage of heterosexual couples. Conservative organizations and their supporters fear that opening marriage to same-sex couples will harm the nation by changing this fundamental institution of society. Therefore, risking negative consequences for American society for such a redefinition of marriage is un-American.

Marriage as a Regulatory Mechanism

Marriage is not only a highly politicized institution; it is also a mechanism for structuring and regulating society as well as for determining the idea of American everyday nationalism.[123] The possibility to marry was a right

[123] Yamin asserts that "[i]n the United States historically, there has been a consistent return to marriage when political questions of inclusion and equality surface. The politics of marriage embody central dynamics in American politics, regarding matters of inclusion and exclusion, the status of citizenship, and the

that was not automatically granted to everyone, thereby making it a tool for the inclusion and exclusion from the American nationhood. The interconnectedness between debates on marriage equality and debates on national identity is unmistakable. In her monograph *American Marriage: A Political Institution* (2012), Priscilla Yamin elaborates on this as follows:

> Marriage is perpetually asserted as basic to American national identity, in both its pre-liberal and liberal expressions. Marriage shapes the grounds for inclusion by enforcing the heterosexual, monogamous expectations about family that apply to all; and marriage defines the hierarchy of citizenship by means of exclusion, in that only particular people may be allowed to marry. . . . In this way, marriage inhabits politics by shaping interests and either promoting or preventing change. (5–6)

Same-sex marriage and the former denial thereof is an example of such regulatory mechanisms of society since they either promote an extended idea of marriage or prevent it. Same-sex couples were deprived of forming a union which is considered to be a basic aspect of American nationalism, making them less American as a result. Consequently, they were placed lower in the hierarchy of citizenship. When accusing marriage equality opponents of un-Americanism, supporters sometimes simultaneously claimed that they were reduced to second-class citizens as they lacked the right to marriage (Bloom). Yamin's observation about the linkage between national identity and the institution of marriage supports these allegations. Marriage is highly politicized, and the discursive power of the issue of marriage in negotiations on American nationalism and national identity is enormous.[124]

meaning of equality" (2). Marriage has served as a tool for exclusion in the case of ex-slaves after the Civil War, immigrants at the turn of the 20th century, disenfranchised women, welfare recipients, and homosexual Americans (2). Yamin borrows from Karen Orren and calls the American marriage practice "belated feudalism" (3).

124 Yamin points out that the investigation of marriage as a "political institution shows how notions of normalization such as the construction of normal sexual practices have been crucial to the development of the nation" (10). This interconnectedness between forces of sexual normalcy and American nationalism is explored in depth in chapter VII.A.

National Stability and the Importance of Marriage

Looking at history reveals that debates on marriage have a certain pattern. It turns out that this basic institution of American life falls most intensely under debate if the perception of national or social stability is low (Yamin 13). People tend to be more open to liberalization or changes when they feel that their sociocultural map is otherwise stable. *Loving v. Virginia* opened marriage to interracial couples at a time when the civil rights movement was still in full swing and when the movement was diversifying ideas of American everyday nationalism in a myriad of areas of American life. African Americans were still fighting for their equal and rightful place in society in the 1960s and attaining the right to marry one's significant other was an essential step in this process. At the same time, some white Americans were struggling to cope with the changes the civil rights movement instigated and were not willing to accept that African Americans were becoming more equal Americans, at least from a legal perspective. A restructuring of who is regarded a full member of society leads to a reconstruction and renegotiation of nationalism. This process involves a temporary instability in society. External factors additionally affecting a nation during this process, for example international conflicts, may contribute to an even stronger feeling of instability. Marriage, and its politicization, is one of the platforms where this instability is mediated. Yamin confirms this hypothesis in her monograph as follows: "At critical moments of political change in the United States, actors turn to marriage to resolve tensions and to justify new political arrangements or maintain hierarchical relationships with regard to the rights, obligations, and social status of specific groups" (13). During times of political change and instability, marriage rights of some groups are promoted whereas those of others are prevented. Through this process, sociocultural change is either integrated into society, as it was the case with interracial marriage, or it is even more strongly prohibited since marriage serves as a regulatory mechanism.[125] The terminology of marriage in crisis occurs at times when other areas of nationalism or individuals' lives are up for reinterpretation and reconstruction.

[125] For instance, when the Hawaiian Supreme Court ruled in favor of the homosexual plaintiffs in *Baehr v. Miike* in 1999, the passing of the Defense of Marriage Act was the conservative reaction (Frank 102). DOMA as well as several "mini-DOMAs" (Adam 259) implemented on state level are examples of a tightening of marriage regulations.

The national debate over marriage equality and the sociopolitical situation at the height of that debate was comparable to the discourse over *Loving v. Virginia*. When marriage equality advocates were celebrating their first victories in state courtrooms, the country was experiencing change and instability in several other areas. For instance, the global financial crisis of 2008 was still affecting the everyday lives of many Americans. Moreover, the United States was involved in two wars and felt threatened by Islamic terrorist organizations. In the domestic sphere, the Obama administration had implemented significant changes in fundamental areas of everyday life, such as a massive regulatory overhaul of the health care system by implementing the Patient Protection and Affordable Care Act in 2010. In addition, there were several efforts for further liberalization in society both on a small scale and at a national level. The marriage equality movement, which aimed at a reconceptualization of something so fundamental to American family life, was simply a step too far for many. This stretched the limits of marriage equality opponents, which resulted in charges of un-Americanism as one means to express their dissent. Thereby, the marriage equality debate had become part of a vicious circle. The movement was rising and becoming an influential factor at a time when there were already other events generating instability. The usual reaction to instability is to protect marriage; however, this institution was about to change as well. Consequently, the urge of some Americans to preserve marriage from being changed by opening it to same-sex couples was much more intense than it may have been under different circumstances. The tone of the debate became harsher as both parties in the conflict were fighting for a concept of American everyday nationalism congruent with their own worldview and their own morals and values. By relying on insults of un-Americanism in order to express their opinion, supporters and opponents alike demonstrated that the debate on marriage equality was about much more than just marriage itself. It was a renegotiation and reconceptualization of core American values and morals as well as American nationalism. The frequent usage of the term 'un-American' was reflective of exactly that process.

C The (Unkept) Promise of Equality

Supporters of marriage equality were often agitated by conservatives arguing against same-sex marriage on the basis of family values and the protection of families. It was as if conservatives forgot or deliberately ignored that same-sex couples were families as well and that they also had children. Many gay couples fighting for same-sex marriage did not demand equal rights solely on ideological grounds, but because they were affected by serious discrimination and the consequences of the lack of equal protection. Furthermore, out of those affected by this inequity, children often suffered most, although it was ostensibly children whom conservatives claimed to protect in their fight for traditional family values. The majority opinion in the landmark civil rights case *Obergefell v. Hodges* elaborated on this absurdity as follows: "Without the recognition, stability, and predictability marriage offers, children suffer the stigma of knowing their families are somehow lesser. They also suffer the significant material costs of being raised by unmarried parents, relegated to a more difficult and uncertain family life" (United States, Supreme Court, "*Obergefell*" 3). In this paragraph, the majority opinion listed the main areas in which the children of same-sex couples and the couples themselves were disadvantaged if full marriage rights were not granted to homosexual partners: They suffered from humiliation and the feeling of not being fully recognized, they were prone to instability due to a lack of legal protection, and they were not entitled to the same benefits and rights as other American families. As Silverman emphasizes in his study on the rights of children with gay parents, "[c]hildren should not bear the burden of this type of legal discrimination against same-sex couples. The state's compelling interest in providing a stable home for the raising of children is a reason to allow, rather than prohibit, same-sex marriages. . ." (457).

Financial Discrimination of Homosexual Couples

More than one thousand benefits in multiple areas of life are automatically granted to heterosexual couples in the United States upon marriage.[126]

[126] According to Phy-Olson, married couples in the United States receive more than 1049 benefits upon marriage. These include employer benefits for spouses of workers, several types of insurance, health care, child or elder care as-

These benefits are intended to privilege couples and families financially as well as in non-material ways (Phy-Olson 75). By contrast, before same-sex marriage became the law of the land in 2015 and provided full equality for all Americans regardless of their sexual orientation, homosexual couples were, in the best case, eligible for some of these benefits depending on the legal situation in their state of residence ("Paying" 78). Thereby, the treatment of same-sex couples was far from consistent within the United States, with gay people living in more progressive states having greater opportunities than couples and families living in conservative parts of the United States.[127] The endless list of protections and benefits that were denied to gay couples and their families before the ruling in 2015 involved the most important areas of life and often resulted in a significant financial discrimination. In the report "Paying an Unfair Price: The Financial Penalty for Being LGBT in America" authored by the Center for American Progress and the Movement Advancement Project, three primary failures of law, which lead to LGBT people being financially penalized for their sexual orientation, are listed: legal discrimination, the lack of family recognition, and hostile educational environments ("Paying" i). Legal discrimination included the areas of employment, housing, healthcare, and credit discrimination. The second area listed in their report, lack of family recognition, was the category where most financial discrimination of gay couples and their families took place. The lack of a proper legal recognition prior to marriage equality led to a lack of health

sistance, inheritance rights, social security benefits, preferential treatment in several areas of life, and the opportunity to file a joint tax return. Furthermore, married couples may refrain from testifying against one another in court, the foreign spouse of a U.S. citizen has immigration rights, and a married couple is usually better off in the case of adoption, foster care, or divorce in terms of child custody rights (Phy-Olson 75).

127 While many liberal states, such as Massachusetts, overwhelmingly provided couples with equal rights on a state level, this did not improve same-sex couples' situation in regard to federal rights or safeguard them against a serious lack of protection when they crossed state borders. When Massachusetts became the first state to allow gay marriage, the life of gay couples who then got married improved significantly in terms of their legal position within the state's borders. However, if they visited or moved to other states with a less progressive stance on gay rights, their marriage certificate was often rendered worthless, since other states were not required to acknowledge their marriage ("Paying" 10–11; 67).

insurance through employers, limited access to government health and insurance programs as well as safety-net programs, unfair taxation, the denial of social security benefits, inequitable access to retirement savings, and an inability to inherit ("Paying" i). This immense financial penalty led to a severe financial discrimination of gay Americans, requiring them to spend significantly more money in the core areas of life such as health care, legal protection and recognition of their families, and taxation.

With this long list of sectors in which same-sex couples were disadvantaged, it comes as no surprise that "[c]hildren of same-sex couples are almost twice as likely to live in poverty compared to children raised by married opposite-sex couples" (4).[128] Of all the child-related spending from the United States government in 2012, 39% of it came in the form of tax credits and deductions for their parents or legal guardians. However, same-sex parents were often denied access to these credits and deductions because only one of them was allowed to have legal ties to the qualifying child (51). Consequently, the families' incomes were often significantly lower than the incomes of traditional families with heterosexual parents. The financial penalization of same-sex couples and their families frequently became a lifelong burden since the unequal social security benefits also meant less income during retirement for a spouse of a gay working partner, less income for a spouse of a deceased partner, less income for a surviving child of a gay working parent, and no assistance with death-related expenses (53). As one can see from the selected examples, the list of disadvantages of homosexual Americans in financial matters alone was incalculable. If another factor for potential discrimination was added to sexual orientation, for example gender or race, the outcome for gay couples was usually even worse: "For example, African Americans in same-sex couples are more than twice as likely to live in poverty as African Americans in married opposite-sex couples; African-American same-sex couples have higher rates of poverty than white same-sex couples"

[128] In the United States, 38% of transgender adults and 37% of LGBT adults are parents and 19% of same-sex couples are raising children. Same-sex couples have a comparatively high labor force participation with 82% whereas only 69% of opposite-sex couples are in labor force ("Paying" 5). Despite this high labor force participation rate, single LGBT adults are three times more likely and married/partnered LGBT families are twice as likely to have incomes near the poverty line in comparison to non-LGBT Americans (6). Moreover, LGBT poverty is significantly higher in states with anti-LGBT laws (8).

("Paying" ii). African American lesbian partners are a group of people who face potential discrimination based on their gender, their race, and their sexual orientation, making them one of the most vulnerable groups as their multiple minority aspects are compounded. Those who suffered the most were not the most vocal in the fight for equal rights. In their quest to find out why African American lesbians often remained unheard in the gay rights movement, Bashir et al. were confronted with the following answer:

> One of the frequent explanations give for their low visibility in this fight is that the blacks as a community have other, higher, and more pressing priorities. Often, we hear that marriage equality is a luxury issue that would provide few tangible benefits to black lesbians. Ironically, many of the most severe economic hardships faced by black lesbian couples and their children would immediately be addressed by the safety net that marriage provides. The fewer resources a couple has, the more that access to marriage makes a real difference. (181)

The argument that marriage equality was a "luxury issue" (181) was not only prevalent in the African American community. This is a view that was frequently uttered by several minority advocacy groups. Unfortunately, the idea of marriage equality being a "luxury issue" (181) was based on the fact that those fighting most fiercely for equal rights were not always those who were most in need of the benefits and protections which marriage would provide. Those who had the means to demand equal rights for gays tended to be Americans who could afford to spend time as well as money on the cause, as the case of Edie Windsor illustrated. Consequently, this created the impression that marriage was not desperately needed by the gay community. In fact, the exact opposite was true.

Interestingly, a national survey experiment conducted by Doan, Loehr, and Miller showed that Americans would be much more willing to extend formal rights to same-sex couples than informal rights.[129] Their results suggest that "heterosexuals do *not* favor heterosexual couples over same-sex couples when it comes to formal rights, but they are less improving of informal privileges for same-sex couples" (Doan et al. 1188). This

[129] In the study conducted by Doan et al., formal rights included family leave, hospital visitation, inheritance rights, and insurance benefits whereas informal rights included the public display of affection, the right to marry, as well as the public recognition of a same-sex relationship (1183).

might explain why some opponents were willing to accept civil unions as in Vermont but not marriage equality. Civil unions had a stronger focus on benefits and protections than on social recognition and on granting same-sex couples their full rights as Americans. In the fight for marriage equality, the focus was just as much, if not more, on informal rights as on formal rights. The argument that marriage equality was important for gay Americans in order to avoid financial penalties and legal burdens did not resonate with opponents, since they were focused on the informal rights that would be given to same-sex couples as soon as marriage rights became equal. For many opponents, this potential acceptance or even endorsement of gay Americans that marriage equality implied was simply a step too far.

The Effects of Insecurity on Children of Same-Sex Parents

The financial burden same-sex couples and their families faced in the United States prior to *Obergefell v. Hodges* was not the only consequence of the lack of protection and equality with which they were burdened. A tremendous problem, especially for couples with children, was the instability that accompanied the denial of nationwide marriage equality. The majority opinion in the Supreme Court ruling in *Obergefell v. Hodges* directly addressed this severe issue.[130] They regarded this unnecessary instability caused by marriage inequality as intolerable for the family, not least because the children, who need all the protection available, usually suffered the most from this unequal treatment of their parents. Furthermore, a series of interviews conducted by Goldberg and Kuvalanka with children of same-sex parents demonstrate that these children experienced instability and insecurity due to marriage inequality in several areas of

[130] They described the difficult situation of the co-plaintiffs DeBoer and Rowse who had welcomed two boys and a girl with special needs into their family, first via foster care and later via adoption. However, the problem with adoption law was that the state of Michigan only permitted adoption to opposite-sex couples or single individuals. Consequently, only one adoptive mother was allowed be the children's legal guardian. If she were to pass away unexpectedly, the children would again be orphaned in a legal sense. This situation created a continuous environment of uncertainty and stress for the family (United States, Supreme Court, "*Obergefell*" 5).

their lives. Many of the adolescents and emerging adults interviewed had experienced minority stress and were acutely aware that a change in law in favor of their parents would increase their feeling of stability (Goldberg and Kuvalanka 41). The situation tended to be easier for children whose parents were granted second-parent adoption which made both parents their legal guardians. The same was the case for families with high educational and financial resources which allowed the parents to offset the disadvantages of being a same-sex couple (42). However, establishing legal ties through second-parent adoption or guardian agreements which enhanced family security usually required parents to spend thousands of dollars. As this typically exceeded the financial means even of middle-class families, this option to reduce family insecurity was open to only a minority of same-sex couples, especially since they were already confronted with additional costs in regard to health care and insurance (42). In addition to the financial burden of having to invest in family stability, many children of same-sex parents "described having to visit lawyers to purchase legal safeguards, an experience that was recalled as humiliating and unfair," Goldberg and Kuvalanka explain (48). The children thought that marriage "would eliminate many of the emotional and financial strains that their parents encountered in their efforts to construct a patchwork quilt of protection for their children" (48). Not being fully recognized as a parenting couple and as a family because of a lack of nationwide marriage equality increased their stress and anxiety when faced with sickness or another crisis. Additionally, the fear of not being able to visit a loved one in the hospital because they would not legally be considered family was expressed by several interviewees, since they knew several people who had experienced this very scenario (41). The fear of losing their biological parent and not having their familial ties to the non-biological parent recognized was a driving factor behind children's demands for marriage equality (43–44). As emphasized by the majority opinion in the landmark ruling *Obergefell v. Hodges*, children of same-sex couples and their parents were suffering from unnecessary humiliation, insecurity, and lack of protection (United States, Supreme Court, "*Obergefell*" 3).

The Symbolic Value of Marriage

Just as important as the legal recognition and protection of these families was "the symbolic value of marriage" (49) as Goldberg and Kuvalanka ascertained through their interviews: Many of the children of same-sex parents noted that "the symbolic recognition associated with marriage would alleviate stresses related to having to explain their families and would encourage others – and in some cases themselves – to recognize their family relationships as real" (49).[131] In addition to that, some "hypothesized that, had they been able to invoke the language of marriage, they may have felt more confident in the legitimacy of their families and more empowered in their interactions with others" (49). Those who have not experienced it themselves can only presume what it meant for the children of same-sex parents to live with the ever-present thought that their families were denied the basic right of marriage because they were somehow regarded as less worthy or less American. Of course, not all opposite-sex parents are married, but they could marry if they wished to do so. This is a crucial difference from same-sex couples for whom marriage was a legal impossibility. Not being fully recognized by society through the denial of an essential American right, the right to marry, not only sent a clear message to homosexual couples and their families but also to opponents of marriage equality. The former felt less American due to their status as second-class citizens, whereas the latter felt confirmed in their view that, in the United States, same-sex couples were not equal to opposite-sex couples and should not contribute to American everyday nationalism to the same extent.

Marriage equality supporters were often in disbelief over claims that gay marriage posed a threat to the traditional concept of marriage. Steve Schmidt, who was a senior advisor in John McCain's 2008 presidential campaign, stated in a speech at the Log Cabin Republicans Convention in Washington, D.C. in 2009 that he believed that labelling marriage equal-

[131] Research has shown that same-sex couples in recognized relationships (partnered or married) experienced lower levels of stress and homophobia than couples whose relationship is not legally recognized, Goldberg and Kuvalanka report (49). They wonder whether the same effect can be measured with the children of these couples (49). The results from the interviews they conducted with children of same-sex parents definitely suggest that they also benefit from the legal recognition of their parents' relationship.

ity as un-American was proof of opponents' weak argumentation, and that there was no compelling reason to exclude gay Americans from the institution of marriage:

> [I]t cannot be argued that marriage between people of the same sex is un-American or threatens the rights of others. On the contrary, it seems to me that denying two consenting adults of the same sex the right to form a lawful union that is protected and respected by the state denies them two of the most basic natural rights affirmed in the preamble of our Declaration of Independence – liberty, and the pursuit of happiness. That, I believe, gives the argument of same sex marriage proponents its moral force. . . . Opponents to giving women the vote argued such a change would undermine marriage and other social institutions. I think the institution would be strengthened by the inclusion of more couples who are genuinely committed to each other. But even if you believe marriage would be changed for the worse by same sex unions, I'm not sure it's a compelling argument for their exclusion. We don't forbid divorce, a more proven and prevalent threat to the health of our society.

Schmidt included points in his statement that reflected the common line of argumentation on which the gay rights movement tended to rely. The constitutional principle of equality was the chief moral principle in the debate on the institution of marriage, as the term 'marriage *equality*' suggests. If one agrees with Steven Schmidt's position, marriage equality would not make the United States un-American but even more American since it brings the nation closer to fulfilling its ideals.

D Fear of Loss and Societal Instability

> Midway between San Francisco and Seattle, in a spectacular verdant valley, is a place I will call Timbertown. Home to eight thousand people, it is in many respects a typical small Oregon community, and a typical small American town, a place that prides itself on the fact that most people know each other, at least by sight, and a place where life goes on and relatively little changes – or so many believe. Yet several years ago, within the space of a few months, the intimate acts of individuals became the subject of a raucous public debate that pitted neighbor against neighbor. Should the community recognize lesbians and gay men as a legitimate minority group, and accord them equal protection under the law? (Stein 1)

This is the beginning of Arlene Stein's socio-ethnographic study *The Stranger Next Door: The Story of a Small Community's Battle over Sex, Faith, and Civil Rights*. In order to execute this project, Stein temporarily moved to a picturesque small town in rural Oregon and spent two years trying to uncover the causes of hostility towards gay Americans and their quest for equal rights (Stein 2–3).[132] Stein draws complex and in-depth portraits of the residents she interviewed; however, it quickly becomes clear that there is one motive that united them in regard to their anti-gay sentiments: a fear of loss.

Timbertown's economic base had been the lumber industry before it rapidly lost importance in the 1990s and left its community struggling with only a few of its members managing to maintain a middle-class income (Stein 47–48). Before its demise, the lumber industry had secured Timbertowners a living free from worry by offering well-paid jobs which men passed on to the next generations and which allowed women to work as homemakers (63; 95). Stein describes Timbertown as a "macho com-

[132] Stein explains that she was drawn to this project because it seemed as if these small towns such as Timbertown had started to define themselves primarily by their stance on homosexuality, and this was also how others defined them. She wondered why the people in this small town see such an enormous problem in homosexuality although they themselves were not confronted with gay and lesbian people. Stein asked how small towns can respond to the question of gay and lesbian rights when homosexuality is basically invisible in their community and people have only a vague idea of what queer life looks like (Stein 3).

munity. . . . where masculinity rules. Autonomy is valued, dependence is seen as negative; father-dominant households are signs of strength, and when wives work, it reflects badly on the family" (111). However, with the vanishing of the lumber mills, men were no longer the sole breadwinners of the family, if they had a job at all (95). The economic structure of the town had changed completely as physical labor had become less lucrative and a college-education rose in importance (63). Whereas some might call this progress, for the majority of Timbertowners, this development was a disaster that completely uprooted their style of living and sense of identity. Many of them had no idea how their situation would develop in the future, and they were left with feelings of deep insecurity.

Homosexuality and Social Change

For many Timbertowners, this rapid social change in their community was already more than they could handle. When the question of homosexuality and equal rights for gay Americans suddenly became a national debate, even this small town in Oregon could no longer avoid this discourse. Stein noticed that "[i]n Oregon, attitudes towards homosexuality appeared to correlate with divisions between a declining working class that felt itself displaced and ignored, and a rising professional class, for whom the declining working class was invisible or irrelevant" (6). For many of those working-class people, homosexual Americans seemed to be rather a phenomenon of this rising professional class than of hard-working small-town folks. They associated gay Americans with high-earning professionals making a good living in San Francisco or other urban centers, estranged from traditional American identity (74). The problem was multifaceted, but these different facets were intertwined. Timbertowners were already struggling socioeconomically and, as a consequence, felt left behind in and by the American nation. In spite of this disenfranchisement, they were then asked to be tolerant and compassionate toward a group of people who they generally located on the other side of the divide and who did not even share their conservative morals and values. This added expectation of attitudinal change on top of their struggles with economic decline was simply too much (217–18). However, the dynamic described here is not unique to Timbertown. Instead, Timbertown is paradigmatic for countless communities and towns all over the United States. This fear of loss, or the actual experience of loss, and the resulting insecurity of a changing individual and community identity is an extremely common phenomenon. Additionally, Timbertowners' response was not an exclusive characteristic of people's attitudes towards homosexuals. In fact, the variable "gay Americans and the quest for equal rights" could easily be replaced by other groups of people or other issues which implied possible further changes to a community that was already reeling from a host of other transitions (4).[133]

"Small rural communities have usually been thought of as the repository of traditional American values, conjuring up images of close, face-to-face relationships among likeminded people" (Stein 2). The closing of the lumber mills and its socioeconomic effects were not the only changes Timbertowners had to accept (47–48). For many decades, the timber industry had served as the glue and the identity-establishing component of this community by providing not only work but also a set of values (64). Consequently, the prevalent understanding of what it meant to be an American was shaped by the idea of working-class, small-town Americans and their traditional conservative mindset. As a result, the decline of the importance of manual labor not only brought changes to the lifestyle of the community but also disrupted it by precipitating an influx of new people, new values, and new discourses (16–17). This, again, was a de-

[133] In Timbertown, homosexuality was the epitome of a scapegoat. The victim could easily have been any other minority (e.g., Jews, Muslims, immigrants), as history has shown us. This employment and marginalization of one group for the sake of the integrity of another's self-concept reminds of Kenneth Burke's theories on what he calls the "scapegoat mechanism" (406). Burke, an American literary theorist and philosopher, reportedly used the term "scapegoating mechanism" in a letter in 1933 when discussing Hitler's scapegoating of Jews, and later elaborated on this concept in his 1945 monograph *A Grammar of Motives* (George and Selzer 202). For Burke, "the scapegoat represents the principle of division in that its persecutors would alienate from themselves to it their own uncleanliness" (406). By "uncleanliness," Burke understands the issue of the persecutors which they want to distract from, which in the case of Timbertown would be socioeconomic problems and people's struggle with changes in their environment. Through the employment of a scapegoat, society "'purifies itself' by 'moral indignation' in condemning" the actual or imaginary scapegoat (Burke 406). The "scapegoat mechanism" was later developed further by the French American philosopher René Girard who focused on the interplay between scapegoating and violence in the victimization process (Leyva 76).

velopment that exacerbated a fear of loss and identity insecurity. Homosexuality and equal rights becoming the outlet for these anxieties was, to some degree, a coincidence as this discourse flared up at a time when Timbertowners were most vulnerable (217–18). However, certain discourses, such as those on sexuality, are more prone to becoming an outlet for channeling fear as a result of their close connection to questions of morals, values, and identity. By contrast, discourses on trade agreements or taxes usually do not carry the same emotional weight. Stein argues that in the case of Timbertown, "sexuality became a resonant symbol upon which a group of citizens projected a host of anxieties about the changing world around them" (4). This was especially prominent among the evangelical Christians who Stein interviewed. She observed that "[t]hey believed that homosexuality posed a threat because it represents chaotic and morally lax behavior, and that growing tolerance for homosexuality is evidence for the community's declining moral values" (6). While religious beliefs may intensify people's negative attitudes towards homosexuality, the idea that acceptance of sexual diversity was symbolic of further moral decline could also be found among less religious Americans. What an issue symbolized overtaking the importance of the issue itself was a problem which Stein witnessed on several occasions during her interviews:

> Even the most pious conservative activists, when engaged in one-on-one discussions, seemed far less certain of themselves and their beliefs than I had anticipated, and the churches in which they placed their trust much more fractious. Rather than announce a sense of certainty and moral fortitude, the campaign seemed to do quite the opposite: it revealed a pervasive underlying sense of insecurity, placelessness, and existential mistrust. If the truth be told, most Timbertowners seemed far less concerned with the moral threat posed by homosexuality than with a host of other problems: the changing roles of men and women and the quickening pace of marital dissolution and family change, the decline of their small community and the fear that global, faceless corporations have more and more power to make decisions about what people will eat, how they will work, and where they will live. (217–18)

Timbertowners, as many other communities and individuals across the United States, were already fighting against what they perceived to be a decline in morals and standard of living. As their social orientation map had already undergone a myriad of substantial changes, these communities or individuals were left feeling uprooted and were compelled to cling firmly to a traditional concept of sexuality, marriage, and family (or at least the promise that an idealized version of the concepts provided). As a consequence, a renegotiation of these concepts was non-debatable and even functioned as a symbol of better times.

Stein describes Timbertowners as having the mindset that everyone was expected to have the same interests and adhere to the same set of values, a characteristic which applies to endless other communities (Stein 53). Being gay was tolerated by the community members as long as it was kept private, did not become too visible, and did not obligate the rest of the community to engage in a discourse about it (60). However, when more and more towns in Oregon started to implement anti-discrimination laws for the protection of homosexual Americans, activist groups in Timbertown questioned why a minority engaging in morally despicable behavior deserved special protection, especially since their acts led to declining values (103–104). Therefore, Stein closely looked at the rhetoric fashioned by these anti-gay groups and came to the following conclusion:

> Such rhetoric was designed to appeal to displaced Timbertowners, especially men, who were battling unemployment, a lack of purpose, a diminished sense of their own capacities. Loggers and their families were the target group: people who hated big government, whose pocketbooks were hurting, but whose "live and let live" attitude tended to stop short of taking stands on social issues. (122)

This rhetoric of asking why gay Americans deserved special rights or privileges targeted those already driven by a fear of loss and who felt left behind by the American nation. Due to these socioeconomic anxieties, people in communities such as Timbertown were reticent to being more open and tolerant towards a group of people who, in their eyes, lived on the other side of the social divide. "As liberals spoke about the importance of inclusion, tolerance, and equality, many longtime Timbertowners wondered, Who was protecting *their* rights, *their* livelihoods?" (Stein 218). Timbertowners increasingly felt that the gay minority had spokespeople championing for their cause all over the nation, whereas they, in rural Oregon, had long been forgotten. Such a mindset was actively encouraged by organizations of the Christian Right which exploited the desperation of people like the residents of Timbertown, Barry D. Adam noticed. In his study on the "moral panic" (266) which gay marriage sparked in the U.S., he explains the strategy of these anti-gay activists:

> DOMA-style campaigns, typically with major financial and organizational resources provided by Christian Right institutions, have frequently succeeded in drawing a discursive cloak of solidarity around rural or small town, less-educated people by constructing gay men and, to a lesser degree, lesbians as privileged, spoiled, and demanding "special rights." The Oregon Citizens Alliance (OCA), which promoted several ballot initiatives, including a Colorado-style embargo on any form of redress for antigay discrimination, mobilized a constituency that identified itself as the victims and outcasts of unfeeling liberal elites, including gay people among them. (Adam 269)

The people in these communities were easy targets for Christian Right institutions since they gave disenfranchised community members the feeling of being heard, protected, and acknowledged. Furthermore, they were told that the socioeconomic difficulties they were experiencing were not their fault. Thus, shielding the residents from the broader national discourse by keeping them under the monodiscursive religious cloak allowed these organizations to become the hailed saviors.

Lack of Community and the Role of the Church

Communities of all sorts provide us with guidelines and a social map for orientation. Situating oneself within a community of like-minded people and defining the self in contrast or in opposition to other groups of people, help people shape their personal as well as national identity. Stein elaborates on this at length in her study:

> We conceptualize the world into those who deserve inclusion and those who do not. Boundaries mark the social territories of human relations, signaling who ought to be admitted and who excluded. The desire to root out others in order to consolidate a sense of self seems universal. How do human beings perceive one another as belonging to the same group while at the same time rejecting human beings whom they perceive as belonging to another group? Why must we affirm ourselves by excluding others? A community's boundaries remain a meaningful point of reference for its members only as long as they are repeatedly tested by people who are on the fringes of the group and repeatedly defended by those within it. Sociologists tell us that in order to create a sense of social order, which all societies must establish, deviants are created and punished. . . . Though the making of collective identities and boundaries is always inherently

> political, at certain moments such processes become explicitly politicized. Symbolic boundaries become more important during periods of rapid social change. (8)

When communities are at risk of falling apart as its social glue of a shared set of morals and beliefs dissolves in times of rapid social change, community cohesion needs to be established by other means. The sociological phenomenon of "othering" or finding a common scapegoat are popular practices to reinforce community solidarity through a demarcation of one's group against a common enemy (Burke 406). A common enemy can be found in unpopular policies but also in other people. In addition, people tend to become more extreme in their beliefs if they surround themselves with like-minded people. Group members tend to mutually amplify the intensity of each other's mindset. Cass Sunstein explains that group polarization is "significantly greater when group identity was emphasized. . . . [P]olarization is highly likely to occur, and to be most extreme, when group membership is made salient" (43). In places like Timbertown, where a new community identity is desperately needed and is supposed to be found by uniting against a common enemy, this polarization occurs because the focus is on the creation of an in-group membership as the ultimate goal. In this time of fear and uncertainty, Timbertowners were ultimately longing for community stability and a sense of belonging. Stein's explanations for the "othering" of homosexuals in Timbertown follows the same line of thought: "The campaign against homosexuality in Timbertown was, too, a quest for belonging and security – and reparation. . . . [T]he campaign emerged at a time when long-standing bonds of trust and reciprocity were eroding" (215). As a result, it was to be expected that Timbertowners would be welcoming of an opportunity to regain a long-lost community spirit. Unfortunately, this new group identity was developed at the expense of another group. Sunstein argues that this kind of group polarization process is interesting because it has the potential to "[reveal] hidden beliefs and desires" (30) as it did in Timbertown. Although a fear of loss seemed to be the overall guiding principle of many opponents of gay rights in Timbertown, not all of these people's fears were directly connected to homosexual Americans. For some, gay rights became the outlet and the host for a number of other insecurities, anxieties, and worries (Stein 4). Efforts of gay-friendly groups to allay these fears were rarely successful. One of the reasons for this lack of success might be that as soon as a new group identity was found, people were not willing to let go of it so easily. Another reason may be the phenomenon described by Sunstein in which efforts to explain why something is not a risk often results in stoking greater suspicions:

> It is well established that when people are given information suggesting that they have no reason to fear what previously seemed to be a small risk, their fear often increases. This mysterious finding might be explained by the fact that the information focuses people's attention on that risk, and when attention is focused on a risk, fear increases. (54)

According to Stein's report, the evangelical churches in Timbertown did their fair share of fostering hostility towards homosexuals and reinforcing people's fears. Church and faith play a central role in Timbertown, as they do in many comparable small towns all over the United States. The church and its congregation offer a community of faith and a feeling of belonging to something larger, something for which many suffering from the town's socioeconomic problems are grateful. Consequently, the influence of the evangelical churches was enormous in shaping the discourse in town. Stein describes the situation in Timbertown as follows:

> With many citizens looking to churches for a sense of connection and belonging, conservative Protestant leaders took up the challenge of reconstructing the community. Evangelical churches provided a vocabulary and infrastructure through which these communal aspirations and ambient fears could be articulated, and a Christian right organization gave these fears a face and a name: homosexuality. To traditionalists, lesbians and gay men epitomized the unencumbered self, and all the flexibility and refashioning that such a self implied. . . . Homosexuals were problematic because they signified a retreat into self-indulgence and individualism and flouted the moral authority of centuries of tradition, the right argued. (216)

Religious leaders offered Timbertowners three things they desperately desired: They gave them a community, they provided them with a common enemy, and they offered them the source and target for their fears. In other words, they gave them their voices back and made them feel heard, which was exactly what they needed.

Timbertown: A Paradigmatic Community

As emphasized earlier on, Timbertown is not a singular example. Much rather, this small town in Oregon is paradigmatic for countless other communities in the United States. An analysis conducted by the sociologists Rory McVeigh and Maria-Elena M. Diaz on attitudes on same-sex marriage as reflected in communities' voting behavior produced similar results to Stein's socio-ethnographical observations. In their essay "Voting to Ban Same-Sex Marriage: Interests, Values and Communities," McVeigh and Diaz attempt to understand opponents' motives for refusing to endorse marriage equality.[134] One explanation they developed is that "[t]he fight over same-sex marriage represents a competition over socially constructed meanings, as groups and individuals on both sides of the issue struggle to define the meanings of marriage, sexuality, morality, and civil rights" (892). They are convinced that people's opinion on homosexuality and marriage equality is heavily influenced by the community in which the voters live: "Varying understandings of same-sex marriage develop through life-long socialization processes and are constructed in churches, college campuses, coffee shops, workplaces, and bowling alleys" (McVeigh and Diaz 893). The phenomena McVeigh and Diaz describe can be seen in the Timbertown community, especially in regard to the dynamics of group polarization and how attitudes towards homosexuality are shaped by socialization processes and the actors involved. The difficult socioeconomic setting, a fear of loss, and the hostile position of the church towards gay Americans in Timbertown intensified the community's anti-gay stance.

The most interesting aspect of McVeigh and Diaz' study is their description of a clear correlation between negative attitudes on homosexuality and economic struggles as well as weak community cohesion. Like Stein, McVeigh and Diaz argue that "[i]n communities where many individuals feel threatened by homosexuality, weak community cohesion can contribute to a general sense that same-sex marriage would further undermine the community's social fabric" (893). Additionally, they write

[134] McVeigh and Diaz conducted an examination of voting data on the county level since they believe this method would provide better evidence on voters' behavior than an analysis based on statewide results. They analyzed voting results from 28 states which had ballot initiatives on same-sex marriage from 2000 to 2008.

that "opposition to same-sex marriage, and to homosexuality more generally, is most likely found in communities where residents are struggling economically" (898). People fear that a further destabilization of their community will result in a loss of values and a still greater decline of a sense of community. Ultimately, this leads to a deterioration in residents' morality as well as an increase in criminal activity. Significantly, "[m]ost of these arguments, however, do not suggest that gay individuals will be the ones committing these crimes. Instead, opponents argue that legalization will undermine the institution of marriage and lead to poorer socialization of the children" (McVeigh and Diaz 897). Areas in which this belief is held are typically characterized by weak community cohesion, low residential stability, and low rates of home ownership (897). A poor educational background as well as a poor financial situation also contribute to this phenomenon. McVeigh and Diaz sum up their core findings as follows:

> [H]olding other factors constant, opposition to same-sex marriage tends to be weaker in counties with high median family incomes, higher levels of education, and higher percentages of the population enrolled in college and employed in professional occupations. Opposition tends to be stronger in counties with higher percentages of workers employed in production and construction occupations, and where higher percentages of households receive public assistance income. . . . Where there is economic deprivation and limited opportunities for social mobility, community residents are more likely to perceive themselves as vulnerable to economic competition that may result when discriminatory barriers are lifted. (907)

The effect described in the last sentence was observable in Timbertown after the proposition of anti-gay discrimination protection policies. The fear of additional competition or of reverse discrimination played an essential role in opposing gay rights and marriage equality. Some heterosexual Americans were afraid that they might find themselves disadvantaged if measures comparable to racial quotas in university admissions were implemented: "[R]esearch suggests that gay rights might be perceived as threatening in working-class and less prosperous communities where many residents may be receptive to arguments about how policies designed to protect or promote gay rights would lead to reverse discrimination" (McVeigh and Diaz 898). Again, McVeigh and Diaz findings based on county-level voting results were consistent with Stein's on-site observations and interviews in Timbertown.

Charges of Un-Americanism and the Fear of Loss

Charges of un-Americanism are prominent in times of crisis and despair, as the quantitative analysis conducted in chapter I indicated, and this rhetoric is most popular when people are afraid of the loss of their identity and their sociocultural framework. As Skey emphasized, symbolic systems of everyday life, which include values and social norms, act as powerful frameworks for orientation in the world (11). As a consequence, Timbertowners' sociocultural map had been turned upside down when their economic and sociocultural environment was subject to severe transformations. The decline of the lumber business forced this community to reconstruct their identity which had been closely connected to this industrial branch. Their profession shaped their identities not only as Timbertowners but also as Americans who stood for conservative American values and ideals. Consequently, the socioeconomic changes that forced them to redefine their personal and professional identity also forced them to reposition themselves as Americans and to reconsider whether their idea of American everyday nationalism was still prevalent in the United States. In the course of this repositioning, these small-town people found themselves feeling left behind by their country. The changes in the community led to a necessary reconstruction of these interests, which required a renegotiation and reconstruction of social discourse on American nationalism as a whole. This is the point when competing concepts of American self-definition, American nationalism, and accusations of un-Americanism come into the picture. It is the fear of loss, rapid changes in society, and the feeling of not being heard which lead to reciprocal accusations of un-Americanism in the fight over good American character and values. As the example of Timbertown and the analysis of the debate over marriage equality in chapter IV demonstrates, in many cases, the term 'un-American' functions as a substitute expression for these fears, thoughts, and worries that people cannot verbalize by other words or means. As a result, it is crucial to look beyond the term 'un-American' in order to understand what initially motivated Americans to attack each other in this fashion. It needs to be understood which social, cultural, and economic problems of American nationhood are at the crux of conflicts that become subsumed under the cover of un-Americanism.

E The Nation as the Family

One of the first to describe the extraordinary status of family in the United States was the French diplomat and political scientist Alexis de Tocqueville. Based on observations from his travels to the United States, the Frenchman praised American family life and encouraged his fellow Europeans to follow the American example as illustrated in his monograph *Democracy in America*:

> In Europe almost all the disturbances of society arise from the irregularities of domestic life. To despise the natural bonds and legitimate pleasures of home, is to contract a taste for excesses, a restlessness of heart, and the evil of fluctuating desires. . . . But when the American retires from the turmoil of public life to the bosom of his family, he finds in it the image of order and of peace. There his pleasures are simple and natural, his joys are innocent and calm; and as he finds that an orderly life is the surest path to happiness, he accustoms himself without difficulty to moderate his opinions as well as his tastes. Whilst the European endeavors to forget his domestic troubles by agitating society, the American derives from his own home that love of order which he afterwards carries with him into public affairs. (335)

The family is the core of American private and civil life. As long as the integrity and stability of the family remain unharmed, the American nation can prosper and Americans can reach their full potential as citizens of this democratic nation. The order, peace, and happiness within the family and the nation are inextricably connected and mutually dependent.

The Traditional Family Ideal and National Stability

For the large majority of Americans, this line of thought continues to ring true in the nearly two centuries since Tocqueville's *Democracy in America* was first published in 1835. The family is still the heart of domestic and private life. How ardently Americans, especially the conservative among them, still cherish the idea of the nuclear family was openly displayed in the debate on marriage equality and on gay rights at large. For some opponents, the possibility that same-sex couples could be granted the same marriage rights and also be considered a family was the first step towards the collapse of American society and the American nation. As iterated in the previous chapter, same-sex marriage is not always the core of people's fears and worries, but it often acts as a symbol on which more general anxieties about the rapidly changing world can be projected (Stein 4). This was the case in Timbertown, which functions as an example for countless other communities all over the United States. What worried conservatives were general changes to family life caused by socioeconomic developments, divorce, or the changing roles of women and men in society (218).

In their analysis of county voting results, McVeigh and Diaz also witnessed this phenomenon. Despite many Americans endorsing anti-discrimination laws on a general basis, they seemed to forget about this belief in equal rights in the debate on marriage equality. Some opponents based their argumentation on the traditional definition of marriage which said that this could only be a union between a man and a woman with no possibility for variation. This attitude is particularly common in communities where traditional gender roles and family ideals are omnipresent: "Psychological studies show that, at the individual level, prejudiced attitudes towards homosexuals are correlated with the adherence to traditional sex roles" (McVeigh and Diaz 893). In addition to that, "traditional sex and gender roles within a community can promote opposition to same-sex marriage in a way that leads many to see a breakdown in social organization as both a cause and a consequence of nontraditional values, including values that promote tolerance of same-sex marriage" (895). Consequently, same-sex marriage sometimes acts as a scapegoat for changes that were already affecting the community before gay marriage even became a topic. As seen in the example of Timbertown, grappling with new gender roles was a problem long before the issue of gay rights entered the sociocultural discourse due to transformations in the Timbertowners' work environment. With men losing their jobs or earning lower wages for manual labor, women increasingly needed to enter the workforce in order to sustain their families. For generations, the men in Timbertown had taken pride in being the breadwinners of the family, which allowed women to stay at home and care for their families (Stein 95). Having to accept that this constellation would no longer be possible was unbearable for many. As a result, they required a coping mechanism for dealing with this blow to their self-concepts. Identifying a cause for their misery that lay outside of their range of influence was a common strategy, and gay rights were the ideal target (217–18). McVeigh and Diaz's discovery that approval of a ban on same-sex marriage was especially popular in communities with a low number of women in the paid labor market was telling of how lived gender-roles had an impact on the perception of same-sex marriage.[135] This strong correlation between traditional concepts of gender and family and attitudes towards gay rights is additionally intensified when community cohesion tends to be weak. McVeigh and Diaz explain this effect as follows:

> Counties characterized by traditional family structures and gender roles tend to show strong opposition to same-sex marriage. . . . In such contexts, the prevalence of traditional arrangements means that individual perceptions of a threat are likely to be continually reinforced through social interaction, as individuals interact on a regular basis with others who share similar views by virtue of their shared circumstances. These conditions, we argue, predispose community members to perceive same-sex marriage as a threat to the community, particularly in locations where community cohesion is already in peril. (907)

Transformations concerning gender roles and the identity concepts associated with them seemed to be especially unsettling. With its untraditional distribution of gender, same-sex marriage was a fitting target for attacks related to insecurity about evolving gender roles.

The Nation as the Family and the Family as the Nation

One's family is not exclusive to the persons to whom we are related by blood. The American family is also the American nation. The metaphor of the nation as family was prominently discussed by the cognitive linguist George Lakoff in several of his publications. He argues that this metaphor for the nation as the family is ubiquitous in the U.S. with names such as the Founding Fathers, Uncle Sam, or the Daughters of the American Revolution. The metaphor of the nation as a family permeates national discourse in the United States (3). In order to instrumentalize this metaphor for analytical purposes, Lakoff distinguishes between two different

[135] As an example, McVeigh and Diaz cite the community of Martin County, Texas where 95% of residents opposed marriage equality and almost half of the county's women did not work in a paid job. The women who were in paid employment primarily worked in a highly sex-segregated workforce. The opposite situation could also be measured in county voting data. In counties where the majority of women contributed to the family income, the approval rate of same-sex marriage bans was low (McVeigh and Diaz 908).

types of family: the strict father family and the nurturant father family. In a strict father family, the father protects the family from the dangerous world outside, gives guidelines for good behavior, and disciplines when there is wrong or immoral behavior. Additionally, he teaches his children to rely on themselves, to obey to rules and respect hierarchies, and to earn their privileges. Lakoff parallels this strict-father family model with a conservative, usually Republican, worldview (6–10).[136] In contrast, the nurturant father family is analogous to a progressive and liberal stance. According to Lakoff, the nurturant model is characterized by three traits: "empathy, responsibility for yourself and others, and a commitment to do your best not just for yourself, but for your family, your community, your country, and the world" (10). This involves the desire to protect vulnerable members of society, promote freedom and equal rights for all, and a belief in opportunity and progress (Lakoff 12). Lakoff claims that these two models act as linguistic frames for the political conversation in the United States. Therefore, they also decide which rhetoric dominates the national discourse. If reduced to a basic system in which liberals and conservatives are employing these frames to fight each other, the fight is one between the strict father family model and the nurturant father family model. These two frames decide the wording that is chosen by the political camps since their rhetoric needs to fit into these frames. Lakoff asserts that facts become secondary to frames: "If the facts do not fit a frame, the frame stays and the facts bounce off" (15–16).[137] Under these circumstances, it is not surprising that the competing parties in the marriage

[136] Lakoff sees the parallels between the strict father and a conservative worldview in an aversion to nurturance and care, i. e., social and welfare programs, a focus on morality, the tendency to reward with incentives (e. g., subsidies and tax cuts for corporations and investors), as well as in a strong focus on self-reliance and independence (i. e., maximizing self-interest, small government, and reckless enforcement of foreign policy interests). Additionally, the strict father as well as the conservative American focuses on the upholding of the moral hierarchy (i. e., Western culture above all others, men above women, Christians above non-Christians, heterosexual above homosexual, and white above non-white) (Lakoff 6–10).

[137] The cognitive linguist Lakoff explains this phenomenon with neuroscientific reasons: "Concepts are not things that can be changed by just someone telling us a fact. We may be presented with them, but for us to make sense of them, they have to fit with what is already in the synapses of our brain" (15–16).

equality debate are completely unmoved when presented with facts from the other side that do not fit into their sociocultural and political frame.

The same word can have completely different connotations depending on a person's worldview and the frame that they employ. Lakoff names the term 'freedom' as an example. Whereas liberals associate equal rights and equal opportunities with the concept of freedom, conservatives rarely share this interpretation and rather understand 'freedom' as the absence of governmental intervention (Lakoff 49).[138] The frames which guide our decision-making processes cannot be changed easily since they are constitutive for our sociocultural map. "To change our frames is to change all of this. Reframing is social change" (Lakoff xii). This hypothesis articulates why changes in opinion are extremely rare in culture war conflicts such as marriage equality. The debate on marriage equality is a clash of values as well as a battle between the strict father family frame versus the nurturant father family frame. Conceptualizing the nation as a family and the family as the nation, the discourse on gay rights is a conflict of two very different interpretations of both personal and national American identity. Therefore, the family as well as the identity concept of each American individual determine the criteria of their idea of American everyday nationalism. For Americans who believe in the strict father family model, same-sex marriage contradicts all the values and morals they hold dear. The problem originates due to same-sex couples lacking someone who could represent a strict father since their union would either be two women or two gay men who are not considered masculine enough to fulfill such a role (Lakoff 130). In addition, all the other factors described previously (moral decline,

[138] A comparable debate was led in the Supreme Court case *Obergefell v. Hodges* regarding the concept of liberty. The majority opinion argued that marriage must be granted to same-sex couples on the basis of the right to liberty. Liberty and marriage are connected because the U.S. Constitution ensures that the American people must be able to freely define and express their identity (United States, Supreme Court, "*Obergefell*" 4). By contrast, the dissenting judges claim that the majority opinion interpreted the principle of liberty wrong (Scalia, "*Obergefell*" 1–2; Thomas, "*Obergefell*" 3; 7; 13; 17–18; Roberts, "*Obergefell*" 10–15). Justice Thomas was most vocal in this regard and accused the majority opinion of inverting the original meaning of liberty (13), of misunderstanding what the concept of liberty means in the U.S. Constitution, namely a freedom from governmental intervention and not an entitlement to certain rights (7), and of risking damage to the constitutional order because of their reckless misinterpretation (13).

changing family and gender concepts, threat to society, etc.) further fortify conservatives in their negative stance towards marriage equality. Lakoff suggests that the culture war is even more intense when conservatives, and especially the right wing, feel attacked due to their strict father family ideal: The right wing wants "nothing less than a radical revolution in how America and the rest of the world functions. That the vehemence of the culture war is provoked and maintained by conservatives is no accident. For strict father morality to gain and maintain political power, disunity is required" (132). In the eyes of conservatives, Lakoff claims, "[t]he hated liberals are threatening American culture and values, and have to be fought vigorously and continuously on every front. It is a threat to the very security of the nation, as well as morality, religion, the family, and everything real Americans hold dear" (134). It must be noted that Lakoff himself is a convinced liberal and has spent a significant amount of his career advising progressive advocacy groups and liberal parties. Nevertheless, the behavior he describes is likely to reinforce political trenches to a certain degree, regardless of political or party affiliation.

The extraordinary connection between the nation and the family in the United States is a theme which has not diminished in importance since Tocqueville's writings. The nation and the family are mutually dependent. Only when both environments are characterized by stability and continuity can people prosper and reach their full potential. Tocqueville described an ideal in which the American carries the peace and order found in family life into the public sphere, which concurrently brings happiness, moderation, and success for the nation (335). The importance of this connection for American life is not least reflected in the fact that the model family is one of the core elements of the American Dream, thereby making it one of the guiding principles of Americanism (Bush and Bush 95). As a consequence, should the fulfillment of the American Dream ever be disrupted by a conflict or threat from outside, the American can still find safety and comfort in the "bosom of his family" (Tocqueville 335). This principle was also observed during the Cold War and the time of the House Un-American Activities Committee. Home and family life provided a safe haven to which Americans could retire in order to shield themselves from the un-American influences from outside (Herbst Lewis 4). Homosexuals were among those classified as un-American since they were believed to pose a threat to national stability and the integrity of the heterosexual family (5). Therefore, denouncing gay Americans as un-American and dangerous for the traditional American family ideal is not a phenomenon stemming from the

21st century's quest for gay rights. Many marriage equality opponents are concerned that changes to the ideal of the nuclear family are the source of all the problems and un-American developments which have led to the gradual decline of the American nation. Consequently, they long for the time in which American social and cultural life was still easy and clearly structured, and when family life was intact as was the nation. However, the question is whether this model of the perfect American family and its positive implications for the nation have ever been a reality or if this has always been more of a pipe dream based on a distorted image of a Frenchman whose only acquaintance with the country was through his travels. For traditionalists, accusations of un-Americanism are often connected to a yearning for better times, times when the United States was "truly American" or at least more American than in current times. In her essay "How 'Un-American' Became the Political Insult of the Moment," Beverly Gage points out that "[t]o label something 'un-American' is to imagine America as it should have been or as it might yet be but not as it ever was."

In the end, this ideal of the perfect connection between the family and the nation in the United States is an image of family which Americans may to aspire to, but which has hardly ever been an obtainable reality. Regardless of the actuality of Tocqueville's descriptions, Americanism remains inextricably interwoven with family values. The family determines many of the values and morals that are cherished by Americans and that they carry into public life. They shape their understanding of a successful nation and of what constitutes American nationalism (Heinemann 7). Consequently, developments in the area of family that are considered unfavorable or even dangerous are prone to accusations of un-Americanism due to the fundamental connection between the family and the nation in the United States. This interconnectedness between family values and American everyday nationalism makes the rhetorical strategy of accusing the opponent of un-Americanism even more attractive. Policies which are labelled un-American are often regarded as not only detrimental to the nation but as potentially harmful for one's private life. The nation is the family and the family is the nation (Lakoff 3). Furthermore, changes in the sociocultural areas of life often require a reframing of one's mindset and one's concept of American everyday nationalism. Denouncing marriage equality or the denial thereof as un-American is much easier than reconceptualizing one's American everyday nationalism and adjusting one's social orientation map.

F Conclusion

In the United States, the right to marriage functions as a regulatory mechanism which helps structure society by operating as a determinant for the inclusion in or exclusion from American everyday nationalism. Consequently, politicizing marriage either enables adherents of the traditional idea of family and marriage to uphold the dominant hierarchy and power structure when they believe political and social stability is at stake or, by contrast, it enables advocates of new concepts of family to challenge these traditional images. As Alexis de Tocqueville noted in his observations of the American people, family and marriage are inextricably linked with the concept of the American nation. This connection between family and nation has not lost any of its importance since Tocqueville's observations.

Sexuality rather functions as a symbol upon which people project anxieties which are often completely unrelated to gay people or same-sex marriage. Opponents' chief concerns are often socioeconomic struggles, declining community cohesion, rapid changes in the world around them, and the feeling that they are losing their self-concept and can no longer identify with their country. They feel voiceless and left behind by their nation. However, they are not the only ones who have experienced this and who have felt compelled to make use of the un-Americanism rhetoric. This impression of being left behind is something that same-sex couples and families know all too well since they long struggled with the thought that the American promise of equality could never come true for them. Before the landmark civil rights case *Obergefell v. Hodges*, same-sex couples and their children suffered from a lack of federal protection and the denial of thousands of benefits that came with marriage in multiple areas of life. Several studies support the claims that marriage in the United States was not a "luxury issue" (Bashir et al. 181) because marriage has the ability to determine the social and economic status that a person can achieve in the American nation.

Smith and Windes claim that American identity is forged in combat (56) and culture wars over marriage equality and other controversial topics thereby operate as a venue where this process of identity formation takes place. According to Prothero's four key features of culture wars (*Liberals* 10), these quarrels over Americanism, un-Americanism, and national identity fit the criteria to be classified as a culture war. The analysis of the reasons behind charges of un-Americanism aimed at uncovering the submerged part of the iceberg, and it revealed that same-sex marriage often functions as a proxy war for conflicts which are not directly related to the issue of gay rights or marriage equality. Thereby, accusations of un-Americanism operate as linguistic auxiliary constructions in these conflicts because the agents involved often struggle to verbalize their fears and concerns or feel as if they need to rely on such a loaded rhetorical weapon in order to be heard. As a result, the true conflicts in disputes over cultural controversies, such as marriage equality, are American nationalism, American national identity, and not least (un-)Americanism. Marriage equality thereby serves as a discursive platform or proxy war while the core of the conflict are discrepancies over what constitutes American nationalism. Whoever holds the upper hand in these debates is able to regulate and decide who is included and who becomes marginalized within the American nation, and how power and cultural capital are distributed.

Chapter VII

VII The Renegotiation of American Nationalism and Its Inclusiveness

A Normalism and Normativity

The ultimate goal of the marriage equality movement was to make gay Americans and their relationships equal to those of their fellow heterosexual Americans. In terms of marriage laws, the Supreme Court secured for gay Americans an equal place in the American nation as opposite-sex couples. However, this change in law did not automatically mean that same-sex couples were also included in people's prevailing notions of American nationalism. Furthermore, many questions regarding the socio-cultural standing of these couples remained open. Are same-sex couples now shaping the common understanding of Americanism and American discourses and practices of nationhood? Have gay couples become an integral part of the American nation or are they still considered too different to fulfill this role? How far has the nation evolved on this issue? Are same-sex couples a part of the "new normal" of American everyday nationalism? What is "normal"?

These questions are crucial for further exploring how the American people handle the challenges posed by diversity and by the demand of minorities to be fully included into what is commonly understood by American nationalism. As the voices of gay Americans continued to grow louder in American national discourse and the concomitant discursive (re)construction of American everyday nationalism, new terms and ideas emerged in this context. Americans realized that this process of a gradual inclusion of gay Americans required new vocabulary to make the discursive negotiation of this development possible. The old binary of homo- and heterosexuality was therefore paired with concepts of normativity and nationalism, which resulted in new terms such as 'homo-' or 'heteronormativity' and 'homonationalism' in order to account for the influence this minority had on these concepts. Traditional hegemonic heterosexual constructions of nationalism and national identity have been challenged by the everyday enactment of gay identity practices and by reconceptualizations of who the un-American in the nation were. This social shift had a lasting and powerful impact on American nationalism, especially since *Obergefell*. A look at new approaches to nationalism, such as homonationalism, reveals how the American nation reacts to sociocultural transformations that require the inclusion of a previously marginalized group of Americans, and how they reconstruct their mental maps in order to comply with this demand.

Normalism, Normalization, and Normativity

When exploring un-Americanism and transformations of American everyday nationalism, one must also talk about 'normalism' because what is considered American or un-American correlates with what is typically regarded as normal, dominant, or characteristic of American behavior or thought at a certain point in time. Normalism usually implies being average, blending into society, and representing the "typical American," whatever it may mean. Influenced by the work of his colleague Jürgen Link, the critical discourse analyst Siegfried Jäger defines normalism as "the entirety of all discursive procedures, dispositives, entities, and institutions" ("die Gesamtheit aller diskursiven Verfahren, Dispositive, Instanzen und Institutionen"; my trans.; Jäger 53).[139] Those are the agents through which 'normalities' are (re-)produced and which then shape the structure of our society. Of course, people's ideas of what is normal as well as accepted behavior changes over time, something that has been observed in the course of the gay rights movement and the marriage equality debate. The concomitant reconfiguration of normalism can provoke a "fear of denormalization" ("Denormalisierungsangst"; my trans.; Jäger 54). Some people are less flexible and tolerant in regard to processes of denormalization. Consequently, they may be inclined to adopt accusations of un-American against those who are expanding the spectrum of normalism in order to make American everyday nationalism more inclusive. Normalism pro-

[139] Reflections on normalism and normalization were prominently made by Michel Foucault in his monograph *Discipline and Punish* and were later taken up by discourse analysists since these notions play a pivotal role in Western societies (Jäger 53). Jäger emphasizes that the concept of normalism is one of the core elements of human discourse and therefore must be paid special attention to in a critical analysis of discourse (55).

vides people with a sociocultural map for orienting themselves in their daily lives so that they do not repeatedly need to invest their cognitive resources in making sense of the world surrounding them.

In the debate over the role of gay Americans in the United States and the changes that came with marriage equality, the terms 'normalism' and 'normativity' emerged in various strands of discourse, not least through concepts such as 'heteronormalism' and 'homonormativity.' Before further inquiring into these new theories and their impact on nationalism studies, it is important to first have a closer look at the terms 'normalism' and 'normativity.' These terms are often used interchangeably by scholars of queer and nationalism studies; however, other disciplines make clear distinctions between the two concepts. Critical discourse studies are not only concerned with the normalism found in Jäger's theories, they also focus on normativity due to overlapping interest in the themes of in-group and out-group constellations, processes of marginalization, and the privilege that results from these dynamics (Koller 573). In the field of critical discourse analysis, Jürgen Link and Mirko Hall are strongly opposed to approaches where "the normal is either a part of the normative or identical with the everyday" ("Contribution" 35). They understand normativity as follows:

> According to concurrent interpretations of ethnology, anthropology, and sociology, all human societies possess and have possessed "norms" and "normativity." Explicit and implicit regulatives, which are reinforced through sanctions, pre-scribe a specific action to materially or formally determined groups of people. "Norms," therefore, always pre-exist (social) action: they are already known to at least a few professionals of the norm before such action. In the large majority of the above relevant discourses, "normativity" is used as a general abstract category for the entire field of the above understood "norms." Here, in a further sense, "normativity" has a legal overtone. (Hall and Link, "Power" 17)

Whereas normativity is an ancient concept, the "normal" is a product of modern society and has separated from the former in the eighteenth century (Hall and Link, "Contribution" 35). Normalism has a stronger statistical component since it makes the data-processing of behavior possible. Hall and Link describe normalism as follows:

> [N]ormalism proves itself – in the sense of the ensemble of discursive dispositives and cultural authorities (or institutions) that produce 'normalities' – as one of the most important regulating authority of modern

> dynamic. In other words, normalism presumes the most complete possible data processing of society to determine the trends of all growth curves (by prognosis) and the ability to normalize them through the intervention of private and state authorities (i.e., by prevention or at least by repair). This power of normalism is based on the fact that its network of dispositives confronts modernity from the outside with neither traditional nor futuristic-utopian imperatives. Rather, normalism shares its fundamental parameters and components with modernity, or it directly "borrows" those of modernity. ("Contribution" 38–39)

Therefore, normativity is a force which exists pre-action since it determines the scope of action, which is possible in a society, whereas normalism can only be determined after action has taken place because only then can its frequency be assessed. In their understanding of normativity, Hall and Link follow the tradition of philosophical ethics insofar as they see normativity as a principle which guides the individual's decision over whether an action is morally accepted. Normativity helps evaluate the social acceptability of an action and also defines what we have reason to do or believe (Wallace 453–54).

This differentiation between normalism and normativity is seldom strictly observed in research on the marriage equality movement and the influence of homosexual Americans on nationalism in the United States. What is normal is frequently also considered normative since normalism dictates what the majority of Americans regard as acceptable behavior and thought, and therefore what they consider to be normative.[140] Nevertheless, the distinction Link draws between these two concepts should be kept in mind because it allows for a better understanding of how people construct dominant views on what is normal and normative. Of particular interest is Link's assertion that norms function as regulatory mechanisms

[140] For instance, the sociologist Diane Richardson defines normalization as "the means by which norms of behavior are identified, encouraged, and (re)produced within populations. This is the process of establishing the normative standards of 'good' (sexual) citizenship" (133). The same linkage can be found in Dean's study on heterosexuality in a post-closeted culture:

> Normalization suggests an ambiguous process. On the one hand, it refers to the acquisition of a moral status as a person or ordinary human deserving of respect, rights, and integration. On the other hand, it reserves this moral status only for individuals who display decidedly culturally specific traits and behaviors such as gender normativity. . . . (6)

and thus determine whether an action is deemed as good or bad, or as American or un-American. Only those sets of belief or actions that are considered American or have become a part of American normativity will ultimately play a role in the construction of American everyday nationalism. Thus, it is worthwhile to explore how 'homonormativity' and 'homonationalism' have once again become relevant terms in the negotiation over American nationalism in the wake of *Obergefell*.

Heteronormativity and Homonormativity

The concept of heteronormativity, the belief that heterosexuality is the societal norm, is most commonly associated with the work of Michael Warner. He introduced the term to the field of queer studies in the early 1990s in order to critically address the gay rights movement's striving for normalism and assimilation (Warner, "Introduction" 3). Despite his criticism, Warner showed understanding for the desire to be "normal": "Nearly everyone, it seems, wants to be normal. And who can blame them, if the alternative is being abnormal, or deviant, or not being one of the rest of us? Put in those terms, there doesn't seem to be a choice at all. Especially not in America, where normal probably outranks other social aspirations" (*Trouble* 53). However, believing that it is necessary to question the dominant and often invisible heteronormativity in society, Warner calls for social theory, and research in general, to "do more than occasionally acknowledge the gay movement because so much of heterosexual privilege lies in heterosexual culture's exclusive ability to interpret itself as society" ("Introduction" 8). Despite public attitudes becoming significantly more positive towards homosexual people, Warner insists that "heteronormativity has a totalizing tendency that can only be overcome by actively imagining a necessarily and desirably queer world" (8). In terms of gay visibility and normalcy, Warner views heterosexuality as a problem when it is turned into a "default heteronormativity" (16) which dictates what society regards as normal and accepted American behavior and what is considered deviant and un-American. His critique targets the process through which heterosexuality receives a normative status in various sectors of everyday life and through which certain ways of living become the norm to which every member of society must aspire: "People are constantly encouraged to believe that heterosexual desire, dating, marriage, reproduction, childrearing, and home life are not only valuable to themselves, but the bedrock on which every other value in the world rests. Heterosexual desire and romance are thought to be the very core of humanity" (*Trouble* 47). Dean agrees that "[l]iving in a heteronormative society, heterosexual individuals are accorded heterosexual privilege. This privilege is often invisible. It is enacted in the view that heterosexuality is 'normal,' socio-psychologically healthy, and complex, as well as through entitlements to 'first-class citizenship'" (26). The marriage equality movement vehemently attacked and denounced this discrepancy in citizenship between heterosexual and homosexual Americans as un-American. The former enjoyed first-class citizenship and the accompanying full rights, and the latter were handed a poor second-class citizenship due to a lack of full equality. The privileging of straight identities leaves little or no room for accepted identity practices outside of heteronormativity. Moreover, it designates a gay identity as abnormal and deviant from the normativity which society postulates. What distinguishes heteronormativity from heteronormalization is, according to Richardson, that the former describes an "assumed norm" whereas the latter is a "process of governance of conduct that fits with prevailing norms" and can follow as the next step after heteronormativity ("Introduction" 17). Richardson regarded naming this problem, as Warner did in his research, as an important first step:

> [T]he concept of heteronormativity was important in shifting away from an analytical focus on homosexuality/heterosexuality, to the specificities of certain sexual/social orders that incorporate a range of assumptions about 'good' sexual citizens who embody normativity and who may be heterosexual *or* homosexual. (Richardson 17)

Warner identified heteronormativity as a powerful system of exclusion, hierarchy, and oppression of those who do not comply with the social codes and norms which heterosexual institutions and agents impose on them. Although his definition of the term 'heteronormativity' is most prevalent in this discourse, a study by Marchia and Sommer has demonstrated that there is "a fairly wide variation in the usages of the term . . . , indicating there has been no clear common or consistent usage of heteronormativity since Warner's original definition" (285).[141] This

[141] Marchia and Sommer investigated the evolution of the term 'heteronormativity' by collecting 58 articles from a wide range of research fields discussing this concept (277). They argue that the articles of their random sample can be assorted to five mutually exclusive themes which are "sexuality," "patriarchal gendered norms," "hegemonic masculinity or idealized femininity," "gender

must be kept in mind when discussing the impact of heteronormativity in the process of negotiating American everyday nationalism.

Heterosexuality and heteronormativity only receive meaning in opposition to homosexuality and homonormativity. Consequently, the coining and popularization of the term 'heteronormativity' resulted in the emergence of the concept of homonormativity. Although 'homonormativity' is most prominently associated with Lisa Duggan, who has used this term in her work published in 2003 and after, Susan Stryker claims that the concept originated much earlier in the transgender grassroots campaigns of the early 1990s in order to "articulate the double sense of marginalization and displacement experienced within transgender political and cultural activism" (145). Transgender people have often been excluded from gay and lesbian rights activism, as well as from government-sponsored health care programs; this exclusion was attributed to homonormativity. In addition to Stryker, an older conception of homonormativity can be found in J. Halberstam's 1998 monograph *Female Masculinity* in which Halberstam uses the term in a critique of both hetero- and homonormative cultures because they pathologize female expressions of masculinity and regard them as abnormal whereas male femininity is fully accepted in homophile cultures (Halberstam, *Female Masculinity* 9). Halberstam uses the term again in a 2003 essay on queer temporalities and subcultures in which Halberstam expresses dismay at "the new patriotism of post-9/11 culture and the new 'homonormativity' of the recent lesbian baby boom" because it could endanger queer subculture ("What's that smell?" 331). Both Stryker's and Halberstam's choice of words surrounding the concept of homonormativity indicate that they do not regard it as a positive development because homonormativity is seen as another mechanism for exclusion and the restriction of personal freedom of expression.

In her monograph *The Twilight of Equality? Neoliberalism, Cultural Politics, and the Attack on Democracy*, Lisa Duggan presents herself as optimistic toward the conflict within the gay rights movement in the United States: "Though the fight for gay equality has been rocked by internal conflict over assimilationist versus confrontational tactics since the emergence

and sexuality," and "power matrix" (279–82). Warner's theoretical framework was attributed to the category of "sexuality" since Warner, along with Seidman and Foucault, link heteronormativity directly to sexuality (279) and understand heteronormativity as a way of thinking where non-heterosexuality is regarded as "unnatural, deviant, or undesirable" (282).

of the homophile movement in the 1950s, the overall goals and directions of change have been relatively consistent" (51). Nevertheless, Duggan is fully aware of the growing influence of what is generally understood as homonormativity on the position which gay Americans occupy within the American nation. In 2003, Duggan conceived a new approach to homonormativity which she terms "the new homonormativity" and defines as "a politics that does not contest dominant heteronormative assumptions and institutions but upholds and sustains them while promising the possibility of a demobilized gay constituency and a privatized, depoliticized gay culture anchored in domesticity and consumption" ("Homonormativity" 179). In this new concept, Duggan not only understands homonormativity as a failure to challenge dominant heteronormative practices, but she also regards it as a product of its time and roots the new homonormativity within the neoliberalist politics of the late 20th century. As already addressed in the discussion of *United States v. Windsor* in chapter V.B, neoliberalism was contradictory because it promised a high level of individual freedom but resulted in a state which regulated the private lives of its citizens.[142] Richardson confirms that, despite the principle that citizens should freely design their individual lives, "[c]entral to such neoliberal modes of governance is normalization, the means by which norms of behavior are identified, encouraged and (re)produced within populations. This is the process of establishing normative standards of 'good' (sexual) citizenship. . ." (133). Duggan confirms that neoliberal America "in fact *has* a sexual politics" and was trying to find a "'third way' rhetoric between the moral conservatism of the religious Right and the 'civil rights agenda' of the progressive Left" ("Homonormativity" 177; 179). While the gay rights movement has been historically associated with the civil rights movements and leftist politics which draw the attention to minority rights, some gays relished the idea of a more conservative neoliberal nationalism into which

142 In terms of economic and trade policy, neoliberalism is a marked-based policy which encourages privatization, deregulation, free markets and free trade, and minimal governmental intervention to the benefit of entrepreneurial freedom. This same freedom provided by a limited government was supposed to be allocated to the private sphere as well. However, this was more of a theoretical idea which did not materialize into the personal freedom for which gay and lesbian Americans had hoped. On the contrary, the nuclear family concept and traditional family values saw a resurgence that was actively propelled by the government despite the neoliberalist philosophy of limited governmental intervention in all areas of life (Long-Droppert 47).

they hoped to assimilate. This mindset is the target of Duggan's criticism which she enunciates in "the new homonormativity" ("Homonormativity" 179). If this subgroup of gay culture encourages homosexual Americans to withdraw from public life and become a demobilized and depoliticized interest group that prefers to seclude itself in the private sphere of domesticity and consumption, those neoliberal gays are not challenging heteronormative structures. Moreover, these gays propel a homonormative lifestyle which accepts the dominance of heteronormativity and aims to comply with the demands of neoliberalism. As Warner claimed, almost everyone wants to be "normal" (*Trouble* 53) and the representatives of the new homonormativity framed what the new gay normal was or what the normal gay should look like.[143] Duggan disapproves of this new homonormativity because of their "rhetorical recoding of key terms in the history of gay politics" ("Homonormativity" 190). She insists that, as a consequence, "'equality' becomes narrow, formal access to a few conservatizing institutions, 'freedom' becomes impunity for bigotry and vast inequalities in commercial life and civil society, the 'right to privacy' becomes domestic confinement, and democratic politics itself becomes something to be escaped" ("Homonormativity" 190). Neoliberal homonormativity undermines the traditional strategy of the gay rights movement which rooted their demands in the American ideal of equality for all citizens and construed a new normativity which gave gay people a new normalism to which they were expected to conform on top of the unchallenged rubric of heteronormativity. The sexual politics of neoliberalism is important to keep in mind since it encourages understanding for the "receptivity or resistance towards demands for equality and rights of (sexual) citizenship" (Richardson 139) as both can be rooted in a neoliberal worldview due to its inner contradictoriness.

Duggan's notion of homonormativity is not uncontested. Roseneil et al. prefer to use the concept of homonormalization "in order to emphasize both the incompleteness of this process, and the historical and ongoing incommensurability of heteronormativity and homonormativity as regulatory and normative regimes" (186). Duggan's theories were primarily

143 Among the forerunners of this new gay politics were the writers of the so-called Independent Gay Forum, an organization which sponsored a website that published pieces by conservative/moderate authors. Those authors simultaneously tried to address both a non-leftist gay public as well as national supporters of neoliberalism in general (Duggan, "Homonormativity" 179).

an answer to the neoliberal politics at the turn of the millennium and do not reflect progress within homonormative influences. Motschenbacher and Stegu bemoan that Duggan's rather restricted definition of homonormativity dominates scholarly discourse. As a result, they suggest a much broader definition of homonormativity for several reasons in order to acknowledge and recognize the diverse influences on this concept and avoid internal conflict within a minority of similar overall goals (524).[144]

The approaches to homonormativity discussed above predominantly address the negative side-effects of this normalization process, particularly Duggan's new homonormativity which is investigated in the rather restricted context of neoliberal politics. However, the concept of homonormativity can also be analyzed from a more neutral perspective that not only acknowledges the costs and negative side-effects of this process but also recognizes the benefits and liberty it has brought to some queer people. The marriage equality movement and the change in law it ultimately achieved were subject to criticism within the gay rights movement for encouraging assimilationist practices and for its uncritical celebration of an old heterosexual institution. Furthermore, the example of same-sex marriage demonstrates that there are different voices and opinions within the queer community. For some, marriage equality brought first-class citizenship, but others are still struggling or experiencing a new form of discrimination. Therefore, homonormativity should be analyzed with a simultaneous consideration of both its benefits and its costs. Only then can its impact on the renegotiation and reconceptualization of American nationalism prior to and in the wake of *Obergefell* be assessed. Despite resistance and dissent from some marriage equality opponents, same-sex

144 The two authors believe using the terms 'heteronormativity' and 'homonormativity' as parallel terms is problematic since heteronormative structures are a given in society and remain largely uncontested whereas homonormativity only exists in certain contexts (525). Furthermore, Motschenbacher and Stegu warn against making such a close connection between homonormativity and the same-sex marriage debate in order to avoid putting same-sex couples who wish to marry and those who do not in contention with each other. This link could result in the former being accused of assimilation and fostering a new marginalization of those previously marginalized (525). In this context, they are concerned that Duggan's definition of homonormativity ignores that there are multiple normativities at work in the development of homonormative values and ways of life besides those prescribed by heteronormativity (Motschenbacher and Stegu 525)

couples are increasingly becoming a constitutive part of American nationalism and American national self-definition. Eventually, homonormativity could also lead to a gradual normalization of gay couples and gay lifestyle in the United States, although same-sex couples are still far from being automatically regarded as first-class citizens as heterosexuals are.

Normativity in Insults of Un-Americanism

Becoming normal, normalized, or even normative was the goal of some same-sex couples in the fight for marriage equality. Their accusations of un-Americanism expressed the wish for homonormalization or homonormativity in the sense that they wanted gay people to be fully accepted citizens who were not regarded as any different from their fellow heterosexual Americans. The vast majority of gay rights advocates did not fight for marriage equality in order to facilitate the exclusion of parts of the queer community who either did not wish to get married or who did not fall within the frame of the same-sex couple which benefitted from the *Obergefell* landmark decision. Therefore, homonormalism and homonormativity should in the following not only be regarded as an instrument which encourages the marginalization of minorities within this minority but much rather as an attempt to make same-sex couples equal citizens with a rightful place within the American nation.

Prior to the hearing of plaintiffs, Jim Obergefell et al., Justice Ruth Bader Ginsburg had already spoken of the massive shift in Americans' attitude toward same-sex marriage. Because of this change, she was positive that a Supreme Court decision in favor of marriage equality would find broad acceptance and "would not take a large adjustment" for the American people (in interview with Stohr and Winkler). Bader Ginsburg saw a realistic chance that same-sex marriage could become as normal to American everyday nationalism as heterosexual marriage, in particular since she was convinced that the United States Constitution granted same-sex couples that right (United States, Supreme Court, "*Obergefell*" 28, majority opinion which Bader Ginsburg joined). Roberta Kaplan, lawyer in *United States v. Windsor*, agreed that the nation had become more accepting and that the pressure on lawmakers and courts was increasing since marriage equality was not only tolerated and accepted but demanded and regarded as American by a growing number of citizens (Krantz). Despite occasional setbacks, Kaplan was convinced that "[n]o American really believes it's OK to treat someone differently and discriminate against them simply because of who they are. Simply because it's un-American" (qtd. in Krantz). Kaplan's insult of un-Americanism signaled that the normalizing of homosexual couples with homonormativity as a next step was the right path for the American nation. The members of the bipartisan coalition Mayors for the Freedom to Marry shared this perspective. As a result, they declared that the discriminatory treatment of gay Americans through the denial of their rightful place within the American nation "is unacceptable, and it is un-American" (Parker et al.). However, they were hopeful that the United States had begun "a journey toward greater acceptance of groups once left behind" by seeing gay Americans as an integral part of America's diverse nationhood (Parker et al.). The former governor of Minnesota, Mark Dayton, also spoke of a "path of social progress, of human compassion and understanding" (qtd. in Andrew) when he appealed to his fellow Minnesotans to reject a proposed amendment which would halt all marriage equality efforts in the state. Regarding marriage equality, Minnesotans should not reverse all of the hard-earned progress which had led to the gradual inclusion of same-sex couples into what Americanism entailed. Robert Redford witnessed the same development in Utah, which, despite being a very conservative and religious state, was changing ahead of *Obergefell* because discrimination of gay people was "un-American," as Redford postulated (qtd. in Thorpe). In a 2014 article published in *The New York Times*' Sunday Review, Frank Bruni went a step further and claimed that equal marriage rights for homosexual couples have become "nonnegotiable," "[e]xpected," and "[a]ssumed," and that anything else would be "un-American." By contrast, the 40 percent of Americans who still opposed same-sex marriage at that time ("Support" 1) would not have regarded this as a nonnegotiable point of contestation and certainly not as something that had become expected or even assumed in 2014. Nevertheless, gay marriage advocates would have agreed that a majority of Americans were comfortable with this change in law since the country had evolved enormously in favor of the issue. However, to regard marriage equality as "assumed" (Bruni), as if same-sex marriage already was an inherent part of American everyday nationalism back then, would have likely even astonished supporters. The word 'assumed' suggests that same-sex marriage had already led to the normalization of homosexual individuals and couples, who consequently had become part of people's idea of Americanism and the United States' diverse national identity.

The impression that the normalization of same-sex couples, and perhaps even a certain degree of homonormativity, was a path that the American nation had already chosen to follow before *Obergefell* is deceiving. Marriage equality opponents were fully aware of the danger posed by homonormalization and homonormativity and were eager to stop gay Americans from being included in American nationalism. For instance, the former House Representative Allen West warned that, if such a path of normalization were to continue, it would only be "a matter of time before we don't have society" (qtd. in Tashman). He was alarmed by the winning streak of gay rights advocates in courts and legislation since he was convinced that integrating homosexual Americans into society would ultimately lead to the downfall of the American people. This development needed to be stopped before homonormalization became established and seized the power to define Americanism. "[S]exual minorities are often perceived as posing a threat to the national community," Mole explained since gays are "undermining the family, failing to adhere to national gender stereotypes, challenging its internal homogeneity and deviating from shared national norms, especially those derived from religious teaching" (660). Bishop Samuel Smith of the Apostolic World Christian Fellowship agreed with West in this regard and advised Christians and marriage equality opponents not to allow the "homosexual agenda" to succeed in their attempts to "redefine morality" (Smith qtd. in Tashman). Smith's statement paints a picture among opponents that marriage equality advocates have a plan to take over American society and that, without intervention, it would only be a matter of time until they dominated the national discourse over what constitutes American values. However, Bryan Fischer, former Director of Issues Analysis for the American Family Association, claimed it was already too late "to stop this press and this push [of marriage equality advocates] toward nationalizing" (qtd. in Wong, "SCOTUS"), as if the marriage equality movement planned on assuming power and creating a homonormative nation. The president emeritus of the Massachusetts Family Institute, Kris Mineau, who believed that this process of the gradual inclusion of same-sex couples "running willy-nilly through our nation" was "un-American," already warned of reverse marginalization and discrimination (qtd. in T. Smith). He dreaded that, as soon as homonormalization and homonormativity reached a certain level, gay marriage opponents would be shut down and oppressed in the United States (T. Smith).

Although supporters as well as opponents did not use the terminology 'homonormalism' or 'homonormativity' in their mutual accusations of un-Americanism, the ideas of these concepts are nevertheless present. As these terms stem from scholarly discourse in queer studies and related areas of research, it is unsurprising that they were not explicitly used in the context of the fight over marriage equality. The statements discussed above show that the theories of homonormalism and homonormativity are negotiated in the debate over marriage equality and the concomitant discursive reconstruction of the nation. Supporters strive for same-sex couples to be regarded as normal and for their stronger inclusion in American everyday nationalism. By contrast, opponents are concerned by this development since they fear that their dominant place in the American society is threatened now that hegemonic heterosexual constructions are being challenged. For them, this reconceptualization of Americanism and American everyday nationalism is tantamount to its decline. Although the terminology of 'homonormalism' and 'homonormativity' is not raised in the public debate over marriage equality, the ideas that lie behind these concepts are an essential part of the negotiation of this issue as it requires the nation to handle the challenges that addressing the demands of a (previously) marginalized group entails. Consequently, the various forces of normalism and normativity are important factors that need to be considered when analyzing the intersections between un-Americanism, gay rights, and its consequences on how nationalism is represented in everyday American life.

A Lack of Locale and Language

The terms 'homonormalization' as well as 'hetero-' and 'homonormativity' provided some of the language which enabled the discourse over the changing role this minority had within the United States; however, a terminology which paved the way for the scholarly debate of the role of gay subjects within American nationalism and the American nation was still missing. In order to allow for an in-depth investigation of queer studies with a stronger focus on (gay) nationalism, Duggan argued "that we need to find a way to close the language gap in queer studies and queer politics. . . . especially with references to the operations of the state" ("Queering" 161). Regarding the role which the nation plays in the process of inclusion of homosexual Americans, Duggan emphasizes that discourses about the nation and the state are deeply rooted in gay and lesbian culture and politics:

> From turn-of-the-century German homosexual emancipationist Magnus Hirschfeld to contemporary radical-feminist philosopher Mary Daly, the 'nation' and its interest have been defined in varying ways. With no geo-

> graphical base or kinship ties to provide boundaries, gay and lesbian nationalists have offered biological characteristics (as in the 'Third Sex'), or shared experience (whether or sexual desire or gender solidarity) as common ground. ("Perfectly Queer" 160)

The difficulties resulting from a missing locale and missing terminology was also broached in Warner's monograph *Fear of a Queer Planet: Queer Politics and Social Theory*: "In the United States, the default model for all minority movements is racial or ethnic. . . . Queer culture will not fit this bill. . . . It cannot even be in diaspora, having no locale from which to wander" (xvii). This conflict makes the question of how the United States as a nation handles the challenges, which the gradual inclusion of this minority entails, unique. The situation of gays is categorically different from those of ethnic and racial minorities despite frequent comparisons to the civil rights movement. Sexual identity cannot be assessed in the same way as the categories of race, gender, and class because it operates differently on several levels, as Warner emphasizes:

> Identity as a lesbian or gay is ambiguously given and chosen, in some ways ascribed and in other ways the product of the performative act of coming out – itself a political strategy without precedent or parallel. In these ways sexuality defines – for most modern societies – a political interest-constituency unlike even those of gender and race. Queer people are a kind of social group fundamentally unlike others, a status group only insofar as they are not a class. (*Fear* xxv)

The default minority language of multiculturalism or class is not suitable to investigate gay people's claims for a full inclusion into the American self-concept and for an equal voice in the discursive negotiation of American nationalism. American nationalism and the American nation as a means of identification have been elusory for most of the gay community's history since gay Americans were marginalized and treated as second-class citizens. This is an aspect which cannot be overlooked when investigating the role of gay Americans in contemporary notions of American nationalism. However, in order to engage in this discussion, we must first address the lack of a concept or term which combines theories from both queer studies and nationalism studies and allows for the discussion of interrelated phenomena and processes of gay life and American nationalism.

B Homonationalism

In 2007, the queer studies scholar Jasbir Puar introduced the term 'homonationalism' in her monograph *Terrorist Assemblages: Homonationalism in Queer Times* and provided scholars in the field with the much-needed terminology to explore and describe the intersection between queer life in the United States and American nationalism. Puar understands nationalism mostly in its traditional sense rather than in the conceptualization of everyday nationalism studies where the focus lies on the agency of the people and their everyday lives.[145] Her understanding of nationalism influences her choice of examples which are situated in the context of U.S. foreign policy; however, it does not diminish the importance of her research for this study. Puar encourages other scholars to regard her work as an "incitement to the debate" over homonationalism and to utilize, adapt, rewrite, critique, and reframe her theories in order to explore new aspects of homonationalism (Puar, "Rethinking" 336). Taking her at her word, the goal of this research project is to develop homonationalism further by analyzing the intersections between queer life and American everyday nationalism as a form of nationalism that is centered on everyday Americans' lived experience within their nation and not exclusively on political considerations. However, before focusing on "homo-everyday-nationalism,"[146] Puar's groundbreaking work on homonationalism must be given a closer look.

[145] Puar understands nationalism in its classical sense whereby it is commonly defined as an "ideology based on the premise that the individual's loyalty and devotion to the nation-state surpass other individual or group interests" (Kohn) or the "[i]dentification with one's own nation and support for its interests, especially to the exclusion or detriment of the interests of other nations" ("Nationalism"). By contrast, everyday nationalism is a subfield of nationalism studies "refocus[ing] attention on the 'masses' and human agency within nationalism studies to consider the role and relevance of the everyday, and relevance of the lived experience of nationalism" (Knott).

[146] The coinage of the term 'homo-everyday-nationalism' is the attempt to shed light on the phenomenon of homonationalism but from the perspective of everyday nationalism studies.

The Instrumentalization of Gay Subjects in the Context of U.S. Foreign Affairs

Reading *Terrorist Assemblages*, one might presume that much more than four years had passed between Duggan's 2003 theories on "the new homonormativity" ("Homonormativity" 179) and Puar's publication in 2007 since Puar's perception of gays within American nationalism is a substantial departure from Duggan's. Whereas Duggan decidedly pursued a focus on the marginalization of the gay minority as a consequence of a heteronormative society, Puar suggests that homosexual Americans already occupy a stable place within the nation and play a significant role in defining what constitutes American nationalism. Puar explains that her increasing frustration "with the standard refrain . . . that the nation is heteronormative and that the queer is inherently an outlaw to the nation-state" led her to "develop the conceptual frame of 'homonationalism' for understanding the complexities of how 'acceptance' and 'tolerance' for gay and lesbian subjects have become a barometer by which the right to and capacity for national sovereignty is evaluated" ("Rethinking" 336). Puar regards homonationalism as a "historical shift in the production of nation-states from the insistence of heteronormativity to the increasing inclusion of homonormativity" (*Terrorist* 231). In her work, it is assumed that gay individuals have already managed to secure themselves a place at the table of national discourse. While this was not yet the case for the majority of the queer community in 2007, it has in the meantime become the reality for at least many gay and lesbian Americans. Puar writes that the goal of her research is to "map out the intersections of confluences, and divergences between homosexuality and the nation, national identity, and nationalism" because "[q]ueer times require even queerer modalities of thought, analysis, creativity, and expression" (*Terrorist* 49; 204). Thereby, homonationalism is "a facet of modernity and a historical shift marked by the entrance of (some) homosexual bodies as worthy of protection by nation-states, a constitutive and fundamental reorientation of the relationship between the state, capitalism, and sexuality" (Puar, "Rethinking" 337).

While homonationalism sounds like a positive process, it has been accompanied by unfavorable side-effects. This historical shift did not just result in the recognition and inclusion of gay people; Puar noticed that the transformation in how queer individuals were treated regarding the American nation also motivated the creation of new normativities. Gay people, their claims and demands, as well as these new homonormativites have become instrumentalized to justify racist, xenophobic, or Islamophobic political positions under the cover of the protection of sexual minorities. Subjects who hold these political positions defend them by claiming that they protect homosexuals and their rights by standing up against others who exclude sexual minorities due to their homophobic beliefs (Puar, *Terrorist* xxi). The (assimilated) gay is portrayed as the ideal American citizen who, as an essential part of American nationhood, needs to be defended against anti-American and anti-gay attitudes from outside. In this regard, nationalism is understood as the identification with one's nation which results in the exclusion of and demarcation from other nations. According to Puar, the result was the emergence of two different forms of homophobia: one was "cast as properly conservative and traditional when it serves the political right and the state" while the other one was "cast as uncosmopolitian and hopelessly provincial when it can fuel anti-immigrant, counterterrorist and antiwelfare discourses" (29). Cheryl Llewellyn, who analyzed sexual orientation-based asylum cases in the United States, discovered in what she calls "an ironic turn of events," that "the very same process of identifying one's sexuality at the border that could previously lead to exclusion is now an important component for gay, lesbian and bisexual (GLB) immigrants seeking asylum in the United States" (683).[147] The tide turned when the protection of gay subjects evolved into "a marker of national progress" (684) and into an opportunity for "racializing the anti-homosexual and elevating powerful nations over weaker ones" (683).

The transition which gay subjects experienced in this discourse is astonishing. Puar explains that "the invocation of the terrorist as queer, nonnational, perversely radicalized other has become part of the normative script of the U.S. war on terror"[148] since September 11, 2001, with

[147] Until 1990, when it was repealed, the McCarren Walter Act of 1952 provided a legal basis for excluding gay immigrants from entering the United States and for deportation if their homosexuality was revealed. Nowadays, immigrants of a sexual minority can seek asylum in the United States if they can prove that they suffered persecution in their country of origin because of their sexual orientation (Llewellyn 683).

[148] The so-called "war on terror" was proclaimed by President George W. Bush as a consequence of the terrorist attacks of September 11, 2001. Jackson describes the war on terror as an "American-led global counterterrorism campaign" which was "multidimensional" and "of almost limitless scope." Mil-

the Gulf War and the Israel-Palestine conflict as early examples of such depictions (*Terrorist* 37). For instance, Saddam Hussein was portrayed as monstrous, deviant, and sexually perverse (38). At the same time, homosexual subjects were instrumentalized in other ways which had not previously been seen in American everyday nationalism. Puar witnessed the following phenomenon:

> [E]ven as patriotism immediately after September 11 was inextricably tied to a reinvigoration of heterosexual norms for Americans, progressive sexuality was championed as a hallmark of U.S. modernity. For despite this reentrenchment of heteronormativity, the United States was also portrayed as 'feminist' in relation to the Taliban's treatment of Afghani women (a concern that had been previously of no interest to U.S. foreign policy) and gay-safe in comparison to the Middle East. (41)

Although some gay American citizens, though certainly not all, experienced a new form of acceptance and social recognition not despite but because of their "progressive" sexuality (41), the Orientalist enemies of the United States were either portrayed as un-American, as sexual perverts, or as unacceptably homophobic. This depiction and line of argument has been employed by the United States government in a variety of contexts, for example in order to explain the torture of Iraqi prisoners in Abu Ghraib (113) or the "racialization of religion" which led to the profiling of certain Orientalist ethnicities (38). Puar insists in her writing:

> For contemporary forms of U.S. nationalism and patriotism, the production of gay and queer bodies is crucial to the deployment of nationalism, insofar as these perverse bodies reiterate the heterosexuality as the norm but also because certain domesticated homosexual bodies provide ammunition to reinforce nationalist projects. (39)

itary operations were primarily conducted in Afghanistan, Iraq, and Yemen. The domestic consequences of the war on terror were the drafting of anti-terrorism legislation (e. g., the USA PATRIOT Act) and the creation of the Department of Homeland Security. By 2004, it was clear that the wars in Iraq and Afghanistan caused massive drawbacks and left the countries in chaos. In 2008, President Obama campaigned on the promise to end the United States' military presence in these countries, a promise which he was able to keep for the most part (Jackson).

Needless to say, homophobia is still omnipresent in the United States and efforts to legalize same-sex marriage were not successful at that time. The instrumentalization of gay rights and the public enshrinement of equality in order to justify U.S. foreign interests was not accompanied by a simultaneous improvement of the lives of queer Americans, especially not in legal terms. Much rather, it led to the whitewashing of the inequality within the nation.

Un-American Bodies and the War on Terror

Whereas Puar depicts the situation of gay Americans after 9/11 as an improvement in their sociocultural status within American nationhood, this perception is not shared by all scholars. In their monograph *Containing (Un)American Bodies: Race, Sexuality, and Post-9/11 Constructions of Citizenship*, Mary K. Bloodsworth-Lugo und Carmen R. Lugo-Lugo also describe an instrumentalization of gay Americans in the war on terror; however, the instrumentalization they describe did not protect domestic gays but bolster the national conservative agenda against marriage equality. Bloodsworth-Lugo and Lugo-Lugo claim that the situation of gays after 9/11 actually worsened, as the categories of what constitutes American and un-American were redefined with the latter becoming understood as being against the war on terror and supporting the opening of the institution of marriage to same-sex couples: "To be *in favor of* same-sex marriage and to be *opposed to* war in Iraq were connected in their exclusion from the category American. A concerted effort unfolded to protect 'America' by containing 'un-American' bodies" (Bloodsworth-Lugo and Lugo-Lugo 1). The "un-American bodies" (1), which needed to be contained for the sake of national security, were not only terrorist subjects but also gay Americans. The rhetoric reported by Bloodsworth-Lugo and Lugo-Lugo is starkly reminiscent of Cold War Era language regarding homosexual Americans. During the time of the House Un-American Activities Committee, the charge of un-Americanism was reserved for two parties: the foreign or foreign-influenced communists and the domestic, American-born security threat of gay Americans. This connection between domestic and foreign threats was echoed in the early 2000s, with Islamic terrorism replacing communism. "Through intermingling international and domestic topics and by placing them within a narrative of threat and containment, Iraq and same-sex marriage became associated with the category 'un-American,'" the two scholars explain in their efforts to make sense of the "perpetual contest between the American and the un-American" (9). In the course of this contest, everything that "has been rendered un-American has been treated with suspicion and 'othered'" (9). Puar speaks of a "folding in of homosexuality into the 'us' of the 'us versus them' nationalist rhetoric" (*Terrorist* 43), but Bloodsworth-Lugo and Lugo-Lugo picture the exact opposite development. The post-9/11 omnipresent 'us vs. them' rhetoric,[149] which was famously exemplified by President Bush's declaration that one was either with the American people or with the terrorists, designated same-sex couples as "them" and thereby placed gay Americans on the same level as the terrorists. During the war on terror, this "binary framing served to reframe the categories of 'American' or 'un-American,' acting to construct them anew" and thereby reminding the American nation of the un-Americanism of same-sex couples and their un-American desire for marriage (Bloodsworth-Lugo and Lugo-Lugo 59). Protecting the United States was equated with keeping un-American bodies under control. Thereby, it put pressure on the American people to comply with what was commonly understood as good Americanism, namely supporting the war on terror, and standing up for heterosexual marriage.[150] People's compliance "served to reinforce the binary constructions of 'un-American' and 'American' (citizenship and

149 In an address to the joint session of Congress and the American nation, President G.W. Bush declared on September 20th, 2001: "Every nation in every region now has a decision to make: Either you are with us or you are with the terrorists" ("Text").

150 During the 2004 presidential election campaign when President Bush spoke about the defense of marriage, he used the same rhetoric as when he spoke about the war on terror. In a 2004 State of the Union Address, G.W. Bush emphasized that the American nation needs to "defend the sanctity of marriage" (qtd. in Bloodsworth-Lugo and Lugo-Lugo 25). "Regarding the homeland, President Bush spoke of 'protecting America,' 'securing our country,' 'provid[ing] resources for our defense,' 'defend[ing] the security of our country,' . . . and upholding the 'unseen pillars of civilization,'" Bloodsworth-Lugo and Lugo-Lugo noticed (25). They noticed that Bush's "use of equivalent language in discussing terrorist threats and same-sex marriage . . . is no coincidence" (25). They insist that this rhetoric "represents a strategic deployment of the discourse of defense whereby terrorism and same-sex marriage are similarly categorized in relation to national security and by which the President is able to clearly articulate the specter of homeland threats – including the threat of same-sex marriage" (25).

nation) at the same time" (60). In contrast to Puar, Bloodsworth-Lugo and Lugo-Lugo assess the time after 9/11 as a decline in the position of gay Americans within American nationalism, which was reflected in the revival of the classification of same-sex bodies as un-American.

Gay Heroism and Homonationalism

During the time of the Lavender Scare and the investigations of the House Un-American Activities Committee, gay Americans were regarded as even more un-American than communists and classified as one of the most imminent risks to national security (D.K. Johnson 2). "Throughout this period, 'security risk' served as a euphemism for homosexual," as Bean explains (55). Homosexuals were deemed a high risk since their weak character made them more vulnerable to blackmail. Furthermore, homosexuality was seen as the psychological aberration which would eventually lead them to communism (D.K. Johnson 16). Consequently, it was believed that it was crucial to detect gays and eliminate them from federal government or comparable civil service positions due to their alleged disloyalty. This association between the communist threat and homosexuality, and consequently of homosexuals and un-Americanism, was instilled so deeply in the mindset of the Americans through HUAC propaganda that it would continue to influence Americans' opinion of the gay community for decades. Homosexuals were said to be untrustworthy, and this led to them being considered a danger to national security. Barry Adam confirms that such a "targeting of gay men as threats to national security has recurred during moments of crises in the United States" (268). Even more, the un-Americanism rhetoric of the Lavender Scare has also been readily employed by citizens who felt threatened by or simply uncomfortable with gay Americans until well into the 21st century, as the analysis of speech acts in chapter IV.C illustrated.

Although it was a gradual transformation, Puar names 9/11 as a turning point in the perception of gay Americans when "progressive sexuality was championed as a hallmark of U.S. modernity" (*Terrorist* 41), not least since they were needed to justify the United States' war on terror as well as invasionist campaigns in Afghanistan and Iraq. Amid the increasing engagement of the nation in the war on terror in post-9/11 America, Puar speaks of an "uneasy yet urgent folding in of homosexuality into the 'us' of the 'us versus them' nationalist rhetoric" of gay Americans (*Terrorist*

43). Simultaneously, these gay Americans "took up the patriotic call in various modalities," for instance by raising the American flag in gay spaces, by embracing patriotic language and symbolism, and by gay conservatives publicly supporting the bombing of Afghan territory (43).[151] In addition to this transformation and the partial integration of gay Americans into the national community, some gays even became national heroes. One of the most prominent examples was Mark Bingham, a gay, white businessman with a masculine rugby-playing physique who was a passenger on board of United Airlines flight 93 which was hijacked in the 9/11 terrorist attacks. Bingham along with three others formed a plan to storm the cockpit in order to overpower the hijackers and eventually managed to crash the plane into a field before it could be used to target a building in Washington D.C. (Hall, "Americanism" 1128). Despite or maybe because of his homosexuality, Bingham was turned into a model hero. Furthermore, he heralded the beginning of a homonationalism which allowed for gay heroism within American everyday nationalism. The events of 9/11 led to an Americanization of some American subjects who were formerly excluded from the national "us" and described as un-American. One could even say that some gays were "un-un-Americanized" through homonationalism since they were finally included into the prevailing concept of what was commonly deemed American at that time. As mentioned beforehand, this inclusion of some gay Americans into ideas of American nationalism and the Americanization of the former un-American was not a process that benefitted everyone in the queer community. Bingham's legacy profited from "his rendering as an exceptional gay (masculine, athletic, Republican, entrepreneurial, patriotic) who fulfilled normative notions of American citizenship" (King 6). In this regard, Duggan also speaks of an "added emphasis on the Americanism of model gay 'heroes' and 'victims'" (*Twilight* 46). It is debatable whether Bingham would have been turned into a gay American hero if he had not conformed with the dominant ideal of the American man. The only point in which he differed from the other men who fit this ideal was in his sexual orientation. If Bingham had been a person of color with an effeminate physique and

151 Andrew Sullivan was one of the most prominent gay conservatives who expressed support for the war in Afghanistan. The major gay rights organizations largely remained silent and did not react publicly, which Puar attributes to the fact that they were too busy with the marriage equality campaign and the role of gays in the military in general (*Terrorist* 43).

had been less compliant with what was generally considered normal or normative, he might not have been adopted as a gay American national hero. "Normativity is comfortable for those who can inhabit it," Ahmed rightly points out (147). Meyer emphasizes that "while more recent articulations of the proper US citizen incorporate some sexual minorities into this ideal" (3), this is not helpful for the "multiply-marginalized groups of LGBTQ people" (15).

While the American nation is now willing to embrace gay heroism, they are not yet ready for every type of hero, particularly if the potential gay hero deviates too much from what is considered normal or normative. The case of the American whistleblower Chelsea Manning (born as Bradley Manning) demonstrates that the Cold War rhetoric and fearmongering regarding homosexual Americans is still an attractive strategy for discrediting gay individuals who are not considered a suitable model for gay heroism. Whether Manning's motives were noble will not be debated in the following.[152] However, what is of interest is that Manning's sexuality, namely Manning identifying as transsexual and transitioning from a male gender identity and the given name 'Bradley' to a female identity and the chosen name 'Chelsea,' seemed to be at the center of the discourse over the classified document disclosure to *Wikileaks*. In his article on U.S. national security culture and queer citizenship, Bean claims that the "interrelated institutional and cultural assumptions about the nature of homosexuals, which arose in early 20th century, have endured in the 21st" (54) as "pre-court-martial media portrayals of Manning often implied that her leaks were caused by queer psychopathology – an ill-defined condition that presumably makes homosexuals prone to disloyalty and emotional instability, and, therefore, more likely to spill secrets" (53). This is the same rhetoric employed by the House Un-American Activities Committee during the Lavender Scare. Manning made herself un-American because she endangered the United States with her traitorous behavior. Homosexuals were also decried as traitors and communist sympathizers during

[152] Manning, a former United States Army soldier who was deployed both to Afghanistan and Iraq, leaked the largest cache of classified or sensitive military and diplomatic documents to the platform *WikiLeaks* in 2010 because she felt that Americans deserved to learn the truth about the war on terrorism (Manning, Tate). As a result of her disclosing secret documents, she was convicted of violations of the Espionage Act and sentenced to 35 years in prison in July 2013 (Tate).

the Cold War. The conservative columnist Ann Coulter described Manning as an "angry gay," one of the "narcissistic hothouse flowers," and a "snit" who "betrayed his country" (Coulter). The reaction to Manning's document disclosure is reminiscent of the case of Daniel Ellsberg who leaked the secret "Pentagon Papers" to the *New York Times* in 1971.[153] Commentators have frequently paralleled the cases of Ellsberg and Manning, especially because of the Nixon administration's deliberate attempts to depict Ellsberg as a homosexual in order to undermine his credibility and classify him a security risk (53). When investigating the treatment of some homosexuals in the United States, in particular in national politics and security culture, Manning appears to be a continuation of Ellsberg. In both cases, their (ascribed) sexuality was used to silence them, which was not markedly different from the treatment of gay Americans during the Lavender Scare Era.

As the example of Chelsea Manning demonstrates, not all queer Americans were considered suitable to be a hero after 9/11. While gay heroism found a model representative in the person of Mark Bingham, Chelsea Manning did not receive the same public recognition but was mostly seen as a transgender traitor. The United States security culture still promotes heteronormative values and a traditional understanding of masculinity. This influences which kind of heroism is allowed by American nationalism. Even before transitioning to a female gender identity, the Army whistleblower Manning did not impress with a Bingham-like rugby player physique but looked rather small and fragile in most pictures. Coming out as transgender made Manning an even easier target for criticism and ridicule. Nevertheless, the process of the American nation opening itself to the idea of gay heroism due to homonationalist efforts was an important first step and a reason to celebrate for gay Americans since this also provided them with heroes from their own ranks who consequently offered a greater potential for self-identification with this hero.

However, this progress did not silence those who still employed the rhetoric of the time of the House Un-American Activities Committee. For

[153] The papers exposed that the Johnson administration had lied to the American public about the diminishing success of the Vietnam War and about the fact that the Americans troops were trapped in a deadlock because Johnson wanted to avoid losing public support for the war. The Pentagon Papers provoked a series of events which resulted in the later resignation of President Richard Nixon in the wake of the Watergate Scandal (Bean 52).

some conservative politicians, the linkage between homosexuality and threats to national security still seems to be an attractive strategy for excluding homosexuals from contemporary American nationalism. Former Senator Rick Santorum called same-sex marriage "the ultimate homeland security issue" (qtd. in Chávez 36), Oklahoma Republican State Representative Sally Kearn claimed that homosexuality was a bigger threat to national security than terrorism (Chávez 36), and Bryan Fischer compared gay sex to domestic terrorism, specifically regarding HIV transmission (qtd. in Mantyla). It remains to be seen whether the American people will be increasingly willing to celebrate gay heroes and accept them as representatives of the American nation both at home and abroad. The marriage equality movement produced their own heroes, such as Edie Windsor. Posthumously as well as following her landmark victory in *United States v. Windsor*, Windsor was lauded as a hero of the gay rights movement, not least by Jim Obergefell, the name-giving plaintiff in *Obergefell v. Hodges* (Obergefell).[154] If the heroes of the gay rights movement were to become the heroes of the American nation at large one day, this would be a milestone in the inclusion of gay Americans as it would indicate that homonationalism had become one of the forces propelling the change of American everyday nationalism. In national perception, some gay subjects have evolved from being the un-American security risk to having the possibility of becoming gay American heroes. This development is evidence of the rehabilitation, or an "un-un-Americanization," of at least a part of the gay community to equal citizens.

[154] In a published eulogy to Edie Windsor, Jim Obergefell wrote:

> *Hero*. Our society has become very free in its use of that word, but if anyone fully deserved the label, it was Edie, who died Tuesday in Manhattan at 88. Her successful career in the male-dominated world of technology and her efforts to inspire and support women in that industry are reasons enough to admire her. But that isn't why so many of us consider Edie our hero. She became our hero because of her courage in fighting to have her lawful marriage to the person she loved treated as equal to opposite-sex marriages, even in a time of great personal loss. Edie is our hero because she moved the LGBT community a giant step closer to full equality as Americans. (Obergefell)

Homo-Everyday-Nationalism

Following Puar's encouragement to develop homonationalism further, I would like to link homonationalism with everyday nationalism studies in order to provide an approach to homonationalism which allows for a perspective on the phenomenon as a bottom-up process, which brings the influence of the gay rights discourse on inner-American nationalism into focus. This is important insofar as homonationalism, as Puar describes it, could theoretically be just a political strategy with no direct impact or effect at all on either American or foreign homosexuals. However, in exploring how the American nation has approached the gradual inclusion of homosexual citizens, one can see how the phenomenon of homonationalism specifically impacts the lives of lesbian and gay people within the country and also how non-elite Americans shape "homo-everyday-nationalism," as I call it, as an everyday lived experience of the nation. In order to allow for this broader perspective, homonationalism, just as homonormativity, should be assessed from a more neutral perspective. The focus of research should not solely be on the controversial side of this phenomenon but also acknowledge that homonationalism led to a rehabilitation of at least some gay subjects in terms of allowing them to achieve a more respected and valued position in people's notions of American nationalism. The instrumentalization of gay Americans for the justification of a dubious foreign policy should be only one aspect of homonationalism. If this term is given a broader definition that permits a look at both its benefits and disadvantages and recognizes its role as both an inner-national process and a strategy to demarcate the United States against other nations, more facets of the interplay between queer studies and American everyday nationalism can be revealed. This broadening of homonationalism means that it is not "another identity politics, not another way of distinguishing good queers from bad queers, not an accusation, and not a position," as Puar suggests, "but a fundamental reorientation of the relationship between the state, capitalism, and sexuality ("Rethinking" 337). Conceptualizing homonationalism as a process and not as a position, which can be attributed to one party or another, keeps the discourse on homonationalism as open as possible and allows for a variety of voices to contribute to the debate. Talking about homo-everyday-nationalism, its manifestations, and its influences is a form of "talking the nation" (Fox and Miller-Idriss 537) whereby American nationalism is renegotiated and reconceptualized. For most American history, gay Americans were the subjects that were talked about while they were mostly silenced through various methods of discrimination and marginalization. This has changed as at least some gay Americans have become active participants in the "the discursive construction of the nation" (Fox and Miller-Idriss 537) and have equal or nearly equal opportunities in determining the direction the nation is heading. Consequently, homonationalism should not be regarded as the parallel nationalism of gay Americans or as the mere instrumentalization of gay people in order to justify questionable foreign policy strategies. Much rather, homonationalism needs to be understood as an essential and integral part of American nationalism, with the latter functioning as an umbrella for this conglomerate of diverse aspects and expressions of American national identity.

(Homo)Nationalism in Trumpian Times

Although this book concentrates on the Obama era, nationalism in the age of President Trump should not be completely ignored. Not least because the developments we have witnessed since the inauguration of President Trump loomed in the last years of the Obama administration. The Obama presidency saw several debates on national identity, and these eight years were strongly characterized by everyday nationalism. The American people engaged in the discursive construction and negotiation of national identity, but the administration itself rather took a backseat in these debates. This changed tremendously during the 2016 presidential election campaign, when Donald Trump set a new tone regarding nationalism in the United States. His campaign strategy was permeated with nationalistic rhetoric which often fostered hostility among Americans. Trump massively changed the sociocultural discourse by turning national identity into a presidential concern. The loud chanting of "U.S.A" by the crowds at his rallies or his premise of "America First"[155] are examples of the blatant nationalism that he

[155] President Trump used the slogan "America First" for the first time in an interview with *The New York Times* in March 2016. In this interview, Trump claimed that he was not "isolationist," but he was "America First" (Trump qtd. in Rothman). "I like the expression," he said, and announced "I'm America First" (qtd. in Rothman). The slogan "America First" has a long history in the United States, mostly in the context of isolationist foreign policy practices. When the famous American aviator Charles Lindbergh, an avid supporter of

encourages (Carothers). The Trump administration promotes an aggressive and angry nationalism which affronts and excludes others, thereby drawing associations with the divisive neo-nationalist movement. He left no doubt to whether he considers himself a nationalist, when he not only confirmed his nationalist stance at a campaign rally but also instigating his supporters to follow his example: "You know what I am? I'm a nationalist, okay? I'm a nationalist. Nothing wrong. Use that word. Use that word" (qtd. in Gearan).

By relying on a clear and overly simplistic diction and constantly reassuring that there was nothing wrong with a nationalistic mindset, he signaled the path his voters should follow. Trump's rhetoric and neo-nationalist stance demonstrate that he had his finger on the pulse of embittered conservative Americans. He was a welcome change for those who felt disenfranchised during the eight years of the Obama presidency and who increasingly felt alienated from their country due to the liberalization these years brought to the nation (Gage). In 2016, which was Obama's last year in office, people's opinion of members of the opposing party were more negative than they had been in a quarter of a century ("Partisanship" 1). The "line between an unthreatening 'other' and one that causes anxiety" (Skey 72), which Skey describes in his work, was already extremely fragile during Obama's second term. For some Americans, it had completely dissolved by 2016. Political opponents are increasingly perceived as a real threat to nationalism, and they are therefore accused of un-Americanism. During Obama's presidency, conservatives felt the need to reassert their position and ensure that they did not lose their national space over liberal efforts such as marriage equality or Obamacare. Liberals were a threat to their national identity because their actions forced them to rewrite their social maps. Since the tide has turned with President Trump, it is now liberals who are struggling to keep their seat at the table of sociocultural discourse (Gage). National identity and its continuous (re)construction have transformed since the change of government. While everyday nationalism is shaped primarily from the bottom up by the agency of the people, with the Trump administration, people's efforts in constructing their nationalism are often overshadowed by the top-down force of Trumpian nationalistic posturing. Fox describes this kind of nationalism as "nationalism on steroids: a juiced up and sometimes menacing nationalism that grabs

the idea of American isolationism, advocated for the non-interventionist organization "America First Committee" at a political rally in 1941, this was widely regarded as "un-American" (Rothman).

newspaper headlines and begs scholarly explanation" (26). However, Fox also adds that "these Trump sorts of nationalist fireworks" are "ultimately, fireworks: intermittent bursts of nationalist fervour that punctuate an otherwise flaccid, humdrum nationalism, the nationalism of everyday life" (26). It remains to be seen how long the American people will accept this top-down nationalism, supported by "alternative facts" and a war on so-called "fake news" produced by non-conservative journalists (Hendricks and Vestergaard 51; 62). Eventually, people will reclaim their agency and direct the development of everyday nationalism in the United States.

More than ten years have passed since Puar's publication and the concomitant popularization of the term 'homonationalism,' but her research has not lost any of its importance. Indeed, it is more relevant than ever "in a political culture ready to instrumentalize queers in one moment, and to viciously scapegoat us in the very next" (Nyong'o xi). In the foreword to the 2017 edition of *Terrorist Assemblages*, Tavia Nyong'o claims that homonationalism has "reached a saturation point, in which even a political candidate as xenophobic as Donald Trump felt the need to begrudgingly embrace gay rights (however in an opportunistic and temporary fashion, as later betrayals would reveal)" (xi). It seems as if the presence and active participation of gay Americans in the continuous process of negotiating and (re)constructing American everyday nationalism has become a matter of course, which not even President Trump dares to contest. Despite his opposition to same-sex marriage and his devastating record on queer rights, Trump has yet to make any attempts to repeal marriage equality and describes this issue as "settled" and "done" (Trump qtd. in Wilstein). However, this attitude and his instrumentalization of the gay community does not mean that he would refrain from persecuting other queer identities as his support of bills targeting transgender people, among others, have proven. While Trump largely leaves gay and lesbian Americans alone, this does not mean that he will not attack other minorities, as his eagerness to build a wall at the border to Mexico to stop immigrants from Latin America and his so-called Muslim ban famously demonstrated. Puar speaks of a "quick-and-dirty rehearsal of post-9/11 racial syllogisms. Homonationalism was alive and well, most certainly as it pivoted both the logic of and the retorts to the Muslim ban" (*Terrorist* 224). Trump repeatedly instrumentalized gays in order to justify his war not only against Islamic terrorists but often the Muslim community as a whole. After the mass shooting at a gay nightclub in Orlando in 2016, when a shooter, who swore allegiance to the Islamic State, killed 49 people and wounded several others, Trump declared in a hypocritical statement: "This time, the terrorist targeted our LGBT community. As your president, I will do everything in my power to protect our LGBT citizens from the violence and oppression of a hateful foreign ideology" (Trump qtd. in Weigel). However, his prime objective was not defending the lives of LGBT Americans. For him, this was a very welcome opportunity to justify his racist attitude towards Muslims and immigrants in general. Trump is not a supporter of LGBT rights, but if he can use LGBT Americans to fuel anti-immigrant and anti-Muslim sentiments, they are useful. In Trumpian times, homonationalism, understood as a phenomenon which instrumentalizes gays in order to defend foreign policies, is in great demand, as Puar spells out: "Queer has now been made productive for biopolitical governance. As an increasingly desirable attribute of modernity it is mobilized as a positive rhetorical function in the struggle over civilizational superiority" (*Terrorist* 227). It even seems as if Trumpian times have led to a revival of homonationalism. Although the interests of gay Americans have been pushed to the background, their role in the context of foreign politics is just as important as in the wake of 9/11. During the Obama era, the fight for marriage equality dominated national discourse; the focus was on achieving measurable advancements in the rights for gay Americans within the nation through opening marriage and other anti-discrimination measures. It is much easier to believe a president who advocates for gay rights not only abroad but also in his own country, as President Obama did, than a president who pretends to fight for gay rights on the international stage but treats queer individuals with contempt when it comes to defending them on the home front. President Obama seems to have understood that "'acceptance' and 'tolerance' for gay and lesbian subjects have become a barometer by which the right to and capacity for national sovereignty is evaluated" (Puar, "Rethinking" 336) and that this does not only apply to how the United States evaluates other countries but also to how the American people themselves are seen in an international context. In the debate over homonationalism, the Obama years allowed for a much stronger focus on American everyday nationalism and the way the nation is experienced by gay Americans within national territory on an everyday basis. By contrast, with Trump's inauguration, Puar's theories on homonationalism suddenly regained importance in the debate over gay rights, and nationalism in its classical sense, as an "ideology based on the premise that the individual's loyalty and devotion to the nation-state surpass other individual or group interests" (Kohn), outweighs everyday nationalism in its influence on Americanism and un-Americanism.

C The Assimilated Americanized vs. the Notorious Un-American

Despite setbacks and backlashes, the gay community in the United States benefits from previously unknown levels of acceptance and participation in the drafting process of American nationalism. Although almost one third of Americans still oppose marriage equality (McCarthy, "Record-High"), some of whom are driven by a "fear of denormalization" ("Denormalisierungsangst"; my trans.; Jäger 54), marriage equality has undergone a process of normalization within the American nation. The gradual renegotiation of American conceptions of nationalism in favor of a more inclusive environment for gay Americans heralded a reconceptualization of the majority perception of un-Americanism. Gay Americans evolved from passive and un-American subjects, who were instrumentalized and talked about without having a strong voice of their own, into active agents in the construction of American nationalism, who assert their right to be treated as equal Americans. They no longer have to accept the place they are ascribed within the nation because they have gained the necessary sociocultural capital in order to insist on their integration into ideas of American nationalism. In the renegotiation over what American everyday nationalism should look like and how the nation handles the challenges posed by minorities' calls for sociocultural equality, new hierarchies and power structures within the American nation unfold. This is caused by the Americanization of some gay individuals through homonormative processes, not least after the success in *Obergefell* which welcomed gay Americans into an institution that was previously an exclusively heterosexual terrain. Marriage equality resulted in the inclusion of some gay couples into American nationalism; however, critics claim that this acceptance was also contingent on the readiness of some to assimilate. Those that preferred not to conform did not receive the same inclusion, which has resulted in new dynamics of marginalization and discrimination.

Same-Sex Marriage Critique within the Gay Rights Movement

Same-sex marriage was not only a heavily contested issue between advocates and opponents of marriage equality but also aroused criticism within the ranks of gay rights supporters (Halberstam, *Gaga Feminism* 97). The institution of marriage has been a target of critique since before the fight for marriage equality directed public attention onto it. Feminists in particular have spoken out against marriage for decades since they see it as a mechanism of oppression which reinforces patriarchal and hegemonical structures within society.[156] Similar concerns have been raised by scholars as well as gay rights supporters who decided against joining the quest for marriage equality. They were worried that same-sex marriage would further enshrine patriarchal and heteronormative relations in American nationalism. Adam Isaiah Green explains that "[q]ueer theorists fundamentally reject same-sex marriage because, in part, the making of the marital subject constitutes a normalizing process that assimilates queers to heteronormativity" (407). Concerning the issue of heteronormativity, Jyl Josephson explains the position of lesbian feminists who warn that "the heteronormativity of marriage will not be easily overcome, given its role historically in the enforcement of compulsory heterosexuality": "[W]hile recognizing the legal advantages and the symbolic equality that marriage might provide for lesbian couples, [they] still see marriage as an undesirable goal" (274). Lesbian feminists argue along these lines since "there is no way for lesbians to avoid being colonized by the institution and its normalizing tendencies" (274). Furthermore, the activist Colin P. Ashley points out that the marriage equality movement "overlooks the interests of most LGBT/Q people and diminishes their potential to build common cause with other oppressed groups" (28). In addition to the lost potential of building alliances with other minorities, "[t]his approach also enshrines marriage as the apex of gay liberation despite marriage being an institution that the women's movement, other left allies, and even the older Gay Liberation movement, have critiqued" (Ashley 28).

The problem of further or new marginalization of some groups of gay Americans was another concern of some gay rights activists:

> For critics of same-sex marriage within the gay community, heteroexclusive marriage, heteronormativity, and homophobia harm queer citizenship, but access to marriage will only benefit straight-acting gays; the secondary exclusions experienced by nonnormative LGBT individuals will be exacerbated. (Josephson 277)

As a result, those then marginalized will lose part of their lobby as soon as marriage equality is achieved since "those in the community who have the

[156] Feminist critique of the institution of marriage started most prominently in 1970 with the works of the radical feminists Shulamith Firestone (*The Dialectic of Sex: The Case for Feminist Revolution*), Kate Millet (*Sexual Politics*), and Germaine Greer (*The Female Eunuch*).

most power because they are the most mainstream may see little reason to engage in further activism to achieve rights for less mainstream community members" (277). This negative side-effect was also raised by DeFilippis, who had collected a variety of voices during the marriage equality discussion within the gay rights movement. Among the most common points of criticism were the concerns that "these very narrow pursuits of equality . . . excluded and further stigmatized queer people who do not comply with the dominant notions of normality," and that "marriage [was] a conservative tool of neoliberalism" (DeFilippis 2). Furthermore, critics worried that "the conservative rhetoric of gay marriage demeaned unmarried people, single mothers, and Black families, and served to control them," and that "resources and energy that were diverted away from other critical issues facing LGBTQ communities and were instead directed to the pursuit of marriage" (2). In the light of the troublesome history of the institution of marriage and the side-effects of marriage equality, Brook J. Sadler proposes civil unions as a third way between the traditional heterosexual marriage and the option of marriage equality:

> Although many liberals and progressives have decried civil unions as a second-class alternative to marriage that would perpetuate the marginalization of gays and lesbians, civil unions could provide an alternative model for both heterosexual and homosexual couples and an opportunity to reconceive the appropriate role of the state in personal and sexual relationships. The idea that civil unions would represent a departure from the (sexist, patriarchal) history of marriage and its accreted social expectations is a reason to favor them (rather than denounce them as an unacceptable substitute for marriage). (590)

Civil unions would allow couples to enter a form of commitment which does not have the same questionable reputation of being patriarchal, outdated, and dogmatic. In addition, civil unions "could allow us to perceive more cleanly the break between church and state in the governing of our personal and familial lives," Sadler argues (592). Many gay rights advocates reminded religious opponents of this principle of the separation of church and state in the discourse over same-sex marriage. Given the ambiguous relationship which same-sex couples have with religion and churches due to the latter's discriminatory practices towards sexual minorities, they might welcome civil unions as a more modern form of commitment that is not historically connected to the institution of the church. However, civil unions would have to be open for both heterosexual and homosexual couples in order to avoid them being labeled as a second-class alternative for same-sex couples.[157] The debate over alternatives to marriage in the United States has been prejudiced from the beginning with civil unions starting out with a bad reputation after the fight for same-sex marriage in Vermont led to civil unions instead of marriage equality. In addition, the politicization of marriage and family in the American nation robbed civil unions of the serious debate which they deserved.

Although the idea of equal marriage rights constituted the only rightful next step on the road to a stronger position of queer Americans within the nation for some, critics of same-sex marriage saw this path as a surrender of queer culture to heteronormative ideals which would ultimately be transformed into homonormative ideals. This inquiry into the debate over same-sex marriage that took place within the gay rights movement before the Supreme Court decision in *Obergefell* may appear superfluous since a ruling in favor of same-sex marriage was reached. However, the opinion of gay people who are not content with the outcome of the national debate over same-sex marriage and who are not convinced that marriage can lead to a greater inclusion of gay couples into the American nation need to be heard. Those who wish to define themselves in their lack of conformity to the heteronormative American nationalism rather than by similarity and equality to the rest of the Americans must also to be considered. Besides, one should not be under the illusion that all gay Americans see an inclusion into the contemporary concepts of American nationalism or homonationalism as a desirable goal for the gay rights movement. Despite having common ground in their wish for anti-discrimination protection and equal opportunities in life regardless of sexual orientation or gender identity, some queer Americans prefer the idea of a queer nation ideologically separate from the dominant representation of American everyday nationalism.[158]

157 An example of this kind of civil union is the Pacte Civil de Solidarité (civil solidarity pact), which has been implemented in France. This domestic partnership contract is open to couples of all sexual orientations and provides legal protection and stability in several areas of life such as social security and housing ("Civil Unions in France?").

158 In the discourse over American national identity and American nationalism, which was debated against the backdrop of marriage equality, gay and lesbian Americans were often treated as a homogenous group which either should be included as a whole through access to equal marriage rights or would be excluded as second-class citizens due to the unequal treatment of this minority. While it is at times necessary to speak of gay and lesbian Americans as one

"Good Gays" vs. "Bad Gays"?

As a consequence of these diverging opinions among queer Americans and their supporters, the problematic dichotomy of "good gays" versus "bad gays" arose in the discourse over the positioning of gay subjects within the American nation. Ashley observed that a lot of the "contemporary gay rights rhetoric works to position good gay subjects versus bad queer others" (29). Influences of heteronormative standards as well as processes of homonormalization play a significant role in this development. In fact, the community itself is uncertain and divided over whether the "un-un-Americanization" and normalization of gay Americans should be regarded as a positive development or whether this is paralleled by a loss of identity. A "gay identity" was for the majority of American history rooted in differentness and opposition to the American mainstream. According to Teal and Conover-Williams, the "separation into a good/ bad queer dichotomy can be understood through the lens of the *politics of respectability*, where members of marginalized groups police their own membership to keep them aligned with mainstream values" (17). Thus, the "good vs. bad gay" dichotomy is not primarily a rhetoric which is imposed on gay Americans by same-sex marriage opponents but also a policing mechanism which they use among themselves. Meanwhile, this infighting is what Motschenbacher and Stegu warn can result from connecting homonormativity too closely with the same-sex marriage debate, as it can place same-sex couples who wish to marry and those who do not in opposition to each other (524–25). Community cohesion within the gay rights movement was higher before the decisive court victories that ultimately paved the way for marriage equality because gay Americans had a common enemy in opponents of the legalization of same-sex marriage. As the support for this form of equality grew within the society and with *Obergefell* being a success for gay marriage advocates, the idea of the common enemy was not as prominent and powerful as before. When gay Americans were no longer only subjects talked about but rather active agents in the continuous (re)negotiation of the American nation, the question of who among the gay community would shape the future direction of American nationalism became more pressing. Accordingly, the declining role of the common enemy and the increased participation of

group for reasons of practicality, one should nevertheless keep in mind that it is a terminology which subsumes highly diverse individuals in one category.

gays in national discourse brought differences within the minority to light to a greater degree than before. This challenge in the process of the inclusion of this minority needs to be addressed both by the minority members themselves as well as by the American people at large. All in all, this is a demanding task as the emergence of new minorities from the larger minority is more prominent than before, which prompts the question of who the "good gays" and the "bad gays" are more frequently. Are the "good gays" those who assimilate to what is commonly believed to be American or are they the "bad gays" since they have betrayed the gay community by no longer insisting on their difference and queerness but preferring to blend in. Puar also notices that homonationalism "has increasingly been used to describe an agenda or a person, or a group/identity, and as an accusation to distinguish good queer subject from bad queer subject," which was never her intention (Puar in interview with Greyser 842). Of course, homonationalism was used in order to distinguish between good and bad queer subjects as a strategy of American foreign policy; however, this approach is increasingly used within the gay minority in order to ostracize those who either assimilate too much or who are too deviant from what is commonly prescribed by homonormativity. Just as charges of un-Americanism were employed among Americans as a regulatory mechanism to police one another, homonormativity and homonationalism serve comparable purposes within the gay minority in the negotiation over which position they should take within American everyday nationalism.

In the debate over whether homonormativity and homonationalism are good for the gay community, doubts are also raised about the strategies of gay rights organizations and their politics. Besides, this is an issue that has existed before the marriage equality ruling, as the analysis of the discussion within the gay rights movement over same-sex marriage has shown. Colin P. Ashley, who bemoans the movement's uncritical stance on marriage equality and the lack of tactical relationships with other minority groups (28), sees the following strategies of the movement as a product of queer mainstreaming: "(1) to advocate for privatized rights granting equal access to traditional social institutions, (2) to make gayness acceptable by portraying it as virtually the same as straightness except for a differential desire, and (3) by advancing a post gay rhetoric that describes gay equality as all but nearly achieved" (31). Ashley regards this approach of the gay rights movement as highly problematic because it fails to address the needs of those within the minority who are less privileged, for instance gay people of color, gay Americans with a low socioeconomic or educational status, or those who do not fit within the gay mainstream for other reasons (31). Regarding intersectionality, Stone believes it is detrimental to the gay rights movement to focus on intersectionality chiefly only "through a corporate diversity culture that reduces diversity to its instrumental functions" (470).[159] This approach is similar to the instrumentalization of gays that Puar describes in her work on homonationalism and is certainly not something that gay rights advocates hoped to achieve.

More assimilated gays are often seen as part of the problem in these new mechanisms of marginalization because they are willing to conform with standards of Americanism and with the American family ideal. In fact, Warner claims that there "has always been a set of hierarchies. Those whose sex is least threatening, along with those whose gender profiles seem the least queer, are put forward as the good and acceptable face of the movement" (Warner, *Trouble* 66). However, all the others who do not fit into this picture are still suffering from a higher degree of discrimination and marginalization than those who manage to fit in. Most Americans are ready to accept gay and lesbian couples in the 21st century; however, this only applies to those couples who do not deviate too far from hetero-homo-normativity and from traditional American family ideals and values. As a result, if the only variance in a couple or a family is that both partners are of the same sex, but they conform in all other areas of life, the majority of the American nation is willing to accept such a difference. However, as Stone, Ashley, and oth-

[159] There has been a lot of critique of the professionalization of the LGBT movement which in particular developed in the course of the fight for marriage equality. In the United States, the marriage equality movement was not just some grassroots activism of Americans caring for the rights of gay and lesbian people, but it was to a large part the effort of professional civil rights organizations (e.g., the Human Rights Campaign as the largest organization, the Gay and Lesbian Advocates and Defenders, or Lambda Legal among others). In 2018, the Human Rights Campaign Foundation and the Human Rights Campaign PAC had an annual budget of more than 45 million dollars ("IRS Form 990 FY18"), which puts the HRC on the same level as other political super PACS. This professionalization was criticized for "weakening the movement and disenfranchising activists who wanted to be involved in movement decision making" (Stone 469). Stone warns that such a strategical professionalization "may increase the legitimacy and effectiveness of the LGBT movement" but, at the same time, these professional organizations "suppress dissent, radicalism, and (in a contradictory fashion) diversity," and their leaders tend to be "white, and middle- or upper-class professionals" (469).

ers witnessed, as soon as intersectionality is involved, acceptance becomes more elusive. As a consequence, some gay people did not feel represented by gay rights movement's strategy, in particular since the marriage equality campaign put a stronger focus on the similarities between heterosexual and homosexual couples, specifically that both types of couples get married for love. Beam criticizes that the campaign's "turn towards the rhetoric of love only intensified this embrace of normativity" (55).[160] Although this tactic proved to be incredibly effective in the end, it came at the price of excluding a minority within the gay minority which was not represented by this normative picture and could face even stronger marginalization as a result.

While more assimilated couples and their lack of willingness to challenge oppressive power structures within society have been the target of criticism, some activists and scholars also defend those who live a more assimilated life, either of their own volition or because they are forced to due to personal circumstance or a lack of resources to combat the marginalization of others. "Some working-class lesbian parents, for example, might not be able to afford being placed outside the kinship networks within local neighbourhoods: being recognised as 'like any other family' might not be simply strategic, but necessary for survival" (Ahmed 153). Ahmed explains that "[a]ssimilation and transgression are not choices that are available to individuals, but . . . effects of how subjects can and cannot inhabit social norms and ideals" (153). Regarding homonormative processes and forces within society, Richardson critically asks: "[D]oes it necessarily follow that by not contesting certain assumptions and institutions one is upholding those same assumptions and institutions simply by omission of critiques of them? Does upholding require certain practices of identification with certain assumptions and institutions?" (155). While some individuals might be in the privileged situation of choosing freely between assimilation and transgression, in an overwhelming majority of cases, this is only possible

160 In several interviews with queer people, Beam found out that they do not feel "included in this vision of the good life the campaign sought to mobilize" and that "the campaign had to *create* the ideal gay and lesbian life narrative based on focus-group research that revealed what straight people wanted to hear – a story that would validate and re-affirm the moral rightness of straight people's own identities and life choices" (55). Indeed, such a strategy makes sense when one considers that many marriage equality opponents were afraid that they would have to give up their identity concept or that their identities could be invalidated.

for those who possess a high amount of sociocultural capital which usually makes them less vulnerable to exclusion and marginalization.

In contrast to many others who see things in black and white, Green emphasizes that the grey area in between can be an opportunity since "the dual socialization of lesbian and gay spouses in both a heteronormative meaning-constitutive tradition *and* a queer meaning-constitutive tradition, may provide the contradictory conditions upon which a substantial contingent of 'first generation' same sex spouses will reimagine the marital form" (430). Thus, gay rights advocates who opposed same-sex marriage because they viewed it as an uncritical continuation of patriarchal and hegemonical structures were in fact calling for such a reconceptualization of marriage. Perhaps the institution of American marriage needs a certain degree of adjustment before it can begin or continue a process of a gradual transformation. Green is convinced that "today's same-sex married spouses are likely to express the cultural contradictions of their lives in the form of complex marital arrangements that bring together tradition and innovation, with the effect of both reproducing and subverting traditional marriage. These are, indeed, *queer* unions" (429).

Expansion of Gay Spaces and Visibility

Despite differing opinions on whether same-sex marriage was the highest goal for the gay rights movement, it must be noted that in regard to American everyday nationalism and American national identity, marriage equality enabled "the expansion of spaces of citizenship to lesbians and gay men" (Richardson 87). It enlarged the space of gay Americans within the American nation because the extension of same-sex couples' federal rights, benefits, and protections led to an increase in their sociocultural capital and power and therefore to an increase in their participation rights in the process of determining what is American or un-American. Gay Americans still have no "geographical base or kinship ties" (Duggan, "Perfectly Queer" 160) and they still have "no locale from which to wander" (Warner, *Fear* xvii). However, it seems as if the empowerment they have experienced over the last decade has allowed them to root themselves within American culture in order to establish their previously missing locale within and all over the American nation. Accordingly, increasing their sociocultural capital has empowered gay Americans to spread out and to claim spaces and territories within the United States outside of gay-dominated areas. Alex Bitterman and Daniel Baldwin Hess, scholars in the field of architecture and urban and regional planning respectively, discovered that this development of gay and lesbian Americans expanding their spaces and moving to new areas can be witnessed in gay urban districts across North America. Therefore, the rehabilitation of gay Americans within the American nationhood and their advance into new terrain is not only a legal and ideological expansion, but one that is also reflected in their living and housing preferences. In their essay titled "Gay Ghettoes Growing Gray: Transformations of Gay Urban Districts Across North American Reflects Generational Change," Bitterman and Hess claim that the success in *Obergefell* fostered "a desire for 'normal' and mainstream adult experiences and lifestyles in which seclusion into gay districts is not needed" (61). Whereas earlier generations of gay Americans preferred to seclude themselves in predominantly gay neighborhoods such as in Greenwich Village in New York City or the Castro district in San Francisco in order to live among likeminded people who would not question their lifestyle or ostracize them, younger generations no longer believe this to be necessary since social acceptance is increasing.[161] Younger gay Americans do not feel the need to stay within certain neighborhoods or even within liberal state lines (Bitterman and Hess 61–62). "This shift mimics the ethnic assimilation that occurred across North America throughout the twentieth century as neighborhoods long identified as homes to immigrant communities . . . were abandoned by second-generation younger residents for more integrated suburbs," Bitterman and Hess explain (61). Nevertheless, they also noticed that, while the younger generation of gay and lesbian adults have dispersed all over North America, the baby-boomer generation still expresses the desire to stay amongst their own community within gay spaces as their demand for gay and lesbian retirement communities proves (61). As those generations of gay Americans did not reach adulthood at a time when the gay rights movement in the United States had already celebrated decisive victories in anti-discrimination protection, the earlier generations appear to need more time to adjust to the idea that homosexual Americans

161 In addition to reasons of security, Bitterman and Hess also name shifting social trends as a reason for younger generations of gays and lesbians no longer feeling the need for secluded gay neighborhoods. They keep in touch and get to know each other via social media and dating apps whereas older generations of gay Americans had to meet in person, which was easier in gay districts and gay communities (59–60).

have become at least partially "un-un-Americanized" and can actively participate in the process of constructing today's American everyday nationalism.

In regard to the visibility, acceptance, and inclusion of gay Americans, American everyday nationalism has evolved significantly. Gay people have largely developed from un-American national security threats to Americanized, active participants in the process of shaping the nation. As a result, everyday nationalism has changed insofar as gay Americans are now omnipresent. Not only are they strong voices in sociocultural national discourse, but they also (re)negotiate and (re)construct the nation by contributing their own language, rituals, symbols, and traditions. Pride parades have turned into huge celebrations of diversity and are no longer solely events for the queer community to protest unequal treatment and marginalization. Rainbow flags are no longer just waving outside gay bars but also from government buildings. Even the White House was illuminated in rainbow colors in celebration of *Obergefell v. Hodges* (Gilman). Gay culture and homonormativity are disseminated throughout the country first and foremost through media, even into the most conservative towns of the country. In regard to television, Gamson witnessed an "explosion of gay visibility on television" (6) over the last fifteen years. Television shows and sitcoms such as *Queer Eye* or *Modern Family* are huge hits with phenomenal ratings figures. In TV formats, as *Modern Family*, "homosexuality is increasingly seen as within the realm of the culturally normative" and the "conservatism that some viewers see in the show could also reflect the shifting mores around marriage and queer culture generally" (Pugh 172). However, regarding which representations of gay life are accepted, TV culture is not much different from gay heroism as the media also offers role models and characters for identification but only if they do not deviate too much from the average heterosexual. Similar to other prominent and widely accepted representations of gay life in American everyday nationalism, TV culture tends to show more assimilated and homonormative gay subjects in order to not deter less progressive viewers.

The depiction of gay subjects on national television has at least improved massively over the last decades. The first portrayals of gay people on television were mostly as curiosities, then as cheaters or targets of ridicule, and later, a little more accurately, with their gay lives shown as a parallel world to that of normal heterosexual Americans (Gamson 6). Meanwhile, a "flattering stage" has now been reached since "gay men are represented as role models for straight people" (7). For instance, in TV shows such as *Queer Eye*, gay men have climbed up the social ladder since they are now "master shoppers, and excellent instructors in upper middle-class urban culture. This is the basis for the reconciliation between gay and straight," Gamson claims (13), but he does not forget the price the gay community pays for this form of depiction of gay life on television:

> There is . . . a huge gap between the cultural situation on television and the political situation outside of it. On television, gay men are treated as models of normality, and as cultural superiors; off television, lesbians and gay men remain excluded from many major social institutions and resources, and regular targets of hostility and violence. The celebratory cultural visibility can make it harder to see the very real political vulnerability. (16)

As this example proves, the American nation is ready for representations of gay lives within their homes on their TV screens, although there are some limitations and downsides to this progress. With television culture playing a tremendous role in American life, the omnipresence of gay characters shows that gay Americans have become an essential and constitutive part of American everyday nationalism. Thereby, this development mirrors the process of the increasing inclusion of gay individuals into dominant notions of American nationalism. Nevertheless, this is not yet the case for all queer people, especially not for those who are perceived as too deviant from "hetero-homo-normativity."

A similar development can be witnessed when it comes to the visibility of same-sex couples in advertisement. So many big American brands have started using gay and lesbian couples and families in their advertising campaigns that some claim that "gay couples in TV commercials became a mainstream phenomenon" (Alcorn). Amazon, American Airlines, IBM, Chrysler, and GM are just a few examples of companies who have opted for commercials with lesbian and gay characters (Alcorn). In an interview with *CNN Business*, Bob Witeck, president of the LGBTQ marketing and communications consulting firm Witeck Communications, explained that featuring LGBTQ-related images in commercials is "not about gay people as much as it is contemporary consumers" because "[o]ne of the ways to be contemporary is to be inclusive of LGBTQ individuals. It's less fraught, I think, even than race. . . . Gay and LGBTQ consumers, Gen Z and Millennials, their attitudes are so different about the ordinariness of same sex marriage today" (Witeck qtd. in Alcorn). Despite this inclusive attitude of younger consumers, having non-heterosexual couples and individuals in commercials is still a bold move, as American consumers continue to prefer advertisement with heterosexual couples who represent "normativity" (El Hazzouri et al.). One obvious problem with such depictions of gay life in advertisement can be explained by social identity theory, that is, heterosexual consumers sometimes do not see themselves as the target of gay-themed advertisement (Um 827).[162] Consequently, companies often opt for a mixture of heterosexual and queer characters in order to reach the broadest audience possible, or they choose the less explicit form of "gay-vague advertising" in which images can be understood differently by different consumer groups as they are less overt (El Hazzouri et al.). While gay Americans are not the prime targets of such advertisements, consumption is regarded as an important step on the path to their full inclusion into American everyday nationalism. "Television ads aren't as important in the digital marketing age as they were a generation ago, but in some ways they represent a final frontier of mainstream cultural acceptance for gay equality," Alcorn believes. As a result, companies would be hesitant to include LGBTQ images in their commercials if they were afraid that this could harm their brand by sparking a boycott from many consumers.[163]

When it comes to advertisement and gay consumption, there is another interesting correlation between purchasing power and American nationalism. Alexandra Chasin explains in her monograph *Selling Out: The Lesbian and Gay Movement Goes to Market*. Advertising has historically held high "significance to national identity, as both a patriotic duty and as a route to Americanization" (104). Chasin critiques that the advertising

[162] Brand commitment (i.e., the emotional attachment to brand) can alleviate the effect of heterosexual costumers not feeling targeted by or having a negative attitude towards a gay-themed advertisement. Um explains that this negative reaction of the advertisement recipient "did not necessarily translate into less positive attitudes towards the brand. This is because the attitude towards the ad is formed quickly after ad exposure. Attitude towards the brand, however, is more stable, accumulated as it is over a long period of time" (827). Consequently, brand commitment "is believed to moderate the relationship between negative information and brand evaluation" (827).

[163] Some companies, however, are not afraid of a conservative backlash as they see it as part of their mission to support LGBT rights. Kraft Foods (with their image of a rainbow-stuffed Oreo cookie), Target, American Apparel, J.C. Penney, and Starbucks were among the first major brands that knowingly opted for gay-themed advertisement and faced massive conservative backlash and customer boycott (Wong, "Oreo").

industry has "long promised that American identity and the mythical privileges attendant to U.S. citizenship – freedom, rights, justice, opportunity – are available to disenfranchised people if they only consume enough" (105). While this promise of Americanization through consumption was not accessible to all minorities, in the case of gay couples, it seems as if this has been regarded as a viable road to "un-un-Americanization" and inclusion. This attitude towards consumption is not surprising as this was exactly the message which the advertisement industry wanted to convey. Chasin confirms this impression when she writes:

> I argue that advertising to gay men and lesbians has played on ideas about national identity in two significant ways. First, such advertising has often appealed to gays on the basis of their identification as Americans. Second, advertising to gay men and lesbians has often promised that full inclusion in the national community of Americans is available through personal consumption. In other words, consumption has been held out as a route to political and social enfranchisement. (101)

Gay Americans who have the means to purchase their way into the American everyday nationalism also have the opportunity to trade their financial capital for sociocultural capital which enables them to participate in the process of shaping the character of the American nation and determine what is considered American or un-American. "[C]onsuming the nation" is also one of the four angles from which Fox and Miller-Idriss suggest analyzing everyday nationalism as they argue that it is also through consumption that the nation is produced and constructed in everyday life (538). Consumption enables gay Americans to be active participants in the drafting of the American nation and American national identity as monetary power can lead to influence as well as to cultural and political power. For some gay Americans, consumption, capital accumulation, and especially the acquisition of property propelled their inclusion into what is commonly considered American. The case of Edie Windsor is a telling example of this phenomenon. It is highly doubtful whether she would have had such a sweeping success in court or whether she would have been treated with the same respect if she had not been this white, successful, influential, and wealthy upper-class New Yorker with considerable property on the Upper East Side. However, this path to Americanization is not open to the large majority of homosexual Americans because a significant proportion of them are not as well-off as many believe. Taken into account that gay people disproportionally suffer from discrimination, including workplace discrimination,[164] the common image of the wealthy gays who are big spenders and travel the world is little more than a myth in the majority of cases. Hollibaugh and Weiss address this fatal misconception in their essay "Queer Precarity and the Myth of Gay Affluence":

> LGBT people are typically depicted as affluent consumers with high disposable incomes, yet this is hardly the norm. The majority of LGBT/Q people are poor or working class, female, and people of color, who struggle to get a job or hold onto one, to pay their rent and care for themselves and the people they love. (19)

As with most processes of homonormalization and homonationalism, this road to inclusion into prevailing understanding of American nationalism is not open and accessible for all gay Americans and ultimately leads to the marginalization of subgroups.

Marginalization of Other Minorities

The history of minorities in the United States has shown that the gradual inclusion of one group into dominant concepts of American nationalism is not accompanied by the greater inclusion of other minorities. By contrast, it can even result in new forms of marginalization as power structures shift and sociocultural capital is redistributed. Time and again, it seems as if one minority must pay the price for the inclusion of another. The dissatisfying situation in which some more assimilated gay individuals have been overwhelmingly welcomed into American everyday nationalism whereas other gay subjects are experiencing even higher levels of marginalization than before is just one example of this. As a result, homonormativity and homonationalism have sparked criticism because some claim that these processes ultimately fostered new forms of discrimination and marginalization. Susan Stryker pointed to the discrimination of transgender people who do not seem to benefit from the inclusion of

[164] About half of all LGBT Americans live in states which provide no state level employment protections or non-discrimination laws. Between 8% and 17% of LGB workers and between 13% and 47% of transgender workers report that they have been denied employment or have been fired because of their sexual orientation ("Paying" 18–19).

gay individuals in American nationalism. Transgender people often not only suffer from discrimination stemming from outside the queer community, but they are also marginalized within the LGBT movement (Stryker 145). Therefore, the double-discrimination they experience makes it even harder for them to find their place within the national community. Since people's attitudes towards gays and lesbians are significantly better than towards the gender non-conforming, transgender people have always occupied a worse position within the American nation (Lewis et al. 862). In the discussion of their study on the public's attitude towards LGBT people, Lewis et al. found out that this group is not perceived as one minority: "Respondents in our survey, on average, expressed warmer feelings towards gays and lesbians compared with transgender people" (871). The gay rights movement's successes in *Obergefell* and its precedents did not improve the position of transgender Americans within the nation or alleviate their suffering. Much rather, transgender people have become new targets of discrimination as the acceptance of gay and lesbian Americans has risen. "[T]he empowerment of one gender, one nation or one sexuality virtually always occurs at the expense and disempowerment of another," Tamar Mayer states in her monograph *Gender Ironies of Nationalism: Sexing the Nation*. This backlash experienced by transgender individuals almost seems as though the anti-LGBT camp in the United States needed a new target or scapegoat as the acceptance of gay and lesbian Americans increased. Subsequently, this led the drafting of anti-transgender bills, as the prominent example of North Carolina's so-called "bathroom bill"[165] demonstrated.

The civil rights movement and the gay rights movement have been strongly connected from the inception of the latter. The gay rights movement has partially adopted the rhetoric of African Americans' fight for equality and demands of both minorities for equality are rooted in the Equal Protection Clause of the Fourteenth Amendment. Simultaneously, gay Americans have often anchored their identity claims in ethnic identity nationalism (Grindstaff 65). However, the advances gay Americans made in becoming more equal members of the American nation and se-

165 The Public Facilities Privacy & Security Act (the "bathroom bill") prevented transgender individuals from using a bathroom that did not correspond to their biological sex as stated on their birth certificate (Tan). In July 2019, a federal judge in North Carolina held that transgender people cannot be prevented from using a public bathroom that matches their gender identity (Levin).

curing a greater number of discrimination protections did not automatically lead to the situations of other minorities improving. For example, despite the striking similarities between the gay rights movement's and the civil rights movement's struggles and efforts, Black Americans did not experience progress as a result of the advancement of gay rights. Meg Wesling even argues that the "apparent advance in gay and lesbian rights is achieved simultaneously to, if not coincident with, a dismantling or regression of advancements toward racial equality" (171). In order to support her allegation, she names the example of *Shelby County v. Holder*, a United States Supreme Court case which was decided the day before *United States v. Windsor* and in which a core element of the 1965 Voting Rights Act was struck down (United States, Supreme Court, "*Shelby County*" 24). Consequently, the ruling in *Shelby County* "has been widely perceived as a critical blow to the progress of racial equality in the United States" because five judges of the Supreme Court decided for revoking an essential section of the Voting Rights Act (Wesling 171).[166] The Supreme Court infringed the rights of a racial minority on June 25, 2013, then one day later, they expanded the rights of a sexual minority by declaring Section 3 of the Defense of Marriage Act unconstitutional. As a result, there is little wonder as to why some believe that race and sexuality are played against each other or that only one minority can receive protection at a time, which has resulted in African Americans paying the price for the advancement of gay Americans. Another problem, which Wesling noticed in her 2014 analysis of the media landscape and their frequent comparisons between civil rights and gay rights, is that racial discrimination has almost vanished from national discourse whereas "gay rights features as the newest horizon in the triumphant march of progress" (172). Wesling's findings are astounding because, in particular since the "Black Lives Matter" movement[167], African American racial struggles

[166] In *Shelby v. Holder*, the United States Supreme Court invalidated Section IV of the Voting Rights Act. Section IV required states which had a history of racial discrimination regarding their voting procedures to present any planned changes in voting procedures to federal authorities for preclearance in order to avoid repeated voting discrimination (United States, Supreme Court, "*Shelby County*" 24). The ruling opened the doors to racial discrimination on voting in the states concerned as they can now change voting procedures without having to submit these changes to federal authorities who could have prevented discrimination in this regard.

[167] The "Black Lives Matter" movement and the associated hashtag, #blacklives

and discrimination were covered extensively by the media. It seems as if national discourse and American everyday nationalism can only incorporate a certain amount of diversity or only give room to one minority at a time. This is highly problematic as it indicates that one minority must pay the price for the advancement of another, and it completely ignores issues of intersectionality.

The inclusion of gay citizens into contemporary notions of American nationalism and into prevailing ideas of Americanism has coincided with the ostracization of Muslims, which has prompted the Raha Iranian Feminist Collective to wonder if "'Gays' vs 'Muslims'" has become the tone of the day (155). They see this "particularly clearly in Donald Trump's cynical inclusion of, as he said, 'LGBTQ citizens' (which implicitly distinguishes citizens from other LGBTQ people) whom he vowed to 'do everything in [his] power to protect'" (155). Jasbir Puar wrote extensively on this development in her studies on homonationalism: "The narrative of progress for gay rights is thus built on the back of racialized others, for whom such progress was once achieved, but is now backsliding or has yet to arrive" ("Rethinking" 337). In U.S. foreign policies, gays have been repeatedly used to justify the discrimination and targeting of racial others and specifically Muslim communities in many cases. In this context, homonationalism can be used to draw attention to "how lesbian and gay rights discourses produce narratives of progress and modernity that continue to accord some populations access to cultural and legal forms of citizenship at the expense of the partial and full expulsion from those rights of other populations" (Puar, *Terrorist* 228).

matter, was started by Patrisse Cullors, Alicia Garza, and Opal Tometi after the killing of the black adolescent Trayvon Martin by a white man who was a self-appointed neighborhood watchman (Spencer and Adrone 79). The movement drew attention to the severe problem of innocent Black deaths as well as police brutality towards Blacks in the United States. The activism took place both on the internet and on the streets.

D Conclusion

The work of Warner, Duggan, and others in the field of hetero- and homonormativity provided the terminology and theories which enabled scholarly engagement with the normalizing and normativizing influences on the positioning of homosexual people within the American nation. Although definitions of hetero- and, in particular, homonormativity differ, the core understandings of these concepts are nevertheless the same.[168] The usage of the term 'hetero-homonormative' instead of just 'homonormative' illustrates that those at the bottom of the hierarchy of queer worthiness possibly experience a double marginalization from two groups with whose norms they cannot comply and therefore experience exclusion. While the homonormative process had some significant negative side-effects, it is important to acknowledge the benefits and freedom which it brought to some gay Americans. For some gay people, homonormativity is an opportunity to become full members of the American nation due to homosexuality being increasingly seen as normal, and some of them never really identified with the queer movement in the first place. By contrast, the normativization process put greater pressure on others who more strongly deviate from what is considered normal or normative, possibly leaving them feeling even more marginalized by dominant ideas of American nationalism than before. Heteronormativity and homonormativity in the United States not only determine what is normal but also what is American. Therefore, discourses in which gay subjects' active participation in the conceptualization process of American nationalism is debated are not only about what is American but also what is normal and normative in American everyday nationalism.

Puar's conceptualization of 'homonationalism' took research on the intersection between queer studies and nationalism studies a step further by allowing for a deeper insight into how the American people handle the challenges posed by the increasing demand of sexual minorities to become an integral component of American nationalism as full and equal American

[168] Heteronormativity is the critique of heterosexuality as the default norm in society which remains largely unquestioned, entails certain privileges, and can cause the marginalization and discrimination of those who deviate from these norms. Homonormativity in a wider sense is the uncritical assimilation of homosexuals to heteronormative standards, which can result in homosexuals marginalizing those who do not assimilate to these new hetero-homonormative standards as well as in a development of hierarchies within the queer community.

citizens. However, homonationalism began with a troubling connotation, as it was mostly used to explore the instrumentalization of gay subjects to legitimize dubious U.S. foreign policies and to expose the concomitant discrimination of racial others. Nonetheless, homonationalism also marked the entrance of at least some gay people into the idea of American nationalism and consequently classified them as worthy of national protection. Gay Americans have developed into active participants in the discursive (re)construction and (re)negotiation of the American nation, and through this acquisition of greater agency, many of them have also become Americanized. More assimilated gays even have the chance to become gay heroes.

Gay American have long suffered from having no geographical base within the United States and from not being a part of American mainstream culture, which goes hand in hand with an exclusion from American everyday nationalism. However, the last years and the fight for marriage equality have led to a tremendous expansion of gay spaces and visibility. This new era in regard to the inclusion, visibility, and participation of gay Americans in American nationalism has even led some scholars to proclaim the "'post-gay'-period" (Richardson 91) where it is no longer necessary to define oneself through sexual orientation. Richardson explains her line of thought, which is based on the assessment of the research of other scholars in this field of study, as follows:

> This notion of a 'post-gay' era has been linked to transformations in sexual politics, as well as to the relative significance of sexual identities. Specifically, this refers to the inclusive logic of contemporary struggles for LGBT equality that emphasize similitude with other (sexual) citizens rather than difference. . . . From this perspective, it is not so much that people are no longer gay; rather it is the disappearance of gay culture that is seen to be occurring through processes of assimilation into mainstream culture alongside greater diversification of LGBT communities. (90)

It remains debatable whether a post-gay era has already begun in the United States, particularly since a significant percentage of queer subjects have not yet had the opportunity to become included into what is commonly understood by American everyday nationalism and American national identity. With some minorities or subgroups, the American nation seems to struggle when it comes to their full inclusion. Therefore, it is important that Richardson and other scholars of the field, despite the all too promising idea of a post-gay era, do not forget to emphasize "that the term 'post-gay' may not translate to post-discrimination or post-(sexual) citizenship" (91).

Conclusion

Renegotiating American Nationalism: The Proxy War over Marriage Equality through the Lens of Un-Americanism has explored contemporary notions of American everyday nationalism and shed light on their manifestation in the context of the marriage equality debate. Operationalizing the term 'un-American' as an analytical tool, I have investigated how the nation addressed the challenges posed by the gay minority's insistence on legal and sociocultural equality as well as their demand to be fully included into everyday nationalism. The book took particular interest in revealing how culture war debates, such as the one over marriage equality, served as proxy wars for conflicts that are ultimately about American nationalism. In the discursive battlefields of these proxy wars, we can observe the continuous renegotiation of American everyday nationalism, in which charges of un-Americanism were employed as a popular rhetorical weapon. My study contributes to the hitherto limited scholarship both on studies on American nationalism as well as on the largely neglected field of un-Americanism and calls for an increase in scholarly attention to the interrelationship between queer and nationalism studies. Focusing primarily on the second term of the Obama presidency, I have examined insults of un-Americanism from both marriage equality advocates and opponents. Furthermore, I have analyzed the slip opinions from the United States Supreme Court cases *United States v. Windsor* and *Obergefell v. Hodges* in order to demonstrate that the marriage equality debate epitomizes conflicts in which the object of dispute becomes incidental to larger discussions of American national identity.

My research into current notions of American everyday nationalism and its continuous renegotiation process was motivated by the following aims: First, I sought to illustrate that sociocultural conflicts, such as the debate over marriage equality, serve as proxy wars for disputes over American nationalism, and that in these debates, insults of un-Americanism serve as a gate-keeping mechanism for regulating who is allowed to shape and define American national identity. Next, I sought to investigate how the American nation handles the sociocultural transformations resulting from the ameliorated status of a minority and how the American people, willingly or by force, reconstruct their everyday nationalism in order to integrate a previously marginalized minority. Finally, my aim was to trace and critique the narrative of homonationalism and to question to what extent this newly found equality regarding marriage translates to a greater equality of gay subjects and their full inclusion into American everyday nationalism.

This cultural studies project has been conceptualized as "a historization of the contemporary moment" (Puar, *Terrorist* xxvii). Therefore, I have situated the discussed reconceptualization of the American self-concept that took place in the lead up to and the fallout from *Obergefell* in regard to the history of un-Americanism and the marriage equality movement. Furthermore, I have operationalized the term 'un-American' and transformed it into an analytical tool since this study benefitted greatly from a methodological approach which reveals how people understand themselves as Americans and whom they are willing to include in their definition of true representatives of the American nationhood at a certain point in time. The term 'un-American,' both as a rhetoric and as a research tool, traces and discloses development, process, and change through American history down to the present day. This methodological approach aligns with the study's theoretical framework of everyday nationalism which understands people as active agents in the process of shaping their nation and of negotiating what their idea of nationalism should entail.

As Beverly Gage established with her proclamation that 'un-American' is "the [p]olitical [i]nsult of the [m]oment," reciprocal accusations of un-Americanism have become a popular rhetoric in 21st century national discourse over sociocultural conflicts. In the debate on marriage equality, its advocates and opponents frequently employed this confrontational language in order to add force to their statements and in order to secure ground in the battle over power and influence in conceptualizing the future of American everyday nationalism. The arguments exchanged in speech acts that included the insult of un-Americanism mostly involved the issues of religion, First and Fourteenth Amendment rights, the American promise of equality for all, questions of judicial activism, as well as of the constitutionality of same-sex marriage. The history of the term 'un-American' and the analysis of the marriage equality debate demonstrate that this lexical choice was an instrument for designating insiders from outsiders and for regulating access to American society. As I showed, the term 'un-American' is to be seen as a highly effective mechanism for determining who can be active agents in the (re)construction and (re)negotiation of American nationalism. Those who are deemed un-American should not be given a voice in defining discourses and practices of American nationhood and may even be excluded from the American self-concept entirely. Gay Americans have for most of the country's history played a passive role in negotiations of American nationalism at best and have even been regarded as security risks during the time of the House Un-American Activities Committee. The United States Supreme Court rulings in *United States v. Windsor* and *Obergefell v. Hodges* were milestones in the gradual "un-un-Americanization" of gay and lesbian Americans. The arguments adduced by the judges in their writings mirrored the concerns and sentiments of the American public and were reflective of how U.S. society tried to cope with the challenges and transformations posed by the gay minority's increasing pressure for equal representation and participation in the contemporary notion of American nationalism. Moreover, *Windsor* and *Obergefell* acted as a stage on which the discursive drafting of the future of the American nation took place. In the majority opinions as well as in the accompanying dissents, the judges discussed the constitutionality of DOMA's Section 3 and whether marriage was granted to same-sex couples by the United States Constitution; however, in addition to their commentary on the issue of same-sex marriage itself, both rulings were also debates over American national identity and the future course of the American nation. The analysis of the public debate over marriage equality and the legal discussion in *Windsor* and *Obergefell* illustrated that the battle over marriage equality in the United States was ultimately a proxy war for a renegotiation of American nationalism in light of the gay rights movement's fight for greater equality.

The level of acceptance of the inclusion of gay subjects into contemporary notions of American nationalism differs vastly. Although seven out of ten Americans now support same-sex marriage according to the latest Gallup poll from June 2021 (McCarthy, "Record-High"), this number also reveals that three out of ten Americans are still struggling to come to terms with this change in marriage law. In fact, support for same-sex marriage has even temporarily decreased slightly from a 67% approval rate in 2018 to a 63% approval rate in 2019 (McCarthy, "U.S. Support") before raising back to a new high at 70% in 2021 (McCarthy, "Record-High"). Consequently, in examining the question of how the American people have addressed the changes instigated by the increasing inclusion of gay subjects into how nationalism is represented in everyday life, scholars should not make the mistake of ignoring the significant portion of Americans who have not accepted a reconceptualization of American nationalism that embraces gay people, despite the majority approval of marriage equality. Opposition to marriage equality and the impact this opposition has on the transformation of American nationalism regarding gay Americans will not fade from public discourse soon. The high degree of politicization of marriage in the United States, the strong ties between family and nation, as well as the fear of loss and societal instability which unsettles communities makes the topic fertile ground for further discussion and negotiation. Same-sex marriage opponents feel as if they had no say in the inclusion of gay Americans and claim that they have been force-fed liberal values and a more progressive American national identity. The massive insecurity that changes in American nationalism implied for opponents of marriage equality constitutes an environment that encourages the use of accusations of un-Americanism. However, an examination of these insults and the circumstances that provoke this lexical choice revealed that same-sex marriage seldomly serves as the core concern for people who engage in the fight against marriage equality. Homosexuality rather functions as a symbol upon which people project their anxieties which are often separate and distinct from gay people and same-sex marriage. My findings, in particular my analysis of the interplay among the polarization in the United States, Americans' ideals and values, and its ideas of the nation, confirmed my hypothesis that the debate over marriage equality serves as a proxy war for other discourses, most notably the renegotiation of American nationalism. Whereas some Americans embraced the turn towards a more inclusive and liberal notion of American nationalism, others felt threatened and overwhelmed by these changes.

In order to trace how the nation addressed the consequences of *Obergefell* and in order to scrutinize to what extent this new legal equality resulted in gay subjects becoming active agents in the transformation of American nationalism, I employed Puar's concept of homonationalism. Homonationalism provided the necessary vocabulary for exploring the intersection between nationalism studies and queer studies. Acknowledging that the further inclusion of gay subjects into American nationalism comes at a price, homonationalism helped to shed light on the advancement of gay and lesbian Americans as well as on the possible downsides of this process, such as the marginalization of other minorities or parts of the queer community. Scholars should not lose sight of these developments when investigating the gay rights movement's continuous success in becoming an integral element of the American nationhood. Although the gay minority has garnered increasing influence, visibility, and power in the process of drafting American nationalism, gay culture in the United States is still subject to the "totalizing tendency" of heteronormativity (Warner, "Introduction" 8), which can produce new expectations on gay subjects through homonormativity. Assimilation was and continues to be a necessary step on the path of receiving social acknowledgement and equal rights in the United States. The contemporary notion of American nationalism integrates gay individuals but only does so to a certain extent. Different gay Americans occupy radically different spaces on the continuum between full integration and multiple marginalization. For some gay people, homonormativity was an opportunity to become full members of the American nation because homosexuality had become increasingly seen as normal. These gay Americans have been "un-un-Americanized," not least through marriage equality, whereas others who deviate from what is considered normal or normative have remained notorious un-Americans. The question whether the *Obergefell* ruling and the concomitant inclusion of some gay Americans into contemporary notions of American nationalism translated to greater equality for the large majority of the gay community cannot be uniformly answered since the extent of the improvements experienced by gay individuals was dependent on each person's sociocultural circumstances. However, it is certain that American nationalism had to transform in the wake of *Obergefell* and the gay rights movement's fight for greater equality. The reaction of the American people to the gay community's demand for equal representation in regard to how the nation is experienced and expressed differs widely.

For the greater part of U.S. history, the un-Americanness of gay people was the national consensus, with very few exceptions. Opinions started to diverge first when the gay rights movement pointed towards the discrepancy between the ideal of equal rights for all Americans and the corresponding reality, with gay rights advocates raising awareness about the severe discrimination and marginalization of homosexual Americans. As a growing number of Americans started to reconsider their stance on gay rights at the turn of the millennium, sexual minority rights and same-sex marriage had developed into a source of conflict that triggered a high degree of polarization. When analyzing polarization in this context, the focus should not only be on political polarization but also on affective polarization. Affective polarization is not tied to political controversies or purely ideological conflicts but has strong elements of emotionality and irrationality (Lütjen 42). The debate over same-sex marriage and the concomitant renegotiation of American nationalism was deeply infused with affective polarization. Consequently, the conflict became nearly intractable as the opposing parties do not seem to speak the same language and were arguing on the basis of different perceptions of reality (Lütjen 43). With the conflict participants operating from opposing positions, everyday nationalism in regard to queer subjects also became more polarized. Americans rarely occupied a middle ground in this debate. They were either in favor of equal rights for gay Americans and also advocated for their inclusion within contemporary notions of American nationalism, or they took a conservative stance on the issue and argued that unequal individuals could not be made equal. Accordingly, they should not be an integral element of what constitutes American national identity.

One answer to the question of how the American nation handled the challenges posed by the necessary integration of gay individuals into concepts of American nationalism is separation. Evangelical churches and deeply religious Americans used to form a united bulwark against same-sex marriage. However, in January 2020, one of the largest denominations, the United Methodist Church, announced that the church would split after years of disagreement over same-sex marriage (Robertson and Dias). The schism appeared to be the only solution to this conflict between liberal and conservative Methodists as "the issue of gay rights [had] proved uniquely divisive in the church" (Williams and Dias). The United Methodist Church was only one example in a line of denominations struggling with disputes over gay rights (Robertson and Dias). This case shows that not even Americans with the same theological perspective manage to find a place of reconciliation or tolerant co-existence regarding this issue. This split in the Methodist church allows liberal and conservative church members to avoid further contact with differently minded believers and to further seclude themselves in their respective echo chambers. This development, as witnessed within the microcosm of one denomination, also takes places on a larger scale in the macrocosm of the American society. The issue of gay rights has proved to be a divisive and polarizing influence on the American nation and the fight over marriage equality appears to have deepened the trenches instead of building mutual understanding between each side's viewpoint. Consequently, people's ideas of what American nationalism should look like have diverged even further.

The growing polarization in the United States and a mutual estrangement among Americans are among the larger developments and shifts in American culture and society that were revealed with the help of this study. In a 2018 poll, 31% of the respondents said that they believed the American nation would experience a second civil war within five years

("31% think"). These 31% perceived American ideas of the nation and who should be permitted to participate in negotiations of American nationalism to be so incongruous that they viewed an outbreak of a civil war as a real possibility. In contrast to preceding decades when there was a much stronger focus on the uniting elements of U.S. culture, Americans now seem to place greater emphasis on difference than on similarities or sameness. This observation aligns with Beverly Gage's hypothesis that "un-American" has become "the [p]olitical [i]nsult of the [m]oment" and reflects the numbers from the Pew Research Center which confirm that partisanship and division regarding personal values "reached record levels during Barack Obama's presidency" which have grown even larger under President Trump ("Partisan Divide"). While Americans used to distribute themselves somewhere on a continuum regarding controversial issues such as marriage equality, they have now started congregating at the ends of the continuum. This process has resulted in the development of two estranged versions of the United States of America which are culturally and politically dissimilar from each other, antithetic even.

The source of this problem is related to what Torben Lütjen calls "paradoxical individualization" ("paradoxe Individualisierung"; my trans.; Lütjen 24). Lütjen claims that our modern and individualized societies do not only implicate a higher degree of freedom and tolerance but have also fostered narrowmindedness and the development of highly homogeneous living spaces, which have allowed Americans to distance themselves from political and sociocultural opponents and dissidents (24). In contrast to earlier generations, today's Americans seem to have lost their ability to compromise and to handle cognitive dissonance. People move to neighborhoods with likeminded people, they consume the news and media outlets which mirror their political opinion, and media algorithms foster the creation of a bubble in which one's own line of thought is continuously reproduced, creating the illusion that one's own opinion is the dominant one. Paradoxical individualization leads to the creation of two political and cultural camps which see the world with completely different eyes (24). In the fight over marriage equality, this effect can be clearly observed in the analysis of accusations of un-Americanism. Often one camp is in complete disbelief over the attitude of the other and insulting the estranged opponent as un-American seems to be the only appropriate lexical choice in times of severe cultural and personal alienation. As a result, Lütjen argues that President Trump's wall is not just a construction at the border of Mexico, rather it is a barrier running right through people's minds (24). Consequently, finding common ground in the renegotiation and reconceptualization of American nationalism has become even more challenging. People's ideas of what constitutes American national identity and their willingness to integrate a new minority depend strongly upon which version of the U.S. they live in.

Making predictions about the future direction of nationalism in the United States is fraught with difficulty. The 2016 presidential election has taught many political scientists and cultural studies scholars a lesson. In the months before the election, many experts argued that an election of a figure such as Donald Trump was impossible, and they substantiated their claims with a series of plausible numbers and theories. Ultimately, many of them failed to correctly predict the outcome of the 2016 election. Consequently, I am hesitant when it comes to hypothesizing about the future direction of nationalism and the situation of queer individuals in the United States as such developments nowadays seem to change with the weather of the day with nothing being impossible anymore. The 2016 election "created a sense of rupture" and "shifted the nation into some dystopian reality that was never meant to be," as Beverly Gage phrased it. Whether this shift towards conservatism that has characterized the past four years, the polarization caused by the retreat of Americans into their echo chambers, and the divisive potency of the issue of gay rights and queer participation in American nationalism will continue can only be answered in hindsight. If the cyclical theory[169] of Arthur M. Schlesinger Sr. and Arthur M. Schlesinger Jr. comes into effect, the country would soon see a turn toward a more liberal American everyday nationalism. Regarding the future of gay rights in the United States, Puar's warning that same-sex marriage is for many a "ground that had never been fully ceded" and that "[h]omonationalism has always been contradictory and in-flux" should be kept in mind in order prevent losing ground that gay rights advocates had already claimed for themselves (*Terrorist* 225). I hope future scholars will continue exploring the intersection between nationalism studies and queer studies. The interconnectedness of these two fields is not only revealing of how queer life shapes American everyday nationalism, but it also sheds light on larger political and sociocultural developments in the United States.

[169] The historians Arthur M. Schlesinger Sr. and his son, Arthur M. Schlesinger Jr., claim that the political climate in the United States alternates between phases of conservatism and phases of liberalism. Their cyclical theory suggests that this alternation repeats itself throughout American history (Schlesinger Jr. 8).

Bibliography

"About." *Family Research Council*, https://www.frc.org/about-frc. Accessed 13 Aug. 2019.

Abramowitz, Alan I., and Kyle L. Saunders. "Is Polarization a Myth?" *Journal of Politics*, vol. 70, no. 2, 2008, pp. 542–55. *JSTOR*, doi:10.1017/S0022381608080493.

Abrams, Kerry. "Citizen Spouse." *California Law Review*, vol. 101, no. 2, 2013, pp. 407–44. *JSTOR*, https://www.jstor.org/stable/23409438.

Adam, Barry D. "The Defense of Marriage Act and American Exceptionalism: The 'Gay Marriage' Panic in the United States." *Journal of the History of Sexuality*, vol. 12, no. 2, 2003, pp. 259–76. *JSTOR*, https://www.jstor.org/stable/3704614.

Agiesta, Jennifer. "Poll: Obama's Approval Ratings Stagnant Despite Economy." *CNN*, 19 Feb. 2015, https://edition.cnn.com/2015/02/19/politics/poll-obama-approval-rating-econo my/index.html.

Ahmed, Sara. *The Cultural Politics of Emotions*. Edinburgh UP, 2014.

Alcorn, Chauncey. "How Gay Couples in TV Commercials Became a Mainstream Phenomenon." *CNN Business*, 20 Dec. 2019, https://edition.cnn.com/2019/12/20/media/hallmark-zola-gay-ad/index.html. Accessed 3 Jan. 2020.

Alito, Samuel. Dissenting opinion. *Obergefell v. Hodges*. 26 June 2015, *Supreme Court of the United States*, https://www.supremecourt.gov/opinions/14pdf/14-556_3204.pdf. Accessed 3 Feb. 2018.

---. Dissenting opinion. *United States v. Windsor*. 26 June 2013. *Supreme Court of the United States*, https://www.supremecourt.gov/opinions/12pdf/12-307_6j37.pdf. Accessed 23 Oct. 2018.

"Alliance for Justice Unveils Cutting-Edge New Website." *Alliance for Justice*, 15 Jan. 2020, https://www.afj.org/article/alliance-for-justice-unveils-cutting-edge-new-website/. Accessed 26 Mar. 2020.

Almasy, Steven, and Darran Simon. "A Timeline of President Trump's Travel Bans." *CNN*, 10 Feb. 2017, https://edition.cnn.com/2017/02/10/us/trump-travel-ban-timeline/index. html. Accessed 8 Dec. 2019.

Anderson, Benedict. *Imagined Communities: Reflections on the Origin and Spread of Nationalism*. Rev. Ed., Verso, 2006.

Anderson, Jeffrey. "Democratic Congresswoman: It's 'Un-American' Not to Fund Obamacare 'Outreach.'" *Washington Examiner*, 22 May 2013, https://www.washingtonexaminer.com/weekly-standard/democratic-congresswoman-its-un-american-not-to-fund-obamacare-outreach. Accessed 20 Feb. 2020.

Andrew, Mike. "Al Franken Speaks Out for Marriage Equality in Minnesota." *Seattle Gay News*, 27 May 2011, http://www.sgn.org/sgnnews39_21/page13.cfm. Accessed 10 May 2018.

Aron, Nan. "AFJ: Now Supreme Court Can Make Gay Marriage Bans 'Relics of a Discarded Past.'" *Alliance for Justice*, 16 Jan. 2015, https://www.afj.org/press-room/press-releases/afj-now-supreme-court-can-make-gay-marriage-bans-relics-of-a-discarded-past. Accessed 15 Feb. 2015.

Ashley, Colin P. "Gay Liberation: How a Once Radical Movement Got Married and Settled Down." *New Labor Forum*, vol. 24, no. 3, 2015, pp. 28–32. *JSTOR*, https://www.jstor. org/stable/24718619.

Ashtari, Shadee. "Alabama Chief Justice: Gay Marriage Is Un-American, Goes Against God And 'All That Is Noble.'" *Huffpost*, 7 May 2014, https://www.huffpost.com/entry/roy-moore-gay-marriage-god_n_5281771. Accessed 10 May 2018.

Associated Press. "Justice Kennedy: Senators Focus on Short-Term." *CBS News*, 14 May 2010, https://www.cbsnews.com/news/justice-kennedy-senators-focus-on-short-term/. Accessed 13 Nov. 2019.

@SamCoyle1. "Alabama Chief Justice: Gay Marriage Is Un-American. . . ." *Twitter*, 5 Jan. 2015, https://twitter.com/SamCoyle1/status/552191554962882561. Accessed 28 Oct. 2018.

Bader Ginsburg, Ruth. "Court Is 'One of Most Activist,' Ginsburg Says, Vowing to Stay." Interview with Adam Liptak. *The New York Times*, 24 Aug. 2013, www.nytimes.com/2013/08/25/us/court-is-one-of-most-activist-ginsburg-says-vowing-to-stay.html. Accessed 15 May 2018.

---. Interview with Greg Stohr and Matthew A. Winkler. *Bloomberg Business*, 12 Feb. 2015, www.bloomberg.com/news/articles/2015-02-12/ginsburg-says-u-s-ready-to-accept-ruling-approving-gay-marriage-i61z6gq2. Accessed 14. Feb. 2018.

---. "Transcript: Interview with Supreme Court Justice Ruth Bader Ginsburg." Interview with John Hockenberry. *WNYC*, 16 Sept. 2013, https://www.wnyc.org/story/transcript-interview-justice-ruth-bader-ginsburg/. Accessed 20 Feb. 2020.

Barbash, Fred. "Muslim Ban Language Suddenly Disappears from Trump Campaign Website after Spicer Questioned." *The Washington Post*, 9 May 2017, https://www.washingtonpost.com/news/morning-mix/wp/2017/05/09/trumps-preventing-muslim-immigration-vow-disappears-from-campaign-website-after-spicer-questioned/. Accessed 8 Dec. 2019.

Barnes, Robert. "Supreme Court Agrees to Hear Gay Marriage Issue." *The Washington Post*, 16 Jan. 2015, https://www.washingtonpost.com/politics/courts_law/supreme-court-agrees-to-hear-gay-marriage-issue/2015/01/16/865149ec-9d96-11e4-a7ee-526210d665b4_story.html. Accessed 8 Dec. 2019.

Bashir, Samiya, et al. "African American Responses to Same-Sex Marriage." *Defending Same-Sex Marriage: The Freedom-to-Marry Movement: Education, Advocacy, Culture, and the Media*, edited by Martin Dupuis and William A. Thompson. Praeger Publishers, 2007, 3 vols, pp. 171–84.

Beam, Myrl. "What's Love Got to Do with It? Queer Politics and the 'Love Pivot.'" *Queer Activism after Marriage Equality*, edited by Joseph Nicholas DeFilippis et al. Routledge, 2018, pp. 53–60.

Bean, Hamilton. "U.S. National Security Culture: From Queer Psychopathology to Queer Citizenship." *QED: A Journal in GLBTQ Worldmaking*, vol. 1, no. 1, 2014, pp. 52–79. *JSTOR*, https://www.jstor.org/stable/10.14321/qed.1.1.0052.

Bergmann, Eirikur. *Neo-Nationalism: The Rise of Nativist Populism*. Palgrave Macmillan, 2020.

Berry, Jeffrey M., and Sarah Sobieraj. *The Outrage Industry: Political Opinion Media and the New Incivility*. Oxford UP, 2014.

Biderman, Chris. "Colin Kaepernick Has Strong Response to Being Called 'Un-American.'" *NinersWire*, 16 Oct. 2016, https://ninerswire.usatoday.com/2016/10/16/colin-kaepernick-has-strong-response-to-being-called-un-american/. Accessed 10 Feb. 2020.

Billig, Michael. *Banal Nationalism*. Sage Publications, 1995.

---. "Banal Nationalism and the Imagining of Politics." *Everyday Nationhood: Theorising Culture, Identity and Belonging after Banal Nationalism*, edited by Michael Skey and Marco Antonsich, Palgrave Macmillan, 2017, pp. 307–21.

---. "Reflecting on a Critical Engagement with Banal Nationalism – Reply to Skey." *The Sociological Review*, vol. 57, no. 2, 2009, pp. 347–52. *JSTOR*, https://doi-org.proxy.ub.uni-frankfurt.de/10.1111/j.1467–954X.2009.01837.x.

Bitterman, Alex, and Daniel Baldwin Hess. "Gay Ghettoes Growing Gray: Transformation of Gay Urban Districts across North America Reflects Generational Change." *The Journal of American Culture*, vol. 39, no. 1, 2016, pp. 55–63. *JSTOR*, https://doi.org/10.1111 /jacc.12523.

Bixby, Scott. "LGBT Couples Can Be Refused Service under New Mississippi Law." *The Guardian*, 5 Apr. 2016, https://www.theguardian.com/world/2016/apr/05/mississippi-law-lgbt-discrimination-religious-moral-grounds. Accessed 8 Dec. 2019.

Blair, Leonardo. "'It's Offensive and Un-American,' Says Lawyer of Ruling Forcing Christian Baker to Produce Cakes for Gay Weddings." *Christian Post*, 2 June 2014, https://www. christianpost.com/news/its-offensive-and-un-american-says-lawyer-of-ruling-forcing-christian-baker-to-produce-cakes-for-gay-weddings.html. Accessed 20 Aug. 2018.

Blinder, Alan, and Richard Pérez-Peña. "Kentucky Clerk Denies Same-Sex Marriage Licenses, Defying Court." *The New York Times*, 1 Sept. 2015, https://www.nytimes.com/2015/09 /02/us/same-sex-marriage-kentucky-kim-davis.html?smid=pl-share. Accessed 20 May 2018.

Bloodsworth-Lugo, Mary K., and Carmen R. Lugo-Lugo. *Containing (Un) American Bodies: Race, Sexuality, and Post-9/11 Constructions of Citizenship*. Value Inquiry Book Series, vol. 219, 2010.

Bloom, Lisa. "The Supreme Court's New Gay Marriage Case Tests MLK's Dream of True Equality." *HuffPost*, 22 Mar. 2015, https://www.huffpost.com/entry/the-supreme-courts-new-ga_b_6503672. Accessed 20 May 2018.

Blue, Miranda. "FRC Spokesman: 'Un-American' LGBT Movement Just Wants To 'Punish People.'" *Right Wing Watch*, 13 Apr. 2016, https://www.rightwingwatch.org/post/frc-spokesman-un-american-lgbt-movement-just-wants-to-punish-people/. Accessed 20 Apr. 2019.

Bonikowski, Bart, and Paul DiMaggio. "Varieties of American Popular Nationalism." *American Sociological Review*, vol. 81, no. 5, 2016, pp. 949–80. *JSTOR*, https://www. jstor.org/stable/44245489.

Briley, Corey. "Argument Against Gay Marriage UnAmerican." *Statesboro Herald*, 29 May 2007, https://www.statesboroherald.com/local/letters-to-the-editor/argument-against-gay-marriage-unamerican/. Accessed 20 May 2018.

Brock, Bernhard L., et. al. *Making Sense of Political Ideology: The Power of Language in Democracy*. Rowman and Littlefield, 2005.

Brubaker, Rogers, and Frederick Cooper. "Beyond 'Identity.'" *Theory and Society*, vol. 29, no. 1, 2000, pp. 1–47. *JSTOR*, https://www.jstor.org/stable/3108478.

Bruni, Frank. "The New Gay Orthodoxy." *The New York Times*, 5 Apr. 2014, https://www.nytimes.com/2014/04/06/opinion/sunday/bruni-the-new-gay-orthodoxy.html. Accessed 20 May 2018.

Buchanan, Patrick Joseph. "Culture War Speech: Address to the Republican National Convention." *Voices of Democracy*, 17 Aug. 1992, https://voicesofdemocracy.umd.edu/buchanan-culture-war-speech-speech-text/. Accessed 15 Sept. 2018.

Burke, Kenneth. *A Grammar of Motives*. California UP, 1945.

Bush, Melanie E. L., and Rod Bush. *Tensions in the American Dream: Rhetoric, Reverie, or Reality*. Temple UP, 2015.

Caiazza, Tom. "Release: Anti-Gay Laws Drive Significantly Higher Rates of Poverty for LGBT People." *Center for American Progress*, 30 Sept. 2014, https://www.americanprogress. org/press/release/2014/09/30/98015/release-anti-gay-laws-drive-significantly-higher-rates-of-poverty-for-lgbt-people/. Accessed 24 Feb. 2015.

"Campaign Exposes Fissures Over Issues, Values and How Life Has Changed in the U.S." *Pew Research Center*, Mar. 2016, https://www.people-press.org/2016/03/31/campaign-exposes-fissures-over-issues-values-and-how-life-has-changed-in-the-u-s/. Accessed 3 May 2020.

Carothers, Cassie. "Trump Calls for 'Americanism, Not Globalism' in RNC Speech." *Global Citizen*, 22 July 2016, https://www.globalcitizen.org/de/content/trump-calls-for-americanism-in-rnc-speech/. Accessed 3 July 2020.

Carpenter, Dale. "Windsor Products: Equal Protection from Animus." *The Supreme Court Review*, vol. 2013, no. 1, 2014, pp. 183–286, https://www.jstor.org/stable/10.1086/6766 40. Accessed 10 June 2019.

"Certiorari." *Cornell Law School, Legal Information Institute*, https://www.law.cornell.edu/wex/certiorari. Accessed 14 May 2020.

Chalfant, Morgan. "Ted Cruz Blasts Jailing of Christian Kentucky Clerk as Un-American." *The Washington Free Beacon*, 4 Sept. 2015, https://freebeacon.com/politics/ted-cruz-blasts-jailing-of-christian-kentucky-clerk-as-un-american/. Accessed 20 Aug 2018.

Chasin, Alexandra. *Selling Out: The Lesbian and Gay Movement Goes to Market*. Palgrave Macmillan, 2001.

Chávez, Karma R. "The Precariousness of Homonationalism: The Queer Agency of Terrorism in Post-9/11 Rhetoric." *QED: A Journal in GLBTQ Worldmaking*, vol. 2, no. 3, 2015, pp. 32–58. *JSTOR*, https://www.jstor.org/stable/10.14321/qed.2.3.0032.

Cherlin, Andrew J. "American Marriage in the Early Twenty-First Century." *The Future of Children*, vol. 15, no. 2, 2005, pp. 33–55. *JSTOR*, https://www.jstor.org/stable/3556562.

"Chick-fil-A Sponsors Anti-Gay Marriage Conference." *PrideSource*, 3 Feb. 2011,https://pridesource.com/article/chick-fil-a-sponsors-anti-gay-marriage-conference-2/. Accessed 4 Apr. 2018.

"Citizens Fight Bill to Bar Uneducated." *The New York Times*, 10 Apr. 1916, https://www.nytimes.com/1916/04/10/archives/citizens-fight-bill-to-bar-uneducated-speakers-declare-exclusion-of.html. Accessed 10 Apr. 2018.

"Civil Unions in France?" *Explore France*, https://uk.france.fr/en/holiday-prep/civil-unions-france. Accessed 10 Oct. 2019.

Confessore, Nicholas, and Michael Barbaro. "New York Allows Same-Sex Marriage, Becoming Largest State to Pass Law." *The New York Times*, 24 June 2011, https://www.nytimes.com/2011/06/25/nyregion/gay-marriage-approved-by-new-york-senate.html. Accessed 14 May 2020.

"Congressional." *Daily National Intelligence*, 24 Aug. 1832. *Nineteenth Century U.S. Newspapers*.

"Constitutional Limitations on the Un-American Activities Committee." *Columbia Law Review*, vol. 47, no. 3, 1947, pp. 416–31. *JSTOR*, https://www.jstor.org/stable/111 8402.

Cooper, R. Clarke. "Chick-fil-A: Empty Calorie Diversion from Equality." *Huffpost*, 30 July 2012, https://www.huffpost.com/entry/chickfila-empty-calorie-d_b_1711185. 12 Apr. 2019.

Coulter, Anne. "Bradley Manning: Poster Boy for 'Don't Ask, Don't Tell.'" *Anne Coulter*, 1 Dec. 2010, http://www.anncoulter.com/columns/2010-12-01.html. Accessed 10 Dec. 2019.

Davis, Brandon A. *Don't Ask, Don't Tell: Background and Issues on Gays in the Military*. Nova Science Publishers, 2010.

De Cillia, Rudolph, et al. "The Discursive Construction of National Identities." *Discourse and Society*, vol. 10, no. 2, 1999, pp. 149–73. *JSTOR*, https://www.jstor.org/stable/10.3366/j.ctt1r26kb.

Dean, James Joseph. *Straights: Heterosexuality in Post-Closeted Culture*. NYU Press, 2014.

"Declaration of Independence: A Transcript." *National Archives*, https://www.archives.gov/founding-docs/declaration-transcript. Accessed 24 Mar. 2020.

DeFilippis, Joseph Nicholas. Introduction. *Queer Activism After Marriage Equality*, edited by Joseph Nicholas DeFilippis, et al., Routledge, 2018, pp. 1–14.

Deming, Adam. "Backlash Blunders: *Obergefell* and the Efficacy of Litigation to Achieve Social Change." *Journal of Constitutional Law*, vol. 19, no. 1, 2016, pp. 271–98, https://scholarship.law.upenn.edu/cgi/viewcontent.cgi?article=1623&context=jcl.

Dijk, Teun A. van. "Cognitive Context Models and Discourse." *Discourse in Society*, http://discourses.org/OldArticles/Cognitive%20context%20models%20and%20discourse.pdf. Accessed 23 Nov. 2019.

Doan, Long, et al. "Formal Rights and Informal Privileges for Same-Sex Couples: Evidence from a National Survey Experiment." *American Sociological Review*, vol. 79, no. 6, 2014, pp. 1172–1195. *JSTOR*, https://www.jstor.org/stable/43187584.

Dodds, Graham D. Crusade or Charade? The Religious Right and the Culture Wars." *Canadian Review of American Studies*, vol. 42, no. 3, 2012, pp. 274–300. *Project Muse*, https://doi.org/10.3138/cras.42.3.002.

Dombrink, John. "After the Culture War? Shifts and Continuities in American Conservatism." *Canadian Review of American Studies*, vol. 42, no. 3, 2012, pp. 301–21. *Project Muse*, https://doi.org/10.3138/cras.42.3.003.

Donner, Frank J. *The Un-Americans*. Ballantine Books, 1961.

Dowd, Maureen. "Presiding at Same-Sex Wedding, Ruth Bader Ginsburg Emphasizes the Word 'Constitution.'" *The New York Times,* 18 May 2015, https://www.nytimes.com/politics/first-draft/2015/05/18/presiding-at-same-sex-wedding-ruth-bader-ginsburg-emphasizes-a-key-word. Accessed 15 Jan. 2020.

Duggan, Lisa. "Making it Perfectly Queer." *Sex Wars: Sexual Dissent and Political Culture*, edited by Lisa Duggan and Nan. D. Hunter, Routledge, 1995, pp. 155–72.

---. "The New Homonormativity: The Sexual Politics of Neoliberalism." *Materializing Democracy: Toward a Revitalized Cultural Politics*, edited by Russ Castronovo and Dana D. Nelson, Duke UP, 2002, pp. 175–94.

---. "Queering the State." *Sex Wars: Sexual Dissent and Political Culture*, edited by Lisa Duggan and Nan. D. Hunter, Routledge, 1995, pp. 179–93.

---. *The Twilight of Equality? Neoliberalism, Cultural Politics, and the Attack on Democracy*." Beacon Press, 2003.

Eaklor, Vicki L. *Queer America: A GLBT History of the 20th Century.* Greenwood Publishing Group, 2008.

Eckholm, Eric. "Federal Judge Strikes Down Michigan's Ban on Same-Sex Marriage." *The New York Times*, 21 Mar. 2014, https://www.nytimes.com/2014/03/22/us/michigan-ban-on-same-sex-marriage-is-struck-down.html. Accessed 8 Dec. 2019.

---. "Oklahoma's Ban on Gay Marriage Is Unconstitutional, Judge Rules." *The New York Times*, 14 Jan. 2014, https://www.nytimes.com/2014/01/15/us/federal-judge-rejects-oklahomas-gay-marriage-ban.html. Accessed 8 Dec. 2019.

Edensor, Tim. *National Identity, Popular Culture and Everyday Life*. Berg Publishers, 2002.

El Hazzouri, Mohammed, et. al. "Out of the Closet: Easing the Backlash against Same-Sex Couples in Advertising." *The Conversation*, 5 Feb. 2019, http://theconversation.com/out-of-the-closet-easing-the-backlash-against-same-sex-couples-in-advertising-110740. Accessed 20 Jan. 2020.

Eleveld, Kerry. *Don't Tell Me to Wait: How the Fight for Gay Rights Changed America and Transformed Obama's Presidency.* Basic Books, 2015.

Erdal, Marta Bivand. "Negotiation Dynamics and Their Limits: Young People in Norway Deal with Diversity in the Nation." *Political Geography*, vol. 73, 2019, pp. 38–47. *Peace Research Institute Oslo*, doi: 10.1016/j.polgeo.2019.05.010.

Eskridge, William N. "The California Proposition 8 Case: What Is a Constitution For?" *California Law Review*, vol. 98, no. 4, 2010, pp. 1235–52. *JSTOR*, https://www.jstor.org/stable/27896710.

"Evil of Native-Ism." *Emancipator and Weekly Chronicle*, 17 July 1844, p. 47. *Nineteenth Century U.S. Newspapers*.

Faderman, Lillian. *The Gay Revolution: The Story of the Struggle*. Simon & Schuster, 2016.

Fairclough, Norman, and Ruth Wodak. "Critical Discourse Analysis." *Discourse Studies: A Multidisciplinary Introduction*, vol. 2, edited by Teun van Dijk, Sage, 1997, pp. 258–84. 2 vols.

Fang, Marina. "Tennessee Passes Anti-LGBT Counseling Bill." *HuffPost*, 11 Apr. 2016, https://www.huffpost.com/entry/tennessee-lgbt-counseling_n_570c4c4de4b0836057a23d63?guccounter=1&guce_referrer=aHR0cHM6Ly93d3cuZ29vZ2xlLmNvbS8&guce_referrer_sig=AQAAAKX3fPsSUnWLTj2MFWFWP51zkig8kKVXLgDoPrx0B64xBYCrjulDwTVx_HJ-l3Um7laqgfA1JLw6kZckJGpHlltL6X20UA9Ig_ZA3D9hv28EC TCPnIoJqfbIxMJ4N3Rbw-7YKU0NqxnBKTd1rMzq_vmb9DX9j9cdAEni1z0QQga X. Accessed 8 Dec. 2019.

Fathali, Heather. "The American DREAM: DACA, DREAMers, and Comprehensive Immigration Reform." *Seattle University Law Review*, vol. 37, no. 1,

2013, pp. 221–54. *HeinOnline*, https://heinonline-org.proxy.ub.uni-frankfurt.de/HOL/P?h=hein.journals/sealr37&i=305.

Felton, Ryan. "Kentucky Clerk Kim Davis Released from Jail after Judge Lifts Contempt Ruling." *The Guardian*, 8 Sept. 2015, https://www.theguardian.com/us-news/2015/sep/08/kentucky-clerk-kim-davis-released-from-jail. Accessed 8 Dec. 2019.

Fiorina, Morris, et. al. *Culture War? The Myth of a Polarized America.* 3rd ed. Longman, 2010.

Firestone, Shulamith. *The Dialectic of Sex: The Case for Feminist Revolution.* Women's Press, 1988.

Fischer, Bryan. "First, It's Unthinkable. Then, It's Permitted. Then, It's Mandatory." *American Family Association*, 21 Feb. 2019, https://www.afa.net/the-stand/culture/2019/02/first-its-unthinkable-then-its-permitted-then-its-mandatory/. Accessed 19 Oct. 2019.

Flores, Andrew R., and Scott Barclay. "Backlash, Consensus, Legitimacy, or Polarization: The Effect of Same-Sex Marriage Policy on Mass Attitudes." *Political Research Quarterly*, vol. 69, no. 1, 2016, pp. 43–56. *JSTOR*, www.jstor.org/stable/44018528.

Flory, Nancy. "Repeal Obergefell: Christian Group Holds Rally at the Supreme Court on the Fourth Anniversary of the Decision." *The Stream*, 26 June 2019, https://stream.org/protesting-obergefell-christian-group-holds-rally-at-the-supreme-court-on-the-fourth-anniversary-of-the-supreme-court-decision/. Accessed 3 Apr. 2020.

Fluck, Winfried. "American Cultural Studies." *English and American Studies: Theory and Practice*, edited by Martin Middeke et. al., Metzler, 2012, pp. 287–300.

---. "Theories of American Culture (and the Transnational Turn in American Studies)." *REAL – Yearbook of Research in English and American Literature*, vol. 23, 2007, pp. 59–77. John-F.-Kennedy-Institut, https://www.jfki.fu-berlin.de/en/v/publications_fluck/2000/fluck_theories_american_culture/Fluck_theorie_American_Culture.pdf.

Fontana, David, and Donald Braman. "Judicial Backlash or Just Backlash? Evidence from a National Experiment." *Columbia Law Review*, vol. 112, no. 4, 2012, pp. 731–99. *JSTOR*, www.jstor.org/stable/23238454.

"14 Supreme Court Cases: Marriage Is a Fundamental Right" *American Foundation for Equal Rights*, 19 July 2012, http://afer.org/blog/14-supreme-court-cases-marriage-is-a-fundamental-right/. Accessed 11 May 2020.

Fox, Jon E. "The Edges of the Nation: A Research Agenda for Uncovering the Taken-for-Granted Foundations of Everyday Nationhood." *Nations and Nationalism*, vol. 23, no. 1, 2017, pp. 26–47. *Wiley Online Library*, doi: 10.1111/nana.12269.

---, and Cynthia Miller-Idriss. "Everyday Nationhood." *Ethnicities*, vol. 8, no. 4, 2008, pp. 536–76. *SAGE*, doi:10.1177/1468796808088925.

---, and Maarten van Ginderachter. "Introduction: Everyday Nationalism's Evidence Problem." *Nations and Nationalism*, vol. 24, no. 3, 2018, pp. 546–52. *Wiley Online Library*, doi:10.1111/nana.12418.

Frank, Nathaniel. *Awakening: How Gays and Lesbians Brought Marriage Equality to America*. Belknap Press of Harvard UP, 2017.

Franklin, Cary. "Marrying Liberty and Equality: The New Jurisprudence of Gay Rights." *Virginia Law Review*, vol. 100, no. 5, 2014, pp. 817–91. *JSTOR*, https://www.jstor. org/stable/24362711.

Friedman, Barry, and Dahlia Lithwick. "What's Left?" *Slate*, 1 July 2013, https://slate.com/news-and-politics/2013/07/whats-left-of-the-progressive-cause-other-than-gay-marriage.html. Accessed 20 Aug. 2018.

Friedman, Max Paul. *Rethinking Anti-Americanism. The History of an Exceptional Concept in American Foreign Relations*. Cambridge UP, 2012.

Gage, Beverly. "How 'Un-American' Became the Political Insult of the Moment." *The New York Times Magazine*, 21 Mar. 2017, https://www.nytimes.com/2017/03/21/magazine/how-un-american-became-the-political-insult-of-the-moment.html. Accessed 23 Oct. 2019.

"A Game Changer – Thomas More Law Center Reveals National Strategy to Defend Traditional Marriage." *Thomas More Law Center*, http://www.thomasmore.org/news/game-changer-thomas-law-center-reveals-national-strategy-defend-traditional-marriage/. Accessed 10 Oct. 2019.

Gamson, Joshua. "The Intersection of Gay Street and Straight Street: Shopping, Social Class, and the New Gay Visibility." *Social Thought and Research*, vol. 26, 2005, pp. 4–18. *JSTOR*, doi:10.17161/STR.1808.5208.

Garner, Bryan A., editor. *Black's Law Dictionary*. 7th ed., West Group, 1999.

Gearan, Anne. "Trump Refuses to Acknowledge the Fraught History of Nationalism." *The New York Times*, 14 Nov. 2018, https://www.washingtonpost.com/politics/trump-refuses-to-acknowledge-the-fraught-history-of-nationalism/2018/11/13/35fd0694-e76a-11e8-a939-9469f1166f9d_story.html?noredirect=on. Accessed 8 Dec. 2019.

Geidner, Chris. "Prop 8 Team, Ted Olson and David Boies, To Fight Virginia Marriage Ban." *BuzzFeedNews*, 30 Sept. 2013, https://www.buzzfeednews.com/article/chrisgeidner/prop-8-team-ted-olson-and-david-boies-to-fight-virginia-marr. Accessed 10 Mar. 2020.

Gellner, Ernst. *Nations and Nationalism*. 2nd ed., Blackwell Publishing, 2006.

George, Ann, and Jack Selzer. *Kenneth Burke in the 1930s*. South Carolina UP, 2007.

George, Robert A. "Expressly Not 'Straight' Talk." *NBC Washington*, 17 Apr. 2009, https://www.nbcwashington.com/local/expressly-not-straight-talk/1889752/. Accessed 20 May 2018.

Gerstmann, Evan. "Litigating Same-Sex Marriage: Might the Courts Actually Be Bastions of Rationality?" *Political Science and Politics*, vol. 38, no. 2, 2005, pp. 217–20. *JSTOR*, http://www.jstor.org/stable/30044278.

Gill, Todd. "Proposed Bill Would Prohibit Future Civil Rights Ordinances." *Fayetteville Flyer*, 3 Feb. 2015. https://www.fayettevilleflyer.com/2015/02/03/proposed-bill-would-prohibit-future-civil-rights-ordinances/. Accessed 24 Feb. 2015.

Gilman, Greg. "Bill O'Reilly Calls White House's Gay Marriage Celebration 'Wrong and Insulting' (Video)." *The Wrap*, 30 June 2015, https://www.thewrap.com/bill-oreilly-calls-white-houses-gay-marriage-celebration-wrong-and-insulting-video/. Accessed 10 Sept. 2018.

Goldberg, Abbie E., and Katherine A. Kuvalanka. "Marriage (In)equality: The Perspectives of Adolescents and Emerging Adults with Lesbian, Gay, and Bisexual Parents." *National Council on Family Relations*, vol. 74, no. 1, 2012, pp. 34–52. *JSTOR*, https://www. jstor.org/stable/41329658.

Goldberg, Carey. "Vermont Gives Final Approval to Same-Sex Unions." *The New York Times*, 26 Apr. 2000, https://www.nytimes.com/2000/04/26/us/vermont-gives-final-approval-to-same-sex-unions.html. Accessed 18 Apr. 2020.

Goldman, Seth, and Paul R. Brewer. "From Gay Bashing to Gay Baiting." *Defending Same-Sex Marriage: The Freedom-to-Marry Movement: Education, Advocacy, Culture and the Media*, edited by Martin Dupuis and William A. Thompson, Praeger, 2006, 3 vols, pp. 103–28.

Goodall, Alex. "Two Concepts of Un-Americanism." *Journal of American Studies*, vol. 47, no. 4, 2013, pp. 925–42. *JSTOR*, doi:10.1017/S002187581 3001461.

Goode, J. Paul. "Guest Editor's Introduction: 'Everyday Nationalism in World Politics: Agents, Contexts, and Scale.'" *Nationalities Papers*, vol. 48, no. 6, 2020, pp. 974–982. *Cambridge Core*, doi: 10.1017/nps2020.73.

Goodman, Walter. *The Committee: The Extraordinary Career of the House Committee on Un-American Activities*. Farrar Strauß & Giroux, 1968.

Gray, Eliza. "Edith Windsor, The Unlikely Activist." *Time*, 11 Dec. 2013, http://poy.time.com/2013/12/11/runner-up-edith-windsor-the-unlikely-activist/. Accessed 10 June 2019.

Green, Adam Isaiah. "Queer Unions: Same-Sex Spouses Marrying Tradition and Innovation." *The Canadian Journal of Sociology*, vol. 35, no. 3, 2010, pp. 399–436. *JSTOR*, https://www.jstor.org/stable/10.2307/canajsocicahican.35.3.399.

Greer, Germaine. *The Female Eunuch*. Harper Perennial, 2006.

Grindstaff, Davin Allen. *Rhetorical Secrets: Mapping Gay Identity and Queer Resistance in Contemporary America*. Alabama UP, 2006.

Grondin, David. "Understanding Culture Wars through Satirical/Political Infotainment TV: Jon Stewart and *The Daily Show*'s Critique as Mediated Re-Enactment of the Culture War." *Canadian Review of American Studies*, vol. 42, no. 3, 2012, pp. 347–70. *Project Muse*, https://doi.org/10.3138/cras.42.3.005.

Guibernau, Montserrat. *Nationalisms: The Nation-State and Nationalism in the Twentieth Century.* Polity Press, 1996.

Haislop, Tadd. "What is the NFL's national anthem protest policy? Here are the rules for kneeling in 2020." *Sporting News*, 20 Sept. 2020, https://www.sportingnews.com/us/nfl/news/nfl-national-anthem-policy-2020-kneeling-protests/1o88fwivdxvqu1d8 nnbiw5dw3z. Accessed 9 Sept. 2021.

Halberstam, J. Jack. *Gaga Feminism: Sex, Gender, and the End of Normal.* Beacon Press, 2013.

Halberstam, Judith. *Female Masculinity.* Duke UP, 1998.

---. *The Queer Art of Failure.* Duke UP, 2011.

---. "What's that Smell? Queer Temporalities and Subcultural Lives." *International Journal of Cultural Studies*, vol. 6, no. 3, 2003, pp. 313–333. *SAGE*, https://doi.org/10.1177/13678779030063005.

Hall, Mirko M., and Jürgen Link. "From the 'Power of the Norm' to 'Flexible Normalism': Considerations after Foucault." *Cultural Critique*, no. 57, 2004, pp. 14–32. *JSTOR*, https://www.jstor.org/stable/4140757.

---."On the Contribution of Normalism to Modernity and Postmodernity." *Cultural Critique*, no. 57, 2004, pp. 33–46. *JSTOR*, https://www.jstor.org/stable/4140758.

Hall, Simon. "The American Gay Rights Movement and Patriotic Protest." *Journal of the History of Sexuality*, vol. 19, no. 3, 2010, p. 536–62. *JSTOR*, doi: 10.1353/sex.2010.0011.

---. "Americanism, Un-Americanism, and the Gay Rights Movement." *Journal of American Studies*, vol. 47, no. 4, 2013, pp. 1109–30. *JSTOR*, doi:10.1017/S00218758 1300145X.

---. *American Patriotism, American Protest: Social Movements Since the Sixties.* Pennsylvania UP, 2010.

Hallowell, Billy. "NFL Player Matt Birk Pens Anti-Gay Marriage Article: Silencing Those Opposed to Same-Sex Marriage Is 'Un-American.'" *The Blaze*, 2 Oct. 2012, https://www.theblaze.com/news/2012/10/02/nfl-player-mark-birk-pens-anti-gay-marriage-article-silencing-those-opposed-to-same-sex-marriage-is-un-american. Accessed 19 Apr. 2019.

Hanisch, Carol. "The Personal is Political." *Carol Hanisch*, Feb. 1969, http://www.carol hanisch.org/CHwritings/PIP.html. Accessed 29 Apr. 2020.

Harrison, Blake A. *The View from Vermont: Tourism and the Making of an American Rural Landscape.* Vermont UP, 2006.

Hawaii State, Supreme Court of Hawaii. *Baehr v. Lewin.* 5 May 1993. *Lambda Legal*, https://www.lambdalegal.org/sites/default/files/legal-docs/down

loads/baehr_hi_19930505_decision-hi-supreme-court.pdf. Accessed 10 June 2019.

Hawkesworth, Mary. "Neoliberalism and the Micropolitics of Domination in the United States." *Post-Neoliberalism in the Americas. International Political Economy Series,* edited by Laura Macdonald and Arne Ruckert, Palgrave Macmillan, 2009, pp. 167–83.

Hawkins, Richard A. "'Hitler's Bitterest Foe': Samuel Untermyer and the Boycott of Nazi Germany, 1933–1938." *American Jewish History*, vol. 93, no. 1, 2007, pp. 21–50. *JSTOR*, https://www.jstor.org/stable/23887264.

Hawley, George. *Making Sense of the Alt-Right*. Columbia UP, 2017.

Hay, Peter. "Recognition of Same-Sex Legal Relationships in the United States." *The American Journal of Comparative Law*, vol. 54, 2006, pp. 257–79. *JSTOR*, www.jstor.org/stable/20454539.

Hearn Jonathan, and Marco Antonsich. "Theoretical and Methodological Considerations for the Study of Banal and Everyday Nationalism." *Nations and Nationalism*, vol. 24., no. 3, 2018, pp. 594–605. *JSTOR*, doi. 10.1111/nana.12419.

Heinemann, Isabel. Introduction. *Inventing the Modern American Family. Family Values and Social Change in 20th Century United States*, Campus, 2012, pp. 7–28.

Hendricks Vincent F., and Mads Vestergaard. *Reality Lost: Markets of Attention, Misinformation and Manipulation*. Springer, 2019.

Herald, Seth. "Bloodshed in Charlottesville." *The Atlantic*, 12 Aug. 2017, https://www.theatlantic.com/national/archive/2017/08/charlottesville-photo-essay/53 6691/. Accessed 8 Dec. 2019.

Herbst Lewis, Carolyn. *Prescription for Heterosexuality: Sexual Citizenship in the Cold War Era*. North Carolina UP, 2013.

Hollibaugh, Amber, and Margot Weiss. "Queer Precarity and the Myth of Gay Affluence." New Labor Forum, vol. 24, no. 3, 2015, pp. 18–27. *JSTOR*, https://www.jstor.org/stable/24718618.

Holmes, David. "The Kim Davis Reality Show Begins and Ends with Discrimination." *Esquire*, 3 Sept. 2015, https://www.esquire.com/news-politics/a37637/kim-davis-discrimination/. Accessed 20 May 2018.

"Homosexuality." *Family Research Council*, www.frc.org/homosexuality. Accessed 12 Dec. 2018.

Hooper, Jeremy. "AFA Sr. Analyst: Marriage Equality 'as Indefensible as Slavery.'" *GLAAD*, 7 Oct. 2014, https://www.glaad.org/blog/afa-sr-analyst-marriage-equality-indefensible-slavery. Accessed 12 Apr. 2017.

Horowitz, Juliana Menasce. "Americans Less Accepting of Homosexuality than Other Westerners – Religion May Be One Reason." *Pew Research Center*, 12 June 2013, https://www.pewresearch.org/fact-tank/2013/06/12/americans-are-less-accepting-of-homosexuality-than-canadians-western-europeans-and-religion-may-be-one-explanation/. Accessed 10 Sept. 2018.

Hunter, James Davison. *Culture Wars: The Struggle to Define America*. 2nd ed. Basic Books, 1991.

"Independence Day in San Francisco." *Daily Evening Bulletin*, 5 July 1864, p. 5. *Nineteenth Century U.S. Newspapers*.

Indiana State, Senate, "Senate Enrolled Act 101." 2015. 119th General Assembly, 1st session. *Indiana House Republicans*, https://www.indianahouserepublicans.com/clientuploads/PDF/RFRA/SEA101%20RFRA%20Law.pdf. Accessed 14 May 2020.

"IRS Form 990 FY18." *Human Rights Campaign*, https://assets2.hrc.org/files/assets/resources/HRC-990-FY18.pdf. Accessed 19 May 2020.

"Is it un-American?" *The New York Times*, 6 July 1881, https://www.nytimes.com/1881/07/06/archives/is-it-unamerican.html. Accessed 10 Apr. 2018.

Jackson, Richard. "War on Terrorism." *Encyclopædia Britannica*, 12 May 2020, https://www.britannica.com/topic/war-on-terrorism. Accessed 19 May 2020.

Jäger, Siegfried. *Kritische Diskursanalyse. Eine Einführung*. 7th ed. Unrast, 2015.

Johnson, David K. *The Lavender Scare: The Cold War Persecution of Gays and Lesbians in the Federal Government*. Chicago UP, 2004.

Johnson, E. Patrick. *Sweet Tea: Black Gay Men of the South*. North Carolina UP, 2008.

Jones, Jeffrey M. "LGBT Identification Rises to 5.6% in Latest U.S. Estimate." *Gallup*, 24 Feb. 2021, https://news.gallup.com/poll/329708/lgbt-identification-rises-latest-estimate. aspx. Accessed 22 Aug. 2021.

Jones, Rhys, and Peter Merriman. "Hot, Banal and Everyday Nationalism: Bilingual Road Signs in Wales." *Political Geography*, vol. 28, no. 3, 2009, pp. 164–73. *SAGE*, https://doi.org/10.1177/0309132516649453.

Josephson, Jyl. "Citizenship, Same-Sex Marriage, and Feminist Critiques of Marriage." *Perspectives on Politics*, vol. 3, no. 2, 2005, pp. 269–84. *JSTOR*, https://www.jstor.org/stable/3688030.

Joynt, Carol Ross. "Michael Kaiser – Newly Married by Justice Ginsburg – on Love, Marriage, and What's Coming Up for the Kennedy Center." *Washingtonian*, 4 Sept. 2013, https://www.washingtonian.com/2013/09/04/michael-kaisernewly-married-by-justice-ginsburgon-love-marriage-and-whats-coming-up-for-the-kennedy/. Accessed 20 Nov. 2019.

Judt, Tony, and Denis Lacorne. *With Us or Against Us: Studies in Global Anti-Americanism*. Palgrave Macmillan, 2016.

"Just 38% of GOP Voters Say Party Would 'Solidly Unite' behind Trump." *Pew Research Center*, 31 Mar. 2016, https://www.people-press.org/2016/03/31/campaign-exposes-fissures-over-issues-values-and-how-life-has-changed-in-the-u-s/. Accessed 3 Mar. 2020.

Kaplan, Roger. "Americanism, Un-Americanism, Anti-Americanism." *Human Rights Review*, vol. 4, pp. 63–71, 2003. *Springer*, https://doi.org/10.1007/s12142–003–1013-x.

Kaplan, Sarah. "Mississippi's Senate Just Approved a Sweeping 'Religious Liberty' Bill That Critics Say Is the Worst Yet for LGBT Rights." *The Washington Post*, 31 Mar. 2016, https://www.washingtonpost.com/news/morning-mix/wp/2016/03/31/mississippis-senate-just-approved-a-sweeping-religious-liberty-bill-that-critics-say-is-the-worst-yet-for-lgbt-rights/. Accessed 10 July 2019.

Kaufmann, Eric. "Complexity and Nationalism." *Nations and Nationalism*, vol. 23, no.1, 2017, pp. 6–25. *JSTOR*, doi: 10.1111/nana.12270.

Kazin, Michael, editor, et al. *Princeton Encyclopedia of American Political History*. Vol. 1. Princeton, 2010. 2 vols.

Kazin, Michael, and Joseph A. McCartin, editors. *Americanism. New Perspectives on the History of an Ideal*. North Carolina UP, 2006.

K. G. S. "Water Colors by Pennell Shown at the Grand Central Galleries Strikingly Un-American in Feeling." *The New York Times*, 2 Aug. 1932, https://www.nytimes.com/1932/08/02/archives/water-colors-by-pennell-shown-at-grand-central-galleries-strikingly.html?searchResultPosition=1. Accessed 18 Apr. 2018.

King, Preston. "Being American." *Government and Opposition*, vol. 42, no. 4, 2007, pp. 593–625. *Cambridge UP*, https://doi.org/10.1111/j.1477–7053.2007.00237.x.

King, Samantha. "Virtually Normal. Mark Bingham, the War on Terror, and the Sexual Politics of Sport." *Journal of Sport and Social Issues*, vol. 33, no. 1, 2009, pp. 5–24. *SAGE*, https://doi.org/10.1177/0193723508328631.

Klarman, Michael J. "Brown and Lawrence (and Goodridge)." *Michigan Law Review*, vol. 104, no. 3, 2005, pp. 431–89. *JSTOR*, www.jstor.org/stable/30044507.

---. *From the Closet to the Altar: Courts, Backlash, and the Struggle for Same-Sex Marriage*. Oxford UP, 2012.

---. "Why Liberals Shouldn't Worry About a Backlash to the Same-Sex Marriage Ruling." Interview with Rick Shenkman. *History News Network*, 3 July 2015, http://historynewsnetwork.org/article/159870. Accessed 29 May 2018.

Klautke, Egbert. "Anti-Americanism in Twentieth Century Europe." *The Historical Journal*, vol. 54, pp. 1125–39. *Cambridge UP*, https://doi.org/10.1017/S0018246X11000276.

Klein, Ezra. "The Un-American Captain America." *Vox*, 18 May 2016, https://www.vox.com/2016/5/18/11692644/unamerican-captain-america-civil-war. Accessed 10 Feb. 2020.

Kmiec, Keenan D. "The Origin and Current Meanings of 'Judicial Activism.'" *California Law Review*, vol. 92, no. 5, 2004, pp. 1441–77. *JSTOR*, www.jstor.org/stable/3481421.

Knott, Eleanor. "Everyday Nationalism." *The State of Nationalism*, 2016, https://stateofnationalism.eu/article/everyday-nationalism/#article. Accessed 10 Oct. 2018.

Kohn, Hans. "Nationalism." *Encyclopædia Britannica*, 19 Feb. 2020, https://www.britannica.com/topic/nationalism/European-nationalism. Accessed 13 Mar. 2020.

Koller, Veronika. "Constructing (Non-)Normative Identities in Written Lesbian Discourse: A Diachronic Study." *Discourse & Society*, vol. 24, no. 5, 2013, pp. 572–89. *JSTOR*, https://www.jstor.org/stable/24441613.

Kortmann, Bernd. *English Linguistics: Essentials*. Cornelsen, 2005.

Krantz, Rachel. "What's Next for LGBTQ Rights After Marriage Equality? The Lawyer Who Defeated DOMA Gives Her Answer." *Bustle*, 27 Oct. 2015, https://www.bustle.com/articles/119673-whats-next-for-lgbtq-rights-after-marriage-equality-the-lawyer-who-defeated-doma-gives-her-answer. Accessed 23 May 2018.

Krieg, Gregory. "Newt Gingrich Wants New House Un-American Activities Committee." *CNN*, 14 June 2016, https://edition.cnn.com/2016/06/14/politics/newt-gingrich-house-un-american-activities-committee/. Accessed 10 June 2019.

Krutnik, Frank, et. al. Introduction. *'Un-American' Hollywood. Politics and Film in the Blacklist Era*. Rutgers UP, 2007, pp. 3–18.

Lambert, Bruce. "Frank J. Donner Is Dead at 82; A Lawyer in Civil Liberties Cases." *The New York Times*, 11 June 1993, https://www.nytimes.com/1993/06/11/obituaries/frank-j-donner-is-dead-at-82-a-lawyer-in-civil-liberties-cases.html. Accessed 11 May 2020.

Lampo, David. *A Fundamental Freedom: Why Republicans, Conservatives, and Libertarians Should Support Gay Rights*. Rowman & Littlefield Publishers, 2012.

Latour, Mark Louis. *American Government and the Vision of the Democrats*. UPA, 2007.

"The Legality of Homosexual Marriage." Anonymous author. *Yale Law Journal*, vol. 82, no. 3, 1973. *Yale Law School*, https://digitalcommons.law.yale.edu/ylj/vol82/iss3/7.

Leonard, Tom. "Tom Hanks Apologises for calling Mormons 'Un-American' for Supporting Gay Marriage Ban." *The Telegraph*, 25 Jan. 2009, https://www.telegraph.co.uk/news/celebritynews/4341062/Tom-Hanks-apologises-for-calling-Mormons-un-American-for-supporting-gay-marriage-ban.html. Accessed 20 May 2018.

Levin, Dan. "North Carolina Reaches Settlement on 'Bathroom Bill.'" *The New York Times*, 23 July 2019, https://www.nytimes.com/2019/07/23/us/north-carolina-transgender-bathrooms.html. Accessed 20 May 2020.

Lewis, Daniel, et. al. "Public Opinion and Judicial Behavior in Direct Democracy Systems: Gay Rights in the American States." *State Politics & Policy Quarterly*, vol. 14, no. 4, 2014, pp. 367–88. *JSTOR*, www.jstor.org/stable/24710973.

Lewis, George. "'An Amorphous Code': The Ku Klux Klan and Un-Americanism, 1915–1965." *Journal of American Studies*, vol. 47, no. 4, 2013, pp. 971–92. *JSTOR*, doi:10.1017/S0021875813001357.

---. "An Un-American Introduction." *Journal of American Studies*, vol. 47, no. 4, 2013, pp. 871–79. *JSTOR*, doi:10.1017/S0021875813001539.

---. "Un-Americans: Ideological Dissent, Patriotic Subversion and Isolating the 'Other' in the USA." *University of Leicester*, https://www2.le.ac.uk/departments/history/research/grants/PreviousProjects/un-americans-ideological-dissent-patriotic-subversion-and-isolating-the-other-in-the-usa. Accessed 1 Feb. 2020.

Leyva, Arturo. "Scapegoat Categories and Conflict Resolution in the History of Sport." *Sport History Review*, vol. 50, 2019, pp. 75–92. *EBSCO*, https://doi.org/10.1123/shr.2017–0036.

Li, Qiong, and Marilynn B. Brewer. "What Does It Mean to Be an American? Patriotism, Nationalism, and American Identity after 9/11." *Political Psychology*, vol. 25, no. 5, 2004, pp. 727–39. *JSTOR*, https://www.jstor.org/stable/3792341.

Lincoln, Mileka. "Judge Rules for State, Says Same-Sex Marriage in Hawaii is Legal." *Hawaii News Now*, 14 Nov. 2013, https://www.hawaiinewsnow.com/story/23971261/breaking/. Accessed 18 Mar. 2020.

Linker, Damon. "Gay Marriage Won. Now Comes the Hard Part: Protecting Religious Freedom." *The Week*, 30 June 2015, https://theweek.com/articles/563691/gay-marriage-won-now-comes-hard-part-protecting-religious-freedom. Accessed 20 Oct. 2018.

Liptak, Adam. "Supreme Court Delivers Tacit Win to Gay Marriage." *The New York Times*, 6 Oct. 2014, https://www.nytimes.com/2014/10/07/us/denying-review-justices-clear-way-for-gay-marriage-in-5-states.html. Accessed 23 Mar. 2020.

Llewellyn, Cheryl. "Homonationalism and Sexual Orientation-Based Asylum Cases in the United States." *Sexualities*, vol. 20, no. 5–6, 2017, pp. 682–98. *SAGE*, https://doi.org/10.1177/1363460716645803.

Long-Droppert, Verity. "When Opposites Attract: The Rise and Fall of the 'Defense of Marriage Act' within a Neoliberal Hegemonic Framework." *Australasian Journal of American Studies*, vol. 34, no. 1, 2015, pp. 43–59. *JSTOR*, https://www.jstor.org/stable/44779752.

Loveland, Ian. "The Sexual Orientation Cases." *British Journal of American Legal Studies*, vol. 6, no. 1, 2017, pp. 59–83. *Sciendo*, doi: 10.1515/bjals-2017–0005.

Lütjen, Torben. *Amerika im Kalten Bürgerkrieg*. Wbg Theiss, 2020.

Maitland, Sarah. *What is Cultural Translation?* Bloomsburg Academic, 2017.

"Majority of Public Favors Same-Sex Marriage, But Divisions Persist." *Pew Research Center*, 14 May 2019, https://www.people-press.org/2019/05/14/majority-of-public-favors-same-sex-marriage-but-divisions-persist/. Accessed 3 Mar. 2020.

Malcolm, Donald. "Talk of the Town. News and Comment." *The New Yorker*, 3 Sept. 1966, https://www.newyorker.com/magazine/1966/09/10/comment-5058. Accessed 19 Jan. 2020.

Manning, Chelsea E. "The Years Since I Was Jailed for Releasing the 'War Diaries' Have Been a Rollercoaster." *The Guardian,* 27 May 2015, https://www.theguardian.com/commentisfree/2015/may/27/anniversary-chelsea-manning-arrest-war-diaries. Accessed 11 Dec. 2019.

Mansfield, Justine. "Victorian Era Not So Golden, Nostalgia for It Found Unjustified and Also Un-American." *The New York Times*, 2 May 1933, https://www.nytimes.com/1933/05/07/archives/victorian-era-not-so-golden-nostalgia-for-it-found-unjustified-and.html. Accessed 18 Apr. 2018.

Mantyla, Kyle. "Fischer: Gay Sex Is 'Domestic Terrorism. I Don't Know What Else You'd Call It.'" *Right Wing Watch*, 15 Sept. 2010, https://www.rightwingwatch.org/post/fischer-gay-sex-is-domestic-terrorism-i-dont-know-what-else-youd-call-it/. Accessed 13 Dec. 2019.

Marchia, Joseph, and Jamie M. Sommer. "(Re)Defining Heteronormativity." *Sexualities*, vol. 22, no. 3, 2019, pp. 267–95. *SAGE*, https://doi.org/10.1177/1363460717741801.

Martin, Edward J. "Healthcare Policy Legislation and Administration: Patient Protection and Affordable Care Act of 2010." *Journal of Health and Human Services Administration*, vol. 37, no. 4, 2015, pp. 407–11. *JSTOR*, www.jstor.org/stable/24459701.

Martin, Ruth. "Operation Abolition: Defending the Civil Liberties of the 'Un-American,' 1957–1961." *Journal of American Studies*, vol. 47, no. 4, 2013, pp. 1043–63. *JSTOR*, doi:10.1017/S0021875813001345.

Massachusetts State, Massachusetts Supreme Judicial Court. *Goodridge v. Department of Public Health*. 18 Nov. 2003. *Massachusetts Supreme Court*, http://masscases.com/cases/sjc/440/440mass309.html. Accessed 10 June 2019.

Mayer, Tamar. *Gender Ironies of Nationalism: Sexing the Nation*. Taylor and Francis, 2012.

McAdam, Doug, and Karina Kloos. *Deeply Divided: Racial Politics and Social Movements in Postwar America*. Oxford UP, 2014.

McCain, Meghan. "Why the New York GOP Should Embrace Gay Marriage." *New York Daily News*, 22 May 2009, http://articles.nydailynews.com/2009-05-22/news/17923273_1_marriage-bill-marriage-equality-log-cabin-republican. Accessed 11 Feb. 2015.

McCarthy, Justin. "U.S. Support for Gay Marriage Stable, at 63%." *Gallup*, 22 May 2019, https://news.gallup.com/poll/257705/support-gay-marriage-stable.aspx. Accessed 23 Feb. 2020.

---. "Record-High 70% in U.S. Support Same-Sex Marriage." *Gallup*, 8 June 2021, https://news.gallup.com/poll/350486/record-high-support-same-sex-marriage.aspx. Accessed 22 Aug. 2021.

McConnell, Jerry. "Five Grossly Un-American Supreme Court Justices Have Ruled Against Traditional Marriages." *Canada Free Press*, 12 July 2015, https://canadafreepress.com/article/five-grossly-un-american-supreme-court-justices-have-ruled-against-traditio. Accessed 19 Apr. 2019.

McDermott, Kevin. "Same-Sex Marriage to Be Legal in Illinois as of June; 15th State to Approve it." *STL Today*, 6 Nov. 2013, https://www.stltoday.com/news/local/govt-and-politics/same-sex-marriage-to-be-legal-in-illinois-as-of/article_fc4d5951-df47-5aa5-bfcf-5f78b4460fa6.html. Accessed 14 Feb. 2015.

McFadden, Robert D. "Edith Windsor, Whose Same-Sex Marriage Fight Led to Landmark Ruling, Dies at 88." *The New York Times*, 12 Sept. 2017, https://www.nytimes.com/2017/09/12/us/edith-windsor-dead-same-sex-marriage-doma.html. Accessed 8 Apr. 2020.

McKay, Hollie. "Tom Hanks Says Mormon Supporters of Proposition 8 'Un-American.'" *Fox News*, 16 Jan. 2009, https://www.foxnews.com/story/tom-hanks-says-mormon-supporters-of-proposition-8-un-american. Accessed 10 Feb. 2015.

McKinley, Jesse. "Same-Sex Marriage Ban Is Tied to Obama Factor." *The New York Times*, 20 Sept. 2008, https://www.nytimes.com/2008/09/21/us/politics/21gay.html. Accessed 16 Aug. 2019.

McVeigh, Rory, and Maria-Elena D. Diaz. "Voting to Ban Same-Sex Marriage: Interests, Values, and Communities. *American Sociological Review*, vol. 74., 2009, pp. 891–915. *SAGE*, https://doi.org/10.1177/000312240907400603.

Messner, Thomas. "Religion and Morality in the Same-Sex Marriage Debate." *The Heritage Foundation*, 20 July 2010, https://www.heritage.org/marriage-and-family/report/religion-and-morality-the-same-sex-marriage-debate. Accessed 12 Dec. 2018.

Metz, Daniel. "Religion Bills Ignite Debate." *Indiana Daily Student*, 17 Feb. 2015, https://www.idsnews.com/article/2015/02/religion-bills-ignite-debate. Accessed 24 Feb. 2018.

Meyer, Doug. "Omar Mateen as US Citizen, Not Foreign Threat: Homonationalism and LGBTQ Online Representations of the Pulse Nightclub Shooting." *Sexualities*, 2019, pp. 1–20. *SAGE*, https://doi.org/10.1177%2F1363460719826361.

"*Miller v. Davis*." *ACLU*, 23 Jan. 2019, https://www.aclu.org/cases/miller-v-davis. Accessed 20 Mar. 2020.

Miller, Zeke J. “More Than 300 Republicans Call on Supreme Court to Recognize Gay Marriage Nationally.” *Time*, 5 Mar. 2015, https://time.com/3734626/gay-marriage-supreme-court-republicans/. Accessed 10 Mar. 2016.

Millet, Kate. *Sexual Politics*. Illinois UP, 2000.

Minnesota State, Supreme Court of Minnesota. “*Baker v. Nelson*.” 15 Oct. 1971. *Justitia US Law*, https://law.justia.com/cases/minnesota/supreme-court/1971/43009-1.html. Accessed 18 Mar. 2020.

Mole, Richard CM. “Homonationalism: Resisting Nationalist Co-Optation of Sexual Diversity.” *Sexualities*, vol. 20, no. 5–6, 2917, pp. 660–62. *SAGE*, doi: 10.1177/1363460716645800.

Montgomery, Peter. “The Fight for LGBT Equality is Not Over.” *The American Prospect*, 16 Apr. 2015, https://prospect.org/justice/fight-lgbt-equality/. Accessed 14 May 2020.

Moreau, Julie. “Longtime Gay-Rights Opponent Tony Perkins Named to U.S. Religious Freedom Panel.” *NBC News*, 17 May 2018, https://www.nbcnews.com/feature/nbc-out/longtime-gay-rights-opponent-tony-perkins-named-u-s-religious-n875016. Accessed 20 Mar. 2020.

Motschenbacher, Heiko, and Martin Stegu. “Introduction: Queer Linguistic Approaches to Discourse.” *Discourse & Society*, vol. 24, no. 5, 2013, pp. 519–35. *JSTOR*, https://www.jstor.org/stable/24441610.

Movsesian, Mark. “Same-Sex Marriage and Our New Religious Politics.” *First Things*, 23 July 2015, https://www.firstthings.com/blogs/firstthoughts/2015/07/same-sex-marriage-and-our-new-religious-politics. Accessed 20 May 2018.

“Multiple Editorial Items.” *Daily National Intelligencer*, 13 Nov. 1865. *Nineteenth Century U.S. Newspapers*.

“Nationalism.” *Lexico by Oxford*, https://www.lexico.com/definition/nationalism. Accessed 10 Feb. 2020.

Neuborne, Burt. “An Overview of the Bill of Rights.” *Fundamentals of American Law*, edited by Alan B. Morrison, Oxford UP, 1996, pp. 83–127.

Nyong’o, Tavia. Foreword to 2017 Edition. *Terrorist Assemblages: Homonationalism in Queer Times*, by Jasbir K. Puar, Duke UP, 2017, pp. xi–xvi.

O’Reilly, Bill. “Playing Chicken with Gay Marriage.” *Washington Examiner*, 3 Aug. 2012, https://www.washingtonexaminer.com/playing-chicken-with-gay-marriage. Accessed 19 Oct. 2019.

Obama, Barack. “Transcript: Robin Roberts ABC News Interview with President Obama.” Interview with Robin Roberts. *ABC News*, 9 May 2012, https://abcnews.go.com/Politics/transcript-robin-roberts-abc-news-interview-president-obama/story?id= 16316043. Accessed 4 May 2020.

Obergefell, Jim. “Jim Obergefell: Edie Windsor, My Hero and My Friend.” *The Washington Post*, 13 Sept. 2017, https://www.washingtonpost.com/opinions/

jim-obergefell-edie-windsor-my-hero-and-my-friend/2017/09/13/51b822de-9896-11e7-87fc-c3f7ee4035c 9_story.html. Accessed 13 Dec. 2019.

"Ohio." *New-York Spectator*, 27 Dec. 1838. *Nineteenth Century U.S. Newspapers.*

Olson, Ted. "Ted Olson on Debate Over Judicial Activism and Same-Sex Marriage." Interview with Chris Wallace. *Fox News*, 8 Aug. 2010, https://www.foxnews.com/transcript/ted-olson-on-debate-over-judicial-activism-and-same-sex-marriage. Accessed 9 May 2020.

Olson, Theodore B. "The Conservative Case for Gay Marriage." *Newsweek*, 8 Jan. 2010, https://www.newsweek.com/conservative-case-gay-marriage-70923. Accessed 10 June 2019.

"Our Un-American Citizens." *The New York Times*, 25 Apr. 1886, https://timesmachine.nytimes.com/timesmachine/1886/04/25/103104465.html?pageNumber=8. Accessed 28 Apr. 2020.

Parker, Annise et al. "Commentary: Same-Sex Marriage Laws Promote Equality, Prosperity." *Houston Chronicle*, 6 Mar. 2012, https://www.chron.com/opinion/outlook/article/Same-sex-marriage-laws-promote-equality-3386910.php. Accessed 20 May 2018.

"The Partisan Divide on Political Values Grows Even Wider." *Pew Research Center*, 5 Oct. 2017, https://www.people-press.org/2017/10/05/the-partisan-divide-on-political-values-grows-even-wider/. Accessed 26 Apr. 2020.

"Partisanship and Political Animosity in 2016." *Pew Research Center*, 22 June 2016, https://assets.pewresearch.org/wp-content/uploads/sites/5/2016/06/06-22-16-Partisanship-and-animosity-release.pdf. Accessed 20 Apr. 2020.

"Paul Ryan Says Gay Marriage Is Not An 'American' Or 'Universal Human Value.'" *Huffpost*, 25 Sept. 2012, https://www.huffpost.com/entry/paul-ryan-gay-marriage-universal-human-value-_n_1914155. Accessed 20 Apr. 2019.

"Paying an Unfair Price: The Financial Penalty for Being LGBT in America." *Center for American Progress* and *Movement Advancement Project*, 30 Sept. 2014, https://www.lgbtmap.org/file/paying-an-unfair-price-full-report.pdf. Accessed 29 Apr. 2020.

Pei, Minxin. "The Paradoxes of American Nationalism." *Foreign Policy*, no. 136, 2003, pp. 30–37. *JSTOR*, https://www.jstor.org/stable/3183620.

Perkins, Tony. "Tony Perkins on CBS Face the Nation." Interview. *Family Research Council*, 25 Mar. 2013, https://www.frcblog.com/2013/03/tony-perkins-cbs-face-nation/. Accessed 13 Aug. 2018.

Peters, Jeremy W. "G.O.P. Senator Says He Has a Gay Son, and Backs Gay Marriage." *The New York Times*, 15 Mar. 2013, https://www.nytimes.com/2013/03/16/us/politics/ohios-portman-says-he-supports-gay-marriage.html. Accessed 10 June 2019.

Phy-Olsen, Allene. *Same-Sex Marriage: Historical Guides to Controversial Issues in America.* Greenwood, 2006.

"Plea for Big Navy Scored by Pastor." *The New York Times*, 4 May 1908, https://www.nytimes.com/1908/05/04/archives/plea-for-big-navy-scored-by-pastor-dr-jefferson-declares-roosevelts.html. Accessed 10 Apr. 2018.

Posner, Richard A. "The Rise and Fall of Judicial Self-Restraint." *California Law Review*, vol. 100, no. 3, 2012, pp. 519–56. *JSTOR*, www.jstor.org/stable/23249564.

"Prop 8: California Gay Marriage Ban Ruled Unconstitutional." *The Guardian*, 7 Feb. 2012, https://www.theguardian.com/world/blog/2012/feb/07/prop-8-california-appeal-live. Accessed 3 Mar. 2018.

Prothero, Stephen. "Why Conservatives Start Culture Wars and Liberals Win Them." *The Washington Post*, 29 Jan. 2016, https://www.washingtonpost.com/opinions/why-conservatives-start-culture-wars-and-liberals-win-them/2016/01/29/f89d0b2c-b658-11e5-a842–0feb51d1d124_story.html. Accessed 10 Jan. 2020.

---. *Why Liberals Win the Culture Wars (Even When They Lose Elections): The Battles That Define America from Jefferson's Heresies to Gay Marriage*. Harper One, 2016.

Puar, Jasbir. "Academic and Activist Assemblages: An Interview with Jasbir Puar." Puar in interview with Naomi Greyser. *American Quarterly*, vol. 64, no. 4, 2012, pp. 841–43. *JSTOR*, https://www.jstor.org/stable/41809535.

---. "Rethinking Homonationalism." *International Journal of Middle East Studies*, vol. 45, no. 2, 2013, pp. 336–39. *JSTOR*, https://www.jstor.org/stable/43302999.

---. *Terrorist Assemblages. Homonationalism in Queer Times*. Duke UP, 2017.

Pugh, Tison. *The Queer Fantasies of the American Family Sitcom*. Rutgers UP, 2018.

Raghavan, Gautam. "Obama Administration Statements on the Supreme Court's DOMA Ruling." *Obama White House*, 27 June 2013, https://obamawhitehouse.archives.gov/blog/2013/06/27/obama-administration-statements-supreme-court-s-doma-ruling. Accessed 10 June 2019.

Raha Iranian Feminist Collective. "After Marriage, Redefining Freedom in the Crosshairs of Empire and Dictatorship: Observations Towards a New Politics of Sexuality." *Queer Activism After Marriage Equality*, edited by Joseph Nicholas DeFilippis et al., Routledge, 2018, pp. 153–61.

Ramírez, Catherine S. "The New Wealth Test for Immigrants Is Un-American." *The New York Times*, 24 Feb. 2020, https://www.nytimes.com/2020/02/24/opinion/trump-immigration-public-charge.html. Accessed 1 Apr. 2020.

"The Reason Why." *North American*, 28 May 1894, p. 4. *Nineteenth Century U.S. Newspapers*.

Reintsma, Mary. *The Political Economy of Welfare Reform in the United States*. Locke Institute Series, 2007.

"Religious Beliefs Underpin Opposition to Homosexuality." *Pew Research Center*, 18 Nov. 2003, https://www.pewforum.org/2003/11/18/religious-beliefs-underpin-opposition-to-homosexuality/. 20 Nov. 2019.

"A Reply to Wm. James." *North American*, 8 Aug. 1894, p. 4. *Nineteenth Century U.S. Newspapers*.

Richardson, Diane. *Sexuality and Citizenship*. Wiley, 2017.

Roberts, John. Dissenting opinion. *Obergefell v. Hodges*. 26 June 2015, *Supreme Court of the United States*, https://www.supremecourt.gov/opinions/14pdf/14-556_3204.pdf. Accessed 3 Feb. 2018.

---. Dissenting opinion. *United States v. Windsor*. 26 June 2013. *Supreme Court of the United States*, https://www.supremecourt.gov/opinions/12pdf/12-307_6j37.pdf. Accessed 23 Oct. 2018.

Robertson, Brandan. "For the SBC, Fighting Marriage Equality Is Actually About Upholding Discrimination." *Patheos*, 13 Feb. 2015, https://www.patheos.com/blogs/revangelical/2015/02/13/for-the-sbc-fighting-marriage-equality-is-all-about-upholding-discrimination.html. Accessed 20 May 2018.

Robertson, Campbell. "Roy Moore, Alabama Chief Justice, Suspended Over Gay Marriage Order." *The New York Times*, 30 Sept. 2016, https://www.nytimes.com/2016/10/01/us/roy-moore-alabama-chief-justice.html. Accessed 20 Aug. 2018.

---, and Elizabeth Dias. "United Methodist Church Announces Plan to Split Over Same-Sex Marriage." *The New York Times*, 3 Jan. 2020, https://www.nytimes.com/2020/01/03/us/methodist-split-gay-marriage.html. Accessed 20 Apr. 2020.

Robinson, Stephen. "At CNN Town Hall, Democrats Talk About LGBTQ People Like They Are People." *Wonkette*, 11 Oct. 2019, https://www.wonkette.com/democrats-talk-about-lgbtq-at-cnn-equality-town-hall-as-if-theyre-equal-people. Accessed 19 Mar. 2020.

Roche, Lisa Riley. "Petition Supporting Traditional Marriage Delivered to Gov. Herbert." *Deseret News*, 5 Sept. 2014, https://www.deseret.com/2014/9/5/20547983/petition-supporting-traditional-marriage-delivered-to-gov-herbert#traditional-marriage-supporters-submit-a-binder-containing-the-first-names-of-18682-people-who-signed-a-petition-to-show-their-support-for-traditional-marriage-at-the-capitol-in-salt-lake-city-on-friday-sept-5–2014-the-petition-was-accepted-by-tiffany-clason-director-of-constituent-services-on-behalf-of-gov-gary-herbert. Accessed 21 Apr. 2019.

Roseneil, Sasha, et al. "Changing Landscapes of Heteronormativity: The Regulation and Normalization of Same-Sex Sexualities in Europe." *Social Politics: International Studies in Gender, State and Society*, vol. 20, no. 2, 2013, pp. 165–99. *Project Muse*, https://muse.jhu.edu/article/510619.

Rosenwald, Michael S. "How Jim Obergefell Became the Face of the Supreme Court Gay Marriage Case." *The Washington Post*, 6 Apr. 2015, https://www.

washingtonpost.com/local/how-jim-obergefell-became-the-face-of-the-supreme-court-gay-marriage-case/2015/04/06/3740433c-d958-11e4-b3f2-607bd612aeac_story.html. Accessed 8 Dec. 2019.

Rothman, Lily. “The Long History Behind Donald Trump’s ‘America First’ Foreign Policy.” *Time*, 28 Mar. 2016, https://time.com/4273812/america-first-donald-trump-history/. Accessed 20 May 2020.

Sadler, Brook J. “Re-thinking Civil Unions and Same-Sex Marriage.” *The Monist*, vol. 91, no. 3/4, 2008, pp. 578–605. *JSTOR*, https://www.jstor.org/stable/27904099.

“Same-Sex Marriage.” *The Church of Jesus Christ of Latter-Day Saints*, Mar. 2014, https://www.churchofjesuschrist.org/study/manual/gospel-topics/same-sex-marriage?lang=eng. Accessed 26 Apr. 2020.

Santorum, Rick. “Rick Santorum: Obamacare Is ‘Un-American.’” Interview with Mike Huckabee. *Fox News*, 18 Nov. 2013, https://video.foxnews.com/v/2847775946001#sp=show-clips. Accessed 22 May 2020.

“SB 10 – Authorizes Same-Sex Marriage – Illinois Key Vote.” *VoteSmart*, https://votesmart.org/bill/16147/46321/authorizes-same-sex-marriage#.Xr0BJBMzai4. Accessed 14 May 2020.

Scalia, Antonin. Dissenting opinion. *Obergefell v. Hodges*. 26 June 2015. *Supreme Court of the United States*, https://www.supremecourt.gov/opinions/14pdf/14-556_3204.pdf. Accessed 3 Feb. 2018.

---. Dissenting opinion. *Romer v. Evans*. 20 May 1996. *FindLaw*, https://caselaw.findlaw.com/us-supreme-court/517/620.html. Accessed 10 Nov. 2019.

---. Dissenting opinion. *United States v. Windsor*. 26 June 2013. *Supreme Court of the United States*, https://www.supremecourt.gov/opinions/12pdf/12-307_6j37.pdf. Accessed 23 Oct. 2018.

Scalia, Antonin, and Bryan A. Garner. *Reading Law: The Interpretation of Legal Texts*. West Academic Publishing, 2012.

Schlesinger, Arthur M. Jr. *The Politics of Hope*. Houghton Mifflin, 1962.

Schmidt, Steve. “Schmidt Steve Biography.” *ProCon.org*, 17 Mar. 2011, https://gaymarriage. procon.org/view.source.php?sourceID=010635. Accessed 12 Dec. 2018.

Schraub, David. “The Price of Victory: Political Triumphs and Judicial Protection in the Gay Rights Movement.” *The University of Chicago Law Review*, vol. 77, no. 3, 2010, pp. 1437–71. *JSTOR*, www.jstor.org/stable/40962091.

Schropp, Abraham S. “Some Words of Championship.” *North American*, 11 June 1894, p. 4. *Nineteenth Century U.S. Newspapers*.

Scudera, Domenick. “That’s Me in the Corner, Losing My Religion.” *HuffPost*, 6 Dec. 2017, https://www.huffpost.com/entry/kim-davis_b_8109914. Accessed 20 May 2018.

Sedensky, Matt. “Justice Questions Way Court Nominees are Grilled.” *Way-*

back Machine, 14 May 2010, https://web.archive.org/web/20100605163057/http://www.google.com/hostednews/ap/article/ALeqM5iWhwP-GmuptNw-uw8t8Z_lb1YV2QD9FMQKRG0. Accessed 10 June 2019.

"Senate Bill 568." *Indiana General Assembly: 2015 Session*, http://iga.in.gov/legislative/2015/bills/senate/568/#digest-heading. Accessed 14 May 2020.

Sensenbrenner, Jim. "The American Health Care Act is a Positive Step Forward for Health Care." *Jim Sensenbrenner*, 23 Mar. 2017, https://sensenbrenner.house.gov/2017/3/the-american-health-care-act-is-a-positive-step-forward-for-health-care. Accessed 1 Apr. 2020.

"A Shameful Veto." *North American*, 26 May 1894, p. 4. *Nineteenth Century U.S. Newspapers*.

Shesgreen, Deidre. "Massie Rallies to Defense of Rowan Clerk." *Cincinnati.com*, 2 Sept. 2015, https://eu.cincinnati.com/story/news/politics/2015/09/02/paul-clerks-gay-marriage-defiance-american-way/71584648/. Accessed 20 Aug. 2018.

Siegel, Reva B. "Community in Conflict: Same-Sex Marriage and Backlash." *UCLA Law Review*, vol 64, 2017, pp. 1730–69. *SSRN*, https://papers.ssrn.com/sol3/papers.cfm? abstract_id=2914674.

Silverman, Lewis A. "Suffer the Little Children: Justifying Same-Sex Marriage from the Perspective of a Child of the Union." *West Virginia Law Review*, vol. 102, 1999, pp. 411–58. *West Virginia University Research Repository*, https://researchrepository.wvu.edu/wvlr/vol102/iss2/7?utm_source=researchrepository.wvu.edu%2Fwvlr%2Fvol102%2Fiss2%2F7&utm_medium=PDF&utm_campaign=PDFCoverPages.

Skey, Michael. *National Belonging and Everyday Life: The Significance of Nationhood in an Uncertain World*. Palgrave Macmillan, 2011.

---, and Marco Antonsich. *Everyday Nationhood: Theorising Culture, Identity and Belonging after Banal Nationalism*. Palgrave Macmillan, 2017.

Smith, Anthony. "The Limits of Everyday Nationalism." Ethnicities, vol. 8, no. 4, 2008, pp. 563–73. SAGE, doi:10.1177/1468796808088925.

Smith, Ralph R, and Russel R. Windes. *Progay/Antigay: The Rhetorical War over Sexuality*. Sage Publications, 2002.

Smith, Tovia. "Lawyer Reflects on Nation's First Gay Marriages: 'The Cage Had Been Lifted.'" *NPR*, 15 May 2014, https://www.npr.org/2014/05/15/312674228/a-decade-of-same-sex-marriage-began-in-massachusetts?t=1580477101806. Accessed 19 Apr. 2019.

Spencer, Leland G., and Helane Androne. "Intersectionality in the Classroom: Black Lives Matter as a Consummate Example." *Journal of Pan African Studies*, vol. 12, no. 9, 2019, p.77–94. *JAPS*, http://www.jpanafrican.org/docs/vol12no9/AJPAS_BLM_Black%20Lives%20Matter_Helane%20and%20Spencer_16%20April%202019_Article%206_III.pdf.

"Statement of Marvin Burrows before the Committee on the Judiciary, United States Senate. Submitted for the Record of a Hearing Entitled 'S.598, The Respect for Marriage Act: Assessing the Impact of DOMA on American Families.'" 20 July 2011, https://www.leahy.senate.gov/imo/media/doc/RFM-Individuals-Packet.pdf. Accessed 30 Apr. 2020.

Steele, Brian. "Inventing Un-American." *Journal of American Studies*, vol. 47, no. 4, 2013, pp. 881–902. *JSTOR*, doi:10.1017/S0021875813001394.

Stein, Arlene. *The Stranger Next Door: The Story of a Small Community's Battle over Sex, Faith, and Civil Rights*. Beacon Press, 2002.

Stern, Marc Joseph. "Attorney General Jeff Sessions Would Spell Absolute Disaster for Civil Rights in America." *Slate*, 18 Nov. 2016, https://slate.com/human-interest/2016/11/attorney-general-jeff-sessions-would-doom-civil-rights-law.html. Accessed 8 Feb. 2019.

---. "Biden's True Legacy: He Was Obama's Conscience on LGBTQ Rights." *Slate*, 21 Oct. 2015, https://slate.com/human-interest/2015/10/joe-bidens-true-legacy-is-as-obamas-conscience-on-lgbtq-rights.html. Accessed 10 June 2019.

Stevenson, Michael R., and Markie Oliver. "Deconstructing Arguments against Same-Sex Marriage." *Defending Same-Sex Marriage: The Freedom-to-Marry Movement: Education, Advocacy, Culture, and the Media*, edited by Martin Dupuis and William A. Thompson, Praeger, 2006, 3 vols, pp. 77–90.

Stewart-Winter, Timothy. *Queer Clout: Chicago and the Rise of Gay Politics*. Pennsylvania UP, 2015.

Steyn, Marc. "Obamacare's Hierarchy of Privilege." *National Review*, 23 Aug. 2013, https://www.nationalreview.com/2013/08/obamacares-hierarchy-privilege-mark-steyn/. Accessed 1 Apr. 2020.

Stohr, Greg, and Matthew A. Winkler. "Ruth Bader Ginsburg Thinks Americans Are Ready for Gay Marriage." *Bloomberg Business*, 12 Feb. 2015, www.bloomberg.com/news/articles/2015-02-12/ginsburg-says-u-s-ready-to-accept-ruling-approving-gay-marriage-i61z6gq2. Accessed 14. Feb. 2018.

Stokes Paulsen, Michael. "The Wreckage of Obergefell. An Analysis of the Supreme Court's 2015 Term." *First Things*, Oct. 2015, https://www.firstthings.com/article/2015/10/the-wreckage-of-obergefell. Accessed 10 June 2019.

Stolberg, Sheryl Gay. "Republicans Sign Brief in Support of Gay Marriage." *The New York Times*, 25 Feb. 2013, https://www.nytimes.com/2013/02/26/us/politics/prominent-republicans-sign-brief-in-support-of-gay-marriage.html. Accessed 20 May 2018.

Stone, Amy L. "Diversity, Dissent, and Decision Making: The Challenge to LGBT Politics." *GLQ: A Journal of Lesbian and Gay Studies*, vol. 16, no. 3, 2010, pp. 465–72. *Duke UP*, doi: 10.1215/10642684–2009–040

Storey, John. *Cultural Theory and Popular Culture*. 4th ed, Pearson, 2006.

Stryker, Susan. "Transgender History, Homonormativity, and Disciplinarity." *Radical History Review*, no. 100, 2008, pp. 145–57. *Duke UP*, https://doi.org/10.1215/01636545–2007–026.

"Students in Kentucky Should Continue Push for Marriage Equality." *Kentucky Kernel*, 13 Nov. 2013, http://www.kykernel.com/2013/11/13/students-in-kentucky-should-continue-push-for-marriage-equality/. Accessed 14 Feb. 2015.

Sunstein, Cass. *Going to Extremes: How Like Minds United and Divide*. Oxford UP, 2009.

Szulc, Lukasz. "Banal Nationalism in the Internet Age: Rethinking the Relationship Between Nations, Nationalism, and the Media." *Everyday Nationhood: Theorising Culture, Identity and Belonging after Banal Nationalism*, edited by Michael Skey and Marco Antonsich, Palgrave Macmilllan, 2017, pp. 53–76.

Tabachnick, Toby. "Jewish Advocates React as SCOTUS Makes Gay Marriage Law of the Land." *Pittsburgh Jewish* Chronicle, 1 July 2015, https://jewishchronicle.timesofisrael.com/jewish-advocates-react-as-scotus-makes-gay-marriage-law-of-the-land/. Accessed 10 May 2018.

Tan, Avianne. "North Carolina's Controversial Anti-LGBT Bill Explained." *ABC News*, 24 Mar. 2016, https://abcnews.go.com/US/north-carolinas-controversial-anti-lgbt-bill-explained/story?id=37898153. Accessed 8 Dec. 2019.

Tashman, Brian. "Anti-Gay Pastor Likens Fight Against Marriage Equality to the American Revolution." *Right Wing Watch*, 25 Sept. 2014, https://www.rightwingwatch.org/post/anti-gay-pastor-likens-fight-against-marriage-equality-to-the-american-revolution/. Accessed 20 Aug. 2018.

---. "West: 'Gay Marriage Is an Oxymoron and Will End Society.'" *Right Wing Watch*, 3 June 2011, https://www.rightwingwatch.org/post/west-gay-marriage-is-an-oxymoron-and-will-end-society/. Accessed 20 May 2018.

Tate, Julie. "Bradley Manning Sentenced to 35 Years in WikiLeaks Case." *The Washington Post*, 21 Aug. 2013, https://www.washingtonpost.com/world/national-security/judge-to-sentence-bradley-manning-today/2013/08/20/85bee184-09d0-11e3-b87c-476db8ac34cd_story.html. Accessed 10 Dec. 2019.

Taylor, Jessica. "Trump: Democrats 'Un-American,' 'Treasonous' During State of the Union." *National Public Radio*, 5 Feb. 2018, https://www.npr.org/2018/02/05/583447413/trump-democrats-un-american-treasonous-during-state-of-the-union?t=15858445476 95. Accessed 1 Apr. 2020.

Taylor, Kate. "For Chick-fil-A, Impact Trumps 'Any Political or Cultural War' When It Comes to Controversial Donations." *Business Insider*, 15 May 2019, https://www.businessinsider.com/chick-fil-a-explains-donations-groups-considered-anti-gay-2019-5?r=DE&IR=T. Accessed 19 Mar. 2020.

Teague, Matthew, and Jana Kasperkevic. "A Divided North Carolina Draws National Attention in Fight over Transgender Law." *The Guardian*, 1 Apr. 2016, https://www.theguardian.com/us-news/2016/apr/01/north-carolina-transgender-bathroom-law. Accessed 8 December 2019.

Teal, Janae, and Meredith Conover-Williams. "Homophobia without Homophobes: Deconstructing the Public Discourses of 21st Century Queer Sexualities in the United States." *Humboldt Journal of Social Relations*, vol. 38, 2016, pp. 12–27. *JSTOR*, https://www.jstor.org/stable/10.2307/humjsocrel.38.12.

"Text: President Bush Addresses the Nation." *The Washington Post*, 20 Sept. 2001, https://www.washingtonpost.com/wp-srv/nation/specials/attacked/transcripts/bush address_092001.html. Accessed 19 May 2020.

"Thea Spyer and Edith Windsor." *The New York Times*, 27 May 2007, https://www.nytimes.com/2007/05/27/fashion/weddings/27spyer.html. Accessed 10 June 2019.

"31% Think U.S. Civil War Likely Soon." *Rasmussen Reports*, 27 June 2018, https://www.rasmussenreports.com/public_content/politics/general_politics/june_2018/31_think_u_s_civil_war_likely_soon. Accessed 10 Apr. 2020.

Thomas, Clarence. Dissenting opinion. *Obergefell v. Hodges*. 26 June 2015. *Supreme Court of the United States*, https://www.supremecourt.gov/opinions/14pdf/14-556_3204.pdf. Accessed 3 Feb. 2018.

Thompson, Ian A. "Jeff Sessions Thinks It Should Be Legal to Fire You for Being LGBT." *ACLU*, 27 July 2017, https://www.aclu.org/blog/lgbt-rights/lgbt-nondiscrimination-protections/jeff-sessions-thinks-it-should-be-legal-fire-you. Accessed 10 Aug. 2018.

Thomson, Irene Taviss. *Culture Wars and Enduring American Dilemmas*. Michigan UP, 2010.

Thorpe, Devin. "Robert Redford Tells Utahns Discrimination Is 'Un-American.'" *Forbes*, 16 Sept. 2013, https://www.forbes.com/sites/devinthorpe/2013/09/16/robert-redford-tells-utahns-discrimination-is-un-american/#7511ffd44ae3. Accessed 10 May 2018.

Tocqueville, Alexis de. *Democracy in America*, edited by Bruce Frohnen, translated by Henry Reeve, Regnerey Publishing, 2002.

"Tonight: Local Legal Experts, LGBT Leaders Discuss Upcoming Marriage Equality Supreme Court Case at Town Hall." *ACLU Florida*, 20 Mar. 2013, https://www.aclufl.org/en/press-releases/tonight-local-legal-experts-lgbt-leaders-discuss-upcoming-marriage-equality-supreme. Accessed 20 May 2018.

Tuchmann, Barbara. *In Geschichte Denken. Essays*. Claassen, 1982.

Tuman, Joseph S. *Political Communication in American Campaigns*. Sage Publications, 2007.

Um, Nam-Hyun. "Does Gay-Themed Advertising Haunt Your Brand? The Impact of Gay-Themed Advertising on Young Heterosexual Consumers." *International Journal of Advertising*, vol. 33, no. 4, 2014, pp. 811–32. *Taylor and Francis*, doi: 10.2501/IJA-33–4-811–832.

"Un-American and Un-Christian." *The New York Times*, 18 Jan. 1921, https://

www.nytimes.com/1921/01/18/archives/unamerican-and-unchristian.html?searchResultPosition=1. Accessed 10 Apr. 2018.

"Un-American." *The New York Times*, 27 Jan. 1892, https://www.nytimes.com/1892/01/27/archives/unamerican.html. Accessed 10 Apr. 2018.

"United States, Congress, House. Special Committee on Un-American Activities (1938–1944). Investigation of Un-American Propaganda Activities In the United States: Hearings Before a Special Committee On Un-American Activities, House of Representatives, Seventy-fifth Congress, Third Session-Seventy-eighth Congress, Second Session, On H. Res. 282, to Investigate (1) the Extent, Character, And Objects of Un-American Propaganda Activities In the United States, (2) the Diffusion Within the United States of Subversive And Un-American Propaganda That Is Instigated From Foreign Countries Or of a Domestic Origin And Attacks the Principle of the Form of Government As Guaranteed by Our Constitution, And (3) All Other Questions In Relation Thereto That Would Aid Congress In Any Necessary Remedial Legislation." Washington: U.S. Govt. Print. Off., 19381944. *Hathi Trust Digital Library*, https://catalog.hathitrust.org/Record/001142900/Home. Accessed 5 May 2020.

United States, Congress. *Defense of Marriage Act*. 21 Sept. 1996. U.S. Government Printing Office, 1996, https://www.congress.gov/104/plaws/publ199/PLAW-104publ199.htm. Accessed 29 Apr. 2020.

United States, Constitution. "Fourteenth Amendment." *Cornell Law School, Legal Information Institute*, https://www.law.cornell.edu/constitution/amendmentxiv. Accessed 11 May 2020.

United States, Supreme Court. *Baker v. Nelson*. Oct. 1972. *The New York Times*, https://www.nytimes.com/interactive/2015/05/13/us/document-baker-vs-nelson-case.html. Accessed 10 June 2019.

---. *Loving v. Virginia*. 10 Apr. 1967. *Legal Information Institute, Cornell Law School*, https://www.law.cornell.edu/supremecourt/text/388/1. Accessed 10 June 2019.

---. *Masterpiece Cakeshop v. Colorado Civil Rights Commission*. 4 June 2018. *Supreme Court of the United States*, https://www.supremecourt.gov/opinions/17pdf/16-111_j4el.pdf. Accessed 7 Nov. 2019.

---. *Obergefell v. Hodges*. 26 June 2015. *Supreme Court of the United States*, https://www.supremecourt.gov/opinions/14pdf/14–556_3204.pdf. Accessed 3 Feb. 2018.

---. *Romer v. Evans*. 20 May 1996. *FindLaw*, https://caselaw.findlaw.com/us-supreme-court/517/620.html. Accessed 10 Nov. 2019.

---. *Shelby County v. Holder*. 25 June 2013. *Supreme Court of the United States*, https://www.supremecourt.gov/opinions/12pdf/12-96_6k47.pdf. Accessed 29 Apr. 2020.

---. *United States v. Carolene Products Company*. 25 Apr. 1938. *Legal Infor-*

mation Institute, Cornell Law School, https://www.law.cornell.edu/supremecourt/text/304/144. Accessed 10 Feb. 2020.

---. *United States v. Windsor*. 26 June 2013. *Supreme Court of the United States*, https://www.supremecourt.gov/opinions/12pdf/12-307_6j37.pdf. Accessed 23 Oct. 2018.

Vermont State, Supreme Court of Vermont. *Baker v. Vermont*. 20 Dec. 1999. *FindLaw*, https://caselaw.findlaw.com/vt-supreme-court/1131833.html. Accessed 10 Apr. 2020.

Vesoulis, Abby. "Steve Schmidt Helped Run Republican Campaigns for Years. Here's Why He Quit the GOP." *Time*, 21 June 2018, https://time.com/5319120/steve-schmidt-republican-party/. Accessed 3 Dec. 2019.

"Voorhees and Turpee Endorsed." *North American*, 16 Aug. 1894, p. 2. *Nineteenth Century U.S. Newspapers*.

Wallace, Jay R. "Constructing Normativity." *Philosophical Topics*, vol. 32, no. 1/2, 2004, pp. 451–76. *JSTOR*, https://www.jstor.org/stable/43154447.

Wallshein, William. "What Does Brenner v. Scott Mean for Same-Sex Marriage and Divorce?" *William Wallshein Law*, 15 Jan. 2015, https://www.wallsheinlaw.com/what-does-brenner-v-scott-mean-for-same-sex-marriage-and-divorce/. Accessed 10 Feb. 2020.

Wallsten, Peter. "NAACP Endorses Same-Sex Marriage." *The Washington Post*, 19 May 2012, https://www.washingtonpost.com/blogs/election-2012/post/naacp-endorses-same-sex-marriage/2012/05/19/gIQA5SFSbU_blog.html?utm_medium=twitter&utm_source=twitterfeed. Accessed 10 June 2018.

Walsh, Clare F. "It Really Is Not Just Gay, but African American Gay: The Impact of Community and Church on the Experiences of Black Lesbians Living in North Central Florida." *Journal of Homosexuality*, vol. 63, no. 9, 2016, p. 1236–52. *Taylor and Francis,* doi: 10.1080/00918369.2016.1151694.

Warner, Michael. *Fear of a Queer Planet: Queer Politics and Social Theory*. 6th ed. Minnesota UP, 2004.

---. "Introduction: Fear of a Queer Planet." *Social Text*, no. 29, 1991, pp. 3–17. *JSTOR*, http://www.jstor.org/stable/466295.

---. *The Trouble with Normal: Sex, Politics, and the Ethics of Queer Life*. Harvard UP, 2000.

Wassermann Schulz, Debbie. "DNC Chair: Santorum Attacks on Same-Sex Marriage 'Un-American.'" Interview with Chris Johnson. *Washington Blade*, 3 Jan. 2012, https://www.washingtonblade.com/2012/01/03/dnc-chair-santorum-attacks-on-same-sex-marriage-un-american/. Accessed 10 June 2018.

Weigel, David. "Trump's 'LGBT Rights' Promises Were Tied to War on 'Radical Islam.'" *The Washington Post*, 26 July 2017, https://www.washington

post.com/news/powerpost/wp/2017/07/26/trumps-lgbt-supporters-defend-him-after-surprise-military-transgender-ban/. Accessed 8 Dec. 2019.

---., and Ed O'Keefe. "Democrats Launch a Full-Scale Opposition Push against Trump's Executive Order." *Washington Post*, 30 Jan. 2017, https://www.washingtonpost.com/powerpost/democrats-across-the-country-join-protests-against-trump-order/2017/01/29/3146fcd0-e4de-11e6-a547-5fb9411d332c_ story.html. Accessed 13 Feb. 2020.

Wendt, Simon. "Defenders of Patriotism or Mothers of Fascism? The Daughters of the American Revolution, Antiradicalism, and Un-Americanism in the Interwar Period." *Journal of American Studies*, vol. 47, no. 4, 2013, pp. 943–69. *JSTOR*, doi:10.1017/S0021875813001321.

Wesling, Meg. "The Unequal Promise of Marriage Equality." *American Quarterly*, vol. 66, no. 1, 2014, pp. 171–79. *Project Muse*, https://doi.org/10.1353/aq.2014.0002.

"What Dan Cathy said." *Atlanta Journal Constitution*, 26 July 2012, https://www.ajc.com/business/what-dan-cathy-said/qOsEwVfhXbUCIp1hnEMQ4N/. Accessed 19 May 2019.

"Who Is Weaponizing Religious Liberty?" *People for the American Way*, http://www.pfaw.org/report/who-is-weaponizing-religious-liberty/. Accessed 13 Aug. 2019.

Wildman, Sarah. "Closed Sessions." *The New Republic*, 30 Dec. 2002, https://newrepublic. com/article/61363/closed-sessions. 13 Oct. 2018.

Willets, Gilson. "Most Un-American Part of the United States." *The New York Times*, 20 Aug. 1905, https://www.nytimes.com/1905/08/20/archives/most-unamerican-part-of-the-united-states-strange-stories-of-people.html. Accessed 10 Apr. 2018.

Williams, Timothy, and Elizabeth Dias. "United Methodists Tighten Ban on Same-Sex Marriage and Gay Clergy." *The New York Times*, 26 Feb. 2019, https://www.nytimes.com/2019/02/26/us/united-methodists-vote.html?action=click&module=Related Links&pgtype=Article. Accessed 20 Apr. 2020.

Wilstein, Matt. "Donald Trump 'Fine' With Same-Sex Marriage." *The Daily Beast*, 13 Nov. 2016, https://www.thedailybeast.com/cheats/2016/11/13/donald-trump-same-sex-marriage-is-settled-law. Accessed 8 Dec. 2019.

Wodak, Ruth, and Michael Meyer. "Critical Discourse Analysis: History, Agenda, Theory and Methodology." *Methods for Critical Discourse Analysis*, 2nd ed, edited by Ruth Wodak and Michael Meyer, Sage Publications, 2009, pp. 1–33.

Wolf, Richard. "Timeline: Same-Sex Marriage Through the Years." USA Today, 26 June 2015, https://eu.usatoday.com/story/news/politics/2015/06/24/same-sex-marriage-timeline/29173703/. Accessed 8 Dec. 2019.

Wolffe, Richard. "Donald Trump is the Most Un-American President in Living Memory." *The Guardian*, 26 June 2018, https://www.theguardian.com/commentisfree/2018/jun/26/donald-trump-immigration-most-un-american-president. Accessed 8 Dec. 2019.

Wong, Curtis. "Oreo Cookies' Gay Pride Backlash: 25 Companies and Products Boycotted for Supporting LGBT Rights." *HuffPost*, 28 June 2012, https://www.huffpost.com/entry/oreo-backlash-companies-anti-gay-boycott_n_1634767?guccounter=1&guce_referrer=aHR0cHM6Ly93d3cuZ29vZ2xlLmNvbS8&guce_referrer_sig=AQAAAD3QMHEonwAFgNAbAdsNByvBI9Rl5GOBiZAZCUgfJSP7zZ1_rnTXCgLhUoDXRpUGfIEuaDiJiwPStNglivK6BjFp1ZaHpvZK1BWi8N9a4HcGd5I8DqCmrABB9pLk7bYse8O2Uv-Se4GBW0Bcbuj4E1OlgcmMxUbpyD1LeFriak49. Accessed 21 May 2020.

---. "SCOTUS's Gay Marriage Decision Is 'Unconstitutional' And 'Un-American,' According to Bryan Fischer." *Huffpost*, 8 Oct. 2014, https://www.huffpost. com/entry/bryan-fischer-scotus-gay-marriage-_n_5953912. Accessed 13 Apr. 2017.

Wright, David. "Trump Jabs at 'Head Clown' Schumer amid Obamacare Fight." *CNN*, 5 Jan. 2017, https://edition.cnn.com/2017/01/05/politics/trump-tweet-schumer-head-clown-obamacare/index.html. Accessed 19 Mar. 2020.

Yamin, Priscilla. *American Marriage: A Political Institution*. Pennsylvania UP, 2010.

Younge, Gary. "California's Supreme Court Declares Gay Marriages Void." *The Guardian*, 13 Aug. 2004, https://www.theguardian.com/world/2004/aug/13/uselections2004. comment. Accessed 10 Feb. 2020.

Zirkle, Brian L. "House Un-American Activities Committee (HUAC)." *Encyclopedia of Privacy*, vol 1., edited by William G. Staples, Greenwood Press, 2007, pp. 282–85.